Testing ASP.NET Web Applications

Testing
ASP.NET Web Applications

Jeff McWherter
Ben Hall

WILEY

Wiley Publishing, Inc.

Testing ASP.NET Web Applications

Published by
Wiley Publishing, Inc.
10475 Crosspoint Boulevard
Indianapolis, IN 46256
www.wiley.com

Published by Wiley Publishing, Inc., Indianapolis, Indiana

Published simultaneously in Canada

ISBN: 978-0-470-49664-0

Manufactured in the United States of America

10 9 8 7 6 5 4 3 2 1

For general information on our other products and services please contact our Customer Care Department within the United States at (877) 762-2974, outside the United States at (317) 572-3993 or fax (317) 572-4002.

Wiley also publishes its books in a variety of electronic formats. Some content that appears in print may not be available in electronic books.

Library of Congress Control Number: 2009935232

To Sarah Jeffreys who loved, supported, and helped me throughout the entire writing process; and a thank you to my family for their support and backing.

— Ben Hall

To my amazing wife, Carla, who has supported me in so many ways; to my mother who has loved and believed in me; and to my father who taught me to work hard and be the best that I can be.

— Jeff McWherter

About the Authors

Ben Hall is a passionate and enthusiastic software developer and tester from the United Kingdom. Ben enjoys exploring different ways of testing software, focusing on how to most effectively test different types of applications, both on the Web and the desktop. He also loves the development side of software — developing web applications using ASP.NET and Ruby on Rails. Ben is a Microsoft C# MVP and maintains a blog at `Blog.BenHall.me.uk`.

Jeff McWherter is the Director of Simplicity at Web Ascender in Okemos, Michigan. Jeff graduated from Michigan State University with a degree in telecommunications, and has 14 years of professional experience in software development.

He is a founding member and current Program Director for the Greater Lansing User Group for .NET (`GLUG.net`). He enjoys profiling code, applying design patterns, finding obscure namespaces, and long walks in the park. His lifelong interest in programming began with *Home Computing Magazine* in 1983, which included an article about writing a game called Boa Alley in BASIC.

Jeff currently lives in a farming community near Lansing, Michigan. When he is not in front of the computer he enjoys rock and ice climbing with his smart and beautiful wife — which leads to his favorite activity of all — road trips. Jeff's blog can be found at `www.mcwherter.net/blog`.

Credits

Associate Publisher
Jim Minatel

Project Editor
Julie M. Smith

Technical Editor
Doug Parsons

Production Editor
Eric Charbonneau

Copy Editor
Tricia Liebig

Editorial Director
Robyn B. Siesky

Editorial Manager
Mary Beth Wakefield

Production Manager
Tim Tate

Vice President and Executive Group Publisher
Richard Swadley

Vice President and Executive Publisher
Barry Pruett

Project Coordinator, Cover
Lynsey Stanford

Assistant Art Director
Michael E. Trent

Cover Photo
© Photos.com/Jupiterimages/Getty Images

Compositor
Craig Woods, Happenstance Type-O-Rama

Proofreader
Nancy Carrasco

Indexer
Johnna VanHoose Dinse

Acknowledgments

First I would like to thank Sarah Jeffreys who supported me during the long, dark, cold nights while writing this book. Without her support, the book would have been near impossible and for that I will be eternally grateful. I also have a lot to thank my family for, who have supported me no matter how strange the decision or request may have been.

I would also like to thank Red Gate Software for sending me to PDC where I met Jeff and for giving me the opportunity and experience required to write this book.

Many thanks go to the entire U.K. development community for putting up with me while writing this book. They have purchased me beer when required while providing advice on key issues. This also extends to my twitter followers who have heard the late-night comments I made while trying to focus on writing something.

Finally, a huge thank you to Jeff for asking me to co-author this book and his hard work throughout the process.

—*Ben Hall*

First and foremost I would like to thank my very patient wife Carla, who sat by my side many nights, late into the night at coffee shops and the kitchen table at our house while I worked on this book. Thank you for all the support, patience, and understanding you have provided.

Throughout the past few years I have had the opportunity to attend hundreds of conferences and user groups targeted at software developers. It was at these events that I was able to meet thousands of developers and learn new things from everyone I met. I would like to thank the organizers of these events, especially the events held within the Microsoft Heartland district. I have had the opportunity to work with so many of you at your events, and I am always impressed at the passion that each and every one of you put into your events. A special thank you goes to all the members of the Greater Lansing User Group for .NET (GLUG.net), my local user group who I have the most interaction with.

Many thanks go to Corey Haines, not only for his invaluable assistance with what should and should not be included in this book, but for his views on life and programming practices. Thank you to Dennis Burton, Jay Harris, Tony Bihn, and Jordan Cobb for helping me with security, load testing, and other random testing questions.

Thank you to the staff at Web Ascender — Ryan Doom, Kevin Southworth, Mike Pardo, and Kyle Schebor — who listened to status updates about this book in the daily stand-up meetings and for answering questions about testing that appeared to come out of nowhere. Special thanks to Matt Hall and Amelia Marshall who helped with the accessibility chapter and any questions that came up about CSS, HTML, or good design. Thanks to Julie Smith and Doug Parsons and the other editors that helped clean up our mistakes; and lastly I would like to thank Ben. Not only have I gained a very valuable colleague, I have made a friend for life.

—*Jeff McWherter*

Contents

Contents

Contents

Contents

Contents

Contents

Introduction

If you are reading this then we have caught your attention and have you thinking about testing ASP.NET web applications. What do you think about when you hear the words *testing ASP.NET web applications*? To some it may mean cross-browser compatibility or accessibility testing. To others it may mean availability and stability. Each is a valid testing discipline, and each is an example of the types of testing that can be found in this book.

It is our intention that while you read this book, you think about web applications that you have developed in the past or are currently building and how each testing discipline can apply to your web applications. We hope that while you are reading each chapter you are able to apply these testing techniques to your daily development processes.

Whether this book was obtained via a bookstore, online store, or you were lucky enough to be given a free copy, we are glad that you see the importance of creating secure, stable, and accessible web applications and we welcome you to the wonderful world of ASP.NET web testing (and we promise you the rest of the book will not be this cheesy).

Who This Book Is For

This book is targeted at beginner and intermediate web developers who are looking to learn about how to test their ASP.NET web applications. This book assumes the reader has created a few websites and has an interest in learning the different testing disciplines that can be applied to web development.

Whether you are a developer, manager, or tester on a web project using C# or VB.NET, this book explains the different disciplines and levels of testing. This book initially introduces unit and functional testing. It then moves on to discuss how you can perform success testing of the user interfaces, acceptance testing, load/stress testing, and accessibility and security testing, which provides the reader with the knowledge required to successfully test ASP.NET web applications thoroughly from start to finish.

What This Book Covers

Testing ASP.NET Web Applications covers the different types of testing that should be performed on Web Applications such as:

- ❑ Unit Testing
- ❑ Integration Testing
- ❑ Automated User Interface Testing
- ❑ Acceptance Testing
- ❑ Manual Testing

❑   Performance Testing

❑   Accessibility Testing

❑   Security Testing

Each section discusses the tools, techniques, and best practices used when implementing that particular type of testing.

How This Book Is Structured

Many readers of Testing ASP.NET Web Applications will not have any experience with creating tests for web applications, while others may have experience with some of the testing disciplines presented in this book. After the first two chapters, which are aimed at technique and design, this book is intended for a reader to "flip around" and read about each testing discipline independent of other chapters.

The following list provides a description of the main topics of each chapter in this book:

Chapter 1: Preliminary Concerns

We start with an introduction into the world of testing, providing a foundation which will be built upon for the rest of the book while dispelling some of the myths which exist around the area of testing.

Chapter 2: Design and Testability

Before jumping straight into how to test ASP.NET websites, we take a look at design and architecture applications to improve testability. We also introduce the core concepts required to start writing automated tests around applications.

Chapter 3: Unit Testing and Test Driven Development

In this chapter we apply some of the techniques discussed in Chapter 2 to an ASP.NET application, highlighting decisions and issues encountered during the process. This chapter focuses on developer testing, including techniques such as unit testing, Test Driven Development, and breaking dependencies within your system.

Chapter 4: Integration Testing

Here we focus on integration testing, ensuring the parts we developed with Chapter 3 work as a group to handle issues such as external systems — databases or mail servers.

Chapter 5: Automated User Interface Testing

In this chapter we take a look at the UI and discuss how you can successfully automate the UI to provide additional confidence in the fact that your system is working as expected.

Chapter 6: Acceptance Testing

Here we focus on the customer and how it is possible to write customer acceptance tests in an automated fashion to ensure that the system meets end user requirements.

Chapter 7: Manual Testing

We now take a step back from automated testing and focus on how and when to perform manual testing, including the main techniques to focus on to perform manual testing in the most effective manner.

Chapter 8: Performance Testing

Are you confident that the web application you have spent the last six months developing will perform well for users when you have deployed it to production? Here we focus on testing the performance of web applications. This chapter discusses commercial tools along with free tools to help ensure your web applications pass their required performance metrics.

Chapter 9: Accessibility Testing

There is a sense of fear that many developers have when they learn they are required to adhere to web accessibility standards for certain web applications. In this chapter, we spend a great deal of time first discussing how to create accessible web applications, and then providing insight on how to test web applications to ensure they are accessible.

Chapter 10: Security Testing

The last chapter of this book discusses the testing of security in web applications. This chapter focuses on the OWASP Top 10 vulnerabilities. It discusses each vulnerability and provides insight about how to test for each vulnerability.

What You Need to Use This Book

The testing disciplines discussed in this book each have a set of tools that are unique to that particular testing discipline. Resources for these tools can be found in each chapter where the particular tool is discussed.

To run the coding examples in this book you will need to be aware of the following guide lines:

❏ Server-side code is written in C#.

❏ Visual Studio 2008 professional or greater should be installed.

❏ A test runner such as Test Driven .NET (http://www.testdriven.net) or Gallio (http://www.gallio.org) should be installed.

Conventions

To help you get the most from the text and keep track of what's happening, we've used a number of conventions throughout the book.

> **Boxes like this one hold important, not-to-be forgotten information that is directly relevant to the surrounding text.**

Notes, tips, hints, tricks, and asides to the current discussion are offset and placed in italics like this.

As for styles in the text:

❑   We *highlight* new terms and important words when we introduce them.

❑   We show URLs and code within the text like so: `persistence.properties`.

❑   We present code as follows:

```
We use a monofont type with no highlighting for most code examples.
```

Source Code

As you work through the examples in this book, you may choose either to type in all the code manually or to use the source code files that accompany the book. All of the source code used in this book is available for download at `http://www.wrox.com`. Once at the site, simply locate the book's title (either by using the Search box or by using one of the title lists) and click the Download Code link on the book's detail page to obtain all the source code for the book.

> *Because many books have similar titles, you may find it easiest to search by ISBN; this book's ISBN is 978-0-470-49664-0.*

Once you download the code, just decompress it with your favorite compression tool. Alternately, you can go to the main Wrox code download page at `http://www.wrox.com/dynamic/books/download .aspx` to see the code available for this book and all other Wrox books.

Errata

We make every effort to ensure that there are no errors in the text or in the code. However, no one is perfect, and mistakes do occur. If you find an error in one of our books, like a spelling mistake or faulty piece of code, we would be very grateful for your feedback. By sending in errata you may save another reader hours of frustration and at the same time you will be helping us provide even higher quality information.

To find the errata page for this book, go to `http://www.wrox.com` and locate the title using the Search box or one of the title lists. Then, on the Book Search Results page, click the Errata link. On this page you can view all errata that has been submitted for this book and posted by Wrox editors.

> *A complete book list including links to errata is also available at* `www.wrox.com/misc-pages/ booklist.shtml`.

If you don't spot your error on the Errata page, click the Errata Form link and complete the form to send us the error you have found. We'll check the information and, if appropriate, post a message to the book's errata page and fix the problem in subsequent editions of the book.

p2p.wrox.com

For author and peer discussion, join the P2P forums at p2p.wrox.com. The forums are a Web-based system for you to post messages relating to Wrox books and related technologies and interact with other readers and technology users. The forums offer a subscription feature to e-mail you topics of interest of your choosing when new posts are made to the forums. Wrox authors, editors, other industry experts, and your fellow readers are present on these forums.

At http://p2p.wrox.com you will find a number of different forums that will help you not only as you read this book, but also as you develop your own applications. To join the forums, just follow these steps:

1. Go to p2p.wrox.com and click the Register link.

2. Read the terms of use and click Agree.

3. Complete the required information to join as well as any optional information you wish to provide and click Submit.

4. You will receive an e-mail with information describing how to verify your account and complete the joining process.

   You can read messages in the forums without joining P2P but in order to post your own messages, you must join.

Once you join, you can post new messages and respond to messages other users post. You can read messages at any time on the Web. If you would like to have new messages from a particular forum e-mailed to you, click the Subscribe to this Forum icon by the forum name in the forum listing.

For more information about how to use the Wrox P2P, be sure to read the P2P FAQs for answers to questions about how the forum software works as well as many common questions specific to P2P and Wrox books. To read the FAQs, click the FAQ link on any P2P page.

1

Preliminary Concerns

The term "software bug" is a common term that even beginning computer users know to be a defect or imperfection in a software application. Software users have become accustomed to finding problems with software. Some problems have workarounds and are not severe, whereas others can be extremely problematic and, in some cases, costly. Sadly, as users, we have come to expect this from software. However, in recent years the quality of software has generally increased as software teams spend countless hours identifying and eliminating these problems before the software reaches the user. The process of identifying these bugs is known as *testing*.

There are many different types of testing that can be performed on your web applications, including functionality of the application, security, load/stress, compliance, and accessibility testing.

If you are new to testing, don't worry: we will explain the fundamental concepts and guide you to the correct actions you'll need to consider for each type of testing discipline. If you already have experience with testing applications, then this book will identify the key areas of the ASP.NET family and pair them with the correct approaches and the tools available to successfully test your web application.

This book is not intended to be the definitive guide to any particular type of testing, but a thorough overview of each type of web testing discipline. Its goal is to get you started using best practices and testing tools, and provide you with resources to master that particular testing discipline. It's our aim as authors to help the reader navigate to a section of this book and learn what and how they should be testing at any point in the development of a web-based application.

Although existing books cover different testing disciplines in depth, this book is unique because it applies today's best testing approaches to the ASP.NET family, including WebForms, ASP.NET MVC Framework, Web Services, Ajax, Silverlight, and ADO.NET Data Services, ensuring that the key technologies relevant today are able to be tested by the reader.

The History of Testing Tools

Tools for testing have been around for as long as developers have been writing code. In the early years of software development, however, there wasn't a clear distinction between testing and debugging. At the time, this model worked. Some argue that this model worked because the system was closed; most companies who needed software had the developers on staff to create and maintain the systems. Computer systems were not widespread, even though developers worked very closely with customers to deliver exactly what was required. In the years between 1970 and 1995, computer systems started becoming more popular, and the relationships between developers and customers became distant, often placing several layers of management between them.

What is the difference between debugging and testing you might ask? Testing *is the process of finding defects in the software. A defect could be a missing feature, a feature that does not perform adequately, or a feature that is broken.* Debugging *is the process of first tracking down a bug in the software and then fixing it.*

Many of the tools developers used for testing in the early days were internal tools developed specifically for a particular project and oftentimes not reused. Developers began to see a need to create reusable tools that included the patterns they learned early on. Testing methodologies evolved and tools started to become standardized, due to this realization. In recent years, testing methodologies have become their own, very strict computer science discipline.

During the past 12 years, many tools have been developed to help make testing easier. However, it's essential to learn about the past and the tools we had previously before diving into the set of tools we have now. It's important to notice that the tools tend to evolve as the process evolves.

The term "debugging" was made popular by Admiral Grace Murray Hopper, a woman who was working on a Mark II computer at Harvard University in August 1945. When her colleagues discovered a moth stuck in a relay, and realized it was causing issues with the system, she made the comment that they were "debugging the system."

The sUnit Testing Framework

It is said that imitation is the sincerest form of flattery; that said, most modern unit testing frames are derived from the principals set forth in the sUnit testing framework primary developed by Kent Beck in 1998. Below are just a small number of frameworks which have built upon Beck's original concept.

- ❑ **sUnit.** Created by Kent Beck for Small Talk, sUnit has become known as the "mother of testing frameworks." Many popular unit testing frameworks such as jUnit and nUnit are ports of sUnit. The key concepts of the sUnit testing framework were originally published in Chapter 30 of Kent Beck's *Guide to Better Smalltalk* (Cambridge University Press, 1998).

- ❑ **jUnit.** A port of sUnit for Java created by Kent Beck and Erich Gamma in late 1998. jUnit helped bring automated unit testing into the main stream.

- ❑ **nUnit.** In late 2000, all the great things about jUnit were ported to .NET allowing C# developers to write jUnit style unit tests against their C# code.

- ❑ **qUnit.** This is the unit test running for the jQuery Framework. In May 2008, qUnit was promoted to a top-level application in the jQuery project. qUnit allows web developers to run unit tests on JavaScript.

❏ **WCAT.** First included in the IIS 4 resource kit in 1998, the Web Capacity Analysis Tool (WCAT) is a freely distributed command-line tool that allows a server to be configured with agents to perform load/stress testing on websites.

❏ **Web Application Stress Tool.** In 1999, Microsoft released a free tool to create GUI browser stress tests. This tool recorded a browser session and scripted the actions into a Visual Basic 6 script that could be modified. Because the tool generated scripts that could be modified, many web developers used the tool not only for stress testing but modified the scripts for user interface functional testing.

❏ **Microsoft Application Center Test.** Included in Visual Studio 2001 Enterprise Edition, Microsoft ACT improved upon the Web Application Stress tool. Microsoft ACT provided a schema in which the tests could be distributed among agents for large-scale load testing.

❏ **Framework for Integrated Test (FIT).** Created by Ward Cunningham in 2002, FIT is a tool for automated customer tests. Examples of how the software should perform are provided by the customer, and automated Test fixtures are created by the developer. The goal of FIT is to help integrate the work of developers, customers, tests, and analysts.

❏ **Fitnesse.** Ported to .NET in 2006 by David Chelimsky and Mike Stockdale, Fitnesse combines a web server, Wiki, and the FIT software acceptance testing framework together. This provides an acceptance testing framework which allows users to define input that can be interpreted by a Test fixture allowing for non-technical users to write tests.

❏ **Watir.** In May 2002, the Web Application Testing in Ruby Watir (pronounced "Water"), a library to automate browser acceptance tests in Ruby, is released.

❏ **Selenium.** Selenium provides a suite of tools for automated user interface testing of web applications. In 2004, Jason Huggins of Thoughtworks created the core "JavaScriptTestRunner" mode for automation testing of a time and expense system.

❏ **WatiN.** In May 2006, Watir, the popular browser acceptance testing framework, is ported to .NET as the WatiN (pronounced "Watt in") project.

❏ **Visual Studio 2005 Test Edition.** In 2005, Microsoft released a version of Visual Studio that included a new unit testing framework created by Microsoft called MS Test. Along with this new unit testing framework, what was known previously as Microsoft Application Center Test (Microsoft ACT) was integrated into this version as Web Unit Tests and Web Load Tests.

❏ **Visual Studio 2008 Professional.** In 2008, the professional version of Visual Studio 2008 included MSTest.

Testing Terminology

As with many different aspects in programming, testing disciplines have their own unique vocabulary. However, because of the number of terms, the barrier to entry is high and can scare new developers. This section is intended to get the reader up to speed on some common terms that will be used throughout the remainder of this book. The terms shown next are only intended to be a brief explanation. Each term will be discussed thoroughly in their respective chapters.

❏ **Test.** A *test* is a systematic procedure to ensure that a particular unit of an application is working correctly.

❑ **Pass.** A *pass* indicates that everything is working correctly. When represented on a report or user interface (UI), it is represented as green.

❑ **Fail.** In the case of a *fail*, the functionality being tested has changed and as a result no longer works as expected. When represented on a report, this is represented as red.

❑ **xUnit.** *xUnit* refers to the various testing frameworks which were originally ported from sUnit. Tools such as jUnit, qUnit, and nUnit fall into the xUnit family.

❑ **Test Fixture.** *Test fixtures* refer to the state a test must be in before the test can be run. Test fixtures prepare any objects that need to be in place before the test is run. Fixtures ensure a known, repeatable state for the tests to be run in.

❑ **Test Driven Development (TDD).** Test Driven Development is an Agile Software Development process where a test for a procedure is created before the code is created.

❑ **Behavior Driven Development (BDD).** Building on top of the fundamentals of TDD, BDD aims to take more advantage of the design and documentation aspects of TDD to provide more value to the customer and business.

❑ **Test Double.** When we cannot, or choose not, to use a real component in unit tests, the object that is substituted for the real component is called a *test double*.

❑ **Stub.** A test *stub* is a specific type of test double. A stub is used when you need to replicate an object and control the output, but without verifying any interactions with the stub object for correctness. Many types of stubs exist, such as the responder, saboteur, temporary, procedural, and entity chain, which are discussed in more depth in Chapter 2.

❑ **Mock.** *Mock* objects are also a form of test double and work in a similar fashion to stub objects. Mocks are used to simulate the behavior of a complex object. Any interactions made with the mock object are verified for correctness, unlike stub objects. Mock objects are covered in depth in Chapter 2.

❑ **Fake.** *Fake* objects are yet another type of test doubles. Fake objects are similar to test stubs, but replace parts of the functionality with their own implementation to enable testing to be easier for the method.

❑ **Dummy Objects.** *Dummy* objects are used when methods require an object as part of their method or constructor. However, in this case the object is never used by the code under test. As such, a common dummy object is null.

❑ **Unit Test.** A *unit test* is a method used to verify that a small unit of source code is working properly. Unit tests should be independent of external resources such as databases and files. A unit is generally considered a method.

❑ **Developer Test.** This is another term for a unit test.

❑ **Integration Test.** This is similar to a unit test; however, instead of being an isolation unit, these test cross-application and system boundaries.

❑ **Functional Test.** *Functional tests* group units of work together to test an external requirement. Testing disciplines such as graphical user interface testing and performance testing are considered functional tests.

❑ **GUI Test.** *GUI tests* test the graphical user interface. GUI tests are considered functional tests. Applications are used to simulate users interacting with the system such as entering text into a field or clicking a button. Verifications are then made based on the response from the UI or system.

- ❏ **Customer Test.** This is another term for an acceptance test.

- ❏ **System Test.** The term *system test* is a term to indicate an "End To End" test of the system. System tests include unit testing, security testing, GUI testing, functional testing, acceptance testing, and accessibility testing.

- ❏ **Load Test.** A large amount of connections are made to the website to determine if it will scale correctly. This type of testing is to ensure that the website can handle the peak load expected when the website is used in production without any errors or failures.

- ❏ **Stress Test.** This is another name for a load test.

- ❏ **Performance Test.** *Performance testing* measures the response of a system in normal use and when it's placed under load. A common metric for Web Applications is Time To First Byte (TTFB) and Requests Per Second (RPS).

- ❏ **Acceptance Test.** This is a formal test to indicate if a function of a software project conforms to the specification the customer expects.

- ❏ **Black Box Test.** A *black box test* is a test created without knowing the internal workings of the feature being tested. The only information you have to base your tests on is the requirements.

- ❏ **White Box Test.** A *white box test* is a test created with knowledge of the inner workings of the code being tested. By using your internal knowledge of the system you can adapt the inputs you use to ensure high test coverage and correctness of the system.

- ❏ **Regression Test.** A *regression test* is a test created to ensure that existing functionality was working correctly previously and is still working as expected.

Testing Myths

Some developers are required to explain every development practice and tool they'll need to create a piece of software to their managers; it's this manager who will then decide if the practice or tool is prudent for use. These managers are often developers that have been promoted, and their focus is no longer on development but managing. Former developers do not always make for the best managers; many times they don't keep their development skills sharp, and they can sometimes deny the use of new techniques and tools just because it's not the way that they do things. These situations do not make sense and are often hard for developers to handle, especially junior developers who are very eager to learn the latest and greatest technology.

> *Unit testing frameworks have been mainstream for roughly 10 years, but still, many managers fight developers who ask to implement unit testing frameworks. This section explores some of the popular myths around testing and helps give advice to the developer who is having issues implementing a testing regiment into their organization.*

Testing Is Expensive

Frederick Brooks stated in his book of essays, *The Mythical Man-Month*, that "A bug found in the field can easily cost one thousand times more to resolve then one found in development."

If this is an argument that your manager uses, create a test to verify the functionality of the method that contains the bug and use it the next time the bug occurs — and time yourself. Then, write the fix for the bug and time yourself again. In most cases, you'll find that it only takes a few minutes to write a test for the functionality and now your argument to your manager can be, "If I was permitted to spend X amount of time creating a test, the customer would have never encountered this bug." Most managers will pay more attention to your requests if you have data to back up your reasons for wanting to do something.

If you continue on the path of creating tests for your system, over time you will form a comprehensive set of test cases. These test cases can then be executed during the development of your system, allowing you to catch regression bugs earlier in the process. By having the tests catch these bugs, you will save time and money in terms of re-testing the application but also in maintaining the system in production.

Only Junior Developers Should Create Tests

This claim is very far from the truth. It's important for junior developers to write tests along with senior developers. This claim is often an excuse for a manager to stick a junior developer on a project just to create a bunch of test plans. However, the test plans and automated testing a junior developer creates is often useless, because of a lack of training and guidance. It's important for senior developers to work closely with junior developers to teach them what makes good tests. Testing is easy; *good* testing is hard. It's difficult to learn how to write good tests and create test plans from books; books help with the concepts, but nothing matches sitting down and pair programming with an experienced developer for the day.

If you are the senior developer and you notice this, take it upon yourself to help educate the junior developer. Ask the manager if you can be responsible for a portion of the tests and help educate the junior developer about the process. In the long run it will make your job easier having multiple people on a team that can perform the task well.

If you are the junior developer, your career is ultimately your responsibility. You should speak to the manager and request that a senior developer work with you for a portion of the tests. If the manager disagrees, take it upon yourself to get the training you need to perform the task. Start with reading as much about testing as you can, then try going to a local user group. Local user groups often have "hack nights," where they get together and write code, allowing you to learn with your peers.

Tests Cannot Be Created for Legacy Code

Testing legacy code is often more difficult, but it's not impossible. Often, legacy code has not been architected in a way that allows unit tests to be created, but in most scenarios functional or acceptance tests can be created for them. During the past few years, many patterns have emerged that make testing legacy code much easier. In the testing world, a code base that contains no tests is oftentimes referred to as legacy code. This means that if you're not writing tests as you write your code, all you are doing is simply creating legacy code from day one.

This myth is generally just another excuse for managers that are uneducated about testing patterns. It's a great idea to write tests for legacy code. Oftentimes the developer who wrote the code is not around to maintain it anymore and creating a test suite for the application will help a new developer learn about the app and give other developers a safety net if they need to make changes in the future.

Tests Are Only for Use with Agile Software Development

Unit testing and Test Driven Development are fundamental processes for XP and many other Agile Software Development methodologies. Just because one process uses a great tool doesn't mean it won't fit into your process.

If your manager doesn't like the word *Agile*, don't refer to the practice of creating unit tests as an Agile process. Just call it unit testing. As a web developer, you may be familiar with Lorem Ipsum. Lorem Ipsum is used as a placeholder for text and is from the Latin work of Cicero's De Finibus Bonorum et Malorum. Lorem Ipsum is intended to have no meaning because customers often focus on the text rather than the layout of the text. Use this trick on your manager. Some managers are not comfortable with Agile processes because of a lack of knowledge or misunderstandings about how the processors work .

Tests Have to Be Created Before the Code Is Written

Test Driven Development (TDD) is a process that we will explore briefly later in this book in Chapter 3, but for now all you need to know is that it's a process where a unit test for a given functionality is created before the code for the functionality is written.

For a TDD purist, this is not a myth and a test has to be created before the code is created. For someone who is new to testing, TDD can be hard. Before a developer thinks about getting into TDD they should first learn what makes a good unit test. In Chapter 4, we will explore what makes good tests and explore both unit testing and TDD.

❏ **It's hard to maintain tests.** As you begin creating tests for your code, your test suites often become quite large and unwieldy. If your tests are written poorly then they will be hard to maintain just as with other code. With the correct architecture and considerations in the correct place as described in this book, you should find that your tests and the overall system are easier to maintain.

Having a large suite of tests that fully test your application is an investment. It's your job as a developer to convince your manager of the importance of having a test suite that fully tests your application.

❏ **You can't automate user interface code.** In the past, creating code to automate user interface code has been difficult. Tools such as the MS Test Web Test and WatiN make automated user interface testing possible.

If a manager states that automated user interface testing is not possible, simply point them to the tools. Be aware, though, that automated user interface tests are often brittle and require more time for maintenance than unit tests. In Chapter 5 you will explore automated user interface testing. With the correct knowledge and time, automated user interface testing can be achieved.

❏ **Unit tests remove the need for manual testing.** Although unit tests will become a valuable resource for your system, they alone do not replace the need for the system to also be manually tested. Unit tests verify isolated blocks, but we need to ensure that the system works as a whole. Manual testing involves ensuring that the system works as expected when everything is deployed correctly. When manually testing the system, not only will you be ensuring that the UI is rendered correctly, but you will also be verifying that the application and UI are actually useable.

Although you can automate different parts of the application, it is not yet possible to automate so that the application can be understood by the end-user and is easy to use. This is a very important stage and has to be performed manually. Without this stage you could create a perfectly working application, however, the end-user may never be able to use it because they simply don't understand the layout and process.

❑ **Unit testing is the latest development fad.** In the last two years, testing has become a very hot topic with new blogs appearing every few days featuring "experts" who preach that if you don't write tests you are writing shoddy code. With the quick rise in popularity, it's understandable why one would perceive this development practice as a fad. This simply is not true with many of the concepts being promoted today originating many years earlier.

As with the Testing Is Expensive myth, most managers listen to facts. Gather facts and present a strong case about why testing is important. In most situations, someone who is telling you that your code is shoddy because you don't practice a certain testing development practice is not someone you should trust in blind faith. The true experts understand why testing is important and will not try to force-feed it to you. They understand why code is written without tests and will help guide you in the right direction if you let them.

❑ **Developers only need to write unit tests.** Unit tests are great to have as they help you design code that is testable and the tests act as a safety net when making architectural changes. However, they should never be considered as a substitution to integration tests, functional tests, and acceptance tests. When a tester/developer understands the purpose of each type of test, thinking that only unit tests are needed will not be an issue.

If someone tells you this, you can assume they do not fully understand the differences between unit tests, functional tests, and acceptance tests. Explain to them the differences, what each type of test is, and where they apply.

❑ **Testing is easy.** Creating tests is very easy, but creating tests that are meaningful is another story. As with many other disciplines learned throughout your development career, the ability to create good tests will come with time and experience. One of the best ways to learn how to create good tests is to do pair programming with a developer who is experienced with creating tests. There are many schools of thought on pair programming: what it is and how best to perform this method of software development. The method I found that works best for me is to work together with another software developer on the same workstation with two monitors, two keyboards and two mice attached. One developer writes the test and the other implements the code to make the test pass. If one developer doesn't agree with exactly what the other is trying to accomplish, they are able to take control of the work station and explain their reasoning. I find that sitting face-to-face works best to keep conversation flowing.

If you have convinced your manager that creating tests is a good practice, it should not be very hard for you to convince them that you need to learn how to create good tests. Chapter 2 includes a section on what makes good tests. Also, there are many training classes put on by top-notch trainers to assist in this area.

Iterative Processes

Have you worked at a company that only performed employee performance reviews yearly? I'm sure most developers have, but during the yearly review have you had a manager say, "On June 13, 2008, you forgot to shut off the kanooter value, and every Friday since then you have not been shutting it off!" or something similar? I'm sure many developers have been in this situation. If the manager had indicated that you were doing something wrong you could have taken measures to correct the issue. This same paradigm happens with software development. Project managers spend a great deal of time working with customers to define exactly what a piece of software should accomplish. However, it's common to find that after the project manager has completed collecting the requirements for an application, the customer doesn't see the application again until development is "finished." This is the reason many software projects fail. In the last few years, Agile Software Development processes have became very popular among developers. One of the key principles in Agile Software processes is iterative development.

Iterative development groups the development of new features together and delivers small chunks of a project to a client, rather than waiting a long time to deliver a very large monolithic system. Agile teams try to keep the iteration period low, perhaps two weeks to a month, and at the end of the iteration they always have something to show. Some attribute the success of Agile to short iterations and constant communication with clients.

Agile developers and managers often speak about reducing the cost of change. Cost of change simply put is this: the longer it takes you to find a defect the more expensive it will be to fix. The cost of change topic is discussed heavily in the project management world; some attribute low cost of change to a very close feedback loop with customers, managers, and developers.

Testing suites can provide many entry points for gaining different types of feedback. At a very low level, testing provides feedback from the code itself about its current state and whether or not it is working correctly. At higher levels, acceptance testing gives developers feedback if the system was developed to specification.

Why Should I Learn about Testing?

You're reading a book about testing for the web, so you're heading in the correct direction.

For Developers

Developers tend to be busy people, what with new technology trends emerging and customers constantly demanding new features. At times, developing software is a very stressful profession. Worrying if the new feature you added this morning is going to break existing functionality should not be something developers are spending time thinking about. Having a test suite that spans from unit tests to customer acceptance tests will help a developer sleep better at night, at peace in the knowledge that the software is functioning as designed.

A well-written test suite will provide the proverbial safety net. With this safety net in place developers are more willing to refactor (changing the internal structure of how code works without modifying its external behavior or functionality) sections of code, experiment more often when getting ready to add more functionality into a system, and be more Agile. The end result is an improved code base and fewer areas within your code base that you are scared to make changes to.

One aspect of unit testing that new developers to automated testing often overlook is the fact that testable code in most circumstances is also well-designed code. Design patterns such as Inversion of Control (IoC), and simple development concepts such as Don't Repeat Yourself (DRY), together with a strict separation of concerns are needed to create testable code (concepts that will be discussed thoroughly in Chapter 2).

A developer who is experienced in writing tests will find that they are more productive actually writing a test as opposed to using the debugger to nail down an issue. Let's take a step back for a moment and think about this. How much time is wasted each day waiting for the browser to load a page just to test a simple change?

> *An informal study conducted by Web Ascender (*http://www.webascender.com*) found that web developers spend 15 minutes per day on average just waiting for web pages to load.*

By investing time in load tests, it will enable developers to choose the correct server infrastructure such as web farms and caching services earlier in the lifecycle. This information is also useful to plan for fiscal year budgeting. Loading tests that are run frequently and appropriately defined will help identify bottlenecks and negate negative customer feedback of a poorly performing website.

The concept of acceptance testing reinforces the importance of communication between developers and customers. The end result of acceptance testing ensures that the customer was delivered what they expected for the system being developed. In most cases, many customers are just happy that a developer cares that they are delivering quality software that is on par with what the customer wanted.

Many web developers are unaware of the accessibility laws that their site must conform to. Countries such as the United States have laws that forbid discrimination against people with disabilities. Accessibility is not just for government websites and in many cases simple accessibility testing could have avoided lawsuits .

For Managers

Different projects and different managers will have different criteria for what they feel makes a project successful. Good managers will see the necessity for each discipline of testing discussed in this book.

❑   **A project should be delivered on time.** Many projects wait until the last possible minute to test an application to ensure it is working properly. One of us has been in a situation where waiting to the last minute to test has caused a project to be delayed because of performance, accessibility, and acceptance issues, all of which could have been avoided if testing was completed through the development process.

This may make sense to many managers; surely you can't test until the system is completed? Plenty of projects have been delivered to customers with very little customer interaction.

❑   **A project should be of high quality.** Managers should put a great deal of time into defining metrics to measure if a project is of high quality. Having a suite of tests is a very strong metric to measure the quality of software. Having a full range of tests means that code is "exercised" often and has a far less chance of breaking because of neglect. How are you currently measuring the quality of the software being delivered? Many managers take the approach, "If it ain't broke, don't fix it," but in reality how do they know it's not broken?

❑   **A project should have low risks.** Managers often speak about the risks of projects. Great managers will manage risks to rewards and only take on projects that they know their team will have success with. In the real world, there is money to be made on projects that are higher risk and many times the highest risk is the delivery date.

Having a range of testing will help lower project risk by ensuring software works correctly conforms to specifications; and in many cases, testing helps keep the customer in the loop of what is going on with a project.

❏ **Have a happy client.** A common measure of success is a happy client. Most clients are very happy when you spend the time with them to make sure you are developing the system they want, not the system you or a manager/developer want. Getting the customer involved early on in the testing is key. Customers should be involved in acceptance testing and can also be leveraged in running manual test plans.

Where to Start

Getting the terminology down is the first hurdle. In the following chapters we will discuss the terminology and different types of testing disciplines. Where applicable, templates will be provided to help get you started. The best way to start testing is to jump in headfirst. Pick a project you're familiar with and create some tests.

Generally, most companies use a common library or framework for various projects. These frameworks take the form of logging, data access, message handling, and so on. A good way to learn how to write good unit tests is to start unit testing this library. You may see that the library you thought had a good architecture is not as easy to test as you expected. Nowadays, most of these frameworks also include their own unit tests that you can use as reference material. Another great way to start is by looking at other peoples' tests with open source projects being a goldmine of useful information. By seeing how other people created tests for these projects, you will be able to pick up some tricks to help you when you start writing tests.

Getting Started with Test Driven Development

Before you dive into TDD, you should spend a great deal of time working with code that was not designed to be tested via automation. Focus on techniques and patterns to write good tests for the code you are able to test. Slowly start to refactor code that is not testable into new abstractions that are testable. Spend time learning how to break dependencies. When you have hit the point where you understand how to abstract code out to make it testable, you will then see that Test Driven Development is a horrible name for the development and it should be named something such as Well Designed Code That Can Be Tested Driven Development (WDCTCBTDD).

Test Driven Development will be covered in more depth in Chapter 2, but readers should understand it's very difficult to decide they are going to practice TDD when they don't have the fundamental testing and software design skills in place.

> *A study commissioned in 2002 by the U.S. Department of Commerce's National Institute of Standards and Technology, found software bugs, or errors, are so prevalent and so detrimental that they cost the U.S. economy an estimated $59.5 billion annually, or about 0.6 percent of the gross domestic product.*

When Should Testing Be Automated?

The discussion about whether and when testing should be automated has been going back and forth for many years. When considering this argument, it is important to remember that testing actually covers a number of different techniques, and as such, this question cannot result in a simple yes or no answer. Instead, you need to look at every feature and type of testing which needs to be performed and decide on a case-by-case basis. But how do you decide?

First, you need to consider what you are asking. You are trying to decide if a test you need to perform should be done using script\code and made into an automatable, repeatable test or if you want to manually perform the test each time you change something. You then need to consider the type of testing you want to perform and consider the cost of automating the process as opposed to the cost of repeating the test. You need to consider the cost of maintaining the automated test compared to our manual test. Finally, you need to think about the cost of it going wrong and a bug ending up in production. With these factors considered, you can decide if you think the cost of automating is worth the cost and effort compared to manual testing.

With that in mind, let's consider some initial problem domains and the general thought process when faced with the question of whether or not to automate.

When unit testing, our main focus will be on the business logic and process. Arguably, this is the most important part of any application as this defines what happens and how it will happen. If this logic is incorrect, it can cause a lot of pain because it generally will only appear in production. We have already discussed that bugs found in production are the most expensive to fix. Having the production that the unit tests in place provide against bugs making their way into production is definitively an important factor. With business logic, if you have designed your system in a testable fashion then you should find that the tests are easy to write and maintain. If you need to make changes to the underlying logic due to the design of the system being testable, then the cost of maintaining the costs should be minimal, especially when combined with the lower cost of ownership of the core system.

Though your automated tests will verify the business logic is correct, you could also manually test this. However, there are a few major blockers to this idea. Firstly, to test the business logic you would need to go via a UI, either the main applications or the custom wrote UI. This has two possible problems: the main application might have bugs, which blocks you from testing the logic. Or, it hasn't been written yet. Combine this with the fact that after every code change you would need to manually re-enter all these values and edge cases into the UI and verify the result was as you expected based on either a specification or previous experience. As far as we're concerned, this makes automating the business logic essential.

The next major parts of most applications are the data access layer and interacting with a database. The levels of interaction with a database can vary greatly. For example, you could be using the database as a simple data store which your application will pull all the information required from and process within the business logic. The other case is that all your business logic actually takes place within stored procedures and your application simply pulls the data and renders it on-screen. In either case, you have similar issues to what you had with the business logic. If you were to manually test the database, you would need to write some custom queries or UI to execute your logic which is expensive in itself. If you were to automate you could insert the required test data automatically and test your logic, and then verify the results in a more effective fashion.

However, database tests have a series of problems. For starters, the tests are a lot slower than if they were simply running in memory, something that we'll discuss in more depth in Chapter 4. Secondly, if our database schema changes, the tests are more likely to break without re-factoring tools to support us as with business logic. Even with this additional overhead, automating your database tests generally still have a lower cost than manual testing.

The final level is the GUI. This is the area that causes most debate about whether it should be automated or not. The GUI has some interesting problems when it comes to automated testing which we will dive into in Chapter 5. The main problem is that when you are automating the UI you are verifying for correctness; however, because you are already testing the business logic, you are actually only verifying the behavior of the UI. Verifying this behavior is an expensive process because you are trying to replicate the UI's logic as steps within the test code. Although it is possible and certainly can lead to success, it can be expensive. If the behavior changes then it means the tests also need to be manually updated.

If you compare this to manual testing, then you are still performing the behavior verification, and, as before, are also performing usability testing, — verifying the rendering is correct — and checking text for spellings. All this is very expensive to automate, and as such, doing it manually could prove to be more effective as you also generally need to perform it less. There is some benefit to automating the UI behavior tests; it can be made more effective and more appealing, which we will discuss in Chapter 5.

But remember, if you don't automate your tests then you will manually need to perform each test for each release. If you think this will be a painful and costly process, then automate.

Introducing the ASP.NET Family

When ASP.NET was released in 2002, there was not much of a "family" to speak of. During the past six years, many new components have been developed under the ASP.NET product umbrella and warrant a brief discussion. Throughout this book, we will apply the testing topics and tools for each type of testing discussed in this book — many of the products in the ASP.NET family.

- ❏ **ASP.NET WebForms.** When people think of ASP.NET, developers think of WebForms. WebForms consist of an ASPX file, designer file, and a code-behind file. The majority of ASP.NET applications are built using this technology. In fact, WebForms is the View Rendering template engine which lives on top of the core ASP.NET runtime built using WebForms.

- ❏ **ASP.NET MVC.** The ASP.NET MVC Framework is an implementation of the Model View Controller (MVC) architectural pattern that isolates business logic, data logic, and user interface logic. In the past, Microsoft developers have thought of this type of architecture as layers, but MVC is more about components than layers.

- ❏ **Silverlight.** In 2007, Microsoft released Silverlight, which is a cross-platform/browser, multimedia browser platform for developing Rich Internet Applications (RIA). The user interface is created using the XAML markup language similar to Windows Presentation Foundation (WPF).

- ❏ **ASP.NET Web Services.** ASP.NET Web Services are components installed on a web server that allow applications to make HTTP requests to the component and receive data back in a standard format such as XML or SOAP.

- ❏ **ASP.NET AJAX Framework.** Included with Visual Studio 2008 by default, and Visual Studio 2005 as a standalone extension, Microsoft has provided ASP developers with an AJAX framework to aid in asynchronous JavaScript calls .

- ❏ **ADO.NET Data Services.** Code named Astoria, ADO.NET Data Services is a framework of patterns and libraries that enable creation and consumption of ADO data in the cloud (the Internet). ADO.NET data services interfaces to data with well-known formats such as JSON and XML.

In 1997, soon after Internet Information Systems 4 (IIS) shipped, Mark Anders and Scott Guthrie began work on the predecessor of ASP 3.0, what many developers now call "classic ASP." One of the main goals of this new project is to address separation of concern much better than the previous version of ASP. Through a few name changes (XSP and ASP+), what we now call ASP.NET 1.0 WebForms was released to the world on January 5, 2002.

Summary

The aim of this chapter is to provide you with some context to the book itself and provide you with an introduction into testing. We introduced you to the various testing terminologies, attempted to solve some of the testing myths, and provided you with some initial starting points to get you on your way.

In the next chapter we will focus more on developing the application and starting to think about the design and testability of applications to ensure they are testable.

2

Design and Testability

When writing code and developing software, one of the most important aspects to keep in mind is, "How am I going to test this?" The *testability* of software (another way of saying how easily the software can be tested), is an important consideration that most software developers forget. If testability is considered from the first line of code, then the testing efficiency and the quality of the software are greatly increased.

To achieve a testable application, you need to be in the mindset of thinking about testing when it comes to writing the code. Whether the code is about new functionality or fixing a bug, you should always be writing tests to reflect the changes. When in this mindset, the process of writing a test and writing code becomes a natural combination of activities. This mindset sometimes requires that you take a step back from your code and consider the effect that the change will have on your code and its overall structure and testability.

One important aspect of testability is your code's design. If you design your code while keeping in mind ways to successfully test it, then the various aspects discussed in this book become easier to take advantage of and implement. This doesn't mean you can't apply the techniques when testing hasn't been considered first; it means that the techniques can be more difficult to use and that you might need to approach them in a different fashion.

In short, considering how the design will affect testing should ensure that your software is of higher quality with lower maintenance costs.

Why Should a Developer Care about Testing?

This is a question that has been a popular topic in the development circles as of late: if I'm a developer, why should I care about testing? Isn't this why there are testers?

We think that every developer should care about *all* aspects of the software development lifecycle, from gathering initial requirements to maintaining the live running systems. As such, a developer needs to care about what happens when the system enters the testing phase because it's an important stage and needs to be as effective as possible.

Testing should also extend to how developers produce the code. As a software developer, you should always verify that the code you've produced matches what you expected it to do. This verification can be done manually or via automated tests. By verifying that the code meets your own assumptions, you can remove those simple, easy-to-solve bugs with very little effort before they enter QA. Testers can then focus on the important issues, such as does the software actually meet the customer's requirements, does it work effectively in production, and more importantly, are any other features broken? The result is improved productivity for the team, because testers are not as concerned with the basic functionality at the class and method level, instead of focusing on the larger picture. As a result, you should be able to fix problems while still maintaining focus on developing the particular block of code. This should result in a lower bug count and higher-quality software for the end-user.

Developer Testing

Developer testing covers a wide variety of techniques; however, the general theme is to create automated tests to verify that the method has been implemented correctly. In other words, developer testing generally involves writing tests using code, generally the same language that the main application has been created in. Because they are in code, they can be run as often as required. These tests should be used to verify that your own assumptions are correct and that the implementation is correct — both when it has just been developed and going forward. There are also many other advantages, such as improved design, readability, and allowing for shared understanding of the code which we will discuss throughout this chapter. The most fundamental technique of developer testing is *unit testing*.

Unit Testing

Unit testing is a very large topic and could easily be a book by itself. However, we want to provide you with a gentle introduction so that you'll have a firm foundation into the technique. Unit testing is when a developer verifies that a small isolated unit of code is working properly. Testing a small, isolated unit, for example, a *method*, is important for a number of reasons. First, unit tests are designed to be run often and as such they need to be fast. Some people run their tests hundreds of times a day and they need to be as quick to execute as possible. If a method accesses the file system or a database, for example, then the additional overhead can quickly add up and cause major problems. Smaller tests are generally easier to write and maintain, which will result in your being able to write them quicker with a lower cost of ownership.

Another advantage for isolated tests is that they are less dependent on a particular file or database being in the correct place at the correct time; this can lead to more fragile tests as they are more likely to fail because of environment issues rather than the code issues. We've found that this results in long debugging sessions attempting to identify why a particular test has failed.

The aim of unit testing is to have a suite of unit tests that each exercise the system in a certain fashion. Each unit test is used to verify a particular action about the system, but also have the positive side effect of providing examples of how to interact with the different objects. These examples could demonstrate the types of arguments, expected returns types, or scenarios when exceptions are thrown — this combines into an excellent form of documentation of the system for the team.

Unit tests are generally created with the support of a unit testing framework. There are various frameworks available for .NET, some of which are discussed in the next section. These frameworks provide the support for knowing which methods to execute as tests and provide additional functionality to support the developer when writing the tests. An example of a unit test for a particular framework might look similar to this:

```
[TestFixture]
public class Name_Of_The_TestClass_Goes_Here
{
  [Test]
  public void Name_Of_The_Test_Goes_Here()
  {
    //Test code goes here
  }
}
```

Fundamentally, there are a few key points to the previous example. First, the test methods must be within a public class that has the attribute TestFixture. Second, the test method itself needs to be public with the attribute of Test. We will discuss the test code in more depth throughout this book.

Different unit testing frameworks will have different syntax. In this book, we use nUnit. Try not to focus on the syntax in general, but on the concepts introduced in this book instead. After you have a firm understanding of the concepts that are involved in creating unit tests, you will be able to use different unit testing frameworks with ease.

When you have your tests, you will need some way to execute them to find out if they pass or fail. Most frameworks come with various different ways of executing their unit tests, some of which are discussed in more depth in the next section.

When creating unit tests, there are a series of best practices that should be followed. The most important practice is to treat test code with the same consideration and importance as you do for application code. This means checking it into source control, building the tests with your product, but also making sure they are readable, no duplicated code and shared logic broken into additional helper methods where required.

The next important factor is around the readability of the tests. Your tests exist for as long, if not longer, as the code they are testing so it is important that they are clear and understandable. The first step is by having a good name for the test. For example, consider these two tests:

```
[Test]
public void Test854()
{
        Assert.AreEqual(1, new Example().Count);
}
```

Compared to:

```
[Test]
public void When_New_Example_Object_Is_Created_The_Count_Should_Equal_One()
{
        Assert.AreEqual(1, new Example().Count);
}
```

Both tests do exactly the same thing, and both will pass\fail if count does not equal one. However, the second test tells you what you are expecting to happen and provides some context, which will help us when reading the test and identifying the reason why it failed. With the first test, you need to think and reverse-engineer the test code before you will know what to expect. This is why naming is important. It's a common practice when creating tests to separate words with underscores to improve readability; however, some people prefer to write the tests without the underscores in place. This is a personal choice between you and your team to decide what format is most readable.

Another important factor is how your tests are structured within the solution. One of our recommendations is to have a separate assembly that contains the tests for your implementation. For example, if your main assembly was called MyApplication.BusinessLogic, then your test assembly would be MyApplication.BusinessLogic.Tests. You should also indicate whether the assembly contained unit tests, integration tests, or UI tests, which we will discuss in later chapters. As a result, the full name would be MyAppliction.BusinessLogic.Tests.Unit. In terms of namespaces and classes, you should follow a similar approach. You should keep the namespaces the same, adding Tests to the end of the class name. If we were creating unit tests for the object Online, which existed in the namespace MyApplication.BusinessLogic.PaymentProcessing, the tests would be in the namespace MyApplication.BusinessLogic.Tests.Unit.PaymentProcess with the test fixture called OnlineTests. As a result, solution explorer would look similar to Figure 2-1.

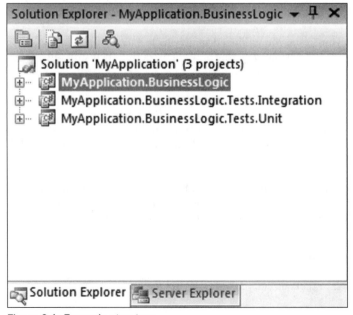

Figure 2-1: Example structure

By having this strict structure, navigating between implementation and tests becomes much easier.

After naming, the next important fact is the test code itself. As previously mentioned, test code should be treated with as much importance as production code. One effective way to achieve this is by using test helper methods. These methods can contain the repetitive logic for use amongst your different tests. If these helper methods are named correctly, then they can actually improve readability. Next you'll see an example of a test helper method called CreateExampleWriter(). This method will construct the object that you use within your unit test. If this logic was located within the unit test itself, then maintenance costs would increase:

```
[Test]
public void When_New_Example_Object_Is_Created_The_Count_Should_Equal_One()
{
        Example e = new Example(CreateExampleWriter())
        Assert.AreEqual(1, e.Count);
}

Public ExampleWriter CreateExampleWriter()
{
        ExampleWriter ew = ExampleWriter();
        Ew.Output = new StringBuilder();
        Return ew;
}
```

An item often overlooked is the fact that each test should only be testing for one thing. This is for two reasons: The first is that if the test fails, identifying why it failed becomes much harder because there could be multiple causes. Ideally, you want the reason why a test failed to be very clear and apparent, because debugging your unit tests to identify the reason it failed is a huge drain on your energy levels and productivity. The second reason is maintainability: If you have large tests, then the maintenance costs will be higher as the code will be more difficult to understand.

After you have your tests in place, the next important question is how much you should test. Although we will discuss this in more detail in Chapter 3, it's important to introduce the concept of code coverage now. *Code coverage* is a percentage of how much code your tests cover. When you execute your tests with the support of a coverage tool, every line executed is tracked. As a result, the tool knows how much code is executed by your tests and the amount of code coverage is the "untested" amount. Different communities take different stances on code coverage and the ideal percentage for the applications codebase (all of the code for the application). Some developers will say that 100 percent coverage is a must; however, I have found that this is extremely difficult to achieve. Personally, I think 80 to 90 percent coverage is a good target to aim for, with 70 percent as the minimum. Although code coverage is a good metric, many people place too much reliance on it. You could very easily get high coverage, although your tests only actually verify the actions of one line of the code.

A more important consideration than coverage is how much confidence you have in your tests. Your tests are verifying that the system is working as expected, and it's important that you trust the result. If you don't trust that your tests are telling you the right result, then they are an expensive artifact to have. In addition, you will have to perform a significant amount of manual testing.

Gaining confidence in other people's and your own tests can be difficult. However, there are techniques you can use to offset these concerns. Each test you write should be self-verifying — meaning there is a check to verify whether the test passed or failed. If you have to manually check the results of a test, then it is definitely not a unit test. To make a test self-verifying, you will generally include an assertion which must hold true for the test to pass. If the assertion fails then the test fails.

Another factor that can help gain confidence in your tests is to include your unit tests in a code review process. Code reviews build confidence within the team and ensure that the tests are focusing on the correct items and following the best practices. The unit tests should also be a useful initial point when starting code reviews. As I mentioned before, unit tests are a form of documentation to describe what the code is doing. As such, they should be able to add value to code reviews.

No matter how good your unit tests are, they are wasted if they are never executed. They should be executed as often as possible, which is one reason why you need to keep them isolated and focused so that they can be run quickly. Ideally, after every change you make you should run your entire suite of tests on your local machine. There should also be a continuous integration server in place that will automatically detect when commits have been made to source control which results in the server automatically building the project and running the unit tests. If a test fails, then the build should fail, informing everyone on the team that something has gone wrong. The developer who caused the build to break should then fix the problem. This is one of the reasons why it is important for code reviews to include unit tests, as it is the team's responsibility to maintain the tests not just the original author.

When most developers/testers hear the phrase "continuous integration," they think of a tool such as Cruise Control or Team City. Continuous integration should be thought of as a process, where development teams integrate their small units of code frequently throughout the day to produce an application that builds successfully.

Tools such as Cruise Control support plug-in models that include tools that will build the application, run the unit tests, copy the build to a directory, send emails based on the status of the build, and even provide code coverage statistics.

Unit Testing Frameworks

The .NET Framework is lucky enough to have a vast number of excellent unit testing frameworks to support you when writing tests. Each framework has a different approach, targeting a different set of users. Choosing which unit testing framework to use comes down to experience and your own goals. Currently, the most common framework is nUnit and this is an excellent starting point.

Another popular testing framework is MbUnit, which focuses on extendibility and data-driven tests while being compatible with the nUnit syntax.

MSTest is the framework included as part of Visual Studio 2005 and 2008 and has slightly different syntax to nUnit. Instead of TestFixture attribute, it is called TestClass and instead of the Test attribute you need to use TestMethod.

Finally, the newest framework is xUnit.NET. xUnit is a very effective framework, which takes a different approach and view to the other frameworks. The syntax is also slightly different; for example you don't need to specify the TestFixture attribute, and instead of specifying the Test attribute, you use the Fact attribute. The reason for this name change is that both Brad Wilson and James Newkirk, the creators of xUnit, feel that unit tests should actually document "facts" about the code. As such, if the unit test fails, then the fact is wrong. Although this is a different view, it is actually logical. The reason for the name change is because the creators do not view each method as a test for the code; instead they view each method as a fact about the code.

When it comes to choosing a framework, if creating tests through code is a new concept, it's recommended that you start with nUnit. nUnit provides a great foundation for learning how to create tests. After you gain some experience with nUnit, start to investigate MbUnit or xUnit. Your initial experience with nUnit will provide a great basis to serve as a comparison to MbUnit and xUnit to see what those frameworks provide.

Unit Test Runners

After you have selected your framework you will need a runner to execute the tests. nUnit, as with MbUnit and xUnit, comes with a console application for executing tests from the command line, with the results being written to the console. It also includes a UI and support for executing your tests from a build script such as NAnt or MSBuild.

Visual Studio includes support for executing tests created with MSTest, and in Visual Studio 2010 this is being opened to other frameworks. There is also a commercial add-in called TestDriven.NET which provides Visual Studio integration allowing you to execute tests for nUnit, MbUnit, and xUnit.

Finally, a framework called Gallio is providing a test automation platform offering a runner, including GUI, command line, TD.NET, Visual Studio integration, and many others.

Test Driven Development

We, along with many other people, feel that unit testing only solves a small part of the problem of testing. Unit testing provides benefits in the fact that you have some verification that the software is working as expected going forward. However, there is one major problem. Adding unit tests to a system after it has been developed is a long process because you are attempting to reverse-engineer the system's implementation. When the code is already in place, then your unit tests' implementation are bound to how the code was written and where the code hasn't been considered for testing. As such, the writing of the tests can be much more difficult and harder to understand.

As a developer, your motivational mindset is also different. You have already written the code, which means taking the additional step of writing the code to verify it works is more difficult to justify. Developers can be more tempted to bypass this stage with the promise of going back and adding unit tests at a later point. Sadly, this is a slippery slope that many developers have been faced with. The more code that is added without unit tests, the harder it will be to go back and add unit tests, until you reach the point where both the code coverage and your confidence in the unit tests are much lower. During this anti-pattern process, all the different considerations that once would have been taken (such as running the tests and designing for testability) have been forgotten, with the code quality deteriorating.

To combat this, *Test Driven Development* (TDD) is used. The concept of TDD can definitely help combat the concerns mentioned previously. Instead of writing the unit tests after you have finished development, referred to as Test After Development (TAD) or Test Eventually Development (TED), you write the unit test first and then implement code to make the test pass. After doing this, you can improve the code to improve maintainability. The TDD community came up with a mantra for this approach that people should follow, called "Red, Green, Refactor."

The red is a reference for creating a new test that will fail when it is executed because the code hasn't been implemented. This first part is a bit obvious on the .NET platform: because the code hasn't been implemented, the application will not compile — hence your first phase of red. The red reference is the first stage of the test. You have written a test based on how you are planning to implement a small section of code. Generally, you the developer, only write one test based on the code you are just about to implement, ideally within the same minute to help you maintain focus. The test should set up the object you are going to interact with, the method you are going to call, and the expected result at the end. If you don't know what the expected result is before you start, it's important to take a step back and think about your code and its requirements. If you start writing code without a clear objective, then it is likely to miss your actual requirement. This is one of the advantages that TDD brings, encouraging you to focus on what is actually happening and how to get it done.

After you have the first stage of the test failing, the next stage is to make it green. The most important fact to remember is that you should only write enough code to make the test pass, nothing more and nothing less. Another point to remember is that you should only write new code if you have an associated failing test. If you need to make a change, then you should write a failing test which demonstrates the change you are about to make and execute the test to verify the change has been done correctly.

Identifying this change from failing to passing is important. First, it tells you that you are finished — if you need to continue, you need another test. Secondly, it comes back to having confidence in your tests. If you only ever see the test as green, how can you be 100 percent sure that it is working correctly and you haven't made a mistake? By seeing it change when you expect, then you have more confidence in both your test and your implementation. Again, this is why the red stage is important, because you want to see the test red (a test failure) before you proceed.

After you have your code implemented and it passes the test, the next stage is to *refactor*. Refactoring is the concept of taking your existing code and improving the quality. At this stage you are not adding or changing any functionality, but you are trying to improve the readability and maintainability of the code going forward. Common scenarios of refactoring are extracting code into a separate method to remove duplication, or moving existing methods into a separate class to improve the isolation. By completing the refactoring at this stage, you are still focused on the small isolated section of code you have just implemented, but you can also take a step back and look at how it fits into the overall picture of your systems architecture. Although you shouldn't be changing the functionality of the code, you have your tests in place to ensure you don't break anything.

> *Refactoring is the process of improving code, but without changing the result that the code produces. If you have ever split large functions into smaller functions, or have renamed a class, then you have refactored code. As with many other computer science techniques and practices, you may have been practicing this process but been unaware that there was a name for it. The term re-factor can be traced to William Opdyke's 1993 Ph.D. dissertation entitled* Refactoring Object-Oriented Frameworks.

> *The practice of refactoring plays a large role in Test Driven Development (TDD), which we cover in depth in Chapter 3.*

After you have implemented a section of code following the Red-Green-Refactor rule, the next step is to repeat it. By following this approach for your entire development process, you will be well on your way to successfully performing TDD.

The problem with following this approach is that it takes a great deal of self-control and willpower, at least at the beginning. As mentioned before, the best approach is to get yourself into the mindset of wanting to develop your code using TDD. If you get into the habit of always wanting to write a test before you write your code, you stand a much better chance of succeeding. After you have been in this mindset for a short period of time, you'll find that it becomes a very natural way to develop software.

You will also find that if you are developing software using TDD, the actual code you write will be very different. Because you are using the tests to guide you, you will find that you are writing much less code because you are only writing exactly what is required. Although this is important, a more important goal is the design of the system. This brings us to an important fact about TDD that is often overlooked. TDD is not about testing! TDD is about designing your software. The tests that are created are just a happy side effect that can be used for regression testing in the future.

Design and Test Driven Development

As we've said, TDD is not about testing; it's more of a design technique. But how can writing tests before you write the code encourage a good design? Simply taking the time to stop and think before you write code can have a huge impact on the design of a system. This leads to an important question: what is a good design?

Well-designed software is the subject of many different books. However, we follow a core set of concepts focused on the SOLID principles outlined by Robert Martin (a.k.a. Uncle Bob). SOLID is a set of five principles based on the best practices for object-oriented development.

> The SOLID design principles started as a reply to a 1995 newsgroup thread entitled "The Ten Commandments of OO Programming." This reply was formed by Robert Martin (Uncle Bob), and has become a great set of standards that many developers follow.
>
> The principles encompassed in SOLID have been around for years, but many developers tend to ignore these principles that have been proven to aid in creating great software.

S — The Single Responsibility Principle

> *"There should never be more than one reason for a class to change."*
>
> — *Robert Martin (Uncle Bob)* `http://www.objectmentor.com/resources/articles/srp.pdf`

The first principle defined in SOLID is that each class should have a single responsibility. A *responsibility* is defined here as being a reason to change. If a class has multiple responsibilities, then there are multiple reasons why it could change. If each class only has its own responsibilities, then they will be more focused, isolated, and easier to test as a result.

For example, consider the Customer class in Figure 2-2.

Figure 2-2: Customer class model with
multiple responsibilities

This class has two different responsibilities which breaks this principle. One role for the Customer class in Figure 2-2 is storing the domain information about the customer, for example their name and address. The second role is the ability to persist this information. If you wanted to add more information about the customer, then that would cause it to change. If you were to change the way you persisted the customer, then that would also cause the same class to change.

This is not ideal. Ideally, there would be two separate classes with each focused on their own roles in the system, as shown in Figure 2-3.

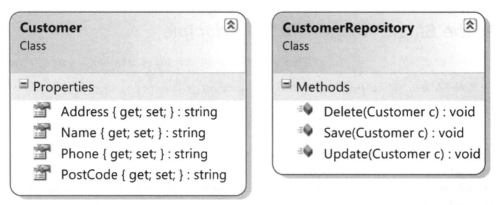

Figure 2-3: Customer class and Repository class model each with separate responsibilities

Figure 2-3 splits the original design into two classes. The system is now more isolated and each class focuses on its own responsibility. As your system is now more decoupled, if you wanted to change how you persisted a Customer object you would either change the CustomerRepository object or create a separate class without having to modify the Customer class.

When you attempt to understand a class to modify it, you tend to attempt to understand *all* the roles a class performs as a whole, even if there are a lot of roles. It can be a daunting task to be faced with a new section of the system because there is so much to understand. If your classes were more isolated, with correct responsibilities, then your code would be easier to understand because you would be able to process the information in small chunks.

From the viewpoint of TDD and testability, the tests you write are now more focused. If you wanted to test either a Customer object or an object dependent on the Customer object, you wouldn't need to be concerned with the persistence side. If you had to initiate a database connection every time you created a Customer object, then your tests would become more heavyweight and take much longer to execute. As with the code, the tests that are created for these objects are now also easier to understand due to the more focused isolation.

However, one of the difficult facts about this principle is identifying the actual requirements. As mentioned, the Single Responsibility Principle defines a responsibility as a "reason for change." If you look at a class and can identify more than one reason why it might need to change, then it has more than one responsibility.

O — The Open Closed Principle

> *"Software entities (classes, modules, functions, etc)*
> *should be open for extension but closed for modification."*

— *Robert Martin (Uncle Bob)* `http://www.objectmentor.com/resources/articles/ocp.pdf`

This principle is focused on creating decoupled, extendable systems so that when changes are required, they can be achieved in an effective fashion with very little impact and overall cost.

The term *open* refers to the fact that an item should be extendable and abstract. This means that if you need to change some of the behavior of the class, you can achieve it without having to change the code. An example of this is to replace the dependencies of different parts of the system by providing a different implementation or take advantage of inheritance and override selected behavior. To do this, you need to think about extensibility and how your application is coupled together.

The term *closed* relates to the first principle of the Single Responsibility Principle (SRP): a class should be closed from requiring modifications to be made when adding new or changing functionality. When reviewing your code, if you find that a section of code needs to be changed every time you implement new functionality, then it isn't closed.

In real-world terms, a class can never be closed from modifications; however, you can make huge gains by thinking about how you structure your code so that it is as closed as it possibly can be. Remember that SOLID is a set of principles, not hard and fast rules.

First, you'll look at an example which violates the open\closed principle, as shown in Figure 2-4. Imagine you have a system that needs to decide which company should be used for shipping a particular order. This could be based on a number of different criteria; however, in this example it is simply based on the postcode.

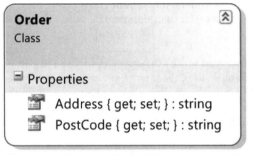
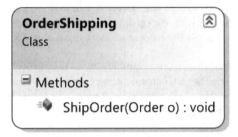

Figure 2-4: Order and OrderShipper class model

In this first example, you have an OrderShipping. The special casing of the terms already clues the reader in to the fact that they are methods and objects with a method called ShipOrder. Based on the Order object, this method decides which company is the most appropriate and starts processing the shipment:

```
public void ShipOrder(Order o)
{
    int i;
    if(o.PostCode.StartsWith("A"))
    {
        //Do processing for CompanyA
    }
    else if (o.PostCode.StartsWith("B") || int.TryParse(o.PostCode, out i))
    {
        //Do processing for CompanyB
    }
    else if (o.PostCode.StartsWith("C"))
    {
        //Do processing for CompanyC
    }
}
```

This method has a number of problems. First, it's breaking the first principle of SRP, but more importantly it is an expensive design to work with when you want to make changes. If you wanted to add a new shipper to the list, you would have to add another additional if statement to the list. If one of your existing shippers changed the rules, then you would need to go back and modify this single method. Imagine if the system grew from three shippers to a thousand shippers. This single method will soon become uncontrollable, not maintainable, and as a result a lot more likely to contain bugs.

Here's the same scenario, but following the open\close principle instead.

In Figure 2-5 you can see that the shipping process has been decoupled. Every company now has its own object within the system, associated together by a common interface. If a new shipper needs to be added, you can simply create a new object and inherit from this interface.

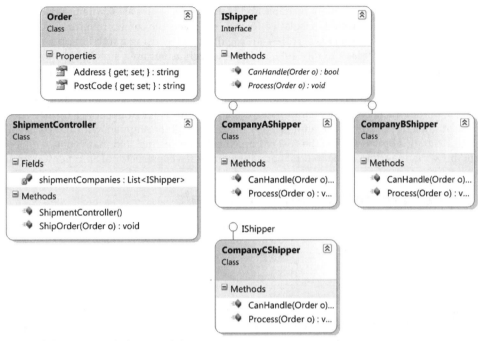

Figure 2-5: Decoupled class model

Each of the objects implements two methods: one is based on whether they can ship the order, and the other is based on processing the actual order. The CanHandle method takes the logic from the previous example and has extracted it into its own class and method:

```
public bool CanHandle(Order o)
{
    if (o.PostCode.StartsWith("A"))
        return true;

    return false;
}
```

Also, Figure 2-5 introduces a ShipmentController. This simply asks all the shippers if they can ship the order; if they can, the controller then calls Process and stops:

```
public void ShipOrder(Order o)
{
    foreach (var company in shipmentCompanies)
    {
        if (company.CanHandle(o))
        {
            company.Process(o);
            break;
        }
    }
}
```

The resulting code is not only more readable and maintainable — it's also more testable. The logic for each company can now be tested in isolation to ensure it meets the correct requirements, and you can test that the ShipmentController is correctly calling the items by using a stub IShipper object. Stubs is a concept that we'll cover later in the Stubs and Mocks section. For now, simply by following this principle, you have made your tests easier to write and maintain and have improved the quality of the code.

Although you have improved the code, there are still problems. If you add a new shipper, you'll need to inform the ShipmentController about the new shipper. This is far from being a disaster, because you could implement support for automatically identifying all the shippers within the system. But you need to weigh this option against the cost of implementation, testing, and maintenance to decide if this would be worth the effort, compared to manually editing the constructor of ShipmentController.

L — The Liskov Substitution Principle

"Classes must be able to use objects of derived classes without knowing it."

— *Robert Martin (Uncle Bob)* `http://www.objectmentor.com/resources/articles/lsp.pdf`

The Liskov Substitution Principle is based on the concept that all implementations should program against the abstract class and should be able to accept any subclass without side effects. Classes should never be aware of any subclass or concrete implementation, instead it should only be concerned with the interface. The aim here is that you can replace the functionality with a different implementation without modifying the code base.

The example in Figure 2-6 violates the principle. You have a simple string formatter and all the formatters inherit from IFormatter. As such, you should be able to use any formatter in exactly the same fashion.

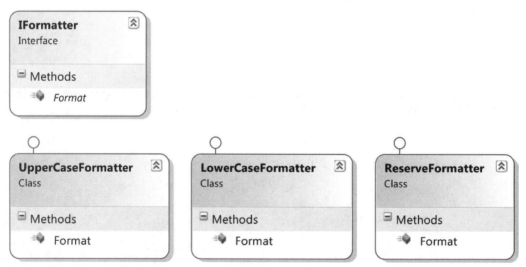

Figure 2-6: Class diagram of principal

However, the Format method for each class handles empty strings in a slightly different way. For example, the uppercase formatter is shown next:

```
class UpperCaseFormatter: IFormatter
{
    public string Format(string s)
    {
        if(String.IsNullOrEmpty(s))
            throw new ArgumentNullException("s");

        return s.ToUpper();
    }
}
```

Although many might consider throwing an exception to be bad practice, in the right scenario this could be acceptable. However, for the lowercase formatter in the same scenario it would return null:

```
class LowerCaseFormatter: IFormatter
{
    public string Format(string s)
    {
        if (String.IsNullOrEmpty(s))
            return null;

        return s.ToLower();
    }
}
```

This breaks the principle. The expectation of how you expect the implementations to work is different. Imagine if you had a large number of different implementations, each behaving slightly differently: your implemented code would be chaos. Instead, you want a consistent view of how the code should work with each implementation being constant. For example, it should return String.Empty:

```
if (String.IsNullOrEmpty(s))
    return String.Empty;
```

Another common cause for breaking this principle is when implementers demand more information than stated by the method signature or interface. In the following class, the correct interface has been implemented, but a new public property has also been added for total width:

```
class PaddingStringFormatter: IFormatter
{
    public int TotalWidth { get; set; }
    public string Format(string s)
    {
        return s.PadLeft(TotalWidth, '_');
    }
}
```

When a developer comes along who wants to use the previous class, they need to cast the formatter argument down to the concrete instance. I'm sure you've encountered code similar to this before:

```
class Implementor
{
```

```
public void OutputHelloWorld(IFormatter formatter)
{
    string s = "Hello World";

    PaddingStringFormatter padder = formatter as PaddingStringFormatter;
    if(padder != null)
    {
        padder.TotalWidth = 20;
        s = padder.Format(s);
    }

    Console.WriteLine(s);
}
}
```

Ideally, you want to move away from code such as this, because it causes a lot more coupling to occur. When it comes to testing, it is also much more difficult, because you need to be aware of the internals of a method and how this affects execution.

The Liskov substitution principle was introduced by Barbara Liskov during a 1987 keynote titled "Data Abstraction and Hierarchy." In 1968, Liskov was the first woman in the United States to be awarded a Ph.D. from a computer science department (Stanford University). More recently, Liskov was awarded with the 2008 Turning Award for her contributions to practical and theoretical foundations of programming languages and system design.

I — Interface Segregation Principle

> *"Clients should not be focused to depend upon interfaces that they do not use."*

— *Robert Martin (Uncle Bob)* http://www.objectmentor.com/resources/articles/isp.pdf

This principle states that interfaces should have high cohesion to allow clients to keep their implementation as minimal as possible. Simply put, clients should not be forced to depend upon interfaces that they do not use.

This principle is often broken without people realizing about the possible implications. For example, it's often broken in parts of the .NET Framework, particularly ASP.NET. The main cause of this principle being broken is when a particular interface is too large with too many unrelated methods. As a result of implementing a simple interface, the concrete implementation must implement nonrequired methods to get the desired effect.

The result of heavy interfaces is a large amount of unwanted boiler plate code, making your objects move heavyweight and memory intensive. The interfaces also tend to be more confusing making it more difficult to know which methods you use.

In an ideal scenario, your interfaces should be lightweight and simple to implement allowing for an accurate description of what the class actually does. As with before, let's start with a simple example that breaks this principle, as shown in Figure 2-7.

Imagine you have extended your shipment options.

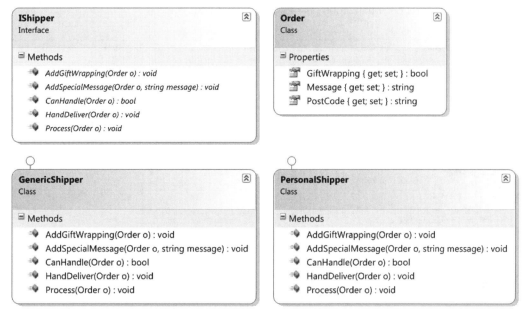

Figure 2-7: Two implementations of the IShipper interface

Next you can see the ability to add some personalization to an item:

```
interface IShipper
{
        bool CanHandle(Order o);
        void Process(Order o);
        void AddGiftWrapping(Order o);
        void HandDeliver(Order o);
        void AddSpecialMessage(Order o, string message);
}
```

The previous listing looks similar to a sensible interface. It defines what a shipper might have to do. However, if you look at the implementation you will notice the problem. Although your PersonalShipper object is fine, because the object requires all the methods to fulfill all the different options, your GenericShipper object doesn't offer any customization, but is still required to implement those additional methods. The result is that the code is littered with the following methods, which throw a NotSupportedException exception:

```
public void HandDeliver(Order o)
{
    throw new NotSupportedException("We do not support this option");
}
```

As the principle states, your GenericShipper object is dependent upon methods that it does not require. Ideally, you want to separate out the interface into two objects: one for the generic shipper and one for a shipper that supports personalization (as shown in Figure 2-8).

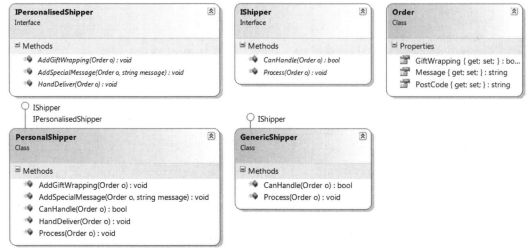

Figure 2-8: Shipper implementations with focused interfaces

With the two separate interfaces, it becomes easier to see what each shipper actually provides in terms of functionality. You have seen the distinction between PersonalShipper and GenericShipper very clearly from looking at the Classes interface. Although the implementation of PersonalShipper is identical, apart from implementing the new IPersonalisedShipper, your GenericShipper code is much shorter and simpler to maintain.

Although this principle is great from the code point of view, how does it affect testing and testability? As your interfaces are more focused, your client classes are also more focused, and as a result you do not have as much code to test. Before, you would have had to test the nonrequired methods and hence waste time or leave them untested, which affects your code coverage.

D — *The Dependency Inversion Principle*

> *"A. High-level modules should not depend upon low-level modules. Both should depend upon abstractions.*
>
> *B. Abstractions should not depend upon details. Details should depend upon abstractions."*

— *Robert Martin (Uncle Bob)* `http://www.objectmentor.com/resources/articles/dip.pdf`

When developing your system, if you have considered the other four principles you would have a decoupled and isolated system. However, at some point, all your isolated components will need to talk to each other. In the situation where you have dependencies within your system, you should then use abstractions as a way to manage them. By depending upon the abstractions and not the concrete class, you can interchange implementations when required.

The first term that needs to be defined in more detail is dependency. What is a dependency? In the context of this book, *dependency* is a low-level class that a higher-level class must use to fulfill its requirements. A simple example is that a text formatter shouldn't be concerned with how to actually obtain the text; if the formatter could only process text from a file called MyImportantDocument.docx, it would be extremely limiting. The formatter should be flexible enough to cope with many different ways of obtaining the text. By removing this lower-level dependency, your higher-level formatter can be more effectively reused.

The inversion part simply says that the dependency should come from outside and be placed into the class to use. Generally dependencies are created inside other classes and as such are closed. Inversion simply states that the dependency should be created outside the class and injected in.

A common example of this is the business logic and data access problem. You have two separate, isolated parts of the application that need to talk to each other. A common pattern is that the business logic would have created an instance of the DataAccess class and callmethods on it as represented in Figure 2-9.

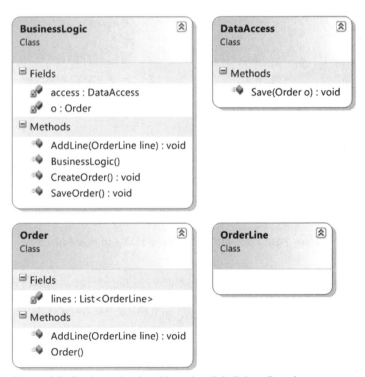

Figure 2-9: Business Logic with an implicit link to DataAccess

The constructor of the BusinessLogic class would reassemble the following listing:

```
private DataAccess access;
public BusinessLogic()
{
    access = new DataAccess();
}
```

A developer using the BusinessLogic class would have no idea how, or even if, the underlying system was accessing data until something went wrong. This common pattern is far from ideal. You want the dependency to be very clear, but also in control of the object which requires the dependency.

An improved example would look similar to Figure 2-10.

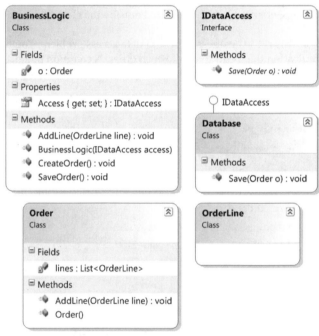

Figure 2-10: Dependency has been split and now explicit

Next, a new interface for defining a DataAccess object is included, as this allows you to have different implementations of the data access. In this case, you simply have the Database class. Your BusinessLogic class has a constructor that takes in an IDataAccess object as shown next:

```
public IDataAccess Access { get; set; }
public BusinessLogic(IDataAccess access)
{
    Access = access;
}
```

Now, the higher-level business logic does not depend on concrete implementation of the lower-level Data Access class.

From the point of view of an implementer of the BusinessLogic class, the dependency is quite apparent. There is a clear boundary between the two different parts of the system. Sometimes dependencies can hide themselves in unusual ways until they start to cause major problems. This is one example of where TDD can identify your dependencies much earlier in the process and change the way you develop software. As you want your unit tests to be nicely isolated and focused, you will find that if you are greeted with a dependency on a more complex or external part of the system then your tests will become much more difficult to write. When you see this issue in your tests, then you will know that you need to do something about it.

In this scenario, if you abstract and decouple the dependencies the DataAccess layer will no longer cause you problems when testing the BusinessLayer, because your tests will be in control of this external dependency.

However, if you have isolated all of your dependencies, and the user of the object is responsible for constructing the dependencies, then your code is quickly going to be difficult to manage.

Imagine the following scenario — your business logic code has dependencies on your Data Access layer, a user management system, and your shipment system. The Data Access layer also depends on a configuration object. The class diagram would look similar to Figure 2-11.

Figure 2-11: Decoupled system design with multiple dependencies

This is a well-designed, decoupled system. In theory, it should be good. However, if you need to construct a BusinessLogic class, then the code would look like this:

```
internal class SimpleUI
{
    public SimpleUI()
    {
```

```
        IConfiguration config = new Configuration();
        IDataAccess access = new ComplexDataAccess(config);
        IUserManagement management = new UserManagement();
        IShippingRules shippingRules = new ShippingRules();

        MoreComplexBusinessLogic logic = new MoreComplexBusinessLogic(access,
    management, shippingRules);
        }
    }
```

You can imagine that this would soon become extremely difficult to manage. If you introduced a new dependency, you would have to change a lot of the code. You could introduce a helper method, or you could have a parameter default constructor, which automatically defines the default objects to use:

```
internal class MoreComplexBusinessLogic
{
    public IDataAccess Access { get; set; }
    public IUserManagement User { get; set; }
    public IShippingRules ShippingRules { get; set; }

    public MoreComplexBusinessLogic(IDataAccess access, IUserManagement user,
IShippingRules shippingRules)
    {
        Access = access ?? new ComplexDataAccess(new Configuration());
        User = user ?? new UserManagement();
        ShippingRules = shippingRules ?? new ShippingRules();
    }

    public MoreComplexBusinessLogic(): this(null, null, null)
    {}
}
```

Managing dependencies via constructor overloading is bad! This is because you still have all the problems you had before as the concrete dependencies are still being hidden. If you removed or changed the ShippingRules object, then this constructor would break — even if you never used the overloaded version. It also causes confusion as you will never be 100 percent sure of which default implementation is being used and if that is even the correct set of objects to use. The result could be that the system only fails at runtime. The only advantage is that you can construct a new BusinessLogic with a single line of code, and this is still not a good enough reason.

Yet, you do want to be able to easily add new dependencies into a system without having to go back and update all the construction set-up code that you want to be a single line. The answer to this problem is to use an Inversion of Control, IoC, framework to support this scenario.

> *Inversion of Control is another one of those principles that has been around for years. A Google search will turn up a bunch of IoC frameworks for the .NET platform, but you don't have to download a large framework that someone else developed to take advantage of IoC. There are many situations where developers cannot use an open source framework. Because IoC is a pattern, don't be afraid to create your own framework.*

As with unit testing frameworks, there are a number of different IoC frameworks, each targeting and solving a particular problem in a particular way, yet the core concept is the same. In the next few examples we will be using a very simplistic 33 line IoC framework created by Ken Egozi.

The first major concept with an IoC has to do with the ways you set up your configuration and the mapping between the interface and concrete implementation. You should simply register all the interfaces using generics. The Register method will keep the mappings in memory, so this method only needs to be called the first time your application is initialized:

```
static class IoCRegister
{
    public static void Configure()
    {
        IoC.Register<IConfiguration, Configuration>();
        IoC.Register<IDataAccess, ComplexDataAccess>();
        IoC.Register<IUserManagement, UserManagement>();
        IoC.Register<IShippingRules, ShippingRules>();
    }
}
```

In the UI for this example, the Configure method is called to set up the mappings. You will need to ask the IoC framework to resolve and initialize an instance of the MoreComplexBusinessLogic class. Under the covers, it will resolve all the dependencies for the constructor of each object based on our configuration:

```
internal class SimpleUI
{
    public SimpleUI()
    {
        IoCRegister.Configure();

        MoreComplexBusinessLogic logic = IoC.Resolve<MoreComplexBusinessLogic>
();
    }
}
```

The result is that the dependency for the ComplexDataAccess object is automatically resolved. If you want to add a new dependency to the constructor, you would simply need to register it in one location for the rest of the system to pick up and use the new object. This makes managing your dependencies very effective and maintainable.

Do You Need SOLID?

At this point you should have an understanding of the principles that are encompassed in SOLID and how it fits into software development. However, do you need it? Yes, you do need these principles in place because they provide a good definition and guideline for object-oriented (OO) design. Many people claim to understand OO design; however, as you've seen demonstrated previously, many people get it wrong and still don't fully understand what makes for a good OO design. By having the principles in place, you create a foundation to build upon.

It is important to remember that these are just principles and shouldn't be simply followed. It is important to understand them and how they apply to your code, becomes sometimes your requirements force you to break a principle. If you do, you need to understand the problems that might occur and, ideally, look at alternative approaches. Your aim is to make the tests as easy to write as possible. This is why you want to keep your code decoupled. Your tests should also be focused on the functionality of the class: if you see your tests are doing lots of different tasks and functions, your class may have too many responsibilities.

Pair Programming and Technical Code Reviews

Sadly, people don't link TDD to Design, they link TDD to testing. TDD is not about testing; it is about design with the tests being a nice side effect. When you're creating your tests, if you don't stop and look at the code in a critical way, you miss a large part of the advantage of TDD. Two concepts that support this process are pair programming and technical code reviews.

Pair programming is focused on two developers sitting at the same workstation helping each other write a certain piece of functionality. One person is typing the code, while the other person is reviewing. The person typing, often called driving, can focus on the code, while the second person can focus on the overall picture, making sure the coder hasn't missed anything and thinking about what is required next. If the reviewer thinks they have a better idea for the implementation, they can swap roles. Swapping roles frequently is an important part of pair programming, with each of the two developers writing code and touching the keyboard. The advantage here is that the developers share their experience and learn together. If you have inexperienced members on the team, getting them to pair program can increase their confidence and experience more quickly than if they were left on their own. It's important to note that pair programming is not just for junior/senior combinations. The spirit of pair programming is that two sets of eyes/brains are working on a problem and therefore are able to help each in a direction that a single mind might not have taken.

Even when pair programming, the code should still be written using TDD. And there are all kinds of different techniques to use: one very popular technique is that one person writes the test while the other person implements the code to make the test pass. All the same coding and design principles apply; there is just the benefit of two heads working on the code, which should result in fewer defects and more code maintainability.

Another technique, often overlooked with pair programming, is that of code reviews. Although pairing is a targeted form of code review, a larger technical code review should still be performed. *Code reviews* are useful points within the project where you can sit as a team and review the tests and the code. It is an opportunity to look at the big picture while still focusing on the implementation and finer details. The aim should be to identify and remove code smells. *Smells* are parts of the code that don't feel right, go against the SOLID principles, and generally show that the code has not been designed in the best possible fashion.

During the review, the tests can help guide the process providing documentation about how the code is expected to work. This is also a good time to verify that the tests are being developed correctly.

Test Smells

Similar to the previously defined code smells, there is also the concept of test smells. As with code smells, *test smells* indicate a problem with your test code. There are varieties of different issues that can affect your test code, some affect the maintenance but others affect the reliability of your tests.

The most common problem is related to the reliability of the tests. As mentioned before, you need confidence in your tests. However, one of the most serious test smells, referenced to as fragile tests, can make you lose this all-important confidence.

Fragile Tests

The term *fragile test* covers a large number of different problem areas, yet the core result is a loss in confidence and increased maintenance with decreased productivity. Fragile tests are one of the main areas why people fail to see the benefit in unit tests.

A common scenario is when tests fail because of the outside environment. This could be due to particular files required to be in a particular location with certain data, for example, configuration files or image files that have to be loaded. When you have this situation, developers may be unaware of the dependent test and change the test file or simply remove it without realizing what they are doing.

Other problems exist when the tests need to interact with external services. External services could range from online web services to inhouse messaging services, but essentially is a service beyond the control of the unit test and the system. When tests have to deal with these services they are at risk of failing because either the service was down or there were network issues or latency issues. When a test fails for this reason, it can be extremely difficult to identify the reason. Sometimes the test will pass, and other times it will fail. Ideally you should decouple the use of the service, allowing yourself to unit test the system and take advantage of mock objects to replicate the external service together with a separate set of integration tests for end-to-end testing, as covered in Chapter 4. Mock objects are a difficult concept to understand; we will spend some time later in this chapter within the Stubs and Mocks section defining exactly what a mock object is.

Databases are similar to both environment and online services. If your tests interact with a database server, such as SQL Server, it could cause them to become fragile. Databases suffer from various problems, such as a nonexistent database or a changed schema. Also, the server itself might not be accessible, credentials might have changed, or it might have simply crashed — all resulting in the test failing.

Problems are not only with the environment. Sometimes it is due to the way that the tests have been developed, oftentimes being too coupled to your implementation. A common problem occurs when you change a piece of functionality that has a knock on effect for tests in a completely different section. This comes back to dependencies. When your code has lots of layers and is communicating between these different layers, changes can have ripple effects throughout the system. However, it sometimes relates to the fact that your tests are over-specified and are testing too much. If you remember the best practices we talked about earlier in this chapter, each test should focus on one fact. If your tests are over-specified, then each test will verify every aspect of the state of the object. For example, the following test should verify that a user can log in successfully:

```
[Test]
public void User_Has_Logged_In_Successfully()
{
    LoginController c = new LoginController();
    bool result = c.Login("username", "password");
    Assert.IsTrue(result);
    Assert.AreEqual("username", c.Username);
    Assert.AreEqual("password", c.Password);
    Assert.AreEqual(DateTime.Now.Day, c.LoginTime.Day);
    Assert.AreEqual(DateTime.Now.Hour, c.LoginTime.Hour);
    Assert.AreEqual(120, c.LoginExpiry);
    Assert.AreEqual("Index", c.RedirectPage);
}
```

Although the first three lines of code in the previous listing implement the entire test, the developer has also verified many other aspects of how they expect the controller to work, moving beyond the scope of the test. Even though all these should be tested, they should be separated into different tests. Imagine if every test within your system had the following assertion: by changing the LoginExpiry property, all your tests would fail, and you would have to modify each test manually to reflect the change.

Production Bugs

It's extremely difficult to remove every last production bug. Airlines and other mission critical systems put a huge amount of focus and energy on ensuring that no production bugs occur. This level of energy is not generally required for most line-of-business applications; bugs are bad, but they are unlikely to kill anyone. However, the more production bugs that occur, the more our users are going to be unhappy — this will reflect poorly on the development team.

Although we have stressed the fact that TDD is predominantly a design tool, TDD should also reduce the amount of regressions and production bugs. *Regressions* are bugs that occur after the feature has already been tested, and they are responsible for a large part of the problems with software. Having your test suite in place should allow you to catch these issues as they occur, allowing you to fix the problems before they ever reach the tester or end-user. If you are still experiencing production bugs, it indicates a problem with your existing unit tests.

When production bugs occur, the first area of concern would be if automated tests actually exist for the system. If they do exist, are they focusing on the correct areas of the application? If you are experiencing many regression bugs around a particular area of the system, it suggests that it may be a good area to provide extra coverage.

Another problem that can cause production bugs is when the tests have been created but they are either not verifying the correct part of the system, or they are not self-verifying. Even if the code does not work, the tests would never alert you to the problem. This is a problem because it gives you false confidence in your system that results in you performing less manual testing, which results in the production bugs appearing.

Even if you have your tests in place, if they are not being executed then you will never be aware of the issues they might discover. Developers should be executing the unit tests constantly while they are making changes, together with your build server on every commit. If a test does fail, then you should react quickly and fix it as soon as possible. A failing test indicates one of two problems, either your code is wrong or the test is wrong. If the test is no longer valid, change it or remove it. Not having a green bar is a major problem as it leads to the broken windows syndrome.

> ### The Broken Windows Syndrome
>
> This syndrome originally related to crime within urban areas. It states that if a building has a few broken windows then vandals are a lot more likely to cause more damage. The same is true for unit tests, if you have broken tests, then developers are a lot more likely to leave more tests broken. To ensure this does not happen, fix tests as soon as possible.

If you have failing tests then it is difficult to identify which tests fail for a particular reason. The tests could always have failed, but they could also be newly failing regression tests. The result is that tests might fail without you realizing, resulting in errors being released.

Slow Tests

One reason why people do not execute their tests is that they are slow. Slow running tests are a problem because they decrease the motivation for running and writing tests. Writing tests is all about being in the mindset of wanting to write the tests, anything to distract from this mindset is bad. Imagine you were happily writing code, but after every new addition or change to a method you had to wait three minutes before you could continue. Imagine it was not three minutes, but thirty minutes or three hours. You would either only run them once a day, or not run them at all, which would lead to production bugs.

You should be running your unit tests constantly. After every method, you'll want to run your tests to verify it worked and nothing else broke. If you cannot do this, then you are going to lose a lot of the benefit.

With this in mind, how can you ensure your tests are quick, or at least not painfully slow? Tests are slow because they have to access external resources. Limiting the amount of interaction with external resources will keep your tests fast. External resources include the external environment, such as the IO, network, or UI. All these cause delays.

One potential solution to this is to separate your unit tests and integration tests into two separate solutions. Your unit tests can stay fast and focused taking advantage of mocks and stubs, and your integration tests can be used for tests that must interact with the external services.

Slow running tests don't just affect the individual developer — they can also affect the entire team. Because the unit tests should be run as part of every build, if your tests are slow, then your builds will take longer to come through, and it will take longer to determine if it failed. The team will start to dislike you because it will affect their productivity.

Long Set-Up Time for Coding

Finally, test smells are not always related to the execution; they can also relate to the development of the tests. This test smell relates to how much effort it takes to have the object constructed in a testable state. You will find that if your system has not been designed with testability in mind, then the amount of set-up code required will overshadow the interaction with the system and the verification that it worked correctly.

This test smell is generally a result of an over-specified test or an over-coupled system. The result may be that the class has too many responsibilities, which results in a lot of set-up code. Other causes could include the set-up of test data, which the test will use when it is interacting with the system.

If all the set-up code is valid then you can limit the fact. By taking advantage of test helper methods, the set-up code can be shared amongst your tests. This has the advantage of reduced maintenance, but will also keep your test readable.

Fundamentally, SOLID is about breaking dependencies within your system. Dependencies are the main reason why people find unit testing and TDD difficult. If you can manage to break down your task and code into small enough blocks, then you will find TDD a much simpler process. As mentioned earlier in this chapter, you still need access to these dependencies when testing. This is where mocks and stubs can help.

Stubs and Mocks

As we briefly mentioned during the section on the SOLID principles, dependencies are a problem. The SOLID principles include techniques and ways of thinking to help us break those dependencies. Stubs and mocks, otherwise known as test doubles, replicate those external dependencies when testing the code that interacts with them.

Going back to the previous Business Logic and Data Access scenario, when you want to test your ProcessOrder method you need an IDataAccess object. The tests want to be in control of this object.

If the tests are not in control of the object, in terms of knowing which methods had been called or what data to return, then you will need to spend a lot of time setting up the environment and running verifications against the Data Access layer to ensure ProcessOrder worked correctly. Ideally you want to know that ProcessOrder correctly called your Save method. You would have other tests focused around the DataAccess object and the Save method. For now, you simply need to verify that the two are communicating correctly and that the logic within ProcessOrder is correct.

This is where mocks and stubs are useful. They allow the test to be in control of the dependency and then verify everything worked as expected. For the system to be in control of this dependency, then it must look like the real implementation. This is achieved by the test double implementing the required interface, in the previous case with IDataAccess. From the viewpoint of implementing code, it would be identical and would treat it the same as if it was the real object. Of course, if you have broken the Liskov Substitution Principle and are attempting to downcast the object to a concrete class, then this will not be possible. After the tests are in control of the double, they can set up the object to behave how it should. For example, this includes setting the expectations for the methods that should be called or setting known return values for certain method calls.

The Difference Between Mocks and Stubs

Although mocks and stubs have a similar task, there is an important difference between them. It's very common that these uses are often confused and used in the wrong situation.

A stub object is the simpler of the two objects. The role of a stub is to simulate input and allow the method or class under test to perform a desired action. Stubs are more about enabling something to happen. For this reason, stubs are generally used for state verification. Your test will create your stub, inject it into the class under test, and perform the desired action. Under the covers, your class will interact with the stub and as a result be in a different state after it has finished. This state could be setting a property or returning a particular return value. The test can then verify that the object is within the expected state.

To create a stub, you don't need a powerful framework or special technique. All you need to know is the interface or abstract class you want to stub and how to inject it into the class under test, be it via the constructor or a public property. The following is a classic example of how a stub might work:

```
[Test]
public void ProcessOrder_sends_Email_if_Order_Is_Successful()
{
    StubMailServer stub = new StubMailServer();
    BusinessLogic b = new BusinessLogic(stub);
    b.ProcessOrder(new Order());
    Assert.IsTrue(stub.MessageSent);
}
```

```
public class StubMailServer: IMailServer
{
    public bool MessageSent {get; set;}
    public void Send(string to, string message)
    {
        MessageSent = true;
    }
}
```

Another possible use of stub objects is to make existing objects easier to test by overriding their default behavior. Given the previous example, you could have implemented your stub object similar to the StubMailServer example. This would have allowed you to keep the rest of the class intact, but replacing the specific part that interacted with the external system, which caused the system to be harder to test:

```
public class StubMailServer: RealSmtpMailServer
{
    public bool MessageSent {get; set;}
    public override void Send(string to, string message)
    {
        MessageSent = true;
    }
}
```

One problem with having a manually created stub for each object is that it can be expensive to maintain. Most of the mocking frameworks we will discuss can also create stub objects using a similar API to the mock object.

A mock on the other hand is a lot more powerful. A mock object provides the same functionality of a stub in terms of returning known results, but mock objects also record the interaction that the class under test performs. The mock objects remember all method calls, arguments provided, number of times a method has been called and the order, along with many other properties. The result is that the test has a huge amount of information that it can use to verify that the system is working as expected. With a mock, you set up your expectations about how you predict your class to interact with the external dependency, which will be the mock. If the class does not interact with the mock in the way it expects, the test will fail. For this reason, mocks are generally used for behavior verification. Behavior verification is verifying that the class under test interacts and behaves with your mock object in the way you expected. Mocks and behavior verification are often used when the state cannot be verified.

Unlike stubs, mocks are created using frameworks to enable them to have the additional functionality previously described. The framework will be responsible for constructing the mock object, remembering the interactions, and verifying that they are correct.

For example in the following listing, you ask the mocking framework to generate an instance of an object which inherits from a particular class — in this case the Mail Server interface. The second line defines how you expect the object to be used. Finally, the last line verifies that all the expectations that were previously defined were met, after you have interacted with your object under test:

```
IMailServer mock = MockRepository.GenerateMock<IMailServer>();
mock.Expect(m => m.Send("Test User", "Order Confirmed"));
mock.VerifyAllExpectations();
```

Given this, a test which uses a mock object might look something similar to this:

```
[Test]
public void ProcessOrder_sends_Email_if_Order_Is_Successful()
{
    Order order = new Order {To = "Test User"};

    IMailServer mock = MockRepository.GenerateMock<IMailServer>();
    mock.Expect(m => m.Send("Test User", "Order Confirmed"));

    BusinessLogic b = new BusinessLogic(mock);
    b.ProcessOrder(order);

    mock.VerifyAllExpectations();
}
```

For the test to pass, the ProcessOrder information would need a method implementation similar to the method in the following listing:

```
public void ProcessOrder(Order order)
{
    MailServer.Send(order.To, "Order Confirmed");
}
```

With this in place, the test would pass. If something changed and the expectations were not met, an expectation would be thrown when you call VerifyAllExpectations, which would cause the test to promptly fail.

With the previous test, a framework called Rhino Mocks was used to create the mock object. Rhino Mocks is an extremely popular open source framework. The framework has two different types of syntax for creating and managing your mock objects; the first is Arrange Act Assert (AAA) with the second being Record\Playback.

Rhino Mocks

The AAA syntax was introduced in Rhino Mocks 3.5 and takes advantage of C# 3.0 features such as lambda expressions and extension methods to improve the readability of your test code when creating mock objects.

Before we hop into Rhino Mocks, let's first define a few C# 3.0 features that help make Rhino Mocks possible. Lambda expressions simply put are anonymous functions that create delegates or expression trees. Extension methods allow you to define additional methods on existing objects without having to subclass the object. This means you can add additional methods without affecting the actual object; however, when reading the code it feels much more natural and human readable.

When using mock objects, the most common use case is to define expected behavior on method calls returning known result values. Using the AAA syntax, an example of defining expectation would be as follows:

```
ICalc mock = MockRepository.GenerateMock<ICalc>();
mock.Expect(m => m.Add(1, 1)).Return(2);
```

With this example, we asked the RhinoMocks MockRepository to generate a mock object which implements the ICalc interface. Due to the namespaces included, the mock objects have a set of extension methods added to them which were not on the original interface. The Expect method allows you to define the method calls in which the object should expect to receive. Rhino Mocks uses the concept of fluent interfaces to join method calls together. The aim is that the method calls should be more human readable as they should flow as a natural language. In this case, the return result of Expect has a method called Return, which we then call with the argument of 2.

If you now call the mock.Add method with the arguments 1,1, then the value returned will be 2:

```
Assert.AreEqual(2, mock.Add(1,1));
```

If you call the mock object with another value, then it will cause an error because the test was not expecting that to happen and as such it should fail the test. This is one of the advantages of a mock object in that it is testing the behavior and the interactions between the class under test and the mock.

Finally, calling VerifyAllExpectations will verify that the previous exceptions were met — for example, the method was called as you expected:

```
mock.VerifyAllExpectations();
```

In certain situations, for example simulating faults when a method is called, you might want to throw an exception instead of returning a value. With the AAA syntax this is very simple. By using the Throw extension method, you can define the exception which should be thrown from the mock object:

```
mock.Expect(m => m.Divide(0, 1)).Throw(new DivideByZeroException("Error"));
```

When it comes to properties and events you need to use a slightly different syntax. First, you need to tell Rhino Mocks to treat the value as a property and then set the value of the property as normal. The next time you call the property, it will be treated as a mock value:

```
SetupResult.For(mock.Value).PropertyBehavior();
mock.Value = 2;
Assert.AreEqual(2, mock.Value);
```

With events, you need to first gain access to the event raiser — in this case the event is called Event — and then use the Raise event passing in the values for the event itself:

```
mock.GetEventRaiser(v => v.Event += null).Raise("5");
```

The other approach with Rhino Mocks is the Record and Playback model. This is a two-stage process; the first stage is Record. This is where you define how you expect the mock to be interacted with. The second stage is Playback — this is where you place your test code and it interacts with the mock object. To make this code easier to understand, it's beneficial to add a using statement to define the scope of the Rhino Mock recording session. This is because the internal stages that Rhino Mocks uses to signal the change between recording and playback is automatically called, as is the statement to verify the expectations that occurred. To manage the state, a MockRepository object is required.

An example of a test using the Record and Playback approach follows. Here you are defining the expectations of how Add should work within the Record using statement. Within the playback section, you have our test and assertion code:

```
MockRepository mocks = new MockRepository();
ICalc mock = mocks.CreateMock<ICalc>();
using (mocks.Record())
{
    Expect.Call(mock.Add(1,1)).Return(2);
}

using (mocks.Playback())
{
    Assert.AreEqual(2, mock.Add(1,1));
}
```

With this in place, you can begin using Rhino Mocks with either syntax to begin mocking your complex external dependencies. However, Rhino Mocks has some limitations on the type of objects it can mock. First, it can only create mock objects for interfaces and abstract classes. Rhino Mocks is unable to mock concrete implementations. Rhino Mocks is also unable to mock a private interface.

TypeMock Isolator

Rhino Mocks is not the only mocking framework available. TypeMock has a product named Isolator which is an advanced mocking framework. TypeMock is fundamentally different than Rhino Mocks in the fact that it uses intermediate language (IL) injection to replace mock real implementations with the mock representations at runtime. It does this by using the Profiler APIs within the .NET Framework to change the IL that is about to be executed by the unit test runner with the mock setup defined previously within the unit test. The advantage of this is that it removes all the limitations which exist with Rhino Mocks.

TypeMock can mock any object used within your system at any point. Unlike Rhino Mocks, with TypeMock you no longer need to worry about how to inject the model into the system, for example, via the constructor as TypeMock you can mock objects at any level. The other advantage is that the mock object doesn't need to inherit from an interface as it can mock the concrete implementations. This means that you can mock objects which aren't in your control, for example in the third-party framework which hasn't considered testability. This also means that you can mock parts of the .NET Framework itself.

However, this leads to a number of concerns of which you need to be aware. Although it shouldn't stop you from using the product, you should be aware that they exist. First, because you don't need to worry about how you inject the mock, you no longer have the same worries about separating concerns and dependency injection. This could lead to some problems when you attempt to replace the dependency with a different implementation. In a similar fashion, because it can mock concrete classes, you no longer need to be concerned with programming against abstracts and your tests don't encourage you to follow this pattern. Finally, due to the depth of access TypeMock has, it can lead to over-specified tests as you can mock methods multiple layers down, where before you might have mocked the dependency at a higher level. This becomes a problem when you change or replace the logic in your code.

However, TypeMock is great for legacy applications. By having more control, TypeMock allows you to start adding unit tests to an existing application with relative ease compared to Rhino Mocks.

Mocking Anti-Patterns

As with all techniques, there are various anti-patterns, or smells, of which you should be aware. We have detailed how TypeMock introduces some concerns for certain people; however, there are more general concerns.

Mocking any part of the .NET Framework is a bad approach to take. As I described in the interface separation principle, most objects are very heavyweight and intercoupled, so mocking objects such as the IDbConnection is going to take a very long time and will be hard to utilize effectively. This is the same for certain third-party frameworks, which have very heavy interfaces with a tight coupling. A more successful approach would be to abstract away from the concrete information using wrappers and abstracts to hide the underlying implementation.

However, for certain parts of the .NET Framework it is not possible because they don't expose interfaces, such as the core parts of ASP.NET. This leads into another anti-pattern when it comes to mocking and that is sealed classes. Even though not providing an interface is limiting, having a sealed class completely closes the door on mocking and stubbing (except TypeMock). By having a sealed class you limit any overriding or extending ability to allow certain parts to be replaced. As such, it can make it increasingly difficult to mock out that particular section.

Another anti-pattern is over-mocking and over-specified tests within a system. This is a common problem within systems where developers think that everything needs to be mocked and as a result the unit tests simply duplicate a large part of the internal implementation. To start with, this is bad because the tests don't actually test that it is working as expected, just that it is working as the tests define. Second, if the internal structure of the code changes then the tests are likely to fail because the two implementations do not match. For example, if you were mocking your data access and your unit tests for the business layer and it replicated exactly the same SQL code which would be executed on the database, then your business knows far too much about the underlying implementation and your tests have over-specified what they expect to happen. Instead, you should consider refactoring your code to improve testability, or look at using a stub object and state verification.

TDD Recap

TDD provides a number of advantages when developing your code, for example, helping you identify code and design smells earlier in the process. However, TDD is not a silver bullet. It will not solve all your design issues and bugs without even trying. TDD requires the correct mindset of the developer to be constantly writing in the test first fashion to get maximum benefit. It also requires the developer to understand good design principles such as SOLID to be able to identify and resolve the problems that TDD brings to the surface. If they are unable to recognize these benefits, then TDD will not seem as beneficial.

TDD also has a problem because of its name. Because the concept includes the term "test," everyone immediately thinks it is another form of software testing. In fact it's a development approach, which has more advantages than just testing software. This confusion around naming is one of the reasons that led to the naming within the xUnit framework: using the Fact attribute to define which methods to execute. The confusion is not only developer-to-developer, but also is passed on to the customer. When talking to customers, customers get confused by having a set of tests which demosrate that their requirements have been implemented as expected. The problem is that customers are generally non-technical and most unit tests reference technical details, and don't provide enough information about the requirement without first understanding the code. As a result, people have come up with a different development approach called Behavior Driven Development or BDD.

Moving Beyond TDD to BDD

Behavior Driven Development (BDD) attempts to build on top of the fundamentals of TDD and the advantages it offers; however, it also attempts to go a step further by making the concept more accessible to developers, to the other members of the team, and to the customer. Dan North is one of the leaders within the BDD community, and he had the realization that the "test method names should be a sentence." The fundamental concept is that if the tests are given an effective name, then they are a lot more focused. This is the same concept he applies with his TDD naming convention for exactly the same reason.

Yet BDD is more than just how you name your tests as it dives deep into agile testing and interacts more with the customer than TDD previously did. One of the core aims of BDD is to take more advantage of the design and documentation which TDD provides by having human readable test method names together with the use of stories and scenarios to provide more context to what is being tested and how.

To provide this level of functionality, BDD has two main types of frameworks: the first type is a specification framework and the second is the scenario runner.

The specification framework is aimed at providing examples and specs about how your objects should work as isolated units. The aim is to provide examples of how the objects are expected to behave. If the objects do not match the defined behavior then it is marked as a failure. If they do meet the desired behavior, then they are marked as a pass. Most of the specification frameworks available for .NET and other languages follow a similar pattern and language when writing the examples. First there is a Because or Describe section, which provides the outline and context to what the examples are covering for the reader. The next sections are It blocks; these provide the examples about what should have occurred after the action happened. Generally you only have one action block with multiple different example blocks to describe the outcome.

Historically, the Ruby community has been the main promoters of the development approach, and due to the readable and dynamic nature of their language means BDD is the perfect fit. For .NET, there has been a number of attempts; however, they are all constrained by the C# language which requires the additional syntax and metadata about classes and methods. Currently machine.specification appears to be the cleanest BDD framework for .NET. By taking advantage of C# 3.0, they have managed to create a syntax that reads very naturally:

```
[Subject(typeof(Account), "Balance transfer")]
public class when_transferring_amount_between_two_accounts:
with_from_account_and_to_account
{
  Because of = () =>
    fromAccount.Transfer(1, toAccount);

  It should_debit_the_from_account = () =>
    fromAccount.Balance.ShouldEqual(0);

  It should_credit_the_to_account = () =>
    toAccount.Balance.ShouldEqual(2);
}
```

However, with the rise of IronRuby you can now use the RSpec and Cucumber BDD frameworks created for Ruby against C# objects. This allows you to have the best of both worlds.

> *Historically the .NET development stack has been criticized by other development communities by not adapting to change very quickly. Ruby developers have been using testing tools such as RSpec since 2007 and more recently the Cucumber framework. With the introduction of the Dynamic Language Runtime (DLR), languages such as Ruby and Python can be run on the .NET platform.*
>
> *Many of the cutting edge testing tools are being developed on these platforms. Don't be afraid to step outside the box, and experiment with languages such as IronRuby and IronPython or with tools such as RSpec and Cucumber. Examples of RSpec and Cucumber can be found in Chapter 6.*

After the tests have been executed using a test runner, the different sections within the example are converted into a readable format, which can then be shown to a nontechnical person to discuss whether the behavior is correct. On the other side is the scenario runner. Although the specification framework focused on objects as isolated units, the scenario runner is focused on the end-to-end tests, otherwise known as integration tests (covered in Chapter 4) or acceptance tests (covered in Chapter 6). This scenario runner is based on describing how the application will be used, sometimes based on how users will interact via the UI but other times simply driving the engine API. Similar to the specification framework, a scenario framework is aimed at describing behavior while taking advantage of design and documentation but this time at the application level.

As with the specification framework, the scenario framework also has syntax to describe the different parts. The first stage is the story itself. This has three different stages:

    As a [. . .]
    I want [. . .]
    So that [. . .]

An example might be

Story: Transfer money from savings account
    As a saving account holder
    I want to transfer money from savings account
    So that I can pay my bills

From the viewpoint of the reader of the story, this example should provide them with some context into what you are doing and the reasons for it. From the viewpoint of the customer, this should match a valid user story that they want the system to implement; as such this should feel very natural and familiar to them. It's important to keep all technical content out of the scenario and use the business domain language to help customers keep with this familiarity.

After you have defined the story, you need to define the scenario and steps. The steps have three separate stages:

    Given [. . .]
    When [. . .]
    Then [. . .]

This example outlines the different stages that need to be set up and then verify that the behavior was correct. The Given step is where you set up your scenario; When is where actions are performed; Then is the verification stage.

Scenario: Savings account is in credit

> Given a balance of 400
> When I transfer 100 to cash account
> Then cash account balance should be 100
> And savings account balance should be 300

The use of And allows you to chain steps together. The previous example provides one scenario about how you expect the story to work — as you progress you would add more scenarios to the story. You can then use the scenario runner to create test methods attached and execute them using the runner in a similar fashion to your specification framework. Then, you can go to your customer with a readable report and ask them if it is implemented correctly.

What Makes a Good Test?

When it comes to the topic of what makes a good unit test, there are as many opinions as there are bugs in production code found with a well-defined set of unit tests. We will start with a concept that most developers believe in.

❑ **There is no point in writing a test if it's useless.** When you are writing your tests, take care to ensure that you have confidence that your unit test tests the code thoroughly. Many developers have good intentions and plan on maintaining tests, but soon get dragged down in the repetitive work of creating a test and making sure it passes. This leads to developers creating tests that are useless and detrimental to the project. These tests can be problematic because they provide a false sense of security. A new developer might come to the project to see that there are unit tests in place and feel that it is safe to begin large refactorings. A developer should be able to depend on the fact that the tests in the system test the code properly and were not blindly thrown together as another cobbled together feature. Unit tests should create confidence in the code you have created. When writing code, always keep in the back of your mind, "How am I going to test this?"

❑ **Unit tests should be fast.** It's a proven fact that if unit tests take a long time to execute, developers will run these tests less frequently. Unit tests are intended to be run often, and as a general rule of thumb every few minutes. Unit tests should run so fast you should never have to hesitate to run them as shown in Figure 2-12.

Figure 2-12 TestDriven.NET output results

❑ **Unit tests should be small.** As with other coding design principles, the amount of code added to unit tests should be very small. Unit tests should be thought of as professional code. Keep clutter out of unit tests and limit what is being tested to a minimum.

❑ **Unit tests should have a descriptive name.** As described previously, unit tests should always have a descriptive name defining what they are verifying and focusing on.

❑ **Unit tests should document your intent.** Unit tests should be thought of as specifications for your code. A developer should be able to determine the aspect of the code the test is testing from the name of the test.

Don't worry about how long the name of the test methods are — the more descriptive the better. This style can be cumbersome at first, but is easy to get used to after you see the benefits of having a set of tests that are very descriptive:

```
[Test]
public void Should_Transfer_From_Checking_To_Savings_Successfully()
{
    Account checkingAccount = new Account(564858510, 600);
    Account savingsAccount = new Account(564858507, 100);

    checkingAccount.Transfer(ref savingsAccount, 100);
    Assert.IsTrue(savingsAccount.Balance == 200, "Funds not deposited");
    Assert.IsTrue(checkingAccount.Balance == 500, "Funds not withdrawn");
}
```

❑ **Unit tests should be isolated.** Unit tests should only test very small units of code; related classes should not be tested in dependant tests, because they should have their own unit tests to go with them. Tests should not rely on external data such as databases or files on a file system. All the data that is needed for a test to pass should be included in the test. A unit test should not be dependent on the order in which it is run. When unit tests are not isolated, the tests become too closely coupled and lead to poor software design. The test in the next listing is an example of a test that is isolated. The test sets up the business logic and the mail server, but essentially it is only testing the MessageSent function:

```
[Test]
public void ProcessOrder_sends_Email_if_Order_Is_Successful()
{
    StubMailServer stub = new StubMailServer();
    BusinessLogic b = new BusinessLogic(stub);
    b.ProcessOrder(new Order());
    Assert.IsTrue(stub.MessageSent);
}
```

❑ **Unit tests should be automatic.** Most developers have created unit tests before and may not have been aware that indeed they were unit tests. Have you ever created a WinForm with a single button, like Figure 2-13, to test a small section of code, maybe how a date was formatted? This is considered a unit test. Most of the time the form is deleted after you figure out how to perform the task you are looking to accomplish, but why throw this code away? Good unit tests can be run automatically with a push of a button. Using one of the frameworks we have discussed allow unit tests to be automatic, hence the name automated testing.

Figure 2-13 Test that many developers don't realize is a unit test.

❏ **Unit tests should be repeatable.** To help ensure that unit tests are repeatable, unit tests should be independent from external environments. Databases, system time, and the file system are examples of environments that are not under direct control of the test. A developer should be able to check out a set of the tests and an application from version control, and expect that the tests will pass on any machine they are working on.

❏ **Unit tests should focus on one behavior per test.** As a general rule of thumb, unit tests should only have one expectation per behavior. In most situations this loosely translates into one assertion per test — hey wait a minute, many of the examples we have shown thus far have had multiple assertions! An assertion doesn't translate strictly to a full expectation. In all our tests, only one behavior has been expected. Take for example the transfer funds test shown previously; there are two assertions, but the expectation is that funds have been transferred from one account to another account. The next listing is an example of a test that tests more than one expectation and should be considered bad practice. This test is expecting that the balance has changed, and also expects that a history transaction item has been added:

```
[Test]
public void Should_Transfer_From_Checking_To_Savings_Successfully()
{
    Account checkingAccount = new Account(564858510, 600);
    Account savingsAccount = new Account(564858507, 100);

    checkingAccount.Transfer(ref savingsAccount, 100);
    Assert.IsTrue(savingsAccount.Balance == 200);
    Assert.IsTrue(checkingAccount.Balance == 500);

    Assert.IsTrue(checkingAccount.TransactionHistory.Count > 0);
    Assert.IsTrue(savingsAccount.TransactionHistory.Count > 0);
}
```

❏ **Unit tests should test the inverse relationship of behaviors.** A common transaction in the financial world is the transfer of money from one account to another. If you have a transfer funds function, ensure you have assertions that enable the funds to be withdrawn from one account and deposited into another:

```
[Test]
public void Should_Transfer_From_Checking_To_Savings_Successfully()
```

```
{
    Account checkingAccount = new Account(564858510) {Balance=600};
    Account savingsAccount = new Account(564858507) {Balance=100};

    checkingAccount.Transfer(ref savingsAccount, 100);
    Assert.IsTrue(savingsAccount.Balance == 200);
    Assert.IsTrue(checkingAccount.Balance == 500);
}
```

❑ **Unit test failures should be descriptive.** Each test should be descriptive about what they are testing and the expected result. This is partly done by the method name, partly by the test code being readable, but also by the assertions having messages which are outputted if they fail.

```
[Test]
public void Should_Transfer_From_Checking_To_Savings_Successfully()
{
    Account checkingAccount = new Account(564858510, 600);
    Account savingsAccount = new Account(564858507, 100);

    checkingAccount.Transfer(ref savingsAccount, 100);
    Assert.IsTrue(savingsAccount.Balance == 200, "Funds not deposited");
    Assert.IsTrue(checkingAccount.Balance == 500, "Funds not withdrawn");
}
```

❑ **Tests suites should test boundary conditions.** If you are working with an object that could have boundary issues, ensure you are testing them. A general rule of testing boundary conditions is the 0, 1 many rule. This rule states you should test your object, with the boundary conditions, with zero elements, one element, and many elements. In most cases, if your object works with two elements it will work with any number of elements. There are cases where your object has an upper limit; in these cases you should also test upper limits:

```
[Test]
public void Should_Sort_Arrary_With_Empty_Element()
{
    int[] arrayToSort = {};
    int[] actual = QuickSort(arrayToSort);

    Assert.IsTrue(actual.Length == 0, "Sorted empty array");
}

[Test]
public void Should_Sort_Array_With_One_Element()
{
    int[] arrayToSort = { 29};
    int[] actual = QuickSort(arrayToSort);

    Assert.IsTrue(actual.Length == 2, "Sorted array count");
    Assert.IsTrue(actual[0] == 29, "Sorted array one element");
}

[Test]
public void Should_Sort_Array_With_Eleven_Elements()
{
    int[] arrayToSort = {100,5,25,11,2,6,29,6,26,7,27};
    int[] actual = QuickSort(arrayToSort);
```

```
        Assert.IsTrue(actual.Length == 11, "Sorted array count");
        Assert.IsTrue(actual[0] == 9, "Sorted array order first element");
        Assert.IsTrue(actual[9] == 100, "Sorted array order last element");
    }
```

Don't think of arrays as the only objects that have boundaries. For instance, if a developer needs to keep track of the age of a person, you would use an integer to keep track of this value. For most applications it does not make sense for a person to be 44,898 years old.

❏   **Unit tests should check for ordering.** Good unit tests verify that the system is working as expected. It's a common enough scenario to mention that if objects are expected to be in a certain order, there should be a unit test to ensure that the expected order is matched:

```
[Test]
public void Should_Sort_Array_With_Eleven_Elements()
{
    int[] arrayToSort = {100,5,25,11,2,6,29,6,26,7,27};
    int[] actual = QuickSort(arrayToSort);

    Assert.IsTrue(actual.Length == 11, "Sorted array count");
    Assert.IsTrue(actual[0] == 9, "Sorted array order first element");
    Assert.IsTrue(actual[9] == 100, "Sorted array order last element");
}
```

How to Cope with Design Changes

Over time, all designs change. The system that you spent countless hours in design meetings for will change. Users will add requirements that do not fit into your original vision of how the application would work and the initial architecture that was designed. Other times you realize that there is a much simpler way to implement a section of code than you had originally thought, and you change the code to reflect this.

This is the process of *refactoring*. Refactoring is the process of improving code, without changing the result the code produces. Improvements include readability, testability, performance, and the general maintainability of your code base.

In Martin Fowler's book *Refactoring: Improving the Design of Existing Code*, he describes the various refactorings that can perform on code bases, when they should be performed, and the advantages they bring. In the refactoring book, Flower introduces the refactoring patterns and gives each type of refactoring a name to allow the concept to be described and shared with other people.

Examples of common refactoring include Extract method, move to class, and pull-up methods. In the next few examples you will apply common refactorings:

```
    private string SetSalesManagers(string phoneNumber)
    {
        int areaCode = int.Parse(phoneNumber.Substring(0, 3));
        string region = string.Empty;

        switch (areaCode)
```

```
    {
        case 248:
            region = "Central";
            break;
        case 818:
            region = "West";
            break;
        case 201:
            region = "East";
            break;
        default:
            region = "Unknown";
            break;
    }

    return GetSalesManager(region);
}
```

Extract Method

Extract method is a type of refactoring where duplicated code is extracted into a shared method to be reused:

```
private string SetSalesManagers(string phoneNumber)
{
    int areaCode = int.Parse(phoneNumber.Substring(0, 3));
    string region = GetRegion(areaCode);
    return GetSalesManager(region);
}

private string GetRegion(int areaCode)
{
    string region;
    switch (areaCode)
    {
        case 248:
            region = "Central";
            break;
        case 818:
            region = "West";
            break;
        case 201:
            region = "East";
            break;
        default:
            region = "Unknown";
            break;
    }

    return region;
}
```

Move to Class

Move to class refactoring involves moving a method into a different or its own class:

```csharp
public static class SalesHelper
{
    public static string GetRegion(int areaCode)
    {
        string region;
        switch (areaCode)
        {
            case 248:
                region = "Central";
                break;
            case 818:
                region = "West";
                break;
            case 201:
                region = "East";
                break;
            default:
                region = "Unknown";
                break;
        }

        return region;
    }
}

public class MySales
{

    private string SetSalesManagers(string phoneNumber)
    {
        int areaCode = int.Parse(phoneNumber.Substring(0, 3));
        string region = SalesHelper.GetRegion(areaCode);
        return GetSalesManager(region);
    }

    private string  GetSalesManager(string region)
    {
        return string.Empty;
    }
}
```

Pull-Up Methods

Pull-up method refactoring takes a method and moves the logic into a super class. This type of refactoring is useful when subclasses share functionality but each implements it separately:

```csharp
public class Employee
{
    public string FirstName { get; set; }
```

```csharp
        public string LastName { get; set; }
}

public class ProjectManger:Employee
{
    public static string GetRegion(int areaCode)
    {
        string region;
        switch (areaCode)
        {
            case 248:
                region = "Central";
                break;
            case 818:
                region = "West";
                break;
            case 201:
                region = "East";
                break;
            default:
                region = "Unknown";
                break;
        }

        return region;
    }
}

public class Developer:Employee
{
    public static string GetRegion(int areaCode)
    {
        string region;
        switch (areaCode)
        {
            case 248:
                region = "Central";
                break;
            case 818:
                region = "West";
                break;
            case 201:
                region = "East";
                break;
            default:
                region = "Unknown";
                break;
        }

        return region;
    }
}
```

The code in the previous example may look familiar to you. You have two different classes (manager and developer) each that inherit from the Employee super class. Both sub classes (manager and developer) have a function included named GetRegion, which provides functionality to get the region where that employee is employed. When this development pattern is encountered, the pull-up methods refactoring should be applied:

```
public class Employee
{
    public string FirstName { get; set; }
    public string LastName { get; set; }

    public static string GetRegion(int areaCode)
    {
        string region;
        switch (areaCode)
        {
            case 248:
                region = "Central";
                break;
            case 818:
                region = "West";
                break;
            case 201:
                region = "East";
                break;
            default:
                region = "Unknown";
                break;
        }

        return region;
    }
}

public class ProjectManger:Employee
{

}

public class Developer:Employee
{

}
```

These kinds of examples can have different impacts on systems depending on at which stage you perform the refactoring. Some refactorings will only affect the internal structure and as such have very little effect on your tests and the rest of the system. Other times, you might have to change a number of different public interfaces that will cause knock-on effects echoing around the rest of the system. Nevertheless, if your refactorings are going to affect your system and your tests, how should you cope with the changes?

Following a similar approach to TDD, your refactoring should also be test-driven. Your refactoring changes should flow from your tests. For example, if you are renaming a method, then you should first rename the method call in the tests to reflect your desired end result in the same way the original test was coded.

You should then perform the Red-Green-Refactor approach where you start with a failing test and refactor your old code into a new passing test. Because you are making your changes in a test-driven style you will know when you are done and when you have finished as the bar will be green. This will keep you focused and provide you with feedback on your changes.

In terms of changes which you will perform, if you're performing TDD and the Red-Green-Refactor, then the refactoring stage is a small focused step and performed very quickly after you have your test passing. As such, the impact on the tests should be minimal.

In terms of large changes, you should still follow TestDriven Refactoring. Similar to the method name changes just described, you should change the tests to reflect your end goal of the system. If the tests are focusing on behavior, then this shouldn't have changed and as such you simply need to change which objects and methods you're interacting with. Any change, to the behavior of the system is not a refactoring step and new tests should be created for them. If you have removed the behavior then you should also remove the associated tests.

To ease the pain and reduce the amount of changes that will be required for your codebase, you should follow the SOLID principles which have been discussed thoroughly previously in this chapter. By isolating your dependencies and each object having its own set of responsibilities, you will find that when you need to refactor the code, both the system and your tests will require fewer changes.

However, while driving your refactoring from unit tests, you also need to consider the implications they have on testers together with your integration and acceptance tests. After making the changes, your testers will need to update their test suites to reflect the updated code. The more testable your code is in terms of isolation and responsibilities, the easier this stage will be because the changes are less invasive.

However, the problem of refactoring changes echoing throughout the code base has been an issue in terms of tests, other methods, and your integration\acceptance. As such, various tools vendors have integrated automated refactoring steps into their development packages that allow the different scenarios to be performed more effectively. For example, when you rename a method, any other methods which are dependent are also updated to reflect this name. As a result, the number of breakages are reduced. By keeping your tests in the same solution as your project you can use the tool to aid in your steps.

In Chapter 3 we will discuss in depth how the various refactoring steps were performed on your sample application and how this affected the tests and the rest of the system.

Wax on, Wax Off

With that in mind, it's useful to take the concepts and quickly write some code to ensure you have a "solid" understanding.

In this exercise, you should create a testable object which calls out to an external service. The service will return a list of items; we need to identify a particular item and return that back to the calling code. The part we want to test is the service obtaining the results and obtaining the particular record.

1. Create a test for a method called GetFirstNode on ServiceResultFilter class and mock a call to a method called GetFeed on a FeedPull object. The call should return "<nodes><node>One</node><node>Two</node><node>Three</node></nodes>."

2. Verify the result of GetFirstNode is the string "One."

3. Ensure the code compiles and execute the test to see it fail.

4. Implement the passing code.

5. Execute the test to see if your code works.

Summary

In this chapter, we covered how to design a system to ensure that it is fully testable. We covered the SOLID principles that can aid your decisions and provide a foundation for you to build your applications. We introduced the various different methods of developer testing such as unit and Test Driven Development. After which, we covered how to take advantage of test doubles to break the dependencies within your system to aid testability. Moving on we discussed test smells and what makes a good test to ensure you have a firm foundation going forward, allowing you to get started writing developer tests.

In the next chapter, we look at applying the techniques discussed to a sample application.

3

Unit Testing and Test Driven Development

With some of the fundamentals of software design and unit testing covered in Chapter 2, you can now move on and start applying these concepts. This chapter looks at how to start writing unit tests and developing in a Test Driven Development fashion when working with ASP.NET. First we'll cover ASP.NET WebForms, and how you can write unit tests against this framework. We will then take a look at the new ASP.NET MVC Framework, which has been designed with testability in mind and solves some of the problems encountered when using ASP.NET WebForms.

By the end of this chapter you should have a good understanding of how to start building your ASP.NET web applications using Test Driven Development techniques.

ASP.NET WebForms

ASP.NET WebForms was released as part of the .NET platform in 2002. The release was a major milestone for developers all over the world, allowing them to produce more powerful web applications using the new C# language and Visual Studio.NET. One of the key advantages to ASP.NET was being able to quickly develop applications by taking advantage of built-in controls that allowed you to quickly display, edit, and delete data from a database and, in later versions, complete membership systems with the hard work already done for you.

The result was developers being able to drag and drop controls onto a page and then release the site. It allowed for a very quick turn around, but at no point was architecture of the application or testability considered. Developers found that as their requirements grew and they needed to move beyond the built-in controls they faced major problems. One of these problems was testability and being unable to effectively test ASP.NET applications. While this is still partly true, with some consideration you can unit test ASP.NET WebForms applications.

Unit Testing ASP.NET WebForms

An ASP.NET application is made up of two main parts. The aspx file contains the ASP.NET markup, which is a mixture of HTML, ASP.NET controls, and ASPX tags that contain code to be executed on the server before being returned to the user. The second part is the aspx.cs file that is the code-behind for a particular page. The code-behind files contain C# code to support the main ASP.NET page, allowing you to hook into the page lifecycle and execute code on the server when the page loads, or more commonly when a user requests some data that needs to be processed by the server.

However, because these code-behind files hook into the lifecycle of the page they have a tight dependency to the core ASP.net runtime. When it comes to testing, this tight dependency causes a huge amount of problems. If you attempt to access the object outside of the ASP.net runtime, such as when writing unit tests then you will receive a number of error messages in and around the core engine. When it comes to the aspx file, any of the code placed in the view is not accessible from another class — as such you wouldn't be able to write any unit tests for it.

In order to be able to unit test ASP.NET WebForms you need to think about how to develop the application in a different way. The most important thing to remember is to keep the view and the code-behind classes as thin as possible. They should contain the minimum amount of code to function and as soon as the code starts to become complex it should be moved to a separate isolated class. We feel that the way Visual Studio and ASP.NET WebForms behave by default encourages you to store a large amount of logic within your code-behind file; however, this is not the correct place for complex logic. If you think back to Chapter 2 and SOLID, The Single Responsibility Principle is broken by code-behind files.

ASP.NET also doesn't help to keep the view lightweight as it encourages controls such as the GridView control. An example of the GridView is next; the control populates the grid and provides built in paging support:

```
<asp:GridView ID="GridView1" runat="server" AllowPaging="True"
    AutoGenerateColumns="False" DataSourceID="ObjectDataSource1">
    <Columns>
        <asp:CommandField ShowSelectButton="True" />
        <asp:BoundField DataField="Name" HeaderText="Name"
                        SortExpression="Name" />
    </Columns>
</asp:GridView>
<asp:ObjectDataSource ID="ObjectDataSource1" runat="server"
                    SelectMethod="GetData"
                    TypeName="WebApplication1.ObjectSourceBusinessObject">
</asp:ObjectDataSource>
```

This kind of code litters your aspx files while also sending over-complex HTML down to the user. This doesn't mean that it needs testing as it's a standard control, but it does mean that there is not a clean separation and no possible way to write unit tests. Even automate UI tests (discussed in Chapter 5) would be difficult.

One way to help encourage you to keep your view and code-behind files clean is to follow the Model-View-Presenter (MVP) design pattern. A design pattern describes some experience or knowledge gained allowing this to be shared with other people. The idea is to allow people to take one person's experience, use the pattern to understand the concept in a high level, and then apply the techniques to their own scenario. Having a pattern in this high-level format allows you to discuss the concepts in the same way, leaving low-level implementation details out of the discussion. The advantage is that the discussion can focus on the technical aspects, without focusing on someone's specific problems. There are many different patterns, and MVP is just one of them.

When it comes to ASP.NET and MVP, the aim is to move all of the normal logic you would find in a code-behind file into a separate class. In order for this class to communicate with the view, the view implements a particular interface defining the view's behavior. The view is then injected into the controller so that it can take advantage of the functionality the view offers. In this example, the view will have two elements, one element is a button and the other is a ListBox. When the user clicks the button, it will request data from the server and populate the result in the ListBox.

If you look at the implementation, you'll see that the view will need to implement an interface. In this example, you need the view to be able to fire an event in order to request data, have a property for the data to be stored and a method to cause the UI to update and display the data:

```
public interface IDisplayDataView
{
    event EventHandler DataRequested;
    List<string> Data { get; set; }
    void Bind();
}
```

After the view has implemented the interface, it can pass the instance of itself into a controller, in this case the DisplayDataController:

```
public partial class _Default : System.Web.UI.Page, IDisplayDataView
{
    private DisplayDataController Controller;
    protected void Page_Load(object sender, EventArgs e)
    {
        Controller = new DisplayDataController(this);
    }
}
```

The controller stores the view instance for future methods calls. Within the constructor, the controller also needs to hook up any events provided by the UI and attach them to the appropriate method to ensure that the functionality is met:

```
public class DisplayDataController
{
    public IDisplayDataView View { get; set; }

    public DisplayDataController(IDisplayDataView view)
    {
        View = view;
        View.DataRequested += GetData;
    }
}
```

Because this code is in an isolated class away from the ASP.NET lifecycle, you can write a test to verify that the functionality is correct. In this case, you are verifying that an event handler is attached to the

DataRequested event, but you don't care which type of handler. After constructing the controller, you verify that this has happened:

```
[TestFixture]
public class DisplayDataControllerTests
{
    [Test]
    public void Ctor_should_hook_up_events()
    {
        IDisplayDataView view = MockRepository.GenerateMock<IDisplayDataView>();
        view.Expect(v => v.DataRequested += null).IgnoreArguments();

        new DisplayDataController(view);

        view.VerifyAllExpectations();
    }
}
```

With the event in place, the next step is to implement the GetData method, which will be called when the event is raised. Again, as you have abstracted away from the ASP.NET code-behind file, you can write the code test-first. The idea is that when GetData is called, it should populate the Data property on the view. To simulate the view, you can use Rhino Mocks to produce a stub object. The controller will then interact with the stub and the Data property as if it was a real page. By having the IDisplayDataView in place you have the control and flexibility to be able to test. If the controller does not populate the data property after a call to GetData, then the test will fail:

```
[Test]
public void GetData_should_populate_data()
{
    IDisplayDataView view = MockRepository.GenerateStub<IDisplayDataView>();
    DisplayDataController controller = new DisplayDataController(view);
    controller.GetData(this, EventArgs.Empty);

    Assert.AreEqual(4, view.Data.Count);
}
```

After the data has been set, the view needs to be alerted in order to refresh the UI and display the data to the user. There are many ways this notification could be made, in this example you expect that the controller will call the Bind method on the view.

In our controller test, you can use a mock object to verify that the call is made correctly after GetData is called:

```
[Test]
public void GetData_should_call_Bind()
{
    IDisplayDataView view = MockRepository.GenerateMock<IDisplayDataView>();
    view.Expect(v => v.Bind());
    DisplayDataController controller = new DisplayDataController(view);
    controller.GetData(this, EventArgs.Empty);

    view.VerifyAllExpectations();
}
```

The results of the implementation via the tests would be next:

```
public void GetData(object sender, EventArgs e)
{
    View.Data = new List<string> { "String A", "String B", "String C",
                                   "String D" };
    View.Bind();
}
```

While MVP is a useful pattern to consider when developing WebForms applications and can definitively improve testability, it's still not perfect. The problem is that the ASP.net application still needs all the events to go via the code-behind file. So, you still have methods containing logic that is unable to be tested. In this example, there are the following two methods that are untested as a result:

```
public void Bind()
{
    ListBox1.DataSource = Data;
    ListBox1.DataBind();
}
protected void Button1_Click(object sender, EventArgs e)
{
    if (DataRequested != null)
        DataRequested(sender, e);
}
```

While two methods won't cause major problems, you can imagine that as the application grows, this untested code will also increase, which might result in more bugs being introduced into the code base. For example, when writing this example you had 100 percent passing tests, but because you didn't call ListBox1.DataBind(), nothing was displayed on the UI.

MVP also doesn't provide much support when attempting to move code from the view into testable classes. While it's possible, it can increase the complexity of the application.

The use of MVP pattern was never a mainstream approach to developing ASP.NET WebForms. People wrote code in the code-behind file and also wanted to be able to unit test it. This became a major issue for Microsoft with developers starting to get frustrated with the lack of testability when compared with other open source frameworks. These open source frameworks offered huge advantages to developers over WebForms, with many people taking advantage and using these frameworks. As a result, Microsoft released a new framework based on the MVC pattern called ASP.NET MVC. This was a huge jump forward in terms of testability support as it solves some of the issues we mentioned with WebForms and the MVP pattern. ASP.NET MVC is the main framework covered in this chapter.

ASP.NET MVC

Due to the problems people encountered with WebForms, Microsoft set their sights on developing a web framework based on the MVC pattern. Since WebForms was released, many other web frameworks such as Ruby on Rails, Django (a web framework for the Python language), and MonoRail (a .NET web framework) have huge main impacts, all with the common theme of being extremely testable and easy to maintain. With pressure from the community, Microsoft released ASP.NET MVC.

ASP.NET approaches the problem of a web framework in a similar manner to the frameworks mentioned previously, focusing on allowing developers to create a testable, decoupled system. This is not meant as a replacement for WebForms, but as an alternative offering for web developers to use. I can imagine some people staying with WebForms and continuing to develop software using that approach, but others will pick up the new framework and run with it.

By having a decoupled web framework you interchange sections of the framework and provide your own. For example, there are now a number of options in terms of the view engine, the component that renders the HTML. Previously, it was extremely difficult to decouple the WebForms view engine from the ASP.NET core engine itself, which limited your choice to WebForms. With the new architecture, you have much more flexibility and choice. Although there are many different view engines available, there appear to be three main engines: NVelocity, Brail, and Spark. NVelocity is a port from the Apache Jakarta Velocity project. It first provided support for MonoRail as a view engine and now supports ASP.NET MVC. MonoRail and the Castle team have since forked the project and have continued to provide functionality and bug fixes. NVelocity aims to provide a similar and cleaner approach to writing your view template, also known as the page that will be converted into HTML.

Brail and Spark are two other view engines available. Similar to NVelocity, Brail also was designed for MonoRail. The aim of Brail is to allow you to take advantage of the Boo language. Boo is a "wrist-friendly language for the Common Language Infrastructure (CLI) aimed at cutting down the amount of code you need to write. With Brail, you can use the Boo language within your View template. Spark allows you to include code snippets within strings within HTML elements. This improves readability and allows you to bind data elements to HTML very simply.

All the view engines take a different approach and are aligned with the different ways people enjoy writing software. The approach you take is a personal choice. In the following example you will use WebForms.

If you wish to learn more about the ASP.NET MVC Framework, check out *Professional ASP.NET MVC 1.0* by Rob Conery, Scott Hanselman, Phil Haack, and Scott Guthrie; published by Wrox 2009.

The Model View Controller Pattern

MVC is a design pattern aimed at describing how you can separate your applications and decouple your system. MVC is the three separate sections of an application. *Model* refers to the domain of the system. This model represents information that will be used by the application. For example, in this system you will have models such as Product, Order, and ShoppingCart. These objects will store all the information related to that section of the problem domain. *View* relates to the UI and displays the model to the user. An example would be a web page, or a desktop form. As MVC is an architectural pattern, it is not constrained to a particular implementation, framework, or language and can be used to describe how to structure both web and desktop applications. Finally, *controller* processes requests from the user and updates the model before returning it to the view to display. The controller will have various methods to control what to display. For example, the controller might be called HomeController, with a method called Index that will set up the model for the Index page before sending the rendered page down to the end-user.

When a request comes in, it will hit the controller first. The controller will construct and populate the model. It will then pass the model to the view. The view will then communicate with the model to display the data. The view might also communicate with the controller to process further questions. Figure 3-1 represents the communication and links between the different parts. The solid lines show associations, while the dashed line indicates indirect associations.

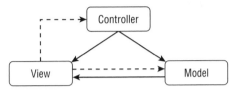

Figure 3-1: Model View Controller

By having your application structured in this fashion, you have separated your concerns (as discussed in The Single Responsibility Principle in Chapter 2. This results in more maintainable software.

Implementing the Pizza Store

The following section will describe how to develop and write unit tests for the ASP.NET MVC application called the Wrox Pizza Store. The concept for the store is simple: a user should be able to navigate to the store, select items from a menu, pay for their purchases, and then expect delivery of their ordered products.

Downloading and Installing ASP.NET MVC

ASP.NET MVC is a free download available from `http://www.asp.net/mvc/`. The installation is a MSI package that contains a collection of assemblies relating to the core framework itself, JavaScript files including JQuery and Microsoft Ajax, and a set of Visual Studio templates to help you create ASP.NET MVC applications.

Structuring Your ASP.NET MVC Applications

The initial structure of your application is important in terms of how maintainable the system will be at the end. If you start off with a good structure it provides a firm foundation for you to build upon.

After downloading and installing ASP.NET MVC, you will have a set of Web Templates within Visual Studio in the same way you had templates for ASP.NET WebForms. By using these templates you can create an ASP.NET application by simply entering a name, in this example HelloWorldMVC; the template will create the structure, and add correct references and initial code to help you get started. After creating and executing the application, it should look similar to Figure 3-2.

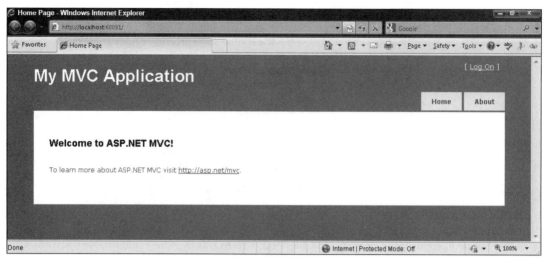

Figure 3-2:The website generated by the MVC template

The solution within Visual Studio created by the template is broken into different sections to indicate the roles and responsibilities as shown in Figure 3-3.

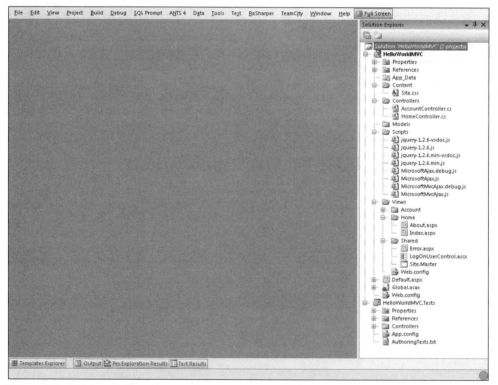

Figure 3-3: Default MVC solution structure

First you'll have two directories for resources: content and scripts. Content is designed to store style sheets, images, and other static resources for the site. The scripts folder contains JQuery and the Microsoft Ajax framework. ASP.NET MVC is the first Microsoft product to ship an open source library in the form of JQuery, which is very exciting news for the open source community and for developers who work on the Microsoft platforms. Both of these frameworks support you when adding JavaScript to your site.

The Models folder is empty, but the Controllers folder currently has two classes: AccountController and HomeController. The AccountController is responsible for the authentication for the system. The HomeController is responsible for handling the logic for the Index and the About pages.

Within the Views folder there are multiple sections. The Accounts folder has the authentication pages. The Home folder contains the About and Index pages. With MVC, unlike WebForms, ASP.NET no longer requires code-behind files as all the logic is within the controller; as a result you simply need the ASPX file. One important item to notice is that the controller's name and the name of the Views folder match. This convention allows the framework to identify which View pages to render based on the controller and action method. The Shared folder contains all the pages or user controls that are shared among the different views in the system; for example, the master page for the site.

The project will be compiled into an assembly called HelloWorldMVC. When creating the project you also have the option to create a test project to store your unit tests. By default, this is the project name with .tests appended, such as HelloWorldMVC.Tests. As described in Chapter 2, the naming of the project, folder, and classes should reflect the names within your main application making it easier to navigate and understand how the tests relate to your implementation. By default, MVC selects an MSTest based project; however, if you've installed the correct extensions you can select from xUnit, MbUnit, NUnit or any other framework.

Although this is the default solution provided by Microsoft, we feel a different structure is more logical. Our main bug-bear with the default structure is how it mixes the business logic and view logic in the same assembly and project structure. We feel better to maintain a clear definition between the two because it helps you think more logically about what belongs where. All the code, actual C# code, should live in a separate assembly to the View templates — the ASPX files.

The folder structure we're recommending for you is shown in Figure 3-4 (found in *3-TDD\Chapter 3 Samples\WroxPizzaStore\v1\WroxPizzaStore*) and is a basic structure for setting up solutions.

All the assemblies are prefixed with the name of the application, in this case WroxPizza. This will help identify assemblies against possible third-party assemblies within the output directory.

In the solution there are four different projects: .Core, .Tests.Unit, .Tests.Integration, and .Web. WroxPizza.Core is a class library that will store all your application logic. There are also three main root folders: Data, for your data access logic (which will be covered later); Model, to store your domain logic; and Web, which stores your controllers, bootstrapping code for the website, and any shared UI logic.

WroxPizza.Web stores all your mark up and content for the web application. This should contain no C# code, with the exception of Global.asax.cs and Default.aspx.cs, which are required due to the core ASP.NET engine. The result of having your application structured this way is that you know everything within .Core needs to be unit\integration tested while everything in .Web should be left to UI automation.

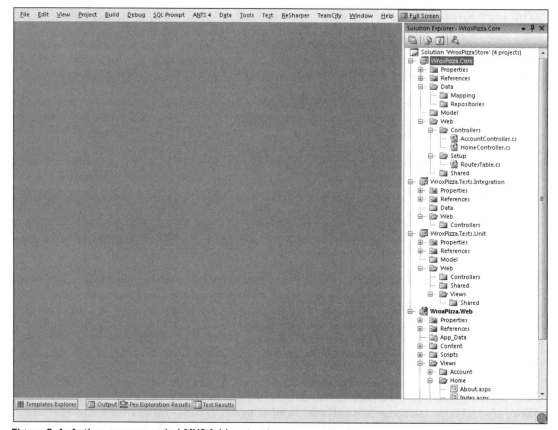

Figure 3-4: Author-recommended MVC folder structure

The final two assemblies are your test assemblies. The assemblies are split into two for an important reason. Your Tests.Unit assembly will contain most of your tests, taking advantage of mock and stub objects where required to break the dependencies. Because this assembly will contain most of your business logic, you want it to be fast to run and to be confident that all the tests will pass every time. If a test fails in this assembly then you must have broken something. Your Tests.Integration assembly on the other hand will be testing against a real implementation; for example, a real database. This assembly will be slower to execute and more error-prone. However, because it's only focusing on your integration tests then it shouldn't need to be executed as often. If you had automated UI tests, these would be stored under WroxPizza.Tests.UI.

With the basic structure in place you can start building your application. As with most applications, the hardest part is figuring out where to start. There are three possible starting points: you can start at the UI and work down to the DB; you can start at the DB and work upward toward the UI; or you can start in the middle and fan out working on UI and DB as required. When using TDD and mock objects, beginning at the middle layer and then fanning out tends to be the easiest. This drives the business value and core functionality more effectively.

As you learn more about your requirements and start interacting with the UI and DB, this layer will be subject to changes. However with tests in place and a decoupled system, this shouldn't be too painful.

Feature 1: Displaying Products from Database

The first feature to develop is one of the core features for the application: displaying products on a web page. Although this sounds like a simple task, it provides a core set of interactions with your system and will allow you to define an initial design and architecture for a core part early on. This will allow you to follow a similar approach when building the rest of the application.

As such, it also provides a great example for explaining the concepts and how to start building features using TDD.

The initial set of samples can be found in 3-TDD\Chapter 3 Samples\WroxPizzaStore\. The final application can be found at Sample\WroxPizzaStore.

Creating the Controller

As previously mentioned, we will be following the fan out approach to software development and with the MVC pattern; the core part is the controller. To start with, you'll be displaying the products to form a menu for your pizza store. The initial name could be ProductsMenu, because it is responsible for displaying the menu. This controller will be responsible for first obtaining the products from the database and then passing them back to the UI to display on the correct page.

When using TDD, your first approach when writing code is to always to create a new test. Your controllers are going to be isolated from all external dependencies as they are going to be unit tested with testability taken into consideration from the beginning. By coding the test upfront, those considerations are easier to implement and get right instead of having to try and retro-fit the problem.

To start, you first create a new class under WroxPizza.Tests.Unit.Web.Controllers called ProductsMenuControllerTests. With the class in place, you can start writing test methods. The first test will verify that the controller is accessing the database correctly and pulling back all the products available. This test is called Index_Returns_All_Products_In_Database.

An initial attempt at the test would be similar to the next code example. The aim of the test is to describe how you are expecting to interact with the controller and method. In this example, the test constructs a controller called ProductsMenu and calls the Index() method:

```
[TestFixture]
public class ProductsMenuControllerTests
{
        [Test]
        public void Index_Returns_All_Products_In_Database()
        {
            //Incomplete
            ProductsMenuController controller = new ProductsMenuController();
            controller.Index();
        }
}
```

This test has two major problems. First, there is no expected data so you don't know what data will be returned. Secondly, the test is not self-verifying and as such it will always pass.

With the first problem, although you know you need to store the products you want to display, you may not know exactly how or where at the moment. A database seems the most logical, but as you move forward you might need to access a web service or an XML data file to obtain the information. Because of this, you should abstract away from this low-level dependency, such as a database, and have your controller talk to a high layer interface. At this point, you should be remembering similar concepts discussed in Chapter 2. By communicating to the abstract implementation, you have the flexibility to replace the implementation during testing allowing you more control.

You know you need to access the data from an external source. For now, you will use Rhino Mocks to create a stub object for an IProductRepository. A class implementing IProductRepository will be responsible for returning all the products within the store. The Repository pattern is a well-known data access pattern, which was defined in Martin Fowler's *Patterns of Enterprise Application Architecture* book, published by Addison-Wesley (2002), and is designed to mediate between domain objects data mapping layers. Your domain objects will be objects such as Product and Order while your data mapping will handle the translation between domain objects and the underlying data store, such as a table.

Although the pattern doesn't define which method a Repository object should have, the .NET community has defined an approach they take and a defacto standard has emerged that people generally follow. The standard set of methods providing core functionality include Get, GetAll, FindAll, FindOne, SaveOrUpdate, and Delete. This standard set of methods generally exists on an IRepository interface with custom methods being defined on the more targeted interface. This keeps the IRepository interface lightweight and focused allowing other interfaces to also remain lightweight while being targeted and providing functionality. This relates to the Interface Segregation Principle as discussed in Chapter 2.

In order to implement this test and have our controller communicate with some data source you will need to stub (as described in Chapter 2) the IProductRepository. This inherits from IRepository; however, it will be the more targeted interface based on how to return product related information:

```
IProductRepository repository = MockRepository.GenerateStub<IProductRepository>();
```

By stubbing this interface, you can define the result you want to be returned when a part of our system calls the particular method. This is how our test can be in control of the data being passed around the object being tested:

```
repository.Stub(r => r.GetAll()).Return(products);
```

In this case, when the GetAll method is called on our Repository object, you want the products' collection defined next to be returned. This collection simply contains a single product; however, it is enough data to allow us to prove if the system is working as expected:

```
List<Product> products = new List<Product>
                        {
                            new Product
                            {
                                ID = 1,
                                Name = "Classic Cheese",
                                Description = "Classic Cheese",
                                BasePrice = 8.00
                            },
                        };
```

You have now defined a test and an interface that will return the data. The next stage is to inject the stub object into the controller so the controller can access the functionality provided via an object implementing IProductRepository. Remember, the controller isn't concerned with the actual details, it just needs an object to provide the functionality requested. The easiest way to handle this is using constructor injection where the external dependency is provided as an argument on the constructor of the object requiring the functionality (as covered by The Dependency Inversion Principle in Chapter 2) as shown next:

```
ProductsMenuController controller = new ProductsMenuController(repository);
```

The controller now has the ability to obtain data. However, the test still doesn't have any way of knowing what data was returned from the controller.

With ASP.NET MVC, any action that should render a view needs to return an object of type ActionResult. The ActionResult is an abstract class with a number of different subclasses within the framework. Each subclass has a number of different options and additional information that controls how the framework processes responses and redirects.

In this example, your Index method will return a ViewResult, indicating the view to render. The first stage is to cast the object in order to obtain the extra information:

```
ViewResult page = controller.Index() as ViewResult;
```

With the ViewResult object you can start verifying that the system is working correctly. One way to achieve this is via the ViewData property on the ViewResult object. ViewData is a collection that allows you to store weak and strongly typed data, and is used to pass data from the controller to the view for rendering. When using the strongly typed part of ViewData, you define a model that allows you to pass data back and forth via objects and properties.

To access the strongly typed object in your tests, you need to cast the ViewData property to your own ViewModel that you are planning to return; in this case the ViewModel is the ProductsMenuModel:

```
ProductsMenuModel model = page.ViewData.Model as ProductsMenuModel;
```

This is how you can verify that the correct data is being returned from the action. When the view renders, it will use the ViewData to obtain the results. Using your tests, you can obtain exactly the same data that the view would receive, allowing you to verify the controller is working as expected:

```
Assert.AreEqual(1, model.Products.Count);
```

The test is now in place and would look like the following:

```
[Test]
public void Index_Returns_All_Products_In_Database()
{
    List<Product> products = new List<Product>
            {
                new Product
                {
                    ID = 1,
                    Category = new ProductCategory {Description =
                                                "Pizza"},
                    Name = "Classic Cheese",
                    Description = "Classic Cheese",
```

```
                                    BasePrice = 8.00,
                                    Image = TestHelpers.GetDummyImage()
                            }
                    };
            stubProductRepository.Stub(r => r.GetAll()).Return(products);
            ProductsMenuController controller = new ProductsMenuController(
    stubProductRepository);
            ProductsMenuModel model = controller.Index()
            .GetModel<ProductsMenuModel>();

            Assert.AreEqual(1, model.Products.Count);
        }
```

However this won't compile because the objects you are interacting with don't exist yet. After you have defined the test and outlined your expectations, the first stage is to get the project to a state where it can compile — this is just a case of creating the classes and methods without any implementation. You just want to compile at the moment.

After you can compile, you can execute your test to ensure that it fails as expected. As mentioned in Chapter 2, you want to see a failing test to provide confidence when you see the test finally pass. Many people say "It doesn't count if you don't see it fail first."

You can now create the implementation using your test as guidance. Remember, you are aiming to implement the minimum amount of code possible to make the test pass. In this case, you need to call a method on your Repository to obtain all the products, assign them to the model, and attach the model to your ViewData. The final implementation is shown next:

```
        private readonly IProductRepository Repository;

        public ProductsMenuController(IProductRepository repository)
        {
            Repository = repository;
        }
        public ActionResult Index()
        {
            ProductsMenuModel model = new ProductsMenuModel();
            List<Product> products = Repository.GetAll();
            model.Products = products;

            return View(model);
        }
```

Now if you rerun the test, it should successfully pass.

The final stage of the process is to refactor your codebase. There are not many changes you could perform to improve your controller code because the code is already clean and legible. However, your test code could be made more readable.

Firstly, the test collection you create doesn't need to be part of the test. It would be more readable if you moved this initialization into a Setup method to keep the test focused on what it is testing. The SetUp method is run before each test and is the ideal position to place any set-up code, such as creating your test data collection. You can take the previous test, and simply extract the logic into the Setup method that has been attributed to indicate to nUnit that it should be executed:

```
List<Product> products;
[SetUp]
public void Setup()
{
    products = new List<Product>
                {
                    new Product
                    {
                        ID = 1,
                        Name = "Classic Cheese",
                        Description = "Classic Cheese",
                        BasePrice = 8.00
                    },
                };
}
```

Another concern with the test is around obtaining the model via the ViewData property. To gain access, you need to first cast the Index result into a ViewResult. You then need to cast the model into its concrete type of ProductsModelMenu. This additional logic causes you to lose focus on what is being tested, instead focusing your attention on this block of code. To keep the tests clean, this logic should be hidden from the test and moved into a different class that can deal with obtaining the model from the ViewData for you. To solve this, you created a generic extension method on the ActionResult object to handle the process of returning the model in the correct format:

```
public static class MVCTestExtensions
{
    public static T GetModel<T>(this ActionResult page) where T : class
    {
        return ((ViewResult) page).ViewData.Model as T;
    }
}
```

With this in place, to obtain the model for the ViewData you simply call the method on the results of your call to Index:

```
ProductsMenuModel model = controller.Index().GetModel<ProductsMenuModel>();
```

The GetModel method keeps your test code more streamlined and focused than it was previously, but also allows you to share this functionality between other tests. After you have completed the refactoring, your test and set-up code looks similar to the following:

```
[TestFixture]
public class ProductsMenuControllerTests
{
    List<Product> products;
    [SetUp]
    public void Setup()
    {
        products = new List<Product>
```

```
                                  {
                                      new Product
                                          {
                                              ID = 1,
                                              Name = "Classic Cheese",
                                              Description = "Classic Cheese",
                                              BasePrice = 8.00
                                          },
                                  };
              }


              [Test]
              public void Index_Returns_All_Products_In_Database()
              {
                      IProductRepository repository = MockRepository.GenerateStub
              <IProductRepository>();
                      repository.Stub(r => r.GetAll()).Return(products);

                      ProductsMenuController controller = new ProductsMenuController(
              repository);
                      ProductsMenuModel model = controller.Index()
              .GetModel<ProductsMenuModel>();

                      Assert.AreEqual(1, model.Products.Count);
              }
      }
```

With your test data being created before each test in the set-up block you can share this amongst future tests and have the advantage that the test itself is clear and focused.

Creating ProductRepository

Even though you have proven that your controller action works as you expected, it still isn't very useful in terms of a real application. Because you have not implemented an object that inherits your IProductRepository you have no way of accessing the real data.

Within your application you are going to use NHibernate, which is an object relational mapping (ORM) framework. You are using a ORM for a number of reasons. Firstly, the framework will handle all of your database communication, creating and executing queries on your behalf, allowing you to code against strongly typed objects instead of handwritten SQL statements. This makes your code more flexible. Because the ORM handles this communication between the database and your domain\business logic, it means it can be more easily isolated because your application is already being developed for different reasons. This isolation makes it much easier for you to create the repositories, which you can stub out and use to improve testability. If you didn't use an ORM and pay close attention to how you communicate with the database, you could have different parts of your code interacting with the database in different ways, making the system much harder to test.

NHibernate will provide you with the mapping to enable you to go from your domain object, for example Product, to your database table called Products. In the example, because you already have a legacy database, NHibernate will allow you to map your domain model and to a different database schema naming convention, allowing you to abstract and hide the underlying schema structure from the application. This allows you to maintain two views on the database without violating any design principals. For example, your Products table in the database will look like Figure 3-5.

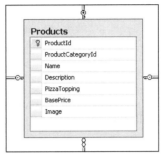

**Figure 3-5: Example Products
table from the WroxPizza
database**

As you already have your domain model and your table, you simply need to create the mapping that links the two together. NHibernate's mapping takes the form of XML, yet a new project called Fluent NHibernate (`http://fluentnhibernate.org`) has been released that allows you to write the mappings as C# code instead of XML. This means that the mappings are now strongly typed, which results in compile time checking and are updated automatically when you perform your refactoring steps. With the mappings as XML, you do not have this level of flexibility.

Based on the structure, all the mapping classes will be stored within WroxPizza.Core.Data.Mapping. A class called ProductMap inherits from a generic class called ClassMap<T>, which is included within Fluent NHibernate. When you inherit from ClassMap, you simply replace the T with the domain class you are mapping to — in this case Product.

After referencing Fluent NHibernate, you can start to create your mapping to map your domain objects onto your database table and columns:

```
public class ProductMap : ClassMap<Product>
```

Fluent NHibernate follows a convention-over-configuration approach. By default, it will expect the class name to map to a table, and properties to map to columns. In this case the naming convention in our model and database are not the same. As such, you can use the WithTable() method to indicate the mapped table:

```
WithTable("Products");
```

Next you need to define your primary key. This is done by calling the ID method providing a lambda expression to define which property on the Product object you want to map. The second argument is the name of the column within the table:

```
Id(x => x.ID, "ProductId");
```

With the ID mapped, you simply need to map your remaining columns. Because the property and the column name are identical on the object and table you don't need to provide the second string argument defining the column name — it will simply be inferred. On the mapping, you'll add a Not Null constraint to indicate rules based on our data in the table:

```
Map(x => x.Name).CanNotBeNull();
Map(x => x.Description).CanNotBeNull();
Map(x => x.BasePrice).CanNotBeNull();
```

At this stage our mapping is complete. However you need to update the product model, because NHibernate requires all properties and methods on the model need to be marked as virtual. This is due to the way NHibernate handles lazy loading; it creates a proxy of the class for managing how and when to populate the collection.

The final stage is to implement the ProductRepository. For a basic Repository like this, most of the logic will be within the generic IRepository implementation. With this in mind, you created a generic NHibernateRepository<T> that inherits from IRepository<T>. ProductRepository will then inherit from NHibernateRepository<Product> and IProductRepository. This allows you to share the core functionality of a Repository amongst different repositories within your system. The implementation of the mapping is shown next:

```
public class ProductMap : ClassMap<Product>
{
    public ProductMap()
    {
        WithTable("Products");
        Id(x => x.ID, "ProductId");
        Map(x => x.Name).CanNotBeNull();
        Map(x => x.Description).CanNotBeNull();
        Map(x => x.BasePrice).CanNotBeNull();
    }
}
```

For additional flexibility with the ProductRepository, I abstract away from the database configuration and created an IDbConfigure allowing me to pass in the relevant configuration when I construct the Repository. The configuration is handled by DefaultNHibernateConfig:

```
public class DefaultNHibernateConfig : IDbConfigure
{
    private Configuration configuration;
    private ISession currentSession = null;
    public DefaultNHibernateConfig()
    {
        configuration = new Configuration();
        configuration.AddAssembly(typeof(ProductRepository).Assembly);

        NHibernateModel model = new NHibernateModel();
        model.Configure(configuration);
    }

    public ISessionFactory GetSessionFactory()
```

```
        {
            return configuration.BuildSessionFactory();
        }

        public ISession GetCurrentSession()
        {
            if (currentSession == null)
                currentSession = GetSessionFactory().OpenSession();

            return currentSession;
        }
    }
```

The resulting ProductRepository implementation is next:

```
    public class ProductRepository : NHibernateRepository<Product>, IProductRepository
    {
        public ProductRepository(IDbConfigure factory) : base(factory)
        {}
    }
```

As the Repository is tightly coupled to the database, there is little point in stubbing any section to unit test the implementation. Because of this, we felt that writing unit tests against this layer didn't add much value. Instead, you write a series of integration tests as you were developing the implementation. You also created a series of tests targeted at the NHibernate mapping files to ensure they are correct.

For more information on the integration tests, please refer to Chapter 4, which covers how you created the Tests.Integration project and tested the Repository.

Integrating IoC with StructureMap

At this point, you are starting to have a number of relationships and dependencies on different parts of the system. The following section describes how you can manage these dependencies within your ASP. NET MVC application. The easier your dependencies are to manage, the more decoupled your application will be, and as a result the easier it will be to test. This is why we feel IoC is an important concept for testability.

As described earlier in the chapter, the ProductsMenuController requires an object that implements IProductRepository to allow the controller to access the database. In turn, the ProductRepository implementation requires an IDbConfigure object for the database configuration. As such, to construct an instance of your controller the following code is required:

```
    DefaultNHibernateConfig config = new DefaultNHibernateConfig();
    ProductRepository repository = new ProductRepository(config);
    ProductsMenuController controller = new ProductsMenuController(repository);
```

Even though this is messy from the point of view of your application's code, having a constructor dependency on the controller also means that the ASP.NET MVC Framework cannot automatically construct the controller. The answer is to use an IoC framework (as discussed in Chapter 2), which can construct instances of the objects and automatically resolve their dependencies. Luckily, ASP.NET MVC is IoC friendly, making it very easy to incorporate a framework into the pipeline.

The first task is to select a framework. Our recommendation is to use StructureMap (http://structuremap.sourceforge.net/) as your IoC framework. StructureMap has two main parts; first is the registration of dependencies with the second part being how it constructs the objects.

StructureMap needs some setup around the interfaces that exist and the concrete implementation that they should use. Although there is an auto mapping feature, manually defining them is equally as successful. This registration happens when the application first starts. In terms of an ASP.NET application, it starts when Internet Information Services (IIS) starts the appdomain for the website. When this occurs, the Application_Start() method is called in the Global.asax. At this point you need to set up StructureMap. This setup will be done within the Bootstrapper object within the Setup method:

```
Bootstrapper.Setup();
```

The Setup method simply initializes StructureMap and provides it with a subclass of the Registry class that configures the mapping:

```
public static void Setup()
{
    ObjectFactory.Initialize(c => c.AddRegistry(new WroxPizzaConfig()));
}
```

The WroxPizzaConfig object overrides the configure method that StructureMap calls during the AddRegistry stage. Within the method there are two important method calls. The first is ForRequestedType; this is the initial call to configure what happens when StructureMap is requested to construct an object with this type — for example, IProductRepository. When IProductRepository is requested, it looks at the value set by the second method. The second method is TheDefaultIsConreteType that defines the concrete implementation to use, in this case an instance of ProductRepository. This is the same for IDbConfigure where it provides an instance of DefaultNHibernateConfig. The initial configuration for StructureMap and the mappings are next:

```
internal class WroxPizzaConfig : Registry
{
    protected override void configure()
    {
        ForRequestedType<IProductRepository>().TheDefaultIsConcreteType<
ProductRepository>();
        ForRequestedType<IDbConfigure>().TheDefaultIsConcreteType<
DefaultNHibernateConfig>();
    }
}
```

StructureMap is a lot more powerful than simply creating objects, however, it can also provide this simple yet effective functionality.

With this mapping in place, StructureMap would now be able to construct instances of your controller. When a request comes in to the ProductsMenu Index page, ASP.NET will ask StructureMap for an instance of the type ProductsMenuController. StructureMap will analyze the constructer of the type and its arguments. When it sees IProductRepository it will attempt to create an instance, again looking at the constructor and parameter. Again, it will see IDbConfigure and provide an instance of DefaultNHibernateConfig before returning the new ProductRepository back to your controller.

While the IoC framework is now configured, you haven't told ASP.NET MVC about how to use the IoC framework and how it can construct objects. When ASP.NET MVC attempts to construct a controller, it will call into the ControllerFactory method that should know how to construct the controller instance. With the new decoupled nature, you can plug in your own ControllerFactory that can talk to your IoC framework to provide an instance of the requested controller.

The first task is to inform ASP.NET MVC that the controller factory exists. Within your Application_ Start method in the Global.asax you simply call the SetControllerFactory method:

```
protected void Application_Start()
{
    RoutesTable.RegisterRoutes(RouteTable.Routes);
    Bootstrapper.Setup();
    ControllerBuilder.Current.SetControllerFactory(
new StructureMapControllerFactory());
}
```

The next stage is to create StructureMapControllerFactory. You have constructed the object within the WroxPizza.Core.Web.Setup namespace to keep everything centralized.

Your new StructureMapControllerFactory first needs to inherit from DefaultControllerFactory. This will provide you with the core functionality. To change the way you construct the actual instance of your controller you need to override the GetControllerInstance method.

The GetControllerInstance method has a parameter that defines the type of controller MVC is requesting. As such you can simply call GetInstance on ObjectFactory that maintains all the information for StructureMap and can create instances of objects requested by their type:

```
protected override IController GetControllerInstance(Type controllerType)
{
    if (controllerType == null)
        return null;

    return ObjectFactory.GetInstance(controllerType) as Controller;
}
```

As you add more controllers, this code doesn't need to be changed as it is flexible enough to cope. If you add a new dependency, you simply need to register it in your WroxPizzaConfig object.

Creating ProductsMenu/Index UI

Based on the previous section you've done, your business logic and data access are complete and you're ready to return all the products. You have taken a number of steps to structure your application in a more effective, testable fashion to allow you to add new features going forward. However, you have one major step missing — the UI. Your business logic is complete and tested, however your poor users still cannot see anything.

You need to create a view to display your model and associated data. The view engine you are going to use is ASP.NET WebForms. Following the MVC structure, as shown in Figure 3-6, you need a folder called ProductsMenu that matches your Controller name as well as a page that will make your Action Method on the controller — in this case, index.aspx.

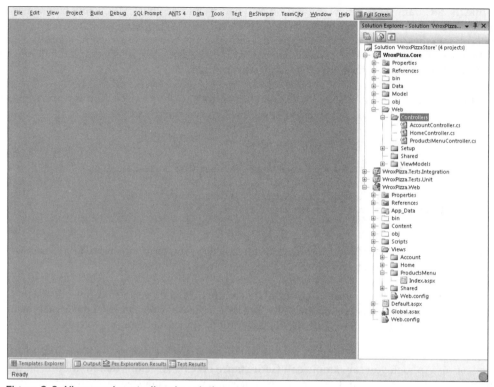

Figure 3-6: Views and controllers in solution

Your ASP.NET view should also be attached to the ASP.NET Master Page Site.aspx. At the moment this is the default ASP.NET MVC blue template that you can modify at a later date to fit in with the style of website you want.

In terms of how you developed your controller, you have a strongly typed model containing a collection of all the products you want to display. This is stored in an object of type ProductsMenuModel. For your view to access this object, the view page needs to inherit from the generic ViewPage<T> page. As such, the page directive will be the following:

```
<%@ Page Title="" Language="C#" MasterPageFile="~/Views/Shared/Site.Master"
    AutoEventWireup="true"
    Inherits="System.Web.Mvc.ViewPage<ProductsMenuModel>" %>
```

You can now access the ViewModel object via the variable model:

```
<% foreach (var product in Model.Products) { %>
        <%=product.Name %>
        <%=product.Description %>
        <%=product.BasePrice %>
    <% } %>
```

The previous code will successfully output the items from the menu. However, instead of the products being listed as a list, they should be side-by-side. To do this you need to have alternative styles for your rows of products. When you have different styles for a pair of rows, you can use CSS to align them side-by-side on the screen. For you to determine which CSS style to use for each side of the list, you need some additional logic that you'll want to test to ensure it works correctly.

With MVC, there are various helper methods included on an object accessed via the Html variable, which is of type HtmlHelper. By using extension methods in C# 3.0, you can extend this object to provide additional functionality while also fitting into the MVC approach to help readability. As these are extension methods, they will be coded in the MVCExtensions class, with the unit tests in the class MVCExtensionsTests.

To test the methods on the HtmlHelper, you need an instance of the actual HtmlHelper object. To create an instance of the HtmlHelper method, you need to provide a ViewContext and IViewDataContainer object. Using RhinoMocks, you can easily generate stub objects to use as parameters on the constructor. In order to keep the test code as clean as possible, there should be a helper method that hides this stubbing and construction:

```
public static HtmlHelper CreateHtmlHelper()
{
    ViewContext context = MockRepository.GenerateStub<ViewContext>();
    IViewDataContainer container = MockRepository.GenerateStub<
IViewDataContainer>();
    return new HtmlHelper(context, container);
}
```

In your Setup method, you can gain an instance of your HtmlHelper:

```
[SetUp]
public void Setup()
{
    helper = MockHelper.CreateHtmlHelper();
}
```

To create alternating styles, you need to provide an even number (0) for a normal-row to be returned. If you provide an odd number (1), then you should expect the alternative style to be returned. This is how you create the side-by-side styles for all your products. This logic is represented in the two test methods shown next:

```
[Test]
public void GetRowClass_Returns_Normal_For_Even_Number()
{
    string rowClass = helper.GetRowClass(0);
    Assert.AreEqual("normal-row",rowClass); //CSS Style
}
[Test]
public void GetRowClass_Returns_Alt_For_Odd_Number()
{
    string rowClass = helper.GetRowClass(1);
    Assert.AreEqual("alternate-row", rowClass); //CSS Style
}
```

Your implementation is then very simple as shown next:

```
public static string GetRowClass(this HtmlHelper helper, int rowIndex)
{
    return rowIndex % 2 == 0 ? "normal-row" : "alternate-row";
}
```

Although this might seem over the top for such simple logic, the reason for the tests is to provide the documentation and verification that it does work as expected. The constantly writing of the tests also keeps you in the TDD mindset, allowing it to become more natural.

The result is that your code now looks similar to the following, with your main complex part in a separate class with associated unit tests:

```
<% for (int i = 0; i < Model.Products.Count; i++) { %>
        <div class="<%=Html.GetRowClass(i) %>">
            <%= Html.Encode(Model.Products[i].Name) %><br />
            <%= Html.Encode(Model.Products[i].Description)%><br />
            <%= Model.Products[i].BasePrice%>
        </div>
    <% } %>
```

In both examples, your view is starting to get messy and confusing. It is difficult to see which part of the code is the main page, which part handles displaying all the products, and which part just handles displaying the single product on the screen. To solve this, you can take advantage of user controls and being able to render partial sections of content. By breaking the different sections of your UI into user controls, you can make the view more readable and open up the possibilities of reusing the actual layout in other parts of the application. This isn't done to improve testability directly, but to improve the maintainability and readability of the code. As a result, issues and bugs should become more obvious as the code is cleaner.

Now, when you output your grid you call the RenderPartial method. As arguments, you provide the user control that you want to render (in this case ProductGrid). The second argument you provide is the list of products that you want to be included on the grid:

```
<div class="Products">
    <% Html.RenderPartial("ProductGrid", Model.Products); %>
</div>
```

Within the ProductGrid control, you have the code to output the grid. Two things to note, first your model is now a strongly typed List<Product> that you provided from the Model.Products variable. The second point is that your product is rendered via the use of the ProductItem user control. You should call this multiple times, once for each product:

```
<% for (int i = 0; i < Model.Count; i++) { %>
        <div class="<%=Html.GetRowClass(i) %>">
            <% Html.RenderPartial("ProductItem", Model[i]); %>
        </div>
    <% } %>
```

Your ProductItem user control then simply outputs the required information to be displayed within the product grid:

```
<div class="productDesc">
        <%= Html.Encode(Model.Name) %><br />
        <%= Html.Encode(Model.Description) %><br />
        <%= Model.GetPrice() %>
</div>
```

Notice your calculation for GetPrice is in a method on a Product domain model, which means that it can be unit tested.

The implementation of GetPrice() is very simple, as it returns the BasePrice variable as a string with the dollar sign prefixed:

```
public virtual string GetPrice()
{
    return "$" + BasePrice;
}
```

As a result, you can create unit tests to implement this functionality.

```
[TestFixture]
public class ProductTests
{
    [Test]
    public void GetPrice_Returns_Price_As_String_With_Dollar_Symbol()
    {
        Product p = new Product();
        p.BasePrice = 4.99;

        Assert.AreEqual("$4.99", p.GetPrice());
    }
}
```

You now have your page in place, which renders multiple user controls to display the different products. The final step is to design your master page. This is the HTML around your content that will be shared among the other pages in the site to provide a consistent view.

The structure of the project now looks like Figure 3-7.

The only thing left is to tell the application the real database to use to serve data from. As mentioned before, your unit tests are running off the App.Config to identify the NHibernate settings. Within a web application, you use the web.config where you can place your NHibernate configuration that you want your application to use. Within the Config section of the web.config, you include a section name:

```
<configSections>
    <section name="hibernate-configuration"
            type="NHibernate.Cfg.ConfigurationSectionHandler, NHibernate"/>
....
</configSections>
```

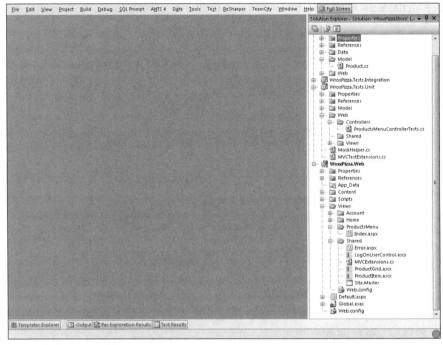

Figure 3-7: Final product structure

Underneath you include your NHibernate configuration, the same as you did for your unit tests, however pointing at a SQL Server 2005 instance:

```
<hibernate-configuration xmlns="urn:nhibernate-configuration-2.2">
  <session-factory>
    <property name="connection.connection_string">
    Data Source=(local);initial catalog=WroxPizza;Integrated Security=True;
    </property>
    <property name="connection.provider">
    NHibernate.Connection.DriverConnectionProvider
    </property>
    <property name="dialect">
    NHibernate.Dialect.MsSql2005Dialect
    </property>
    <property name="connection.driver_class">
    NHibernate.Driver.SqlClientDriver
    </property>
    <property name="connection.release_mode">
    on_close
    </property>
    <property name="show_sql">
    false
    </property>
  </session-factory>
</hibernate-configuration>
```

With everything in place, your application should work as expected. The final stage is to ensure the database has been created and populate it with test data, for the example in Figure 3-8 you used a tool from Red Gate called SQL Data Generator (http://www.red-gate.com/products/ SQL_Data_Generator/index.htm).

If you visit the ProductsMenu Index page, you see a list of products in a similar fashion to Figure 3-8.

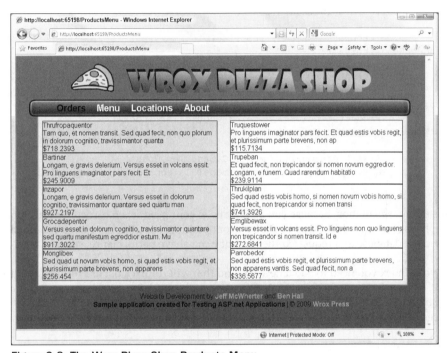

Figure 3-8: The Wrox Pizza Shop Products Menu

As you might have noticed, you didn't unit test all your UI — but you tested some logic such as the GetRowClass method. The aim should be to keep the UI as simple and maintainable as possible; breaking complex logic into user controls helped readability and kept it simpler, while moving logic into separate classes to support testability.

To verify that the UI is working as expected in an end-to-end process, you will have a set of UI tests that will be covered in Chapter 5.

Feature 2: Adding Categories

The first feature was to list all the products on the page. The second feature is to have different categories for products and only display certain products for a particular category.

To add this new functionality you need to modify various parts of your application. First of all, the controller will need to return a list of categories and will also need to take a category and return only the certain products within that category. Your ProductRepository will need to be modified to allow you to filter our query. Finally, your UI will need to be modified to display links to the different categories together with a page to show the filtered list of products.

The first change you need to make is to the controller in order to return a list of categories. When you access the Index page, you want the list of categories to be attached to the ProductsMenuModel that you can then use in the UI. The test you are aiming to make pass is as follows. The main points of this are that you are stubbing your implementation for the Repository; after that you verify that the categories are returned as expected based on the products' list you created in the set-up block:

```
[Test]
public void Index_Can_Get_Categories_As_List_Of_Strings()
{
        IProductRepository repository = MockRepository.GenerateStub<
IProductRepository>();
        repository.Stub(r => r.GetAll()).Return(products);

        ProductsMenuController controller = new ProductsMenuController(
repository);
        ProductsMenuModel model = controller.Index()
.GetModel<ProductsMenuModel>();

        Assert.AreEqual(1, model.Categories.Count);
        Assert.AreEqual("Pizza", model.Categories[0].Description);
}
```

In terms of implementation, because you already have your products returned from the database, you can simply use these products to form the base for obtaining the different categories available. You could have used the database and requested the list, but it may have performance issues.

Within your Index you need to add a new method that will return a list of ProductCategory. ProductCategory is a domain object that maps onto a table without your database and is referenced by your product. To keep the code clean, you need an additional method called GetCategoriesFromProductList that will take a list of products and return the categories:

```
[Test]
public void GetCategoriesFromProductList_Should_Return_Pizza()
{
        ProductsMenuController controller = new ProductsMenuController(
stubProductRepository);
        List<ProductCategory> categories = controller
.GetCategoriesFromProductList(products);
        Assert.AreEqual("Pizza", categories[0].Description);
        Assert.AreEqual(1, categories.Count);

}
```

The implementation for this is as follows.

```
        private List<ProductCategory> GetCategoriesFromProductList(
List<Product> products)
        {
        List<ProductCategory> list = new List<ProductCategory>();
        foreach (var product in products)
        {
                list.Add(product.Category);
```

```
        }

        return list;
    }
```

You then need to add a new property onto the ProductsMenuModel to store the categories that are populated with the value of the previous method call:

```
public ActionResult Index()
{
    ProductsMenuModel model = new ProductsMenuModel();
    List<Product> products = Repository.GetAll();
    model.Products = products;

    model.Categories = GetCategoriesFromProductList(products);
    return View(model);
}
```

However, this implementation has one bug. If you have two products in the same category, then the category will be returned twice. You want the list to be unique as this will be used in your navigation system on the web page. The first stage is to write a test that highlights the bug and defines the desired behavior:

```
[Test]
public void GetCategoriesFromProductList_Returns_No_Duplicate_Categories ()
{
    products.Add(new Product
    {
        ID = 2,
        Category = new ProductCategory {Description = "Pizza"}, //Duplicate
        Name = "Classic Four Cheeses",
        Description = "Classic Four Cheeses",
        BasePrice = 9.00
    });

    ProductsMenuController controller = new ProductsMenuController(
stubProductRepository);
    List<ProductCategory> categories = controller
.GetCategoriesFromProductList(products);
    Assert.AreEqual(1, categories.Count);
}
```

On the first line, you are adding an additional product to your base test data. This helps define the specific test while keeping the other tests generic. If this was going to be regularly required, then you might want to look at other ways of creating test data such as Object Mothers (discussed in Chapter 5). Now that you have the failing test, you can fix the bug and make the test pass.

In terms of changes to your UI, at the top of your index page, your categories will be rendered via a separate user control (again to keep your UI clean):

```
<div class="menu">
    <% Html.RenderPartial("CategoriesMenu", Model.Categories);%>
</div>
```

The user control will loop around and output a link:

```
<%  foreach (var s in Model) { %>
    <%=Html.CreateShowLink(Html.Encode(s.Description))%> |
<% }%>
```

Similar to how you extended the HtmlHelper object before, you have done the same with your CreateShowLink. This takes in the description and constructs the correct link to your Show page to show all the products in the category:

```
[Test]
public void CreateShowLink_Returns_ConstructedUrl_String_With_Desc_As_
LinkText()
{
    string t = h.CreateShowLink("Test");
    Assert.IsNotNullOrEmpty(t);
    Assert.IsTrue(t.Contains("Test"));
}

public static string CreateShowLink(this HtmlHelper html, string text)
{
    return html.ActionLink<ProductsMenuController>(c => c.Show(text), text);
}
```

If you launch the application, then your category links will appear like in Figure 3-9.

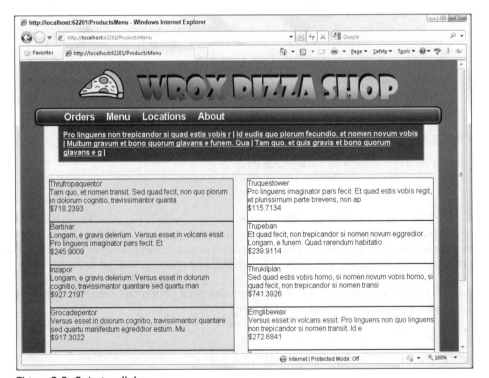

Figure 3-9: Category links

With the links being rendered at the top of the page, you now need to make a page that just displays those products. Your users can now visit the Show page, providing the category as a parameter to the page. The next step is to implement the Show action method and view. Again, you stub your IProductRepository, however this time you stub a new method called GetProductsByCategory. This takes a category as a string, in this case pizza. This should return a list of products which are within the category "pizza." In this test, you want the GetProductsByCategory to return our Products test data collection.

As you did before, in our test you call the Show method and then obtain the ViewData model from the result. After you verify that only one product was returned:

```
[Test]
public void Show_Return_Product_For_a_Single_Category()
{
    string category = "Pizza";
    IProductRepository repository = MockRepository.GenerateStub<
IProductRepository>();
    repository.Stub(r => r.GetProductsByCategory(category))
.Return(products);

    ProductsMenuController controller = new ProductsMenuController(
repository);
    ProductsMenuModel model = controller.Show(category)
.GetModel<ProductsMenuModel>();

    Assert.AreEqual(1, model.Products.Count);
}
```

Although this test covers the core functionality, there is only have one item in your collection — as such you are not filtering the list and might be confusing to readers of the test. To provide more clarity, you can add an additional test:

```
[Test]
public void Show_Only_Returns_Products_For_a_Single_Category_When_Two_Exist()
{
    products.Add(new Product
    {
        ID = 2,
        Category = new ProductCategory { Description = "Starter" },
        Name = "BBQ Chicken Wings",
        Description = "4x BBQ Chicken Wings",
        BasePrice = 4.00
    });

    string category = "Pizza";

    IProductRepository repository = MockRepository.GenerateStub<
IProductRepository>();
    repository.Stub(r => r.GetProductsByCategory(category))
                        .Return(products.Where(p => p.Category
.Description == category).ToList());

    ProductsMenuController controller = new ProductsMenuController(
repository);
```

```
                ProductsMenuModel model = controller.Show(category)
    .GetModel<ProductsMenuModel>();

                Assert.AreEqual(1, model.Products.Count);
        }
```

Although this test is longer, it adds value to the overall suite. A new product is added to your base test data. You then use LINQ to Objects to filter your expected return data based on the category description. This should make it very easy to understand what you expect to happen.

In terms of the implementation, all you need to do is create your ProductsMenuModel and attach the results from your Repository:

```
        public ActionResult Show(string category)
        {
            ProductsMenuModel model = new ProductsMenuModel();
            model.Products = Repository.GetProductsByCategory(category);
            return View(model);
        }
```

The new method, GetProductsByCategory, will only be used by your ProductRepository. Because you have the IProductRepository already in place, you can simply add the method to this interface without affecting your other repositories:

```
        public interface IProductRepository : IRepository<Product>
        {
            List<Product> GetProductsByCategory(string category);
        }
```

With your Repository tests and implementation in place, you need to implement your Show view.

Your view simply needs to output all the products reusing the ProductItem control you built earlier. The first approach is to simply iterate over the Products collection and render the partial control in your div tags:

```
    <% foreach (Product p in Model.Products) { %>
        <div class="normal-row"><%=Html.RenderPartial("ProductItem", p) %> </div>
    <% } %>
```

However, this starts to become difficult to read with the multiple opening and closing ASP.NET tags. Remember, you want to keep your code as clean as possible. By creating another extension method, called WithDiv, you can output a div with a particular Partial control rendered inside, in the same way as shown previously. The advantage of this is that you only have a single set of open and close tags. On the WithDiv method, the first parameter is the style to attach to the div, while the second parameter is an action that should be invoked to produce the content. In this example, the action is to render the partial method:

```
    <%
        foreach (Product p in Model.Products)
            Html.WithDiv("normal-row", () => Html.RenderPartial("ProductItem", p));
    %>
```

This method can also be unit tested to verify it works as you hope. In the first test, you want to verify that the WithDiv method correctly outputs the div with the style attached. You need to mock the HttpResponse as this is where you need to write content to, in order for the data to be returned to the user for rendering by their web browser. By using a mock you can verify that the correct calls were made with the correct data, and as such verify that the test passes:

```
[Test]
public void WithDiv_Writes_Div_Tags()
{
    HttpContextBase httpContext = MockRepository.GenerateStub<
HttpContextBase>();
    HttpResponseBase httpResponseBase = MockRepository.GenerateMock<
HttpResponseBase>();
    httpContext.Stub(c => c.Response).Return(httpResponseBase);

    httpResponseBase.Expect(r => r.Write("<div class=\"styleClass\">"));
    httpResponseBase.Expect(r => r.Write("</div>"));

    HtmlHelper helper = MockHelper.CreateHtmlHelper(httpContext);

    string t = string.Empty;
    helper.WithDiv("styleClass", () => t = string.Empty);

    httpResponseBase.VerifyAllExpectations();
}
```

The second test, verifies that the action was called correctly. An action is a delegate, which means they are easy to test. As the action, you simply set a variable to true that you can test against in order to know if the call was successful. When you use the method in your main system, you can be confident that the action will be called as expected:

```
[Test]
public void WithDiv_Executes_Action()
{
    HttpContextBase httpContext = MockRepository.GenerateStub<
HttpContextBase>();
    HttpResponseBase httpResponseBase = MockRepository.GenerateMock<
HttpResponseBase>();
    httpContext.Stub(c => c.Response).Return(httpResponseBase);

    HtmlHelper helper = MockHelper.CreateHtmlHelper(httpContext);

    bool called = false;
    helper.WithDiv("row", () => called = true);

    Assert.IsTrue(called);
}
```

You have created two tests because they are verifying two different things. The first test is verifying that the correct HTML is written to the correct output. The second test is verifying that the action is called correctly. By having them as two separate tests, you can verify that each logical section is working.

When it comes to the implementation, the tests have already defined your expectations, so you simply need to fill in the gaps:

```
public static void WithDiv(this HtmlHelper helper, string style,
Action action)
    {
        helper.Write(string.Format("<div class=\"{0}\">", style));
        action();
        helper.Write("</div>");
    }
public static void Write(this HtmlHelper helper, string text)
    {
        helper.ViewContext.HttpContext.Response.Write(text);
    }
```

With this in place your web page works as you want it to. However, you still have a problem with your URL. The link you created earlier results in the URL looking similar to /ProductsMenu/Show?category=Pizza. With MVC, you want a cleaner looking URL that is more similar to /ProductsMenu/Show/Pizza. This can be solved by modifying your Routing table.

In your RouteSetup object, you need to add a new entry above the default route. In the new entry, you define that for the controller ProductsMenu, when the action Show is called, the category parameter should be included as an additional slash and parameter instead of as an entry on the querystring:

```
routes.MapRoute(
        "ShowProductCategory",
        "{controller}/Show/{category}",
        new { controller = "ProductsMenu", action = "Show",
category = "" }
            );
```

When you have your products being listed, it would be nice to give them a header, the logical choice is to use the current category. The test for this simply verifies the CurrentCategory property is what you expected based on your test products list — in this case pizza:

```
[Test]
public void Show_Returns_The_Category_As_A_Property()
    {
        string category = "Pizza";
        IProductRepository repository = MockRepository.GenerateStub<
IProductRepository>();
        repository.Stub(r => r.GetProductsByCategory(category))
.Return(products);

        ProductsMenuController controller = new ProductsMenuController(
repository);
        ProductsMenuModel model = controller.Show(category)
.GetModel<ProductsMenuModel>();

        Assert.AreEqual(category, model.CurrentCategory);
    }
```

Within your Show method, you simply assign the parameter to the property:

```
model.CurrentCategory = category;
```

You can then use this property within your UI:

```
<h2><%= Model.CurrentCategory %></h2>
```

The reason you have a unit test for such a small piece of functionality is all about Test Driven Development. No matter how small, a test should still be written to cover the implementation and verify it works as expected.

Feature 3: Adding Items to the Shopping Cart

Now that you have your products displayed on the screen, the next stage is to add a product into the basket that the user can then proceed and purchase.

The aim is that you will allow users to add multiple products into a shopping cart. This cart is persisted across sessions using their username as an identifier. This means the next time they visit the site, the cart will still be available. When the user is happy with the products in the cart, they should be able to proceed and complete their purchase. Other features include the ability to update the shopping cart quantity and remove unwanted products.

To handle the basket\shoppingcart you need to assign the responsibility. In a similar way to your Products menu, you are going to need a ShoppingCartController to support your shopping cart implementation. The most complex part of the implementation is around adding an item to the basket. This is where you will start.

The idea is that you will have a link on your menu that will add the particular product to the basket. The link will be a button that will submit a form to a particular action on your ShoppingCartController. Within your ProductItem control, wrap your existing code into a BeginForm. As part of this, provide an action method that should be called when the form is submitted. In this case, you need to send the request to the AddToBasket method on the ShoppingCartController. So that the controller knows which product to add to the cart, you need to provide the Product ID as an argument. From a testability point of view you can replicate exactly how the form will submit requests to the controller, meaning your tests will accurately reflect the functionality.

The final argument is the ID of the style sheet to use. This style sheet will make the button look like a hyperlink instead of a button:

```
<% using(Html.BeginForm<ShoppingCartController>(p => p.AddToBasket(Model.ID))) { %>
        <%= Html.Encode(Model.Name) %><br />
        <%= Html.Encode(Model.Description) %><br />
        <%= Model.GetPrice() %>
        <%= Html.SubmitButton("Add to basket", "Add to basket",
new {id = "submit"}) %>
<% } %>
```

You can now start implementing the method by using TDD. The first task is to get the shopping cart for a user. You will do this by requesting the cart from your IShoppingCartRepository implementation as shown next:

```
public interface IShoppingCartRepository : IRepository<ShoppingCart>
{
    ShoppingCart GetCart(string username);
}
```

Again, the implementation of the concrete Repository will be discussed in Chapter 4, but for now, you can simply mock this. GetCart will return your cart and that's all the test needs to worry about.

The first test is to verify that the 'Add To Basket' method under test correctly calls into your IShoppingCartRepository. To write this you need to mock your Repository as done before. After this, you call the method with a productId as a parameter and verify that your expectations occurred:

```
int PRODUCT_ID = 1;
[Test]
public void If_Cart_Already_Exists_Then_AddToBasket_Should_Use_It()
{
    ShoppingCart shoppingCart = new ShoppingCart();
    IShoppingCartRepository shoppingCartRepository = MockRepository
.GenerateMock<IShoppingCartRepository>();
    shoppingCartRepository.Expect(r => r.GetCart()).Return(shoppingCart);

    ShoppingCartController controller = new ShoppingCartController(
shoppingCartRepository);
    controller.AddToBasket(PRODUCT_ID);
    shoppingCartRepository.VerifyAllExpectations();
}
```

Once you have your cart object, you need the product from the database. You can reuse your existing IProductRepository to gain this. In a similar fashion, verify that the Repository was correctly called:

```
[Test]
public void AddToBasket_Pulls_Product_From_Database_Based_On_ID()
{
    Product product = new Product { ID = PRODUCT_ID, Name = "ProductName",
Description = "ProductDesc" };

    IShoppingCartRepository stubShoppingCartRepository = MockRepository
.GenerateStub<IShoppingCartRepository>();

    IProductRepository mockProductRepository = MockRepository.GenerateMock<
IProductRepository>();

    productRepository.Expect(r => r.Get(PRODUCT_ID)).Return(product);

    ShoppingCartController controller = new ShoppingCartController(
stubShoppingCartRepository, mockProductRepository);
    controller.AddToBasket(PRODUCT_ID);
    mockProductRepository.VerifyAllExpectations();
}
```

To keep our tests clean and more focused, some of your set-up logic can be moved. By having the construction done in the setup, your tests are left to focus on getting your expectations\stubs and verifying that everything worked as expected:

```
ShoppingCart shoppingCart;
Product product;
IProductRepository stubProductRepository;
IShoppingCartRepository stubShoppingCartRepository;
[SetUp]
public void Setup()
{
    shoppingCart = new ShoppingCart();
    product = new Product { ID = PRODUCT_ID, Name = "ProductName",
Description = "ProductDesc" };

    stubShoppingCartRepository = MockRepository.GenerateStub<
IShoppingCartRepository>();
    stubProductRepository = MockRepository.GenerateStub<
IProductRepository>();
}
```

This allows us to refactor our initial test to look more like this, which I'm sure you would agree is more readable:

```
[Test]
public void AddToBasket_Pulls_Product_From_Database_Based_On_ID()
{
    IProductRepository mockProductRepository = MockRepository.GenerateStub<
IProductRepository>();
mockProductRepository.Expect(r => r.Get(PRODUCT_ID)).Return(product);

    ShoppingCartController controller = new ShoppingCartController(
stubShoppingCartRepository, mockProductRepository);
    controller.AddToBasket(PRODUCT_ID);
    mockProductRepository.VerifyAllExpectations();
}
```

The reason you created the Product Repository mock inside the test is that mocks are only used in a small number of tests, while stubs are used in the majority:

```
public ActionResult AddToBasket(int productID)
{
    Product product = ProductRepository.Get(productID);

    ShoppingCart cart = Repository.GetCart();
    return View();
}
```

Now that the AddToBasket has the cart and a product as shown next, we simply need to join the product and cart together.

Because the tests are no longer verifying the interactions, the stub implementations, already created in the Setup method, are set for how the objects should behave. This test verifies that the product is correctly added to the ShoppingCart object, which was created in the Setup method:

```
[Test]
public void Cart_Should_Contain_ShoppingCartItem_With_Product_Attached()
{
    stubProductRepository.Stub(r => r.Get(PRODUCT_ID)).Return(product);

    stubShoppingCartRepository.Stub(r => r.GetCart()).Return(shoppingCart);

    ShoppingCartController controller = new ShoppingCartController(
stubShoppingCartRepository, stubProductRepository);
    controller.AddToBasket(PRODUCT_ID);
    Assert.AreEqual(product, shoppingCart.Items[0].Product);
}
```

In order to implement this functionality, you need to add an additional method onto our ShoppingCart model. As such, you need a test that will define the functionality required in order to be able to add items into the basket:

```
[TestFixture]
public class ShoppingCartTests
{
    [Test]
    public void AddItems_Adds_Shopping_Cart_Item_To_Collection()
    {
        ShoppingCart cart = new ShoppingCart(username);
        cart.AddItem(new Product { ID = 1, BasePrice = 1 });
        Assert.AreEqual(1, cart.Items.Count);
    }
}
```

This test verifies that the AddItem method does in fact add an item into the Items collection. With this in place, you can use your AddItem method in the same way in our AddToBasket method.

The final stage is to save the cart back to the Repository, and hence, back to your database for future use. In this test, simply set the expectations on our mock to define that you expect a call made to the SaveOrUpdate() method:

```
[Test]
public void AddToBasket_Saves_Cart_Back_To_Repository()
{
    IShoppingCartRepository mockShoppingCartRepository = MockRepository
.GenerateMock<IShoppingCartRepository>();
        mockShoppingCartRepository.Expect(r => r.SaveOrUpdate(shoppingCart))
.Constraints(Is.TypeOf(typeof(ShoppingCart)).Return(shoppingCart);

    ShoppingCartController controller = new ShoppingCartController(
mockShoppingCartRepository, stubProductRepository);
        controller.AddToBasket(PRODUCT_ID);
        mockShoppingCartRepository.VerifyAllExpectations();
}
```

In the previous test, you add a constraint onto your expected call. These constraints simply define some additional rules about what to expect. In this case it is just a particular type; however, they can be complex rules such as defining particular data within a property on the object (for example, `Property.IsNotNull("Username")`). At this point, your implementation should look like this:

```
public ActionResult AddToBasket(int productID)
{
    Product product = ProductRepository.Get(productID);

    ShoppingCart cart = Repository.GetCart();
    cart.AddItem(product);

    Repository.SaveOrUpdate(cart);
    return View();
}
```

However, there is a problem. After you have added the item you will be redirected to a view called AddToBasket. Ideally, you want to be redirected to a particular page that will show the cart itself. Again, writing test, first you verify that the page goes to the correct location. By casting the result of the AddToBasket to a RedirectToRouteResult you can test to verify that the correct Action was called, in this case Show:

```
[Test]
public void After_Adding_Item_To_Basket_It_Redirects_To_Cart()
{
    ShoppingCartController controller = new ShoppingCartController(
shoppingCartRepository,productRepository);
    RedirectToRouteResult view = controller.AddToBasket(PRODUCT_ID) as
RedirectToRouteResult;

    Assert.AreEqual("Show", view.RouteValues["action"]);
}
```

Within your AddToBasket method, instead of returning View(), you return RedirectToAction("Show").

With your happy path complete, you need to implement edge-case scenarios. The first being what happens if the cart doesn't already exist. In the case where a cart doesn't exist, you want your Repository to return null. When this happens, you expect a new cart to be created and used as normal without any problems, and then saved back to the database for future use.

Your stub object represents this. First you define that you expect a call to be made to your Repository that will return null. Then you define that you expect a call to be made to the SaveOrUpdate method with an additional constraint saying that the object should be a ShoppingCart object. After you call AddToBasket from your test, you can verify that the expectations were met:

```
[Test]
public void If_Cart_Does_not_Exist_Then_Null_Should_Be_Returned_And_A_Cart_
Created()
{
    IShoppingCartRepository mockShoppingCartRepository = MockRepository
.GenerateMock<IShoppingCartRepository>();
```

```
        mockShoppingCartRepository.Expect(r => r.GetCart()).Return(null);

        mockShoppingCartRepository.Expect(r => r.SaveOrUpdate(shoppingCart))
                .Constraints(Is.TypeOf(typeof(ShoppingCart)))
                .Return(shoppingCart);

        ShoppingCartController controller = new ShoppingCartController(
mockShoppingCartRepository, stubProductRepository);
        controller.AddToBasket(PRODUCT_ID);

        mockShoppingCartRepository.VerifyAllExpectations();
    }
```

You now have your basket working, with items being saved into either a new or existing shopping cart.

The final requirement is that all the shopping carts should be associated with a username. To get the username, you need an additional service to obtain the current username from the ASP.NET membership provider. You need to create a service that will wrap this functionality in order to make it testable. This service will implement the ICredentialsService interface that has a single method that returns the username. By having your own CredentialsService you don't need to be dependent upon the built-in ASP.NET membership provider. It allows you to mock\stub the service, which isn't possible with the built-in provider. The implementation details for the service will be discussed in Chapter 4:

```
public interface ICredentialsService
{
    string GetUsername();
}
```

The test now ensures that the controller accesses the service; you mock object the ICredentialsService, setting it to return the username as a string. The test then verifies that this call was made:

```
        private string USERNAME = "TestUser";
        [Test]
        public void When_Creating_A_Cart_It_Should_Ask_Credentials_Provider_For_
Username()
        {
            ICredentialsService mockCredentialsService = MockRepository
.GenerateMock<ICredentialsService>();
            mockCredentialsService.Expect(r => r.GetUsername()).Return(USERNAME);

            ShoppingCartController controller = new ShoppingCartController(
stubShoppingCartRepository, stubProductRepository, mockCredentialsService);
            controller.AddToBasket(PRODUCT_ID);

            mockCredentialsService.VerifyAllExpectations();
        }
```

To provide the controller with access to the CredentialsService, you should use constructor injection. However, you will need to revisit the other tests that also use the controller, which means that the other tests also required a CredentialsService. These tests simply want a stub ICredentialsService object that will always return a particular username. To keep the code as clean as possible you should use a helper method to provide this functionality:

```
        public static ICredentialsService CreateCredentialsService(string username)
        {
```

```
        ICredentialsService credentialsService = MockRepository.GenerateStub<
    ICredentialsService>();
        credentialsService.Stub(r => r.GetUsername()).Return(USERNAME);
        return credentialsService;
    }
```

As part of this change, IShoppingCartRepository and the GetCart method was modified to accept the username to use in the query:

```
public interface IShoppingCartRepository : IRepository<ShoppingCart>
{
    ShoppingCart GetCart(string username);
}
```

As a result, the mock objects were changed to reflect this:

```
        mockShoppingCartRepository.Expect(r => r.GetCart(USERNAME))
    .Return(shoppingCart);
```

Going back and changing your tests is something that will occur during their lifetime. As long as you keep the changes small and targeted, the impact should be minimal. Constantly running the tests can help identify changes and failures faster, which should also result in the fixes being much quicker to make.

Finally you are constructing your own shopping cart object with some defaults that you should test to ensure they're correct to be set correctly. In your WroxPizza.Tests.Unit.Model.ShoppingCartTest you have your tests for the model itself. You simply want one test that will verify that the defaults are set correctly as shown next:

```
[Test]
public void Default_Object_Has_Date_NoItems_And_Username_Attached()
{
    ShoppingCart cart = new ShoppingCart(USERNAME);

    Assert.AreEqual(USERNAME, cart.Username);
    Assert.AreEqual(0, cart.Items.Count);
    Assert.AreEqual(DateTime.Now, cart.Created);
}
```

While the test looks straight forward it will never pass. The reason is because the Created date on the cart will never be the current time when the check is made. In fact, the tests don't know what time it might be. You want your tests to be repeatable and deterministic — having a date based on the system clock causes problems because the test becomes non-deterministic. You need a way to freeze time within your unit tests. The answer is to create a SystemTime class (http://ayende.com/Blog/archive/2008/07/07/Dealing-with-time-in-tests.aspx). The class will have a C# 3.0 function attached to return the current DateTime. On the SystemTime object, there will be a method called Now(). When this is called, it will return the result of DateTime.Now:

```
public static class SystemTime
{
    public static Func<DateTime> Now = () => DateTime.Now;
}
```

This doesn't sound like it will solve the problem, however the function can be redefined at runtime. In your test setup, you can redefine SystemTime.Now to return a predetermined date instead of the DateTime.Now. This means you can now handle dates in your unit tests as long as your code uses SystemTime:

```
DateTime testDate;
[SetUp]
public void Setup()
{
    testDate = new DateTime(2000, 1, 1);
    SystemTime.Now = () => testDate;
}
```

With this in place, the date the application uses will always be 1/1/2000 during your unit tests, while your live system will use the correct DateTime.Now value.

At this point you can add products to your basket, but you have no way to show them. If you remember, your add method will redirect to your Show action after it has completed; this action will result in a page being displayed to the user.

The first test you need to write for your show method is actually obtaining your shopping cart when you first visit the page. As with your Products menu, you have a ShoppingCartModel that will have the shopping cart as a property:

```
[Test]
public void Cart_Action_Gets_Cart_For_User()
{
    shoppingCartRepository.Stub(r => r.GetCart(USERNAME))
.Return(shoppingCart);

    ShoppingCartController controller = new ShoppingCartController(
shoppingCartRepository, productRepository,
MockHelper.CreateCredentialsService(USERNAME));

    ShoppingCartModel model = controller.Show().
GetModel<ShoppingCartModel>();
    Assert.IsNotNull(model);
}
```

Because you already have the core functionality in place testing, your implementation is very simple.

```
public ActionResult Show()
{
    ShoppingCartModel model = new ShoppingCartModel();
    model.Cart = CreateOrGetCart();

    return View(model);
}
```

You can reuse the CreateOrGetCart() method extracted from your AddToBasket implementation.

```
private ShoppingCart CreateOrGetCart()
{
```

```
        ShoppingCart cart = Repository.GetCart(CredentialsService
.GetUsername());

        if(cart == null)
            cart = new ShoppingCart(CredentialsService.GetUsername());
        return cart;
    }
```

After extracting the CreateOfGetCart method, you could return and add some additional unit tests focused on this particular method. However, the tests already provided good coverage on this block of code and as such additional tests were not required.

The next stage is to output the cart. If the cart has items then you want to displayed them; however. if the cart is empty then you want a message to be shown to the user informing them of this. Your initial solution is to determine which control to render within the view itself. The first attempt at the code looks like this:

```
    <%
        if (count == 0)
            Html.RenderPartial("CartEmpty");
        else
            Html.RenderPartial("DisplayCart", Model.Cart.Items);
    %>
```

Although that was fairly simple, there is a way to remove the `if` condition from your view and move it into testable code. The result is that an extension method is created again, which would determine if it should output an empty user control or output the cart. The result is a method which takes in the list together with two action items. One action is what to do when the list is empty; the other is if the list is populated:

```
    <% Html.RenderShoppingCart(Model.Cart.Items, () => Html
.RenderPartial("CartEmpty"), () => Html.RenderPartial("DisplayCart", Model.Cart));
    %>
```

The tests for your implementation follow the same approach as the tests for the WithDiv implementation. You want to verify that the correct action is being called at the correct point in time based on how many items are in the list:

```
    [Test]
    public void RenderShoppingCart_Renders_Empty_Cart_When_Empty()
    {
        HttpContextBase httpContext = MockRepository.GenerateStub<
HttpContextBase>();
        httpContext.Stub(c => c.Response).Return(MockRepository.GenerateStub<
HttpResponseBase>());

        bool called = false;

        HtmlHelper helper = MockHelper.CreateHtmlHelper(httpContext);
        helper.RenderShoppingCart(new List<ShoppingCartItem>(),
() => called = true, null);

        Assert.IsTrue(called);
```

```
        }

        [Test]
        public void RenderShoppingCart_Renders_HasData_Action_When_It_Contains_Data()
        {
                HttpContextBase httpContext = MockRepository.GenerateStub<
HttpContextBase>();
                httpContext.Stub(c => c.Response).Return(MockRepository
.GenerateStub<HttpResponseBase>());

                bool called = false;

                HtmlHelper helper = MockHelper.CreateHtmlHelper(httpContext);
                helper.RenderShoppingCart(new List<ShoppingCartItem> {
new ShoppingCartItem() }, null, () => called = true);

                Assert.IsTrue(called);
        }
```

The result is a very simple and straightforward implementation — one that is more readable than the alternative and is tested:

```
        public static void RenderShoppingCart(this HtmlHelper helper,
IList<ShoppingCartItem> items, Action empty, Action hasData)
        {
            if (items.Count == 0)
                empty();
            else
                hasData();
        }
```

As for the controls that are actually rendered, the CartEmpty control simply outputs text. The DisplayCart control outputs a table as shown next. The ShoppingCartLine control is rendered for each item in the cart and outputs a row for the table:

```
<table>
    <tr>
        <td><small><b>Product</b></small></td>
        <td><small><b>Quantity</b></small></td>
        <td><small><b>Price</b></small></td>
        <td></td>
    </tr>
    <%  foreach (ShoppingCartItem item in Model) { %>
        <% Html.RenderPartial("ShoppingCartLine", item); %>
    <%} %>
</table>
```

Within the ShoppingCartLine control you output the name and the price. You also attach the Quantity property to a textbox. Attaching the property in this way is important for when users want to update the quantity amount, as you will be able to take advantage of the framework itself:

```
<tr>
        <td><%=Model.Product.Name%></td>
```

```
            <td><%=Html.TextBox("Quantity", Model.Quantity)%></td>
            <td><%=Model.Product.GetPrice()%></td>
    </tr>
```

With your items now being displayed, the next task is to allow the user to update the quantity. To update the shopping cart item you need some additional logic. First, you need a second Show method that will accept the cartItemId as a parameter to allow you to identify which particular row in the cart you are modifying. The second parameter is the form post data. This will contain any updated values such as the quantity. You can then use this to update your model and your cart.

To simulate this, our tests can creates a FormCollection within the Setup method to provide the result you would expect for the particular form post request; in this case you can simulate the users of the quantity 2 in the form:

```
formWithQuantityOf2 = new FormCollection();
formWithQuantityOf2.Add("Quantity", "2");
```

This allows you to simulate how the method will behave when the form is submitted.

Next is the verification that this new method correctly retrieves and saves your cart. You pass in the ID of the item in the shopping cart together with our test form collection:

```
[Test]
public void Show_Can_Update_Quantity_Of_Item_In_Shopping_Basket()
{
    shoppingCart.AddItem(product);

    shoppingCartRepository.Expect(r => r.GetCart(username))
.Return(shoppingCart);
    shoppingCartRepository.Expect(r => r.SaveOrUpdate(shoppingCart))
.Return(shoppingCart);

    ShoppingCartController controller = new ShoppingCartController(
shoppingCartRepository, productRepository,
MockHelper.CreateCredentialsService(username));

    int cartItemId = 0;
    controller.Show(cartItemId, formWithQuantityOf2);

    shoppingCartRepository.VerifyAllExpectations();
}
```

You then have a second test to verify the quantity was updated correctly for the correct cart item:

```
[Test]
public void Updating_Quantity_Modifies_Item_In_Cart()
{
    shoppingCart.AddItem(product);

    productRepository.Expect(r => r.Get(PRODUCT_ID)).Return(product);
    shoppingCartRepository.Stub(r => r.GetCart(USERNAME)).
Return(shoppingCart);
```

```
            shoppingCartRepository.Stub(r => r.SaveOrUpdate(shoppingCart))
    .Return(shoppingCart);

            ShoppingCartController controller = new ShoppingCartController(
    shoppingCartRepository, productRepository,
    MockHelper.CreateCredentialsService(USERNAME));
            int cartItemId = 0;
            controller.Show(cartItemId, formWithQuantityOf2);

            Assert.AreEqual(2, shoppingCart.Items[0].Quantity);
        }
```

In terms of implementation, you obtain the shopping cart and then the particular shopping cart item based on the ID.

```
    public ActionResult Show(int cartItemId, FormCollection form)
    {
        ShoppingCart cart = CreateOrGetCart();
        ShoppingCartItem item = cart.Items.Single(i => i.ID == cartItemId);
        UpdateModel(item, form.ToValueProvider());

        Repository.SaveOrUpdate(cart);

        return RedirectToAction("Show");
    }
```

In the previous method you provided the ID as a parameter. You were able to do this when your ID was a hidden field on the form. As a result it was submitted as a parameter. The updated quantity value was submitted back to the server because you used a form around your input:

```
<% using (Html.BeginForm()) { %>
        <%= Html.Hidden("cartItemid", Model.ID) %>
        <td><%=Model.Product.Name%></td>
        <td><%=Html.TextBox("Quantity", Model.Quantity)%></td>
        <td><%=Model.Product.GetPrice()%></td>
        <td><%=Html.SubmitButton("Update", "Update", new { id = "submit" })%>
<% } %>
```

With the ability to update the quantity of your products, you need to change the behavior of your Add To Basket method. If the item already exists then you want to increment the quantity or otherwise add it as a new value. Your test asserts that the number of items in the cart is still one, while the item quantity is in fact 2:

```
        [Test]
        public void If_Item_Already_Exists_In_Basket_Then_Quantity_Is_Incremented_
    Instead()
        {
            shoppingCart.AddItem(product);

            stubProductRepository.Expect(r => r.Get(PRODUCT_ID)).Return(product);
            stubShoppingCartRepository.Stub(r => r.GetCart(USERNAME))
    .Return(shoppingCart);
```

```
        stubShoppingCartRepository.Stub(r => r.SaveOrUpdate(shoppingCart))
.Return(shoppingCart);

        ShoppingCartController controller = new
ShoppingCartController(stubShoppingCartRepository,stubProductRepository,
MockHelper.CreateCredentialsService(USERNAME));
        controller.AddToBasket(PRODUCT_ID);

        Assert.AreEqual(1, shoppingCart.Items.Count);
        Assert.AreEqual(2, shoppingCart.Items[0].Quantity);
    }
```

For the test to pass you modify your logic slightly to see if the cart already contains the item:

```
        if (cart.Contains(product))
            cart.IncrementQuantity(product);
        else
            cart.AddItem(product);
```

The final method is adding the ability to remove items from the cart. Your test follows the same approach as the update test. You first add a product into your cart and then stub your Repository to return this item. After you have called the remove action on your controller, you assert that the cart no longer contains any items:

```
        [Test]
        public void Remove_Should_Remove_Item_From_Shopping_Cart()
        {
            shoppingCart.AddItem(product);

            shoppingCartRepository.Stub(r => r.GetCart(username))
.Return(shoppingCart);
            shoppingCartRepository.Stub(r => r.SaveOrUpdate(shoppingCart))
.Return(shoppingCart);

            ShoppingCartController controller = new ShoppingCartController(
shoppingCartRepository, productRepository, MockHelper.CreateCredentialsService(
username));
            controller.Remove(PRODUCT_ID);

            Assert.AreEqual(0, shoppingCart.Items.Count);
        }
```

Your implementation simply obtains the cart, removes the item from the collection, and saves the updated item back to your Repository. Your Repository will work the rest out for you:

```
        public ActionResult Remove(int productId)
        {
            ShoppingCart cart = CreateOrGetCart();
            cart.RemoveItem(PRODUCT_ID);
            Repository.SaveOrUpdate(cart);
            return RedirectToAction("Show");
        }
```

To execute the action you need a link on your cart page. However, you are already using the form, which means you can't use another Submit button. Instead, you are going to use a hyperlink with a JQuery script attached to the onclick event that will call your action method. In order to keep the UI clean, another helper method should be created to generate your link:

```
<%=Html.DeleteShoppingCartItemLink(Model)%> </td>
```

The actual implementation of the link is as follows:

```
public static string DeleteShoppingCartItemLink(this HtmlHelper html,
ShoppingCartItem item)
    {
        string js = @"$.post(this.href, function(){
                                    window.location.reload();
                        });
                    return false; ";

        return html.ActionLink<ShoppingCartController>(s => s.Remove(item.
Product.ID), "Remove", new { onclick = js, id = "submit" });
    }
```

Your users can now happily add, update, and remove items from the shopping cart. All your methods have been tested and everything appears to work as expected. Your shopping cart screen is shown in Figure 3-10.

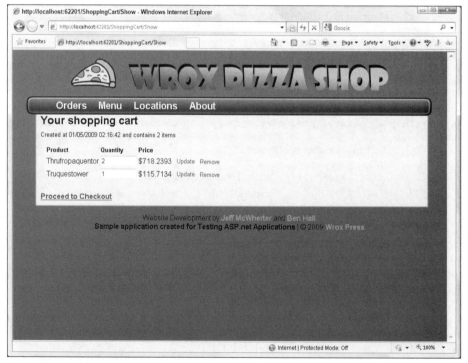

Figure 3-10: Shopping cart

Feature 4: Displaying Addresses

The next stage is to allow the users to select a delivery address. The user will be able to enter a new delivery address if they wish; however, if they have used the site before then you want to provide them with their recently used address to save them from having to enter the address again — in terms of functionality the page is similar to the other three features, yet the implementations are quite different.

To enable this functionality, you need to be able to save address objects into the database. For this to work effectively, you should create another controller, which has the reasonability to handle any address-related functionality. This is to separate the concerns of your system, keeping your responsibilities correct, which improves the readability of your code, but also allowing for the tests to be more focused and readable as a result.

To support the ability for the system to handle addresses, there needs to be an AddressController. This should be capable of ensuring that users can select addresses to use for delivery. After a user has selected an address, it will need to be saved into the database for future use. The following test will verify that the Select method can accept an address object, and that it will correctly call into the Repository, which will handle the saving of the object:

```
[SetUp]
public void Setup()
{
    address = new Address
            {
                StreetAddress1 = "Test1",
                StreetAddress2 = "Test2",
                City = "City",
                State = "State",
                PostCode = 123
            };
}

[Test]
public void Address_Can_Save_Address_To_Database()
{
    IAddressRepository repository = MockRepository.GenerateMock<
IAddressRepository>();
    repository.Expect(r => r.SaveOrUpdate(address)).Return(address);

    AddressController controller = new AddressController(
repository, MockHelper.CreateCredentialsService(USERNAME));
    controller.Select(address);

    repository.VerifyAllExpectations();
}
```

The following test then verifies that after a user has selected an address they are redirected to the summary page:

```
[Test]
public void After_Adding_Address_Should_Redirect_To_Summary()
{
```

```
            IAddressRepository repository = MockRepository.GenerateStub<
IAddressRepository>();
            repository.Expect(r => r.SaveOrUpdate(address)).Return(address);

            AddressController controller = new AddressController(
repository, MockHelper.CreateCredentialsService(USERNAME));
            RedirectToRouteResult result = controller.Select(address) as
RedirectToRouteResult;

            Assert.AreEqual("Summary", result.RouteValues["action"]);
            Assert.AreEqual("Checkout", result.RouteValues["controller"]);
        }
```

Based on your database schema you also need to attach the current UserID to the address before it can be saved. By extending your Credentials service you can return the current UserID from the user who is logged in. This is provided by the ASP.NET membership provider; we will go into more detail in Chapter 4. In your test, you can first set your UserID on the object to be empty — this is to ensure you are testing against a known value. In your assertion, simply verify that the value of the object is as you expect. Lever stub objects make testing your system easier:

```
        [Test]
        public void When_Saving_Address_It_Gets_UserID_To_Attach_To_Address()
        {
            Guid userId = Guid.NewGuid();
            address.UserId = Guid.Empty;

            IAddressRepository repository = MockRepository.GenerateStub<
IAddressRepository>();
            repository.Stub(r => r.SaveOrUpdate(address)).Return(address);

            ICredentialsService credentialsService = MockRepository.GenerateStub<
ICredentialsService>();
            credentialsService.Stub(i => i.GetUsername()).Return(USERNAME);
            credentialsService.Stub(i => i.GetUserID()).Return(userId);

            AddressController controller = new AddressController(
repository, MockRepository.GenerateStub<ICacheService>(), credentialsService);
            controller.Select(address);
            Assert.AreEqual(userId, address.UserId);
        }
```

The final stage is to allow users to actually enter their address and then construct your Address object. In the Address/Select view, you will have a header and then render your partial control:

```
    <h3>New Address</h3>
    <% Html.RenderPartial("NewAddress"); %>
```

The NewAddress control renders a fieldset collection. Each textbox has the same name as the property on your address object:

```
    <fieldset class="address-form">
        <legend>Enter your Address</legend>
        <ol>
```

```
            <li>
                <label>Street Address 1</label>
                <%=Html.TextBox("StreetAddress1")%>
            </li>
            <li>
                <label>Street Address 2</label>
                <%=Html.TextBox("StreetAddress2")%>
            </li>
            <li>
                <label>City</label>
                <%=Html.TextBox("City")%>
            </li>
            <li>
                <label>State</label>
                <%=Html.TextBox("State")%>
            </li>
            <li>
                <label>Post Code</label>
                <%=Html.TextBox("PostCode")%>
            </li>
        </ol>
    </fieldset>
```

When the form is submitted, it goes to the Select method you tested previously. Because you use the fieldset with the correctly named input fields, your Address object is automatically constructed and populated for you. The result is that the implementation of the action method can be as follows:

```
public ActionResult Select(Address address)
{
    address.UserId = Credentials.GetUserID();
    Repository.SaveOrUpdate(address);

    return RedirectToAction("Summary", "Checkout");
}
```

With the ability to add new addresses into the database for a particular user, the next feature you need to implement is the ability to display existing addresses. This allows users to select a previously entered address instead of having to enter the same address each time.

For this to work effectively, a user should be able to select an address when he visits a page, and it should also have a list of his existing addresses. To have this information you need to return it as part of your view model page.

```
[Test]
public void Select_returns_addresses_for_customer_attached_to_model()
{
    Guid userId = Guid.NewGuid();

    IAddressRepository repository = MockRepository.GenerateStub<
IAddressRepository>();
        repository.Stub(r => r.GetAllAddressForCustomer(userId)).Return(
new List<Address> {address});

    ICredentialsService credentialsService = MockRepository.GenerateStub<
ICredentialsService>();
```

```
        credentialsService.Stub(c => c.GetUserID()).Return(userId);

        AddressController controller = new AddressController(repository,
MockRepository.GenerateStub<ICacheService>(), credentialsService);
        AddressSelectorModel addressModel = controller.Select().GetModel<
AddressSelectorModel>();

        Assert.IsTrue(addressModel.Addresses.Contains(address));
    }
```

After you have the addresses on your model, you can output the information on the page. For each address returned, create a new radio button that is assigned the address ID as the value with the address text next to it. With this wrap it in a form, when the form is submitted the SelectExisting action will be called on your Address controller.

```
    <% using (Html.BeginForm("SelectExisting", "Address")) { %>
        <% foreach (Address a in Model.Addresses) {%>
            <%=Html.RadioButton("addressId", a.ID)%>
            <%= Html.Encode(a.GetAddressText()) %> <br />
        <% } %>

        <%=Html.SubmitButton("Proceed", "Use this address", new { id = "submit"})%>
    <% } %>
```

If the user has previously entered an address, then this will be selectable on the UI, as shown in Figure 3-11.

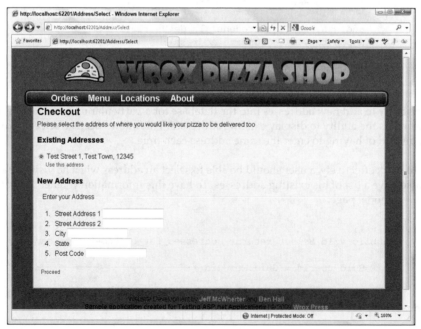

Figure 3-11: Previous address is selectable

With the form sending the request, the next stage is to implement the SelectExisting method. The test for this method is shown next; you need to mock the IAddressRepository and state that you expect a call to the FindAddressByUserIdAndAddressId method. This is what will be called in order for the method to identify the Address object based on the ID provided by the form:

```
[Test]
public void SelectExisting_Address_Pulls_It_From_Repository()
{
        Guid userId = Guid.NewGuid();
        IAddressRepository addressRepository = MockRepository.GenerateMock<
IAddressRepository>();
        addressRepository.Expect(r => r.FindAddressByUserIdAndAddressId(
userId, 1)).Return(address);

        ICredentialsService credentialsService = MockRepository.GenerateStub<
ICredentialsService>();
        credentialsService.Stub(c => c.GetUserID()).Return(userId);

        AddressController controller = new AddressController(
addressRepository, MockRepository.GenerateStub<ICacheService>(),
credentialsService);

        int addressId = 1;
        controller.SelectExisting(addressId);

        addressRepository.VerifyAllExpectations();
}
```

Your implementation then calls your method:

```
[AcceptVerbs(HttpVerbs.Post)]
public ActionResult SelectExisting(int addressId)
{
        Address address = Repository.FindAddressByUserIdAndAddressId(
Credentials.GetUserID(), addressId);

        return RedirectToAction("Summary", "Checkout");
}
```

To allow your checkout controller to access this information you need a way to store the object. There are multiple ways to handle this; in this example, you're going to use System.Web.Caching.Cache that is a builtin part of the framework. The cache object is accessible via HttpContext.Current, which is a singleton for your current http request. By adding an object to the cache the object will be available across multiple requests. This means you can temporarily store your address to access later in the process. The implementation of the cache is very similar to the implementation of the credentials service (which will be discussed in Chapter 4), as they both reply on the core ASP.NET Framework and external entities. For now, you will take advantage of being able to stub the interface shown next:

```
public interface ICacheService
{
    void Add(string cacheID, object cache);
    object Get(string cacheID);
}
```

To verify objects are being added to the cache correctly you can use a mock object. The two tests for new and existing addresses are as follows:

```
[Test]
public void New_Address_Is_Added_To_The_Cache_For_The_User()
{
    IAddressRepository repository = MockRepository.GenerateStub<
IAddressRepository>();
    repository.Stub(r => r.SaveOrUpdate(address)).Return(address);

    ICacheService cache = MockRepository.GenerateMock<ICacheService>();
    cache.Expect(r => r.Add(USERNAME + "ShippingAddress", address));

    AddressController controller = new AddressController(repository, cache,
MockHelper.CreateCredentialsService(USERNAME));
    controller.Select(address);

    cache.VerifyAllExpectations();
}

[Test]
public void SelectExisting_Adds_Address_To_Cache()
{
    IAddressRepository repository = MockRepository.GenerateStub<
IAddressRepository>();
    repository.Stub(r => r.FindAddressByUserIdAndAddressId(Guid.Empty, 0))
.IgnoreArguments().Return(address);

    ICacheService cache = MockRepository.GenerateMock<ICacheService>();
    cache.Expect(r => r.Add(USERNAME + "ShippingAddress", address));

    AddressController controller = new AddressController(repository, cache,
MockHelper.CreateCredentialsService(USERNAME));
    int addressId = 1;
    controller.SelectExisting(addressId);

    cache.VerifyAllExpectations();
}
```

With these tests passing, you can be confident that the object will be stored correctly in your cache for later use. The implementing code required is next:

```
Cache.Add(Credentials.GetUsername() + shippingAddresskey, address);
```

With your cache in place, the final task is to display a summary screen together with a confirmation screen to confirm that the order has been successful.

Feature 5: Displaying Confirmation

By now you should see a very common theme with unit testing\TDD. Outline your expectations for a targeted feature or problem then write the implementing code. By having your controller testable and your dependencies injectable, you have control over what you expect to happen. The final feature is to show the confirmation screen. This was implemented following a similar pattern to previous features.

After the user has entered their address they will see the confirmation page, as shown in Figure 3-12.

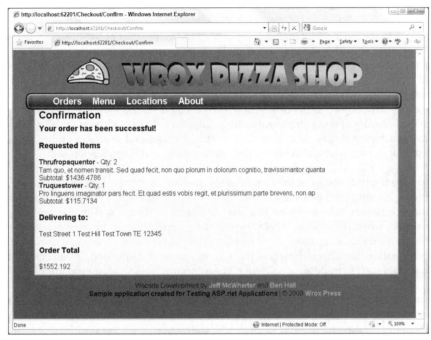

Figure 3-12: Confirmation screen

To see the final implementation please refer to the sample project.

Applying Unit Tests to Legacy ASP.NET WebForms Code

In this chapter we have covered how to write tests for both ASP.NET WebForms and ASP.NET MVC as you are designing and developing the system. However, if you already have an ASP.NET WebForms application you might not have unit tests already in place. Working with legacy code is a very common problem and could be an entire book, in fact it is as Michael Feathers wrote *Working Effectively with Legacy Code* and is a highly recommended read. But before you head off and read that book, we wanted to provide you with some initial considerations about how you can add unit tests to an existing ASP.NET application that hasn't been developed with testability in mind.

When you start writing unit tests for legacy code you will face some initial issues. You find yourself in a catch-22 position where you want to add tests to ensure the code works correctly; however, you will generally need to change (or refactor) the code in order to make this happen — or at least you will if you want useful, non-fragile tests. In order to mitigate the risk of changing the code and not breaking anything there are a few techniques to try. Firstly, there are many refactoring tools available to support this type of activity for ASP.NET based applications. Two of the popular tools are JetBrains ReSharper (`http://www.jetbrains.com/resharper/index.html`) and DevExpress Refactor! (`www.devexpress.com/Products/Visual_Studio_Add-in/Refactoring/`). These tools can take blocks of code and extract them into different classes and methods, adding parameters as required. By using a tool you can eliminate the chance of making a simple mistake and perform the change in a much easier fashion. However, even when using a tool you still have the possibility of breaking some functionality while attempting to move your code into a testable state.

One approach to take is to write higher level tests covering the part of the functionality that you plan to refactor in order to add unit tests. You want the tests to cover the existing functionality so that when you refactor the code you can re-run the tests to ensure that the functionality is still in place. Ideally, you want the tests to be as close and targeted as possible, and because parts of the system haven't been refactored yet, the tests will be integration tests (discussed in Chapter 4). Sometimes this isn't possible due to a too tightly coupled dependency, in which case you should look at even higher level tests such as UI testing (Chapter 5) and acceptance testing (Chapter 6) to provide you with an initial safety net during the refactoring stages. After you have written the tests and made the code change, you still have the tests in place to support and continue the development of the application.

Once you have the tests covering the functionality you can start taking steps to improve the code. You should then write unit tests in a similar way to how you would with TDD in order to define how you want your architecture to be and how you want to interact with the system. This will give you something to aim for when refactoring, while also allowing you to remain focused and know if you are finished with the refactoring stage. Once this new unit test is passing, you can re-run your higher-level tests to ensure the other affected parts of the system still work as desired. If you continue this process, then you should start to build up a collection of acceptance tests around your application.

However, you need to ask yourself a question — why are you adding the test cases? Retrofitting test cases is a costly process, especially when you need to refactor the code to support it. As such, you need to be clear about the advantages you want to add to the code by taking the effort to write the your tests.

If you want to ensure you don't cause any regressions, then you are better looking at techniques such as acceptance testing (discussed in Chapter 6) that allow you to add automated tests without having to refactor large parts of the application. If your aim is to support adding new functionality and improve maintenance of the system, then it is worth making the effort to write the tests and improve areas of your code as you're working on. However, if it's just to say you have unit tests or that you have 70 percent test coverage, then you should ask if it is worth the effort to retrofit these tests. Instead, it might make more sense to put your time and effort into refactoring the code as we have described only when you actually need to change the code instead of spending three months attempting to add the tests. It will mean you don't have as much coverage straight away, but it will allow you to target your time and efforts more effectively.

Summary

This chapter covered how to start unit testing and writing code using Test Driven Development. By expressing your expectations ahead of time you can ensure that your code meets them after you have implemented the features. After you change the code and add new features, you can use the tests to verify that the application is still working as you expect. The most important item to remember is how to keep everything separated, isolated, and think about how you are going to test the system and write the test before you write any code to ensure that the first two items are achieved.

By stubbing and mocking your dependencies, you can be confident that your controllers are working as expected. Chapter 4 will cover how you implement the layer underneath. Chapter 5 will cover the UI layer.

4

Integration Testing

Chapter 3 covered unit testing and Test Driven Development, but there are times when you need to cross application boundaries and go beyond testing your application as a single, isolated unit. This is where integration testing comes in. *Integration testing* is very similar to unit testing, with a few major differences. The main difference is that integration tests are much more likely to access external systems such as databases or web services. An integration test would combine the two components and verify that they work together.

Integration Tests versus Unit Tests

As integration tests cross boundaries they are more fragile than unit tests. This is one of the reasons why you should always store your integration tests in a separate assembly from your unit tests. The aim for your unit tests is to run consistently and to always be green. If your unit tests are not green then you have broken something. Integration tests are different. They might fail for other reasons outside of your control. For example, if the database is not in the expected state or even accessible, then the test will fail. This is why they are fragile and why you want to separate the two types — so that you can keep the warm feeling of seeing the green bar for as long as possible. By dividing, you have more chance of always seeing a totally green bar. This is important, and it comes back to the broken window syndrome mentioned in Chapter 2. If you always see some tests are broken, then you'll become used to it and let things slide. If you have your unit and integration tests together, you'll be used to seeing red appear every now and again. As a result, you won't notice when unit tests have failed. As discussed in the previous chapter, the name of your project would be ProjectName.Tests.Integration.

The other reason is for speed, because integration tests are generally slower than unit tests. You'll generally be running your unit tests more often because they contain all your logic, so you'll want these tests to run much faster. To give you an indication of this, a more complete version of the application has 93 unit tests. To execute them, it took 2.49 seconds:

```
93 passed, 0 failed, 0 skipped, took 2.49 seconds (NUnit 2.5).
```

In terms of integration tests, executing 26 tests took 27.46 seconds:

```
26 passed, 0 failed, 1 skipped, took 27.46 seconds (NUnit 2.5).
```

As you can see, the time difference soon adds up when you start crossing boundaries and external systems.

Now you might be thinking that integration tests are pointless if they are this slow and fragile. But it isn't as bad as it sounds. Remember, this is only compared to unit tests; if you architect your tests in the correct fashion — as will be explained later in this chapter — then you will be able to speed up your tests and take advantage of them failing less often.

Finally, after you have the tests in place you'll need to execute them. Ideally, you should be running the tests as often as possible. However, if this is not possible then you should at least run the tests after making a change — which is covered by the tests themselves — to verify that you haven't broken anything. When it comes to the build, your integration tests should be executed as a separate build after your main build has completed successfully. This means that you build and run your unit tests as normal; if this is successful, you start a second build which runs your integration tests. As before, you'll want to separate tests which might fail for different reasons. You don't want to fail the main build because your database server was restarted.

Although this defines integration tests, what they actually cover varies from application to application. In terms of your example application WroxPizza, the integration tests will cover three main sections:

❑   NHibernate mapping between domain objects and tables

❑   Repositories implementation

❑   ASP.NET security and caching

Alongside this, it would also be common to see integration tests focusing on the following:

❑   Email communication

❑   Web services

These all share the common traits of being potentially fragile compared to your nicely isolated unit tests. However, the tests around these sections of the application are important as you still need to verify that they work as expected. During the following sections, you will take the same features as discussed in Chapter 3 but explain them with regard to the integration tests and how you can verify the additional functionality required by the application.

Feature 1: Displaying Products from Database

In your first feature, you created a domain mapping for your Product object. This enabled NHibernate, likewise with other ORM frameworks, to understand how to communicate between your object and the underlying table. With Fluent NHibernate, you can verify that these mappings are correct. You'll use a PersistenceSpecification object that can verify that your object, mapping, and schema are configured correctly. The following example demonstrates how to create a test which will verify the mapping for your Product entity model:

```
[TestFixture]
public class ProductMapTests : NHibernateFixtureBase
```

```
        {
            [Test]
            public void Product_Mappings_Are_Set_Correctly()
            {
                new PersistenceSpecification<Product>(Session)
                    .CheckProperty(x => x.Name, "Cheese Pizza")
                    .CheckProperty(x => x.Description, "A Cheese Pizza")
                    .CheckProperty(x => x.PizzaTopping, true)
                    .CheckReference(x => x.Category, new ProductCategory {ID = 1,
Description = "Pizza"})
                    .CheckProperty(x => x.BasePrice, 13.23)
                    .VerifyTheMappings();
            }
        }
```

This is another useful verification to ensure that your mapping behaves as you might expect. This becomes more useful when you have relationships to other domain objects. In the previous example you have a Category reference which should accept a Category object that already exists in the database. This test will verify that the relationship between the two objects has been set up correctly, which we found to be very useful during development.

For these mappings to verify, they need a Session object. A Session is an active connection to a database which NHibernate uses. To provide this, you should create a NHibernateFixtureBase. This base fixture will create your Session which can be used by all your mapping tests. The most important part of the fixture is the Setup method. Within the Setup method, you create your session to the database as defined in our App.Config config. You can then take advantage of your NHibernate mapping to build the schema. NHibernate has enough information about your database to build a complete schema. This allows you to rebuild your schema for every test — this means you're confident about the expect state of your database. You don't have to worry that it will be attached to an older version of your database. Below is the NHibernateFixtureBase which the tests inherit from:

```
public class NHibernateFixtureBase
{
    protected SessionSource SessionSource { get; set; }
    protected ISession Session { get; private set; }

    [SetUp]
    public void Setup()
    {
        SessionSource = new SessionSource(new NHibernateModel());
        Session = SessionSource.CreateSession();
        SessionSource.BuildSchema(Session);
        CreateInitialData(Session);
        Session.Flush();
        Session.Clear();
    }
}
```

The other object you'll be working with is the NHibernateModel, which is part of your main assembly as it is used in DefaultNHibernateConfig created earlier. This model simply defines how to find the assembly containing your fluent NHibernate mapping objects.

```
public class NHibernateModel : PersistenceModel
{
```

```
public NHibernateModel()
{
        addMappingsFromAssembly(typeof(ProductMap).Assembly);
}
}
```

The final part of the puzzle is the app.config configuration for your database connection. This is automatically picked up by NHibernate and looks similar to the following example but looks different than the configuration used in Chapter 3 as you are no longer connected to a SQL Server instance. Instead, to improve the performance and reliability of your tests, you can use SQLite. SQLite is a database implementation; however, it has the advantage of being able to store the database in memory. This means that the database is extremely quick as well as being easy to create and destroy:

```
<hibernate-configuration xmlns="urn:nhibernate-configuration-2.2">
    <session-factory>
        <property name="connection.provider">
            NHibernate.Connection.DriverConnectionProvider
        </property>
        <property name="dialect">
            NHibernate.Dialect.SQLiteDialect
        </property>
        <property name="connection.driver_class">
            NHibernate.Driver.SQLite20Driver
        </property>
        <property name="connection.connection_string">
            Data Source=:memory:;Version=3;New=True;
        </property>
        <property name="connection.release_mode">
            on_close
        </property>
        <property name="show_sql">
            true
        </property>
    </session-factory>
</hibernate-configuration>
```

By taking advantage of NHibernate's provider model, you can point your connection to either SQL Server or SQLite without affecting the previous layers. This is amazing for testing purposes as you can use the correct database type at the correct point in time.

This means that you can test your mappings against a SQLite database in a very quick fashion without having to worry about setting up servers, instances, databases, and so on — NHibernate can do all this for you.

The foundation you have laid down can be reused and taken advantage of when you test your Repositories. The Repositories will also take advantage of using the in-memory SQLite instance for the same reasons.

In the next step you will implement the ProductRepository. As discussed in Chapter 3, this has the responsibility of returning different products from the database to the controller. The most important logic happens within the setup stage.

The Setup method constructs the ProductRepository object, calling a helper method to do similar setups to the previous Setup method. After you have the Repository, you can construct two test objects, which you will use as known data. Having known data in the database is a must as you need to use this to verify the results. If your tests do not define the database content, then your tests will become fragile. They generally become fragile because of outside influences — for example, other tests, or developers, changing the data:

```
[SetUp]
public void Setup()
{
    repository = new ProductRepository(Helper.GetTestDatabase());

    Product p = new Product { Name = "FirstTestProduct",
                              Description = "FirstTestDesc",
                              BasePrice = 123 };

    Product p2 = new Product { Name = "SecondTestProduct",
                               Description = "SecondTestDesc",
                               BasePrice = 123 };

    repository.SaveOrUpdate(p);
    repository.SaveOrUpdate(p2);
}
```

However, you need a way to insert data into your Repository. You need a way to insert your two products into the Repository so that you can retrieve them. The most appropriate solution would be to use a different mechanism to insert the data such as using ADO.NET directly. The reason for using a different mechanism is that you remove the dependency on the Repository implementation, plus you can be more confident that it works as expected as you set up your known state via a different route. However, setting up a known state is complex and made even more difficult with SQLite in-memory databases. Due to this, the example uses the Repository to insert your known data. As discussed in the next section, this logic is shared across multiple Repositories — this reduces your risk, and if it breaks, then you can be confident you will be alerted quickly.

Yet, as you are using the Repository in your test code, you still need to test the implementation. You now have a tight coupling. You need to insert data to verify "Get" works; however, you need to retrieve data to verify insert works. Given this situation, you need to somehow break the decoupling. In this situation, I like to find a way to verify that one works without being dependent on the other method. Our ProductRepostiory will inherit a base class called NHibernateRepository. This will be a generic class to allow you to share the common functionality across mulitple different implementations.

When we originally started to code the NHibernateRepository, we were testing the object via the ProductRepository as if the two were a single unit. This was wrong. The two are separate; the fact that they share functionality doesn't matter. The base class needs to be tested and verified in its own right. With this in mind, we created a NHibernateRepositoryTests class. This class follows the same pattern of the ProductRepository where you have your Setup method to define your Repository and a sample. You still need to provide a concrete type to test against, however this is irrelevant to the actual tests:

```
[SetUp]
public void Setup()
{
    repository = new NHibernateRepository<Product>(Helper.GetTestDatabase());
    p = new Product {ID = 0, Name = "TestName", Description = "TestDesc"};
}
```

Your NHibernate Repository can now be tested. As mentioned, you need a way to insert the SaveOrUpdate method without having to "Get" the item, as this hasn't been implemented yet.

When NHibernate inserts an item into the database, if it has an auto increment ID, as the Product object does, then NHibernate will increase the value of the ID. If the insert worked as you expected, then the ID would not be 0 as you initialized the variable to. This is how you test to verify that the insert worked without having to retrieve the item:

```
[Test]
public void SaveOrUpdate_Inserts_New_Product_Into_Database()
{
    Product update = repository.SaveOrUpdate(p);
    Assert.AreNotEqual(0, update.ID);
}
```

When you are confident that the SaveOrUpdate() method works as expected, you can implement your GetAll method and use the previous SaveOrUpdate method to help verify it worked as expected. The test method in your NHibernateRepositoryTests will first insert your temporary Product, and then call GetAll and verify that the count is 1:

```
[Test]
public void GetAll_Returns_All_Known_Items_In_Repository()
{
    repository.SaveOrUpdate(p);
    List<Product> products = repository.GetAll();

    Assert.AreEqual(1, products.Count);
}
```

The implementation to ensure these tests pass looks like this:

```
public List<T> GetAll()
{
    ICriteria criteria = Session.CreateCriteria(typeof(T));
    return criteria.List<T>() as List<T>;
}

public T SaveOrUpdate(T entity)
{
    using(Session.BeginTransaction())
    {
        Session.SaveOrUpdate(entity);
        Session.Transaction.Commit();
        return entity;
    }
}
```

With these two methods in place, you have your core functionality for your first feature implemented and tested. Because your ProductRepository inherits from NHibnerateRepository, your Repository has inherited the GetAll and SaveOrUpdate functionality. Your class definition is similar to the following:

```
class ProductRepository : NHibernateRepository<Product>, IProductRepository
```

In both your Setup methods, you take advantage of a GetTestDatabase() method. This constructs the DefaultNHibernateConfig object that is responsible for configuring NHibernate, adding mapping files, and creating a session factory. To create your schema for testing, the object has been extended to have a custom method called GenerateSchemaCreationScript:

```
public static IDbConfigure GetTestDatabase()
{
    DefaultNHibernateConfig db = new DefaultNHibernateConfig();
    string[] script = db.GenerateSchemaCreationScript();
    executeScripts(script, db.GetCurrentSession().Connection);

    return db;
}
```

This GenerateSchemaCreationScript is what will produce your table and create scripts, which you can execute against your database to produce your schema:

```
public string[] GenerateSchemaCreationScript()
{
    return cfg.GenerateSchemaCreationScript(GetSessionFactory().Dialect);
}
```

After your GetTestDatabase method has been executed, you have a new database with an up-to-date schema together with a SessionFactory waiting for your tests to start executing.

NHibernate provides you with a number of nice features which you can take advantage of during testing. However, if you are using another method of data access then you might not be able to take advantage of this. In this case, what should you do?

First, it depends on how you develop your data access. No matter which framework you use to develop your layer, there are some concepts which you must follow:

❑ **Ensure you are testing against the latest database schema.** If you are not using NHibernate, then you will manually create the schema. The best advice is to keep the creation script in a file or set of files. For every test, or at least every Test fixture, you should create the database from these creation scripts. You can then use these same creation scripts to deploy to your production database. There are tools available to help manage this stage. Microsoft offers Visual Studio for Database Professionals (Data Dude), while Red Gate Software has SQL Compare. Both products provide support for managing your database schema.

❑ **Ensure the tests are responsible for generating test data.** Similar to your database schema, it's important to test against a known data set. Again, Data Dude can help while Red Gate has a tool for SQL Data Generator for producing large amounts of test data. The other approach is to insert the data within the Setup block in a similar fashion to those shown previously. The final approach is to use Test Data Builders, as discussed in Chapter 5.

How you achieve this depends on your implementation, but as long as you keep this in mind you should be able to successfully test against the database.

In summary, in order to test this feature that interacts with the database we had to create a number of different helper methods and base classes to support creating the database and forming a connect. By taking advantage of NHibernate we could use the framework to create our database based on our mapping files created in Chapter 3 and use SQLite to store the database in memory.

Feature 2: Adding Categories

After you have created your NHibernateRepository you can start extending your ProductRepository to meet more of your requirements.

The second feature implemented was the ability to return categories for the products. As you are now implementing features on the ProductRepository, your tests should live within the ProductRepositoryTests class.

The first test is to ensure that the category is returned for each product in your Repository — you've already inserted your two products in the Setup method. After you return the products from the database, loop around and verify that they have a Category object and a valid description:

```
[Test]
public void When_Product_Returned_The_Category_Object_Is_Also_Returned()
{
  List<Product> products = repository.GetAll();
  foreach (var product in products)
  {
    Assert.IsNotNull(product.Category);
    Assert.IsNotNullOrEmpty(product.Category.Description);
  }
}
```

After this passes you can be confident that the relationship is set up correctly. The rest of the logic is handled by the controller to determine which products to display.

The next feature is for returning products within a certain category. For this feature, you don't want to return all the products and then display only certain products. Instead, you only want certain products to be returned from the database for a particular category, and as such improve performance.

The test is as you would expect by now. The method is called GetProductsByCategory, which returns a collection. Within the Setup method, you inserted two products with different categories. As such, when you request the products for one of those particular categories you only expect one to be returned:

```
[Test]
public void GetProductsByCategory_Returns_Only_Products_In_Category()
{
  List<Product> products = repository
                  .GetProductsByCategory("FirstTestCategory");

  Assert.AreEqual(1, products.Count);
}
```

In terms of what you pass to the controller, if no products are found, then you expect a list to be returned with a product count of 0 instead of null. To define this behavior you need a test. This will ensure that if this behavior changes, it will be caught:

```
[Test]
public void ProductRepository_No_Products_Returns_Empty_List()
{
```

```
        List<Product> products = repository
                    .GetProductsByCategory("NonExistentCategory");

        Assert.AreEqual(0, products.Count);
}
```

With the behavior defined within the tests, you can implement the query against your NHibernate layer to pull back the required results as a List<Product> collection:

```
public virtual List<Product> GetProductsByCategory(string category)
{
    ICriteria criteria = Session.CreateCriteria(typeof (Product))
                        .CreateAlias("Category", "c")
                        .Add(Expression.Eq("c.Description",
                                            category))
                        .SetResultTransformer(resultTransformer());

    return criteria.List<Product>() as List<Product>;
}
```

With this method in place, the control will be able to use and interact with the Repository and return the required information from the database.

Feature 3: Adding Items to the Shopping Cart

If you remember back to Chapter 3, when adding an item to the shopping cart you either get an existing shopping cart for the user or if null was returned then you should create a new cart.

For the first part of your Repository you need to create the ability to retrieve a cart for a particular user. To add a cart, you simply need to insert an instance of a ShoppingCart object. As this is part of the shared functionality it has already been tested and implemented.

The second stage is a custom method on the IShoppingCartRepository which is similar to how the GetProductsForCategory method worked — where you query the database and select a single object.

After the test inserts a cart you need to retrieve the cart before verifying that the two are equal:

```
[Test]
public void GetCart_Returns_Cart_Based_On_Username()
{
  repository.SaveOrUpdate(cart);

    ShoppingCart cart1 = repository.GetCart(username);
    Assert.AreEqual(cart, cart1);
}
```

To match the second part of the implementation, if the cart cannot be found, then you need to return null. Again, you need to define the expected behavior as a test to ensure that it doesn't change without you being aware, which could potentially cause other parts of the system to break:

```
[Test]
public void If_cart_does_not_exist_then_getcart_should_return_null()
```

```
        {
            ShoppingCart cart1 = repository.GetCart(string.Empty);
            Assert.IsNull(cart1);
        }
```

The implementation to match this method is shown in the following:

```
        public ShoppingCart GetCart(string username)
        {
            ICriteria criteria = Session.CreateCriteria(typeof (ShoppingCart))
                                 .Add(Expression.Eq("Username", username));

            return criteria.UniqueResult<ShoppingCart>();
        }
```

To verify that the implementation of NHibernate and your mappings are working correctly, you want to verify that a product is also returned as an item in your cart when the cart is retrieved. Although you aren't testing any code directly, you are verifying that your system is working as expected and defining the behavior. This is an important stage of development and testing. The test is shown here:

```
        [Test]
        public void GetCart_Returns_Products_Within_Cart()
        {
            cart.AddItem(p);
            repository.SaveOrUpdate(cart);

            ShoppingCart cart1 = repository.GetCart(username);
            Assert.AreEqual(1, cart1.Items.Count);
            Assert.AreEqual("productName", cart1.Items[0].Product.Name);
        }
```

In terms of the feature, this is your implementation complete. The other functionality is inherited.

The next major problem you face doesn't have to do with your Repositories, instead it relates to your ASP.NET membership security provider. To obtain the shopping cart, you need to access the user's credentials. You do this by asking the ASP.NET built-in membership provider. This handles all the authentication and credentials for you. However, because the ASP.NET pipeline stores this information, it makes it very difficult to test.

In terms of your systems implementation, you already have an ICredentialsService which will return a username for the currently logged-in user. The ASPnetCredentialsService object implements ICredentialsService to provide this functionality:

```
        [Test]
        public void GetUsername_Returns_Current_Logged_In_User()
        {
          ISecurityContext context = MockRepository.GenerateStub<ISecurityContext>();
          context.Stub(c => c.GetUser()).Return(new StubMembershipUser("TestUser",
                                                                  Guid.Empty));
          ASPnetCredentialsService service = new ASPnetCredentialsService(context);
          Assert.AreEqual("TestUser", service.GetUsername());
        }
```

As you can see from the test for ASPnetCredentialsService, you need an ISecurityContext which has a GetUser() method. This is where you hit your first major problem. The GetUser method needs to return a MembershipUser object which is part of ASP.NET. However, you are unable to construct this object in your tests as it has a private constructor which means you also can't mock CredentialsService. You also need to create a manual StubMembershipUser. This inherits from MembershipUser to allow you to use it; however, you have to override the username property so you can set the value in your constructor:

```
public class StubMembershipUser : MembershipUser
{
    public StubMembershipUser(string username, Guid userKey)
    {
        _username = username;
        _userKey = userKey;
    }

    private string _username;
    public override string UserName
    {
        get { return _username; }
    }
}
```

The result is that you can verify that the ASPnetCredentialsService correctly talks to the ISecurityContext object and can obtain the data from a MembershipUser object.

After you have done this, you need to actually obtain a live instance of your MembershipUser based on the user currently logged in. As your tests don't run in the ASP.NET lifecycle, you don't have information available. During your tests, you need to mock this information; in the real system you need to access ASP.NET. This can be done in a similar way to your SystemTime and DateTime where during test execution you can override the current user.

To verify that the HttpSecurityContext, which implements ISecurityContext, is working as you expect you want to verify that the object correctly calls the function, accesses the ASP.NET Membership Provider as expected, and returns the correct MembershipUser object.

To make this happen, your test needs to replicate the information ASP.NET provides. ASP.NET provides an Identity object. One of the properties on this object is called Name, which contains the username to use. Within your test, you create a stub of this object. You then reassign a function on the object of CurrentUser to use your stub Identity object instead of ASP.NET. After calling GetUser, you verify that the user was correct:

```
[Test]
public void GetUser_Calls_HttpContext()
{
    HttpSecurityContext httpSecurityContext = new HttpSecurityContext(null);
    //Mock current user so it attempts to get access to a username of our
    //choice in our tests but actual implementation will go via ASP.net
    var stub = MockRepository.GenerateStub<IIdentity>();
    stub.Stub(i => i.Name).Return(username);

    httpSecurityContext.CurrentUser = () => stub;
```

```
        MembershipUser user = httpSecurityContext.GetUser();
        Assert.IsNotNull(user);
        Assert.AreEqual(username, user.UserName);
    }
```

The test is not complex. The complex section is generally getting the system into a testable state. To make this testable, you abstract away as much as possible from the dependency on ASP.NET. This allows the tests to be more focused and flexible. If you had merged ICredentialsService and ISecurityContext into one, the overall complexity would have increased.

After you have abstracted, you created a CurrentUser hook function that allows you to change the implementation of the object under test, making it easier to test. Accessing this method is key to making the feature testable as you can remove the dependency on ASP.NET.

The implementation of the method isn't very complex either:

```
    public Func<IIdentity> CurrentUser = () => Current.User.Identity;
```

An alternative solution to using a Func in C# 3.0 would have been to create a TestableHttpSecurityContext for use during the testing. This object would inherit from HttpSecurityContext but override the method for obtaining the CurrentUser, leaving GetUser untouched.

However, you do have a problem with how the Membership object behaves. The Membership system needs access to a real SQL Server instance with the correct schema and data setup to access the Membership information. To make it more complex, the Membership system doesn't use NHibernate for data access and instead uses ADO.NET. As discussed in the previous section, there are a few rules to follow when tests need to connect to databases. First, the test should create the schema. Secondly, the test should create the data to test against.

In this case, you should create an ASPnetDBHelper method which knows how to construct the database and populate it with the data required by ASP.NET — not your test data:

```
    [SetUp]
    public void Setup()
    {
        ASPnetDBHelper.ReCreate();
        ASPnetDBHelper.ExecuteSchema();
        ASPnetDBHelper.ExeuteData();
    }
```

You need to re-create the database itself. This is done by attempting to drop the database in case it already exists and then calling the create command:

```
    public static void ReCreate()
    {
        ExecuteDbCommand("DROP");
        ExecuteDbCommand("CREATE");
    }
```

Within the ExecuteDbCommand method, you replace the database name in the connection string to master. This is because you don't want your initial catalog to be the database you're creating as it doesn't exist yet. You then use ADO.NET to execute the command:

```
static void ExecuteDbCommand(string start)
{
      string dbname = "WroxPizzaTestDB";
      string connToMaster = connString.Replace(dbname, "master");
      SqlConnection sqlConnection = new SqlConnection(connToMaster);
      SqlCommand command = new SqlCommand(start + " DATABASE " + dbname,
                                          sqlConnection);

      try
      {
         sqlConnection.Open();
         command.ExecuteNonQuery();
      }
      catch (Exception)
      { }
      finally
      {
         if (sqlConnection.State == ConnectionState.Open)
            sqlConnection.Close();
      }
}
```

In terms of generating your schema and data, SQL Compare and SQL Data Compare from Red Gate are used. This allows you to script schema creation scripts and data insertion commands into two single .sql files.

Your DB Helper will simply read in the file and call Execute:

```
public static void ExecuteSchema()
{
    string path = Path.Combine(location, @"Schema.sql");
    string schema = new StreamReader(path).ReadToEnd();
    Execute(schema);
}
public static void ExecuteData()
{
    string path = Path.Combine(location, @"Data.sql");
    string data = new StreamReader(path).ReadToEnd();
    Execute(data);
}
```

Because SQL Compare and Data Compare produce scripts with GO statements, it means you cannot use ADO.NET to execute them. A GO statement indicates to the execution process that it is the end of a batch. ADO.NET does not understand this and will fail if it sees a GO statement. However, SQL Server Management Objects (SMO) can understand a SQL Script with GO statements. As such, you can use SMO objects to execute the SQL generated by the Red Gate tools:

```
private static void Execute(string script)
{
    SqlConnection sqlConnection = new SqlConnection(connString);
```

```
        Server server = new Server(new ServerConnection(sqlConnection));

        try
        {
            server.ConnectionContext.ExecuteNonQuery(script);
        }
        finally
        {
            if (sqlConnection.State == ConnectionState.Open)
                sqlConnection.Close();
        }
    }
```

So the tests can access the scripts, they are included as a linked item in the Visual Studio Solution. You can then access the path based on where the assembly is being executed from:

```
private static string codebase = Assembly.GetExecutingAssembly().CodeBase;
private static string cbReplace = codebase.Replace("file:///", "");
private static string location = Path.Combine(Path.GetDirectoryName(cbReplace),
                                              @"Data\Schema");
```

The connection string is stored in the app.config and accessed via the ConfigurationManager in your tests:

```
<connectionStrings>
  <clear />
  <add name="LocalSqlServer"
   connectionString= "Data Source=(local);
                    initial catalog=WroxPizzaTestDB;
                    Integrated Security=True;"
   providerName="System.Data.SqlClient"/>
</connectionStrings>

private static string connString = ConfigurationManager.ConnectionStrings
                                   ["LocalSqlServer"].ConnectionString;
```

After you have your database, you need test data. The easiest way is to use the Membership object to create a new user. In your Setup method, you simply have the following lines of code:

```
MembershipCreateStatus status;
Membership.CreateUser(username, "test||1236", "test@user.com", "Book Title",
                    "Testing ASP.net", true, out status);
```

After you have finished, make sure to clean up by deleting the user:

```
[TearDown]
public void Teardown()
{
    Membership.DeleteUser(username);
}
```

With this in place, your test will now connect to the Membership service and query the provider for a user with a username of your choice, which you have created. When it's found, it will return it back to the test for you to verify to ensure it is the correct user and that the HttpSecurityContext is correct. Put this together with ASPnetCredentialsService and your authentication system will work as required for obtaining the shopping cart.

From this feature, hopefully you can see the types of processes you need to perform when testing certain features. Sometimes you will be faced with problems which don't look testable; however, with certain considerations it is generally possible to test a feature or at least be confident it will work as expected.

Feature 4: Displaying Addresses

Feature 4 involves letting the user enter a new address, or selecting an existing address for delivery. This address would then be stored in a cache for later use in the checkout process. Caching is a very simple task in ASP.NET as the foundation is built into the framework. As such, you just need to use it as required. However, testing the cache is not as simple.

First you read an InMemoryCacheService which implements the ICacheService we described in the previous chapter. This has two methods, Add and Get. In your implementation, you simply call the appropriate methods on your ActiveCache object, which is provided as a parameter to your constructor:

```
public class InMemoryCacheService : ICacheService
{
  //Cache is sealed.
  private static Cache ActiveCache { get; set; }
  public void Add(string cacheID, object cache)
  {
    ActiveCache.Insert(cacheID, cache);
  }

  public object Get(string cacheID)
  {
    return ActiveCache.Get(cacheID);
  }
}
```

The main problem when testing this is getting access to the Cache object. The Cache object is generally accessed via the current HttpContext. However, as the HttpContext doesn't exist you can't use it. If you initialized a new instance of Cache, and attempt to add items you will get a null reference exception. However, you can access a constructed and isolated version of the Cache object via the HttpRuntime object. You can then use this object to provide the backing for your InMemoryCacheService, allowing you to test the implementation:

```
[Test]
public void Add_Calls_Add_On_HttpContext()
{
    Cache c = HttpRuntime.Cache;
    InMemoryCacheService service = new InMemoryCacheService(c);
    service.Add("test", 123);

    Assert.AreEqual(123, c.Get("test"));
```

```
    }

    [Test]
    public void Get_can_return_object_from_cache()
    {
        Cache c = HttpRuntime.Cache;
        c.Insert("test", 123);

        InMemoryCacheService service = new InMemoryCacheService(c);
        Assert.AreEqual(123, service.Get("test"));
    }
```

The reason for abstracting your Cache object into a separate class is to enable you to add an interface, allowing you to stub out the implementation in higher layers meaning you don't have to worry about getting access to the object and having this hanging around in your tests. By breaking it out, you reduce the complexity of your tests while creating a more decoupled system.

External Systems

While the WroxPizza sample doesn't interact with external systems, it is very common for web applications to need external systems such as email servers.

Email Servers

Although your WroxPizza application doesn't have any email implementation, you could easily imagine that when an order is placed an email confirmation is sent. This is a very common feature and has certain issues when it comes to testing the implementation.

Imagine your implementation has a controller which contains some logic and is required to send an alert via email. You then have an EmailService object which implements the INotificationService interface. The EmailService will communicate with your SMTP Server and send the email.

As described in Chapter 3, testing your higher level controller logic is very easy as you can simply use a mock object to verify the two are implemented as expected:

```
    [TestFixture]
    public class ControllerTests
    {
        [Test]
        public void CanSendEmail()
        {
            var notification = new Notification {Text = "Test"};

            var mock = MockRepository.GenerateMock<INotificationService>();
            mock.Expect(i => i.SendNotification(notification)).Return(true);

            Controller controller = new Controller(mock);
            controller.SendAlert(notification);

            mock.VerifyAllExpectations();
```

```
        }
    }
```

However, the problem is testing your EmailService to verify that it works as expected; you need to actually connect to an SMTP Server. There are two major problems with this. First is the fact you need to set up and figure an SMTP Server. This has administration problems but also security concerns — as spammers gain access to the test server they can use it to spam people — not ideal. Secondly, you don't want emails being actually sent to people. The solution is to use a fake SMTP Server.

There are a few implementations of a fake SMTP Server online. The concept is similar to using SQLite as an in-memory database. Your tests will start your fake server, you send the email to this server, and then use your fake server to verify the email was sent as expected before stopping it. The next example is from Phil Haack and the implementation he used for his SubText open source project. The code can be downloaded from http://haacked.com/archive/2006/05/30/ATestingMailServerForUnitTestingEmailFunctionality.aspx.

The concept is simple. Imagine you have the following test:

```
[Test]
public void CanSendEmail()
{
    var notification = new Notification {Text = "Test"};
    EmailService service = new EmailService("localhost", 25);
    bool result = service.SendNotification(notification);
    Assert.IsTrue(result);
}
```

At the moment this will fail because localhost doesn't have an SMTP Server setup. To solve this, use your Setup method to start your Test\Fake server. You need to ensure that the two are communicating on the same port number:

```
[SetUp]
public void Setup()
{
    receivingServer = new TestSmtpServer();
    receivingServer.Start("127.0.0.1", 25);
}
```

After you are done, stop the server in your Teardown method:

```
[TearDown]
public void Teardown()
{
    receivingServer.Stop();
}
```

To verify your email was sent, ask your fake server for its inbox count. If it is 1, then the email sent was expected:

```
Assert.AreEqual(1, receivingServer.Inbox.Count);
```

You now have your EmailService object fully tested at both levels.

Summary

In this chapter we covered integration tests. We discussed the issues when having to interact with a database and how you can still successfully test your system. We also spoke about how external systems and how dependencies can have an impact on how you test your code, and we defined steps you can take to mitigate the impact and still be confident your system works correctly. In the next chapter we focus on how you can successfully test the UI.

5

Automated User Interface Testing

In this chapter you learn the different approaches, advantages, and disadvantages to automated UI testing. After we discuss the concepts of automated UI testing, you'll be able to see how they apply to the rest of the ASP.NET family and learn about the various problems and solutions for the different technologies.

Can UI Automation Be Achieved?

User interface (UI) testing is often thought of as a manual process because of the many problems associated with this type of testing. To ease the repetitive nature of this manual testing, developers and testers often resort to third-party tools to "record" mouse positions and raise click events on the screen. The test scripts created from these third-party tools are very difficult to read, because the tool that generated the script created a script so complicated that a human would have a very difficult time maintaining it. Again, because of this fact, UI test scripts begin to rot, and are deleted because they no longer work. Although these tests are easy to set up, they often make the UI tests very brittle because any change to the UI can invalidate the positioning and logic recorded within the test. As a result, most testers and developers have started to abandon these types of record\playback tests.

> Is it okay to delete tests? There are strong advocates on both sides of the fence of this issue. Many believe that tests should never be deleted, that it can be reworked if the code being tested has been refactored, but a test should never be deleted. Others believe that if a test is no longer useful, the test should be removed. We think that deleting test code should only be done if it won't increase the cost of finding a defect or add documentation regarding the behavior of the application.

As you read through this chapter, you will learn not to fear automated user interface testing and learn that it can be successfully applied to a project. However, it's important to keep in mind that there is a cost to automation. In almost all situations it will take you much longer to write a program that clicks a button and reports the result than it would to manually click that button and see what it does. Many testers and developers assume that automated UI testing will replace manual testing, but this is never the case. Manual testing will not go away.

Great testers/developers are able to weigh their experience with the benefit of what automation will buy them. After you have read through this chapter you will realize that UI testing is easy, but that creating meaningful tests is a difficult skill that can only be obtained by practice. Some development shops have very few automated UI tests and use them as smoke tests (you can read a definition of these in the list of functional tests in the next section). If the automated UI tests they have created run without failures, the application is good enough for manual testing to be performed. Other development shops have created very elaborate test suites to test every aspect of the application covering very fine details, such as the background color of a web page. Both of these cases are acceptable, and the testers/developers have decided what they need to get out of automated testing.

With all that said, what does UI testing do for web applications? Automated UI testing is great for those few moments after code is checked in to tell you if something in the UI is broken. If something *is* broken, you'll know that the quality of the code is not sufficient to run the manual tests on this code. As with other types of tests, UI testing helps flush out bad requirements, finds issues with features that don't match requirements, and provides a nice safety net to prevent against regression.

Functional Testing

Functional tests have many different responsibilities. Part of their role is to ensure that the system being developed meets the requirements set out by the customer. In some circumstances they ensure that goals and metrics — such as performance metrics — are met. Functional tests can also allow customers to monitor the system while it's being developed. At a low level, functional tests will be created by testers to test functionality, such as the UI and performance testing. At a higher level, acceptance tests may be created by the customer to ensure that the software meets the external requirements. Functional tests should pick up where unit tests left off and start testing the system with concrete implementations and in a more end-to-end process with the aim of catching integration problems and missing requirements. When acceptance tests have been well written, they can act as a specification because they are readable by a customer. This concept will be covered in more depth in Chapter 6.

Functional tests can be invaluable during a major refactoring of a system. When large refactorings occur, a large number of unit tests can break and it can be hard to determine which tests were expected to fail. Functional testing will help indicate to you when the application is restored to a known state and indicate if manual testing should begin.

Unlike unit tests, functional tests can take a long time to run. Often a well-defined suite of functional tests will run overnight and, in some cases, will run for days. Because functional tests take a great deal of time to run, it's imperative that some type of continuous integration system is put into place to schedule when the functional tests are run. Without such a system in place, functional tests are not run often enough and degrade over time. Although it is common practice to run unit tests upon every commit to the source control repository, functional tests are more likely to be run every night.

Many types of tests fall under the functional testing umbrella. It's understandable if you find the term *functional testing* confusing, because many developers/testers/customers substitute the precise name of the testing discipline with the generic term "functional test." Let's take a moment and define each type of functional test:

- **Accessibility testing.** In this context, accessible can be thought of as the ability to access. Accessibility testing ensures that the functionality of the application is available to people with disabilities. Many organizations have published standards that applications should meet to maximize accessibility.

- **Ad hoc testing.** Ad hoc testing is a concept that is applied to tests that are created with the intention to only be run one time. Ad hoc tests are considered exploratory tests. It is often argued that ad hoc tests should be more structured and be contained in the test harness.

- **Acceptance** testing. Acceptance testing tests that the system does exactly what it is supposed to do. They can be used as a "sign-off" to indicate that the vendor has delivered what the customer has asked for. Acceptance tests are created from the customer's requirements and result directly in the acceptance or rejection of the final system

- **Capacity testing.** This type of test is used to determine the maximum number of resources that can be contained inside the application under test.

- **Deployment testing.** This type of test ensures that the package created to deploy the application works as expected. Often deployment testing occurs on virtual machines to ensure that the application will install on multiple operating systems.

- **Exploratory testing.** Exploratory testing is a manual test that can be thought of as a style of testing that allows a developer/tester the freedom to explore a black box system by creating tests to find out how the system works.

- **Graphical user interface software testing.** UI testing includes tests that ensure the UI meets the specifications of how the application should perform. UI tests can be automated or manual tests.

- **Load testing.** This is another name for performance testing.

- **Performance testing.** Performance testing measures the response of a system when it's placed under load. Common metrics for web applications is Time to First Byte (TTFB) and Requests per Second (RPS).

- **Recovery testing.** Recovery testing simply tests how well the application under test recovers from a software crash or hardware issue.

- **Regression testing.** Regression tests ensure that functionality that was previously working correctly has stopped working as intended.

- **Sanity testing.** A sanity test is a quick check to ensure the validity of a function. Sanity tests help determine whether it is reasonable to continue with more thorough tests.

- **Scalability testing.** Testing for scalability ensures that the web application under test is able to maintain the same performance characteristics (requests per second) as traffic, users, or the amount of data on the page increases.

- **Security testing.** Security testing ensures that data and functionality is protected on the application under test.

- **Smoke testing.** Smoke tests are the first tests run on the application under test, to provide assurance that the application will not catastrophically fail. If the application does not catastrophically fail, more in-depth tests can be run on the system. Smoke tests are often used to help flush out errors.

❑   **Stress testing.** This is another name for performance testing.

❑   **Usability testing.** Usability testing focuses on how users use the system. Usability testing cannot be automated, and testers have a very close communication line with the users in the test scenario.

❑   **Volume testing.** Volume testing ensures that the system being tested can handle a certain amount of data. Databases or files are examples of items that would be tested under a volume test. Volume testing is also closely related to performance testing.

Some software development processes place a barrier that is stricter than we have discussed thus far between unit and functional tests. XP processes state that unit tests should be created by developers, while functional test specifications should be created by the customer with the guidance of developers and testers.

Importance of Automated UI Testing

We feel that UI testing is an important part of a project. Though the tests are still automated, they have to be handled in a slightly different fashion and different considerations need to be taken into account when creating them.

With unit tests, the focus is on an isolated and targeted method with a clearly defined set of inputs and outputs, and as such, it is easier to understand the flow of the test and the interactions it is performing. With UI tests you lose this ability. This means that you need to combat this by reconsidering how you write and structure your tests to take this into account. As with most parts of software development, if you lose something — such as readability or automation — then you need to react by replacing or mitigating the impact. This is solved by paying more attention to another area that will help combat this. Because it is more difficult to understand the internals of the system when dealing with a black box, you need to make UI tests even more readable.

UI tests also have a different focus and role than unit tests. They both focus on catching regression bugs, but unit tests, and in particular TDD, focus on design and improving testability of the code base. Sadly there isn't this relationship to the UI. The UI tests can provide a form of documentation for your UI and the UI interface about how the software should work. If you combine this with your BDD or acceptance testing then you can create a very effective form of documentation for the customer.

The focus of the tests should be to ensure that the core functionality is working as expected. Every application has a core set of scenarios and features that must work for the application to be tested or demoed to a customer. This should be the initial focus for your automated tests because if this core functionality doesn't work as you expect you'll want to know as soon as possible. Common core-use cases could include being able to log in to an authenticate-only system. Of course, if you can't get past this initial screen then you can't do much else, so it's important to know if this breaks in an automated fashion as we discussed earlier. Just as with other core features of the application, if they fail you'll want to know very early on.

This is the most important point of UI tests. They provide you with early warning signs for when parts of your system have changed. With unit tests, you want high code coverage, while with UI tests you want high value systems that provide the most value for identifying breakages. If they can provide you with this level of confidence that they will catch the major showstoppers, then they're worth investing the time and effort you'll spend in creating and maintaining them.

Having this level of confidence is a great comfort, especially for testers. Although developers continue to provide code and implement new features, having the UI tests along with unit and integration tests means that the testers can remain focused on the same features as the developers are working on. Having developers and testers focus on the same feature or scenario at the same provides a huge productivity boost. Testers can start testing features as soon as the developer commits the changes, reporting bugs earlier in the lifecycle allowing them to lower the cost. Automation helps this. By having automation, testers are not as concerned with regression bugs on existing features as there will be some automation cover.

This is especially relevant in agile practices such as Scrum. One of the important parts of the scrum process is that all the team focuses on implementing a story and making sure it's finished. If the testers are focused on making sure that no regressions have occurred, they can't focus on moving the application forward.

After you have your UI testing automated, the next ideal stage is to automate the tests across multiple platforms and browsers to take full advantage of the tests you have invested in. With the right structure and UI automation, this is possible and can be a great time return on investment.

However, although UI tests are greatly important and can have great benefits, they are not without their problems.

Problems with UI Automation

Testing the UI is a heated topic in testing circles. Many will argue that testing the UI is a waste of time as there are too many problems associated with this type of testing. You have learned that fragile tests increase maintenance tasks by requiring the developer to modify many tests each time the functionality of the system being tested is changed. UI tests are fragile tests and in most projects require the most maintenance, more than all other types of tests. UI testing is considered black box testing; as a tester you will supply the input and only verify the expected outcome without looking at the code that provides the outcome. With black box testing you are not expected to see how the inputs are processed or how the output is generated. There is no way to ensure that each code path is effectively tested (see Figure 5-1).

Input 1 — Output

Input 2

Figure 5-1: Black box testing

Fragile tests *are tests that are very sensitive to the functionality of the system being tested. Fragile tests break often and require a great deal of maintenance. Fragile tests require the most maintenance of any other type of test. Because of the close relationship with the function of the system, and how frequent functionality can change, functional tests are considered to be fragile tests.*

❑ **Fragility Due to Layout Changes.** When a developer learns that automated testing of a UI can be performed, many of them jump right in to creating tests for existing systems that have not been designed with testing in mind. Tools such as Visual Studio Team Test, Selenium, and WatiN have recorders, which allow for creating scripted tests without much thought. The developer may develop hundreds of UI tests using these tools without any issues, but one morning they may come into the office, run their tests, and see a sea of red, meaning many test failures. This situation is common when a designer or another developer makes a change to the UI, such as changing a menu on the master page; suddenly all your tests are broken. You may spend an hour or so fixing your tests to get them running correctly again, only to find the changes to the menu were not finalized and your tests are broken again. Many developers get into this vicious circle and soon abandon the concept of UI testing.

The problem with the previous example could be solved by knowing exactly what is being tested in the UI and how. Is it important to test that the background color for the page is #0C1911, perhaps? It would be important to create a test for this if some function of the application being tested changed the background color to #0C1911. Another time you might want to create a test like this is if there is a process problem. Perhaps the background color of the application used to be #FFFFFF, and a recent feature changes the background to #0C1911 — developers are forgetting to conform to this standard. By creating a test to ensure that the background color is correct, you will save a few calls from the customer.

❑ **Timing Problems.** There are two types of timing issues that developers and testers should be concerned about. The first type of timing issue occurs on the machine where the test is being run, and has to do with the testing framework and not specifically the system being tested. Functional tests are often not run on hardware that is similar to the hardware the production system is running in. Because many developers do not use a known set of production data for functional tests, the system will not perform as expected and application timeouts will occur that are unexpected. These are issues you may not see in production, but are causing your tests to fail.

The other type of timing issue to be aware of is that web applications perform differently under different connection speeds, and because of this, timing issues will occur. This issue tends to appear most often when you are testing the AJAX functionality of an application that uses AJAX. Because of these connection timing issues, it is essential that developers/testers create tests that account for this issue. It's very common that developers will add "Sleep's" into their tests, but there are better ways which we will explore later in the WatiN and Ajax section of this chapter.

❑ **Hard-to-Test UI Elements.** As you have probably come to realize, testing a UI is hard but testing some elements are harder than others. Testing when a label appears is much easier than testing that a message on the screen fades in and then fades out at a certain speed. You may find yourself in a situation where you cannot create an automated test to test a certain functionality of the system. UI testing requires the developer/tester to think outside-the-box in many situations. Hard to test UI elements can be overcome with a combination of automated and manual confirmation techniques.

❑ **Tight Coupling to Other Parts of the System.** For years, numerous sources have been trying to educate developers about separation of concern, but for some reason it is still commonplace for developers to insist on placing business logic inside of UI logic. As we learned in Chapter 2, it's difficult to create tests for systems that are tightly coupled, sometimes impossible without some sort of refactoring. Creating functional tests is just as hard for tightly coupled systems. Developers/testers will find themselves creating tests that should be created at the unit test level.

❑ **Unsolicited Events.** Web applications can contain logic to raise events that are not based on user interactions. Examples could be when the price of a product reaches a certain amount the product should be displayed differently on the screen. Another example that most web developers have encountered is automatic user logic. In this situation the system will log out the user after a certain time period has expired. Events such as these are difficult to re-create using functional tests.

❑ **Many Ways In, Many Ways Out.** Because of the nature of web applications, there are many ways to access pages and features inside the application. Did the user access the feature from a menu, a URL, button, or perhaps an external link? How many different ways can a user access a particular feature of your system? Because access to a feature is acyclic, only a finite number of paths exist — should we test each path? Depending on the size of your application, you could spend a great deal of time creating functional tests to test the paths to each function of a system. This topic will be discussed later in the chapter, but will always pose a problem for functional testing.

❑ **Infinite Input Sequence.** As a general rule-of-thumb, web applications allow users to enter form data in any order they wish. The application will have a default tab order, but the sequence is the choice of the user using the system. As forms become more complex, the number of sequences of how the data can be entered onto the form will increase exponentially. If conditional logic has been applied to fields, such as field 1 must be greater than field 2, then what would happen if field 2 is entered before field 1? As addressed in the previous UI testing issue, testing for these situations can generate a great number of tests that will need to be maintained.

❑ **Random Failures.** When performing UI tests, it is common to receive random errors that are hard to reproduce. It's common for these errors to be timing issues, or issues with the machine the test is running on. Many developers will ignore these errors and either delete the test or let the test stay red. Not resolving these types of errors make their UI test suite lose value. It's important to track down these random errors and resolve them.

The Pareto principle (also known as the 80–20 rule) states that roughly 80 percent of the effects come from 20 percent of the causes. With automated UI testing, expect 80 percent of the benefit to be obtained from 20 percent of the tests. Don't waste time on complex tests at the expense of high-volume tests.

Tools for UI Testing

It's important to keep in mind that when you're testing the UI, you are testing human activity. Because of this, you should let the computer perform the tasks it is good at, and you should perform the types of tasks you are good at. When developers and testers first learn about the tools that can be used to test the UI, they often think that everything can now be automated, and this is very far from reality. Chapter 7 talks about manual testing in depth, but for now it's important that we understand that manual testing is still a very important testing discipline in the testing cycle.

Frederick Brooks taught software developers in the 1987 paper entitled "No Silver Bullet — Essence and Accidents of Software Engineering," that there is no silver bullet in software development, meaning there is not one tool that will solve the entire job you are looking to accomplish. UI testing should not be thought of as the end-all-be-all of testing. When performed properly UI testing is a very strong testing tool.

After you realize the importance of automated UI testing, the next most important decision to make is which tool you will be using to create your tests. There are three schools of thought on how to test the UI.

Impersonating the Browser

This is a set of headless scripts that sends the same type of requests to impersonate the browser, but measures the response times without looking at the content that was sent back. This type of UI testing is great to find bottlenecks inside web applications. The downside of this type of testing is that you are not examining the response and verifying test cases. This type of testing can only be used for volume, stress, and load testing scenarios.

The Web Capacity Analysis Tool (WCAT) is a lightweight HTTP load generation tool that is designed to simulate thousands of concurrent users, making requests to a site. WCAT uses simple scripts to impersonate the browser and fully exercise a website:

```
NEW TRANSACTION
    classId = 1
    NEW REQUEST HTTP
        Verb = "GET"
        URL = "http://www.google.com"
```

The preceding example is a WCAT test script at its simplest. Notice in this script there are no verifications to ensure that the page loaded successfully or contained a certain element; the script just navigates to the Google homepage.

Parsing the HTML Ourselves

This concept first starts with an impersonation of browser by opening a web request to the application, then parsing the HTML returned in the response looking for the criteria that will make the test succeed. This method of UI testing is the middle ground between browser impersonation and driving a web browser. This UI testing method is great when you have a set of tests that impersonate the browser, but you need to start moving into a method of testing to start validating responses:

```
using NUnit.Framework;
using System.Net;
using System.IO;

namespace ParseHttp
{
    [TestFixture]
    public class ParseHttp
    {
        [Test]
        public void Should_Navigate_To_Google_And_Return_Results_For_AspNet()
        {
            string urlToTest = "http://www.google.com/search?hl=en&rlz=1G1GGLQ_
ENUS295&q=asp.net&btnG=Search";
            string result = GetPage(urlToTest);
            Assert.IsTrue(result.IndexOf("The Official") >0, "Asp.net Page ");
        }

        private string GetPage(string urlToTest)
        {
            // create a web client object to load the page from local server
```

```
        WebClient client = new WebClient();
        string result = string.Empty;

        // dump the contents of the page we navigated to into a stream
        using (StreamReader reader = new
            StreamReader(client.OpenRead(urlToTest)))
        {
            result = reader.ReadToEnd();
        }

        return result;
    }
  }
}
```

Driving the Browser

In this method of UI testing (shown in the next listing), the test will open a physical browser, perform a behavior, and then the test will verify the HTML based on the test criteria you have entered. This type of automated UI testing is the closest to manual testing you will get. Because the test needs to open a browser, perform a test, and report the results back this type of test is very fragile. These types of tests are often complex, and if your plan is to only stress test your application this type of testing would be overkill:

```
using NUnit.Framework;
using WatiN.Core;
using WatiN.Core.Interfaces;

namespace SimpleWatinTest
{
    [TestFixture]
    public class SimpleWatinTests
    {
        [Test]
        public void Should_Click_Search_On_Google_And_Return_Results_For_AspNet()
        {
            using (IBrowser ie =
                BrowserFactory.Create(BrowserType.InternetExplorer))
            {
                ie.GoTo("http://www.google.com");
                ie.TextField(Find.ByName("q")).Value = "asp.net";
                ie.Button(Find.ByName("btnG")).Click();
                Assert.IsTrue(ie.ContainsText
                    ("The Official Microsoft ASP.NET Site"));
            }
        }
    }
}
```

The previous listing contains test code that drives the browser. In this example the WatiN library is used to drive the browser. In this test, a physical instance of Internet Explorer will open on the computer, navigate to the page we are testing, and then ensure that certain text exists on the page that was rendered.

With the different types of automated UI testing methods laid out, you may be wondering which method to use. You may realize you have the need to use all three methods. The decision of which UI testing tool to use depends on which method you have decided fits best with the application you need to test. Hopefully you will see a need to use a tool that will enable you to create tests that fit into each of these testing methods.

To get the feel about how the tools work, we will create a test using multiple tools that go out to www.google.com, searches for the term "ASP.NET," and returns a set of results.

WatiN

WatiN is an open source library inspired from the Watir library developed for Ruby. WatiN is an abbreviation for "Web Application Testing in .NET" and the project is currently maintained at http://watin .sourceforge.net/. WatiN is known for its very easy to read syntax that drives the browser. WatiN supports tests that drive both Internet Explorer and Firefox. The WatiN API has a very rich API that includes very easy to use functions that map HTML to WatiN to allow for easy searching of the DOM.

To drive Internet Explorer, WatiN uses COM automation that is built into Internet Explorer. One drawback of the WatiN framework is that HTTP status codes are not exposed, which is currently a limitation of the COM automation in Internet Explorer.

Version 2.0 of WatiN has added support to Firefox. For WatiN to drive the Firefox browser, the JSHH plug-in must be installed. JSSH is a plug-in that exposes a telnet server that allows automation commands to be pushed to Firefox.

In the next listing, an Internet Explorer object is used to open a connection to www.google.com and then ensure that the string Official Microsoft ASP.NET Site appears on the page:

```
using NUnit.Framework;
using WatiN.Core;
using WatiN.Core.Interfaces;

namespace SimpleWatinTest
{
    [TestFixture]
    public class SimpleWatinTests
    {
        [Test]
        public void Should_Click_Search_On_Google_And_Return_Results_For_AspNet()
        {
            using (IBrowser ie =
                BrowserFactory.Create(BrowserType.InternetExplorer))
            {
                ie.GoTo("http://www.google.com");
                ie.TextField(Find.ByName("q")).Value = "asp.net";
                ie.Button(Find.ByName("btnG")).Click();
                Assert.IsTrue(ie.ContainsText
                    ("The Official Microsoft ASP.NET Site"));
            }
        }
    }
}
```

Below is a table of how HTML elements can be obtained using the WatiN framework.WatiN HTML Mapping:

HTML ELEMENT	WatiN Class	Example
<a />	Link	Ie.Link(linkId)
<button />	Button	Ie.Button(buttonId)
<div />	Div	Ie.Div(divId)
<form />	Form	Ie.Form(formId)
<frame />	Frame	Ie.Frame(frameId)
<iframe />	Frame	Ie.Frame(iframeId)
<img />	Image	Ie.Image(imageId)
<input type=button/>	Button	Ie.Button(buttonId)
<input type=checkbox/>	CheckBox	Ie.CheckBox(checkboxId)
<input type=file/>	FileUpload	Ie.FileUpload(fileuploadId)
<input type=image/>	Image	Ie.Image(imageId)
<input type=password/>	TextField	Ie.TextField(passwordId)
<input type=radio/>	RadioButton	Ie.RadioButton(radioId)
<input type=submit/>	Button	Ie.Button(submitId)
<input type=text/>	TextField	Ie.TextField(textId)
<label />	Label	Ie.Label(elementId)
<option />	Option	Ie.Select(selectId).Options
<p />	Para	Ie.Para(pId)
<select />	Select	Ie.Select(selectId)
<span />		
<table />	Table	Ie.Table(tableId)
<tbody />	TableBody	Ie.TableBody(tablebodyId) Ie.Table(tableid).TableBodies
<td />	TableCell	Ie.TableCell(tablecellId) Ie.Table(TableId).TableRows[0] .TableCells[0]
<textarea />	TextField	Ie.TextField(textareaId)

145

HTML ELEMENT	WatiN Class	Example
<tr />	TableRow	Ie.TableRow(tablerowId) Ie.Table(TableId).TableRows[0]
All elements, also the ones not mentioned in this list	Element and ElementsContainer	Ie.Element(elementId) Ie.Element(tagname, elementId)

`http://watin.sourceforge.net/htmlelementmapping.html`

Screen Capturing

Because UI tests are fragile, it's often difficult to figure out exactly why a test is failing. You have learned that tests should be descriptive, and that developers/testers should be able to drill into the behavior that is failing with ease, but often it's not that easy when testing the UI.

Many UI testing frameworks include methods that can take a screen capture to indicate the state of the system during the test. The next listing is an example using WatiN to capture the screen after the browser has navigated to the page, but before checking that the text exists on the page.

The next example only takes one screen capture, but depending on the test, it's acceptable to capture multi-images during the test. It's important to adopt a naming standard that makes it easy to find the screen capture images when needed. The name of the screen capture is the exact name of the test. If multiple captures were taken, then the state would be appended at the end of the capture name:

```
string capturePath = m_testCapturePath + fileName;

using (IE ie = new IE())
{
    ie.GoTo("http://www.google.com");
    ie.CaptureWebPageToFile(string.Format("{0}_After_Browser_Launch.jpg",
        capturePath));

    ie.TextField(Find.ByName("q")).Value = "asp.net";
    ie.CaptureWebPageToFile(string.Format("{0}_After_Text_Is_Entered
.jpg",capturePath));

    ie.Button(Find.ByName("btnG")).Click();
    ie.CaptureWebPageToFile(string.Format("{0}_Before_Results_Are_Parsed.jpg",
        capturePath));

    Assert.IsTrue(ie.ContainsText("The Official Microsoft ASP.NET Site"));
}
```

Although the WatiN screen capturing functionality is very useful, it can also be problematic at times. The release of Internet Explorer 8 has caused issues with this functionality of some older versions of the WatiN framework. The images rendered will be solid black. If you encounter these issues, please refer to the WatiN documentation (`http://watin.sourceforge.net/documentation.html`) for more detailed information:

```
using System;
using System.Diagnostics;
```

```
using System.IO;
using NUnit.Framework;
using WatiN.Core;

namespace WatinTestWithScreenCapture
{
    [TestFixture]
    public class WatinTestWithScreenCapture
    {
        private string m_testCapturePath = string.Empty;

        [SetUp]
        public void setup()
        {
            DirectoryInfo appBasePath = new DirectoryInfo(AppDomain.CurrentDomain
                .BaseDirectory);
            m_testCapturePath = string.Format("{0}/Captures/", appBasePath.Parent
                .Parent.FullName);
        }

        [Test]
        public void Should_Click_Search_On_Google_And_Return_Results_For_AspNet()
        {
            StackFrame stackFrame = new StackFrame();
            string fileName = string.Format("{0}.jpg", stackFrame.GetMethod().Name);
            string capturePath = m_testCapturePath + fileName;

            using (IE ie = new IE())
            {
                ie.GoTo("http://www.google.com");
                ie.TextField(Find.ByName("q")).Value = "asp.net";
                ie.Button(Find.ByName("btnG")).Click();
                ie.CaptureWebPageToFile(capturePath);

                Assert.IsTrue(ie.ContainsText("The Official Microsoft ASP.NET
                    Site"));
            }
        }
    }
}
```

It's important to note that screen capturing is an expensive resource and should not be abused. Even though it's acceptable to have multiple captures in the same test, please use this functionality with care. Remember that the longer a test takes to run, the less frequently it will be run.

Visual Studio Web Tests

Visual Studio web tests first appeared in Visual Studio 2001 Enterprise Edition. In recent years, the Microsoft Application Center Test application was discontinued, and web tests have found a home in the Visual Studio Team System Test. Visual Studio web tests are another type of test that drives the web browser. The power of Visual Studio web tests comes from the test recorder that is provided. The code that is generated from the recorder is much more difficult to read than other tools, but with a little practice a developer would not have much trouble writing the web tests manually:

```
using System;
using System.Collections.Generic;
```

147

```
using System.Text;
using Microsoft.VisualStudio.TestTools.WebTesting;
using Microsoft.VisualStudio.TestTools.WebTesting.Rules;

namespace SimpleVSWebTest
{
    public class SimpleVSWebTest: WebTest
    {
        public SimpleVSWebTest()
        {
            this.PreAuthenticate = true;
        }

        public override IEnumerator<WebTestRequest> GetRequestEnumerator()
        {

            WebTestRequest request1 = new WebTestRequest("http://www.google.com/");
            WebTestRequest request2 = new WebTestRequest(
                "http://www.google.com/search");
            request2.QueryStringParameters.Add("hl", this.Context["$HIDDEN1.hl"]
                .ToString(), false, false);
            request2.QueryStringParameters.Add("q", "asp.net", false, false);
            request2.QueryStringParameters.Add("aq", "f", false, false);
            request2.QueryStringParameters.Add("oq", "", false, false);

            if ((this.Context.ValidationLevel >= Microsoft.VisualStudio.TestTools
                .WebTesting.ValidationLevel.High))
            {
                ValidationRuleFindText validationRule2 = new
                    ValidationRuleFindText();
                validationRule2.FindText = "The Official Microsoft";
                validationRule2.IgnoreCase = false;
                validationRule2.UseRegularExpression = false;
                validationRule2.PassIfTextFound = true;
                request2.ValidateResponse += new EventHandler<ValidationEventArgs>(
                    validationRule2.Validate);
            }

            yield return request2;
            request2 = null;
        }
    }
}
```

Automating the UI Using Record and Playback

So far in this chapter, you've learned about creating UI tests by hand, meaning that each behavior is coded by hand. This next section will discuss the Record and Playback model, where a tool is used to record the steps and let an application play back performing test cases on each page being played back.

Recorded Tests

Tests that are recorded are the most brittle and many developers don't like to work with them because they are so fragile. Many scripts follow the same pattern: navigate to a page, poke some buttons, and then look at the results. UI tests can be hard to work with because of a lack of clarity. You start with a small script and you keep adding to it. Code in the middle of the script may depend on code that happens in the beginning, and there is seldom an indication for why a keystroke is happening. Most test recorders don't follow the 'Don't repeat yourself' (DRY) principle and duplicate logic from test to test instead. When working with an application that has no UI tests created, using a test recorder can save a great deal of time. It can be very overwhelming to try to create handwritten UI tests for an application that has only 10 web pages, let alone hundreds. We have discussed the negatives of recording tools, but some tools available create scripts that are very easy to use and do not include unneeded code. Well-written test recorders are also great to help a developer new to the UI testing tool learn how to use the API.

WatiN Recorder

The WatiN test recorder (`http://watintestrecord.sourceforge.net/`) is an automatic web test recorder for the WatiN UI testing framework. The WatiN recorder is not maintained by the same set of individuals who created the WatiN framework and therefore is not included with it. It is, however, an open source tool. As the user navigates through a website, the WatiN recorder will record the session and then convert it to WatiN framework calls that can be saved into your unit tests. The WatiN recorder creates very clean code, making it a great tool for beginners to learn how the WatiN framework works.

In Figure 5-2 the WatiN test recorder was used to navigate to Google; enter **ASP.NET** in the text box, then press the Search button.

Figure 5-2: WatiN test recorder

The WatiN test recorder produced the following code:

```
IE ie = new IE("about:blank");
ie.GoTo("http://www.google.com");
ie.TextField(Find.ByName("q")).TypeText("asp.net");
ie.Button(Find.ByName("btnG")).Click();
```

```
StringAssert.Contains("The Official Microsoft ASP.NET Site",
    ie.Link(Find.ByUrl("http://www.asp.net/")).Text, @"innerText does not match");
```

The code may not be exactly the way you would have performed the task if you were writing the code yourself by hand, but nonetheless the test recorder produced working WatiN code that could be entered into a unit test.

The WatiN recorder contains a great deal of features allowing you to perform validation on page elements contained in the DOM. The following code was generated by right-clicking the Official Microsoft ASP.NET link, and using the options contained in Figure 5-3 to create an assert to ensure that the phrase Official Microsoft ASP.NET was contained in a link on the results page:

```
StringAssert.Contains("The Official Microsoft ASP.NET Site",
    ie.Link(Find.ByUrl("http://www.asp.net/")).Text,
    @"innerText does not match");
```

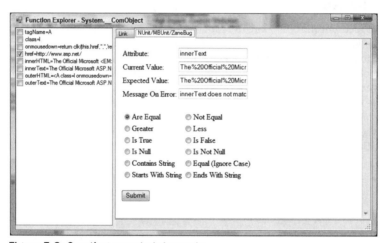

Figure 5-3: Creating assert statements

When using a test recorder, you might make a mistake and need to delete an action or you might want to add an action without having to do it through the browser. The WatiN recorder takes this into account and provides an interface for deleting the WatiN commands that were generated, or even for adding events to help aid in driving the browser.

Right-clicking the browser page while using the WatiN test recorder will present a list of options to assist with your test creation. These options will help you create a powerful WatiN script to drive the browser.

Figure 5-4 shows the options available when right clicking the browser window in the WatiN Recorder.

❑ **Visual Studio Web Testing.** The roots of Visual Studio web tests started in 1999, when Microsoft introduced a tool called the Web Application Stress tool, also known as Homer. Homer recorded a browser session that was saved to a Visual Basic 6 script using COM Automation to drive Internet Explorer. Although it's not the same code base, and does not remotely generate code similar to Homer, the concept of recording the browser session is the same.

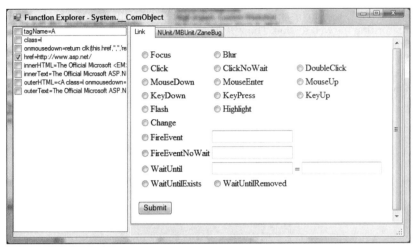

Figure 5-4: WatiN Recorder options to assist in creating tests

The ability to create Visual Studio web tests has bounced around between different versions of Visual Studio, but currently makes its home in Visual Studio Team System Test Edition (2005, 2008, and 2010). Visual Studio Team System Test (VSTS) allows creation of unit tests — test types such as web tests, load tests, manual tests, and database tests are introduced in this version of Visual Studio. Web tests are very closely linked to load tests which will be covered in depth in Chapter 8.

In this section you'll be introduced to the web testing tool included in VSTS, and cover many of the concepts that are supported. It is our intention that you focus more on the concepts and not how VSTS implements the concept. It's important to understand that the concept exists and relate the implementation to tools in the future. Having a firm knowledge of the concepts will allow you to transfer the knowledge to different tools. New web tests can be added to test projects from the Test Menu, and then by selecting "New Test." Figure 5-5 shows the Visual Studio Team System Team Edition Add test screen.

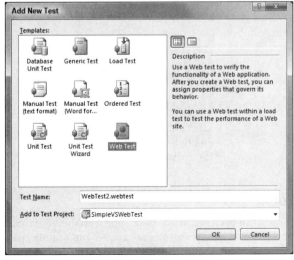

Figure 5-5: Creating a new test

When you select a web test, an instance of Internet Explorer will appear with a toolbar that contains the options for recording the web session. The VSTS web test browser tools are very simplistic, allowing for pausing of the current test, stopping the test entirely, inserting a comment between requests and deletion of requests. Although simplistic, this tool is very powerful and can be of great use when having to create web tests for a system where testing was an afterthought. Having the ability to pause the testing session and delete responses are there in case you make a mistake. With early test recorders, if you made a mistake you need to start over. Figure 5-6 shows the web test browser tools docked on the right side of the browser.

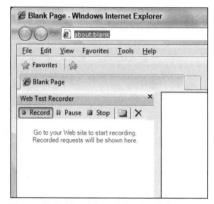

Figure 5-6: The Visual Studio Web
Test Recorder

Navigation Requests

After the web test has been created and the browser appears with the tools available, as shown in Figure 5-7, your navigation requests will be recorded. When you are finished with the testing session, you can either close the browser or click the Stop button available on the web test toolbar.

After the session is stopped, the results from the test will appear in Visual Studio as a new web test. Figure 5-7 shows the requests that were generated when navigating to www.google.com and searching for "ASP.NET."

Figure 5-7: List of HTTP Requests
for a Visual Studio Web Test

The Web Test Editor

After the requests to a site have been recorded, they appear in the Visual Studio web test editor. Figure 5-8 the web test editor is where your tests are added and maintained. Figure 5-9 is a contexts menu containing options specific to the test such as allowing for tests to be run, credentials to be set, and the parameterization of the web server URL.

Figure 5-8: Visual Studio Web Test Editor

Figure 5-9: Options
obtained by right clicking
a Visual Studio Web Test

Validation Rules

A web test *Validation Rule* will perform a validation on a request to ensure that the request is valid. Think of a Validation Rule as a type of assert statement that are special to VSTS.

Validation Rules are used to determine whether the response in the test is valid; generally Validation Rules check for the existence of an HTML control or that an HTML control is set to a certain value. By default, web tests will also determine if a step in the test failed based on the HTTP status code it returned. Any return code between 400 and 599 is considered a failure. Web tests are great at finding 404 Page Not Found errors. If you forget to include an image or a script file in the application you are testing, then the web test will fail because of the 404 error.

Figure 5-10 shows the six different types of Validation VSTS supports for you to ensure your website is performing as expected:

❑ **Form Field.** This type of Validation Rule will verify the existence and value of a form value on the request.

❑ **Find Text.** The Find Text Validation Rule will parse the request and search for the text specified in the Validation Rule. The Find Text Validation Rule will take plain text or a Regular Expression. The Pass If Text Found property allows the test to pass if text is not found. For example, creating

153

a FindText rule with the {FindText="Error" and PassIfTextFound="false"} and set for the properties will ensure that the word error is not found on the page.

❑ **Maximum Request Time.** This Validation Rule will ensure that a response does not exceed a maximum value in milliseconds set on the rule. If the maximum time is exceeded then this Validation Rule fails.

❑ **Required Attribute Value.** This type of Validation Rule verifies the existence of a specified HTML tag that contains an attribute that is set on the rule.

❑ **Required Tag.** This Validation Rule simply tests the occurrence of a specified HTML tag. The minimum number of occurrences property on this Validation Rule can be tested to ensure that a HTML tag appears a certain number of times in the request.

❑ **Response URL.** The Response URL Validation Rule verifies that the response URL is the same as the recorded response.

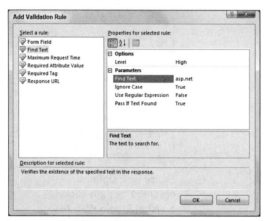

Figure 5-10: Adding a Validation Rule to a Visual Studio Web Test

Inserting Comments

Comments are a great way of keeping track of what is happening during the test. The VSTS web test editor does not list the requests in a very descriptive way. Having the ability to stick comments between the requests will greatly increase the readability of the web test in the VSTS web test editor. We have talked about the importance of only testing one behavior per test. Sometimes when testing an application that was not designed with testing in mind, we are forced to test more than one behavior. It's important no matter which tool you are using, to keep track of exactly what is happening during the test. As illustrated in Figure 5-11 and Figure 5-12, there is nothing complex about comments, the interface provided only allows you to create text about the current request you are working with.

Figure 5-11: Adding a comment to the web test

Figure 5-12: Comment in VSTS web test

Properties of a Request

Each request in the web test contains a set of properties that provide close control of how the request acts. Figure 5-13 shows the properties that are available for a web request.

❑ **Cache Control.** Cache control should be set to true if you would like the web test to simulate the standard browser caching behavior. For example, resources on the website you are testing such as shared images will only be requested once when the cache control property is set to true. The default value of this property is false, but it's important for tests to imitate a user session. Setting the cache control property to false can be useful for load testing, but for functional tests it should be set to true.

❑ **Encoding.** This property sets the text encoding format to be used for the requests. The default is set to UTF-8.

❑ **Expected HTTP Status Code.** This property will allow the web test to validate against the HTTP status code that is returned, for example if you need to test specific HTTP error codes, such as a 404 page not found error.

❑ **Follow Redirects.** This property allows the web test to follow HTTP redirects (300–307 HTTP status codes). The default option is true, and in most cases you should leave this setting to true. There may be cases where your site is performing complex redirects and you need to validate the redirect response; you can set this option to false.

❑ **Parse Dependent Requests.** This property determines whether the internal requests that belong to the response page should be executed and parsed or just ignored. Downloading of images is an example of a dependent request, and if this property is set to false then images would not be downloaded. As stated before, VSTS web tests should imitate a browser as closely as possible, so this property should be set to true.

❑ **Record Results.** The record results property is a property that is used only for load tests. If set to true, the response timings will be included in the load test results.

❑ **Response Time Goal.** Another property that is only used for load testing, the response time goal is a goal set in seconds that the tester is expecting the website to respond in.

❑ **Think Time.** A think time is an amount of time to pause on the page before processing the next request.

❑ **Timeout.** The timeout property of requests is the maximum time in seconds to wait for the response before causing a timeout and marking the test as a failure.

❑ **Method.** Transport method of the request, either GET or PostMethod

❑ **Version.** The version property sets the HTTP version to be used in the request. This option can be used to simulate a user hitting your site using an older version of the HTTP protocol. For most tests, this test should remain at the default of 1.1.

❑ **URL.** This is the URL of the request.

Two properties that are important to single out in this section are the timeout and think time properties. A think time is an amount of time to pause on the page before processing the next request. Think times are an important concept to keep in mind when creating load tests. If you decide to add a think time at this level, ensure that the request timeout is not exceeded.

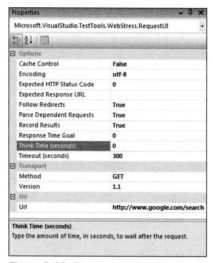

Figure 5-13: Properties of a web test

Context Parameters

How tests are run vary greatly from organization to organization. There are dramatic differences from only running manual tests, or the tests only run on one developer's machine, to having a machine dedicated for testing and builds. Ideally, organizations will have a continuous integration process in place, but how do you manage settings that are specific for a test to run? We have talked about how unit tests should not require any external dependencies, but functional tests are a bit different, often requiring settings that are specific to the environment where the testing is taking place.

A common dependency for web testing is the web server, which we have introduced you to (the Cassini pattern) to help avoid having to set this type of external dependency. In some organizations the web server dependency will be required. VSTS provides a concept called Context Parameters to help manage this requirement. Think of Context Parameters as variables that can be easily changed depending on which environment the test is being run in. A common example would be the web server URL. When you create the test the WebServer1 Context Parameter may be `http://localhost`, but when the test is run on a different machine it may be `http://CompanyTestServer`. Figure 5-14 shows the interface that allows you to change the parameterized values of a web test. In this case, the test is being pointed to `www.google.com`.

Running a Web Test

After you have created your VSTS web tests, click the Run Test button (the icon with the green arrow pointing to the right) on the Web Test editor toolbar, and your test will run. A new tab will appear inside Visual Studio that contains the results of your test. Figure 5-15 is the final product of the simple example of navigating to Google and searching for ASP.NET.

Figure 5-14: Changing the value of a parameterized option in a Web Test

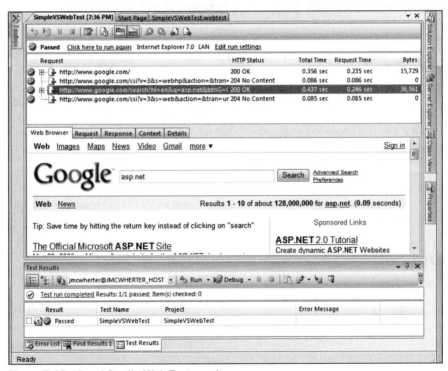

Figure 5-15: Visual Studio Web Test results

Because testing procedures differ greatly from organization to organization, VSTS provides an interface so web tests can be run from the command line. Figure 5-16 shows the call to mstext.exe, specifying the web test name to accomplish this task.

Figure 5-16: Calling mstest.exe to execute a web test

VSTS *Final Thoughts*

The ability to record a browser session, set a few Validation Rules, and then play the session back is a very powerful tool to have in your testing toolbox. Previously in this chapter we discussed the downfalls of automation tools, but VSTS does a good job of keeping tests organized and easy to change in the future. If a web test needs to change, the VSTS web test editor toolbar includes options to delete responses, change Validation Rules, and even insert new browser recording sessions. Behind the screens, the automated scripts are generated as C# code, and if you choose, you can generate the code for each script and make modifications to the test script code.

We've only scratched the surface features that are included in VSTS web tests, but have provided an overview of web testing concepts you can apply to other web testing tools.

Selenium Suite

The Selenium Project is a suite of open source tools used for automated testing of web UIs on multiple platforms. Selenium has the ability to drive Internet Explorer, Firefox, Opera, and Safari. Selenium uses JavaScript and Iframes to embed the test automation engine into the browser. Because browsers handle JavaScript differently, the automation engine is tweaked to support browsers on Windows, Mac, and Linux. The Selenium Project was originally started by Jason Huggins of Thoughtworks in 2004 while he was working on an internal time and expense application.

The Selenium suite has became a very popular option for web UI testing because of the support for multiple browsers and support for creating tests in many languages such as C#, Java, Python, and Ruby. The three parts of the Selenium Project we are going to discuss are the Selenium IDE, Selenium Remote Control (RC), and Selenium Grid.

In 2004 when Selenium was first created, there were only a few record/playback tools on the market. Major tools such as Quick Test Pro and Test Director, were developed by the company Mercury, who were purchased by Hewlett-Packard in 2006. The tools from Mercury were expensive, complicated to learn, and the scripts were hard to maintain.

As an astute chemist may have already noticed, the Selenium element is the antidote to mercury poisoning; the name of the Selenium software suite may have been chosen for this reason.

Selenium IDE

The Selenium IDE is a Firefox plug in that it can be used for creating and running Selenium tests to drive the web browser. The Selenium IDE has support for recording a browser session, setting break points/stepping over test code, and the playback of tests. Figure 5-17 shows a simple test that involves navigating to Google and typing in **ASP.NET**.

Figure 5-17: Selenium IDE Firefox plugin

Looking at the image in Figure 5-17, you may be thinking, "Would I use the Selenium IDE to run a large test suite with hundreds of tests?" The answer is no — that's where the other tools in the Selenium suite come into play. When you have a number of tests, more than likely you will run the tests in an xUnit testing framework, such as nUnit with references to the Selenium Client Libraries. The Selenium IDE is great for recording the session and saving the output into an xUnit test. Figure 5-18 shows the languages that the Selenium IDE will export the tests into.

Selenium RC

The Selenium Remote Control (RC) contains the Selenium server which acts as a proxy for the browser and will run your Selenium tests. The Selenium tools included in Selenium RC will automatically launch and kill browsers as the tests require. The following code creates a connection to the Selenium server (which in this example is running on the local host) and will navigate to www.google.com:

```
ISelenium browser = new DefaultSelenium("localhost", 4444,
    "*firefox", "http://www.google.com/");
```

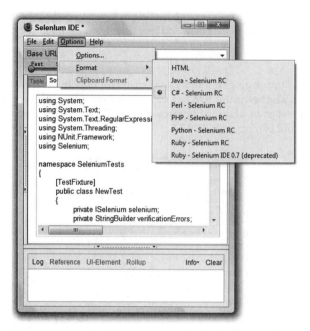

Figure 5-18: Setting the language the Selenium test is rendered in

The Selenium RC makes it possible to write automated tests for a web application in just about any programming language. Having this ability allows Selenium to be integrated into existing test frameworks easily.

It's important to note that the Selenium RC comes in two parts, the server portion and the client libraries that allow you to create Selenium tests in your language of choice.

Selenium Server

The server portion of Selenium RC is written in Java and requires version 1.5.0 or higher of the Java Runtime Environment. The server accepts commands for the browser via HTTP and will launch browsers and follow the HTTP commands passed to the server:

```
Usage: java -jar selenium-server.jar [-interactive] [options]
```

Option	Description
port <nnnn>	Port number the Selenium server should use (default 4444)
multiWindow	Puts the server into a mode where the test website executes in a separate window, and Selenium supports frames.
forcedBrowserMode <browser>	Sets the browser mode (e.g. "*firefox") for all sessions, no matter what is passed.

Option	Description
browserSessionReuse	Stops the initialization and creation of the browser between tests.
htmlSuite <browser> <startURL> <suiteFile> <resultFile>	Runs a single HTML Selenese (Selenium Core) suite and then exits immediately using the specified browser (e.g. "*firefox") on the specified URL (e.g. "http://www.google.com"). You need to specify the absolute path to the HTML test suite as well as the path to the HTML results file you'll generate.

Selenium Client Libraries

To make writing tests easier, the Selenium Project currently provides client drivers for Python, Ruby, .NET, Perl, Java, and PHP. The Java driver can also be used with JavaScript (via the Rhino engine).

```
[Test]
public void Should_Click_Search_On_Google_And_Return_Results_For_AspNet()
{
    ISelenium browser = new DefaultSelenium("localhost", 4444, "*firefox",
        "http://www.google.com/");

    browser.Start();
    browser.Open("/");
    browser.Type("q", "asp.net");
    browser.Click("btnG");
    browser.WaitForPageToLoad("30000");

    Assert.IsTrue(browser.IsTextPresent("The Official Microsoft ASP.NET Site"));
    browser.Close();
}
```

The Selenium core uses a language named Selenese to drive the browser. The Selenium RC client library is a wrapper to this language, and will translate commands created in your favorite language into Selenese to be transported via http. Using the Selenium RC client libraries, makes it so the end user of the APIs does not need to learn the specific syntax to Selense, but it is useful to learn about how Selenese and its commands work. The commands come in three types:

❑ **Actions.** These are commands that manipulate the state of the application such as click this link.

❑ **Accessors.** These look at the state of the application and store the results.

❑ **Assertions.** These verify that the state of the application conforms to what is expected. Selenium has three types of modes for assertions:

    ❑ **Assert.** When assert fails the test is aborted.

    ❑ **Verify.** When verify fails the test will continue to execute, but the failure will be logged.

    ❑ **Wait For.** Wait For assertions wait for a condition to become true. These types of assertions are very useful for testing AJAX.

Element Locators

When creating automated UI web tests, a good portion of your time will be spent using the testing framework to locate tags in the returned HTML to verify whether the test has passed. The Selenium RC client library has a concept of Element Locators that tells Selenium which HTML element a command refers to. Understanding how to specify Selenium Element Locators will help you build tests that are reliable and are easy to maintain if the application changes. Currently Selenium supports the following strategies for locating elements:

❑ **Identifier.** Selects the element with the specified id attribute. If no match is found, selects the first element whose name attribute is id.

❑ **Id.** Selects the element with the specified id attribute.

```
selenium.click("id=btnClickMe");
```

❑ **Name.** Selects the element with the specified name attribute.

```
selenium.click("name=myButton");
```

❑ **Dom.** Selects the element by evaluating the specified string. Using this type of locator allows JavaScript to be entered to traverse the DOM.

```
selenium.click("dom=document.images[2]" );
selenium.click("dom= function GetMyLink() { return document.links[4]; };
GetMyLink();");
```

❑ **XPath.** XPath is a language for addressing parts of an XML document, designed to be used by both XSLT and XPointer:

```
selenium.click("xpath=//img[@alt='Alt text of my image']");
```

❑ **Link.** Selects the anchor tag element which contains the following text:

```
selenium.click("link=My Link");
```

❑ **CSS.** Selects the element using CSS selectors:

```
selenium.click("css=div#MyButton");
```

Below is a table defining some of the methods you can use with Selenium together with the selectors above in order to identify different parts of the web page

Command	Description
captureScreenshot("File name")	Captures a PNG screenshot to the specified file.
Check("Locator")	Checks a toggle-button (checkbox/radio).
click("Locator")	Clicks on a link, button, checkbox, or radio button.
close()	Simulates the user clicking the "close" button in the title bar of a pop-up window or tab.
doubleClick("Locator")	Double-clicks a link, button, checkbox, or radio button.

Command	Description
getAlert()	Retrieves the message of a JavaScript alert generated during the previous action, or fails if there were no alerts.
getAllButtons()	Returns the IDs of all buttons on the page.
getAllFields()	Returns the IDs of all input fields on the page.
getAllLinks()	Returns the IDs of all links on the page.
getBodyText()	Gets the entire text of the page.
getTable("Table Cell Address")	Gets the text from a cell of a table.
getText("Locator")	Gets the text of an element.
getTitle()	Gets the title of the current page.
goBack()	Simulates the user clicking the "back" button on their browser.
isAlertPresent()	Has an alert occurred?
isChecked("Locator")	Gets whether a toggle-button (checkbox/radio) is checked.
isTextPresent("Pattern")	Determines whether some option in a drop-down menu is selected.
isVisible("Locator")	Verifies that the specified text pattern appears somewhere on the rendered page shown to the user.
open("URL")	Determines if the specified element is visible.
openWindow("URL","WindowID")	Opens a URL in the test frame.
refresh()	Opens a pop-up window (if a window with that ID isn't already open).
Start()	Launches the browser with a new Selenium session.
Stop()	Ends the test session, killing the browser.
submit("Form Locator")	Submits the specified form.
waitForCondition("JS","Timeout")	Runs the specified JavaScript snippet repeatedly until it evaluates to "true".
waitForFrameToLoad("Frame Address","Timeout")	Waits for a new frame to load.
waitForPageToLoad("Timeout")	Waits for a new page to load.
waitForPopUp("WindowID","Timeout")	Waits for a pop-up window to appear and load up.

Selenium Grid

Testing a Web UI with automation is a slow process. Automated UI tests are much slower than unit tests, and as you build a large test suite the time it takes to execute all the tests could range from a few hours to a few days. We have learned that the longer it takes to run a suite of tests, the less frequently they will be run. Selenium Grid is a tool that allows you to run Selenium tests in parallel, cutting down the time required for the entire test suite to run. Selenium Grid runs on top of the Selenium RC, and can be configured to run your tests on multiple machines.

Figure 5-19 is a representation of a traditional Selenium test. A test script in a framework such as nUnit makes a call to Selenium RC, which in turn spawns a new web browser with the application under test and then the test steps are executed. Selenium RC is slow at driving the browser and in most situations will be the bottleneck of the test suite. There is also a limitation of the number of concurrent tests that can be run on the same Selenium RC instance before the Selenium RC instance becomes unstable. The Selenium team currently recommends no more than six tests with a single instance of Selenium RC. These limitations can cause tests suites to not run as effectively as they could.

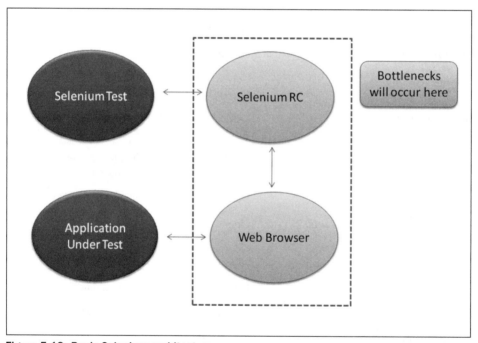

Figure 5-19: Basic Selenium architecture

Selenium Grid builds upon the traditional Selenium test setup by adding a component called the Selenium Hub. The Selenium Hub exposes an external interface that is the same as the Selenium Remote Control, meaning an existing Selenium test suite that is using the Selenium RC can be switched to the Selenium Grid without any code changes. The Selenium Hub will allocate instances of Selenium RC for each incoming test. Figure 5-20 is a representation of using the Selenium Grid.

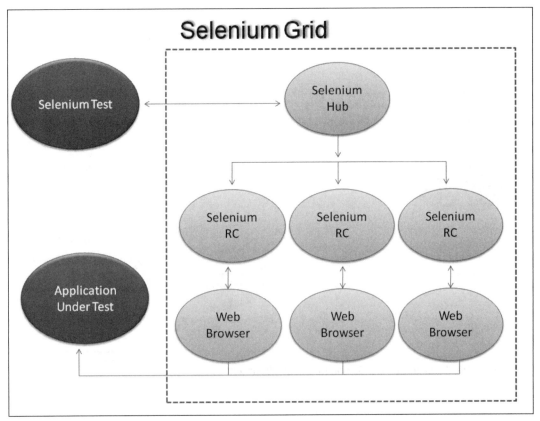

Figure 5-20: Selenium Grid architecture

Another great feature of Selenium Grid is that tests can be configured to run against a specific environment. Selenium Grid Environments can be configured in the grid_configuration.yml file found in the root directory of the Selenium Grid binary file. To take advantage of specific environments in the Selenium Grid, an existing test that created an instance of Firefox could be modified to only test with Firefox on Windows. Figure 5-21 is a visualization of how a Selenium Grid environment may look.

An example of an existing Selenium test:

```
new DefaultSelenium("localhost", 4444, **'*firefox'**, 'http://www.Google.com');
```

An example of the same tests configured to use an instance of Selenium Grid that only runs Firefox on Windows:

```
new DefaultSelenium("localhost", 4444, **'Firefox on Windows'**,
    'http://www.Google.com);
```

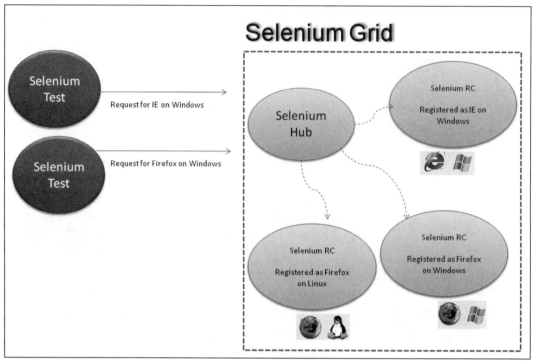

Figure 5-21: An example of a Selenium Grid Environment

Figure 5-22 shows what the entire Selenium suite looks like working together.

UI Testing Patterns

To help with UI testing, there are a number of different patterns which people follow to help organize their testing.

The Test Monkey

A *test monkey* is a test whose only purpose is randomness. Test monkeys will enter random strings into text boxes and then randomly click on the screen. When using a test monkey, your hope is that it will help flush out those quirky integration issues. Test monkeys may also be called stochastic tests, which is really the same testing pattern, but sounds more technical. Test monkeys are often used for destructive testing. There are two types of test monkey patterns: the dumb test monkey and the smart test monkey.

Dumb test monkey tests are black box tests. They don't know how the application works and they only subject the applications to random user activity. Dumb test monkeys may not realize they caused an error, but are valuable because of their randomness.

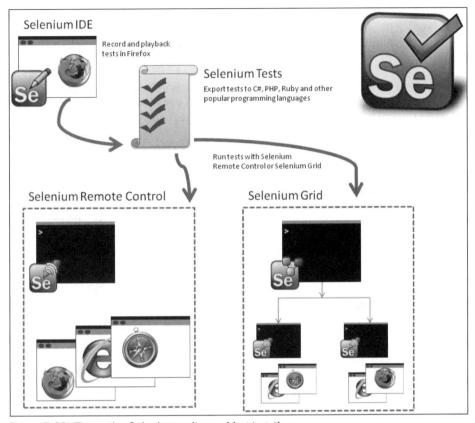

Figure 5-22: The entire Selenium suite working together

Smart test monkeys are not as random. Their inputs are generated from data that is reflective of user data. This data is often gathered from log files or data that has been obfuscated from the database.

You may have heard of the infinite monkey theorem: the idea is that a monkey (or other object perform-ing the same task) hitting keys on a typewriter at random for an infinite amount of time has a very good chance of typing a particular text, such as the complete works of William Shakespeare. The term "test monkey" is based on this theorem.

Cassini Testing Pattern

As you may have noticed, the samples shown previously are testing websites via external URLs. You learned in previous chapters that tests should be self-contained, but with the pattern used earlier, are your tests really self-contained? The answer is, not really; the tests are dependent on the external URL functioning correctly. When testing the UI, the URL should not be the production URL. This would mean that your set of UI tests only runs against the production system, which goes against everything we've been talking about thus far. The URL of the application being tested needs to be some type of test machine that you have control over. Most of the time, teams have a system just for this: some call it a "staging system," some call it a "test system," and some teams even bring up a web server on the build/ test machine to host the application under test.

This pattern of UI testing raises issues. How do you copy the latest version of your app to the test server? Do you really want to install a web server on the build server? Sure there are solutions to these problems, but these issues can be avoided by using a UI design pattern that brings up a small, lightweight web server for each UI test that is being run.

In Visual Studio 2005 you saw the first version of Cassini. Cassini is the lightweight web server that is used for debugging ASP.NET applications in the IDE. Both Visual Studio 2005 and 2008 come with two Cassini parts: Cassini.exe and Cassini.dll. For your purposes here, you'll only need to work with the dll.

You'll want to bring up an instance of Cassini for each test fixture, run your tests, and then destroy the instance of Cassini. It's important to note that you're only bringing up an instance of Cassini once per test fixture and not per test. This is because Cassini requires a bit of overhead to start up, and you don't really need to bring one up for each test.

The next listing creates an instance of the Cassini web server, tests a web, and then destroys the instance of the Cassini web server. In this example, you'll see that the Cassini web server is created in the TestFixtureSetup method, and destroyed in the TestFixtureTearDown method. The path for where the web application is stored is set in the pathToAppToTest variable:

```
using System;
using NUnit.Framework;
using Cassini;
using System.IO;
using System.Diagnostics;
using WatiN.Core.Interfaces;
using WatiN.Core;

namespace CassiniDemo
{
    [TestFixture]
    public class CassiniPatternTests
    {
        private Server m_webServer;
        private string m_serverURL;

        [TestFixtureSetUp]
        public void Setup()
        {
            DirectoryInfo appBasePath = new DirectoryInfo(
                AppDomain.CurrentDomain.BaseDirectory);

            string serverPhysicalPath =  appBasePath.Parent.FullName;
            int webServerPort = 8090;
            string virtualDirectory = "/";
            string pathToAppToTest = "AppToTest";

            try
            {
                m_webServer = new Server(webServerPort, virtualDirectory,
                    serverPhysicalPath);

                m_serverURL = String.Format("http://localhost:{0}/{1}",
```

```
                    webServerPort,pathToAppToTest);

            m_webServer.Start();

            Debug.WriteLine(String.Format("Started Port:{0} VD:{1} PD{2}",
                webServerPort, virtualDirectory, serverPhysicalPath));
        }
        catch (Exception ex)
        {
            Debug.WriteLine(string.Format("Error starting web service {0}",
                ex.Message));
        }
    }

    [TestFixtureTearDown]
    public void TearDown()
    {
        try
        {
            if (m_webServer != null)
            {
                m_webServer.Stop();
                m_webServer = null;
            }
        }
        catch (Exception ex)
        {
            Debug.WriteLine(string.Format("Tearddown error {0}", ex.Message));
        }
    }

    [Test]
    public void Should_Load_The_Default_Page_And_Find_Results_For_AspNet()
    {
        string expectedText = "The Official Microsoft ASP.NET Site";
        string urlToTest = string.Format("{0}/{1}",
            m_serverURL, "default.aspx");

        using (IBrowser ie = BrowserFactory.Create(
            BrowserType.InternetExplorer))
        {
            ie.GoTo(urlToTest);
            Assert.IsTrue(ie.ContainsText(expectedText));
        }
    }
}
}
```

This example uses WatiN to test the page for a specific test, but other UI testing methods could be used as well, such as parsing the HTML manually.

It's important to note some of the lines found in the previous listing. This is the code that creates the instance of the Cassini web server and then starts the service:

```
m_webServer = new Server(webServerPort, virtualDirectory, serverPhysicalPath);
m_webServer.Start();
```

What is this testing pattern getting you? Using this pattern will ensure that your tests are self-contained and that the machines where the tests are run will not require that a web server be installed. Using this pattern will also resolve the need to create complex build scripts that copy the application you are testing to another machine. Another nice side effect of this pattern is not having to worry about networking issues. Many times when testing the UI, tests will fail due to network latency or network errors that are out of the developer's hands and are not really considered errors.

Many owners of the build machine believe that it should be kept as clean as possible, meaning that no third-party software should be installed on the machine. This forces developers to include any third-party binary files with their application; if they don't, the build server will not have these files, and therefore the build will break. For some build machine owners, this includes web servers.

What Goes into a Good UI Test?

In the previous chapter you learned what makes a good test. Many of these same principles apply, but there are a few key concepts pertaining to UI testing that we haven't covered yet

Tests should be created using the same concepts that an end user would see. When creating UI tests, think in terms of behaviors that encompass the problem domain, instead of thinking of the IDs of text boxes and edit controls. Think of these tests as small unit tests that test the behavior of a feature.

Randomness

You may have already come to the realization that when you are testing UIs, you have to think outside-the-box. Great testers think outside-the-box all the time, which brings us to the topic of randomness.

When creating UI tests, it's important to randomize how the data is entered into the UI. Let's take a step back and think about this for a moment: in Chapter 2 you learned that tests should be repeatable, but if you randomize how the data is entered into the UI, is the test going to be repeatable? The answer is yes. If, eventually, a test fails, that test will be run again in the test cycle, so therefore it is repeatable. Having a log of what the test has done is invaluable for re-creating the random test that failed.

What sort of tasks should be random? The quick answer is behaviors. For example, you could create automated UI tests that drive the user interface into the browser using a mouse, but then also create tests that drive the browser using keyboard navigation. Then, mix up the way they are run. Having both sets of tests will help find those weird integration issues that are extremely difficult to track down later. On smaller systems, this type of random testing may not be needed; if you are only testing a few pages your tests will run fast enough so that you don't need to choose which method of accessing the UI you need. On larger systems, where tests may take hours or even days to run, it's very beneficial to have the ability to test behaviors randomly to help cut the time in which the tests run down.

How Random Should You Be?

User interface bugs have a very bad habit of hiding, meaning that the quirks of the interface are hard to flush out. Most developers have witnessed the weird types of integration issues that users report. Most of the time, these issues are hard to track down mainly because the user neglected to inform you of a key piece of data, such as they were using the tab key to navigate form fields when the error occurred.

There is a level of randomness for each application that is acceptable, and that level is dependent on the application. Testing random characters and mouse vs. keyboard movement randomly is acceptable for most applications, where randomly clicking around on the screen is not for most applications.

Special Characters

As a developer, we're sure you have manually tested web forms by entering garbage text such as "foo," into the fields. Tests such as these do not fully exercise your application. Good UI tests involve entering copious amounts of text, such as Lorem Ipsum, as well as a sample of the full range of alpha numeric characters. Characters such as <>?/_+ are great at breaking applications. You'll test special characters and large amounts of text for edge cases where the application has issues accepting these types of text inputs. You will be surprised at the amount of errors you will find when exercising these types of tests.

The next listing creates a test that enters three paragraphs of Lorum Ipsum into the text search text field on www.google.com. After the text is entered, the tests verify that at least 10 results were found.

Notice the GetLorumIpsum function. This function takes in an integer value of the number of paragraphs you would like to generate. As your application gains more tests, this function could be abstracted into a Test Helper class, because multiple test fixtures should be using this concept:

```
using NUnit.Framework;
using WatiN.Core;
using WatiN.Core.Interfaces;
using System.Text;

namespace LorumIpsumTest
{
    [TestFixture]
    public class LorumIpsumTest
    {
        private const int MAX_PARAGRAPHS = 3;

        [Test]
        public void Should_Enter_Large_Amount_Of_Text_On_Google_Search()
        {
            using (IBrowser ie = BrowserFactory.Create(BrowserType
                .InternetExplorer))
            {
                ie.GoTo("http://www.google.com");
                ie.TextField(Find.ByName("q")).Value = GetLorumIpsum
                    (MAX_PARAGRAPHS);
                ie.Button(Find.ByName("btnG")).Click();
                Assert.IsTrue(ie.ContainsText("Results 1-10 "));
            }
        }

        private string GetLorumIpsum(int numParagraphs)
        {
            StringBuilder lorumIpsum = new StringBuilder();

            if (numParagraphs > 0 )
            {
                lorumIpsum.Append("Lorem ipsum dolor adipiscing elit. Maecenas ");
                lorumIpsum.Append("eu nibh. tum in, aliquam at, massa. Maecenas");
                lorumIpsum.Append("non sapien et mauris tincidunt cursus. In hac");
                lorumIpsum.Append("ante ipsum primis in faucibus orci luctus et");
```

```
            lorumIpsum.Append("vehicula. Lorem ipsum dolor sit amet,");
            lorumIpsum.Append("nec felis ultricies venenatis. Ut mollis mi s");
            lorumIpsum.Append("eros. Suspendisse felis nunc, malesuada eu, ");
            lorumIpsum.Append("dolor at magna.\n");
        }

        if (numParagraphs > 1)
        {
            lorumIpsum.Append("Fusce mauris enim, semper quis, accumsan eget");
            lorumIpsum.Append("rutrum condimentum orci. Duis libero. Suspen");
            lorumIpsum.Append("Donec gravida nulla vel felis elementum lobo");
            lorumIpsum.Append("ultrices non, ipsum. Fusce et arcu non urna");
            lorumIpsum.Append("elementum eu, semper a, mauris. Suspendisse");
            lorumIpsum.Append("aliquet. Vestibulum gravida, ipsum id pretiu");
            lorumIpsum.Append("euismod neque nunc ut erat. Pellentesque habi");
            lorumIpsum.Append("fames ac turpis egestas. Nunc hendrerit elem");
            lorumIpsum.Append("interdum mi sit amet justo. Etiam augue. Ph\n");
        }

        if (numParagraphs > 2)
        {
            lorumIpsum.Append("Praesent id enim. Praesent tortor. Phasellus" );
            lorumIpsum.Append("convallis in, imperdiet eu, eleifend vel, nu" );
            lorumIpsum.Append("elementum viverra. Integer nec nibh ut erat" );
            lorumIpsum.Append("ullamcorper. Praesent porta tellus mauris. \n");
        }

        return lorumIpsum.ToString();
    }
  }
}
```

The next listing is very similar in concept to the Lorem Ipsum test. If more than one test fixture calls the GetSpecialCharacters function, then this method should be abstracted into a test helper class:

```
using NUnit.Framework;
using WatiN.Core;
using WatiN.Core.Interfaces;
using System.Text;

namespace SimpleWatinTest
{
    [TestFixture]
    public class SpecialCharacterTest
    {
        [Test]
        public void Should_Enter_Special_Characters_On_Google_Search()
        {
            using (IBrowser ie = BrowserFactory.Create(
                BrowserType.InternetExplorer))
            {
                ie.GoTo("http://www.google.com");
                ie.TextField(Find.ByName("q")).Value = GetSpecialCharacters();
```

```
            System.Threading.Thread.Sleep(6000);
            ie.Button(Find.ByName("btnG")).Click();
            Assert.IsTrue(ie.ContainsText("Results 1 – 10 "));
        }
    }

    private string GetSpecialCharacters()
    {
        return @"""""!'@#$%^&*(){}[]-=_+:;<>,.?/|\~`";
    }
    }
}
```

When testing your application for special characters, don't only test characters, but think outside-the-box and also test character patterns. Special character testing is a great time to test for cross-site scripting attacks, as shown next. We will cover cross-site scripting attacks thoroughly in Chapter 10, but for now it's important to know that a cross-site scripting attack is where a user of your application injects malicious HTML or JavaScript into form fields.

```
using NUnit.Framework;
using WatiN.Core;
using WatiN.Core.Interfaces;
using System.Text;

namespace XSSTest
{
    [TestFixture]
    public class XSSTest
    {
        [Test]
        public void Should_Check_For_XSS_Attack_Google_Search()
        {
          using (IBrowser ie = BrowserFactory.Create(BrowserType.InternetExplorer))
          {
                ie.GoTo("http://www.google.com");
                ie.TextField(Find.ByName("q")).Value = GetXSSAttack();
                ie.Button(Find.ByName("btnG")).Click();
                Assert.IsTrue(ie.ContainsText("Results 1 – 10 "));
          }
        }

        private string GetXSSAttack()
        {
            return "<script>alert('xss attack');</script>";
        }
    }
}
```

This is a very simplistic cross-site scripting attack. There are many different ways to inject scripts into a page and Chapter 10 will cover these methods. For the moment, please note that the test in the previous listing is just a simple example, and more thorough tests encapsulating the techniques discussed in Chapter 10 should be used as true cross-site scripting tests.

Tests Should Be Focused

It's very important to stress (again) the fact that developers and testers should be creating small tests. As a rule of thumb, tests should fit inside your head, meaning the code for the test methods should never be physically longer than the size of your head. Another good example would be that tests should fit on a cocktail napkin.

When using the record/playback method for automated UI testing, tests can become very large. This is a common code smell, leading you to realize that it's time to refactor the test into smaller pieces. Also, it's more than likely that there are sections of the recorded test that can be reused.

Along with test patterns, there are also a number of other tools and frameworks which are designed to help drive the browser.

Automating the UI as an Object Model

Although the first approach is good for single isolated tests, it is not very scalable when it comes to full UI testing. The main problems are that the tests are difficult to read because they are very tight in controlling the browser and the UI — this means the actual test is hidden behind this. Secondly, if you need to make a change, then you will need to reflect this in a lot of different places. Because of the browser control nature, you have to duplicate a lot of the steps.

The second approach is to treat the UI as an object model. The aim is abstraction. You want to abstract away from the underlying browser control and from interaction with the UI framework, such as WatiN. Instead, you want your tests to be interacting with objects with meaningful names and methods that in turn interact with the UI framework. Next you'll see how the previous test could be rewritten taking the object model approach. Notice that there is no mention of the browser, buttons, click events, or waiting for pages to finish loading. Instead, you'll talk in terms of how Google works. You create an instance of a Google object, you set the search term, and you call the Search method. You can then verify that the result contains the text you expect:

```
[Test]
public void Search_Google_For_ASPNet()
{
    using (Google google = new Google())
    {
        google.SearchTerm = "asp.net";
        google.Search();
        string expectedString = "The Official Microsoft ASP.NET Site"
        Assert.IsTrue(google.Result.Contains(expectedString));
    }
}
```

In terms of how the Google object was implemented, you'll see that it takes exactly the same code as you had written before but splits it into reusable methods. For example, in the constructor you initial the browser as the following:

```
public Google()
{
```

```
        ie = BrowserFactory.Create(BrowserType.InternetExplorer);
        ie.GoTo("http://www.google.com");
    }
```

In your search term and search method, you'll use exactly the same code that is used in previous examples, but provide more context to what it does by using a property and method:

```
public string SearchTerm
{
    set { ie.TextField(Find.ByName("q")).Value = value; }
}

public void Search()
{
    ie.Button(Find.ByName("btnG")).Click();
}
```

The advantage is improved readability and reusability. If Google changes, then you'll only have to change this layer and object model. As a result, your tests can remain untouched while your abstract object model changes to reflect this.

Creating UI Tests for Wrox Pizza

To demonstrate how to use the object model, you'll apply the patterns and concepts discussed in the Wrox Pizza store example. The aim is to create an object model and a test structure that will allow you to interact with the UI while achieving readable and maintainable tests.

Because you are interacting with the UI, it means you need to have the UI hosted and running. As such, you will take advantage of the Cassini pattern, as we discussed in the patterns section, to host the website. This is different from unit tests, because with unit tests you only interact with objects. With UI tests you are interacting with the actual application.

For this application, you are going to create a CassiniWebServer class, which will have the responsibility of starting and shutting down the web server. To do this, you will use the [TestFixtureSetUp] attribute, which is used to identify the method that should be executed before all the tests within that Test fixture are executed. As such, the website will be running before any tests are executed. When the tests have finished executing, the method with the attribute [TestFixtureTearDown] will be called. Here the test will stop and dispose of the server:

```
public abstract class CassiniWebServer
{
        [TestFixtureSetUp]
        public void Setup()
        {
            DirectoryInfo buildPath = new DirectoryInfo(Path
.GetDirectoryName(Assembly.GetExecutingAssembly().Location));
            string serverStartPath = buildPath.Parent.FullName;
            string virtualDirectory = "/";
            int port = 8090;
```

```
        CopyCassiniToBinDirectory(serverStartPath);

        try
        {
            server = new Server(port, virtualDirectory, serverStartPath);
            url = String.Format("http://localhost:{0}/", port);
            server.Start();

            Debug.WriteLine(String.Format("Web Server started. Port: {0}
Physical Directory: {1} @ {2}",
                port, serverStartPath, URL));
        }
        catch (Exception ex)
        {
            Debug.WriteLine(string.Format("Error starting web service {0}",
                ex.Message));
            throw;
        }
    }
}
```

As you want all your tests to take advantage of this functionality, your tests will inherit from the CassiniWebServer class. Because you've defined the attributes then these will also be inherited and executed as part of your tests. As such, your Test fixture would be defined as the following:

```
[TestFixture]
public class List_Products_On_Menu_Tests: CassiniWebServer
```

With this in place, you can start interacting with the website.

Creating Tests for Listing Products

When you have the server in place you can start interacting with the website via test automation. The first page you are going to be testing is the product menu as shown in Figure 5-23. This is an important feature within the application because you want to tell people what you offer. If this doesn't work, then it doesn't matter what else does or doesn't work as no-one would be able to progress past this.

The first issue you face when creating your tests is naming. With unit tests you could name the tests based on the particular class and method you were thinking about. With UI automation you need to name your tests differently because you are working at a higher level. We always name the tests based on the feature that is currently under test. For example, one of the test classes for the page would be called List_Products_On_Menu_Tests.

An example of a name for an actual test would be Products_Menu_Displays_All_Products_On_Webpage. This will cover the scenario and ensure that the page correctly contains all the products. Notice you are not testing that they are displaying correctly or in the correct position. Instead, you just want to ensure the data is being returned and rendered in some form.

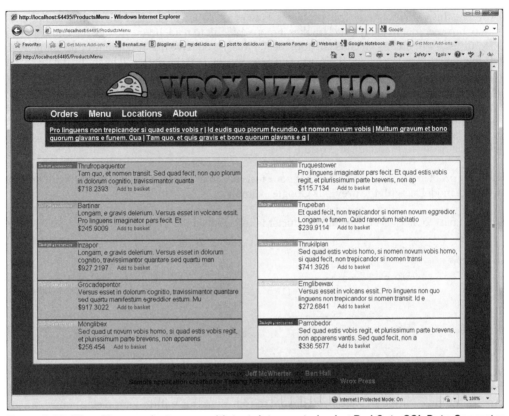

Figure 5-23: Wrox Pizza products page with test data created using Red Gate SQL Data Generator

At this point you can start writing your test. If you didn't follow the object model approach, your test would look like this:

```
[Test]
public void Products_Menu_Displays_All_Products_On_Webpage()
{
    using (IBrowser ie = BrowserFactory.Create(BrowserType.InternetExplorer))
    {
        ie.GoTo(URL);
        var link = ie.Link(Find.ByText("Menu"));
        link.Click();
        Assert.IsTrue(ie.ContainsText("Thrufropaquentor"));
    }
}
```

You'll start by first creating an instance of the browser and telling it to go to your URL. The URL is a variable set within the Cassini superclass when the server is started. After this, you'll need to link your menu to navigate to the correct section of your site to get to the particular page in question. After you click the link as a user would, you'll verify that a product name was returned in the text.

However, this test has a number of problems. First of all, what you are actually testing is hidden behind a lot of browser interactions, which makes it more difficult to read. If you change the name of the menu, all your tests will break, which is far from ideal. Finally, you have this random product name within your test that you're expecting to be there and you're expecting that the data will be in the database in the correct order every time. As a result, if anyone removes this item from the database then your tests will start to fail, even if no changes have been made to the code base. These types of problems are extremely difficult to identify and track down. The final problem is that when you're reading the test, you come across this magic string, which will be confusing and will not actually relate to anything with no indication as to how it got there. During the next sections we explain how you can solve these problems and make the tests easier to write, maintain, and read.

The first problem to solve is the fact that your tests are interacting directly with the browser instead of an object model as with the previous Google example.

The first part to model is the actual ProductsMenuPage itself:

```
public class ProductsMenuPage
{
    IBrowser Browser;
    public ProductsMenuPage(IBrowser browser)
    {
        Browser = browser;
    }
}
```

When this is constructed, you provide a browser instance that the object should use. The next thing you need to do is have access to the Menu link and the ability to click it. Because the same menu crosses multiple, different pages, you'll want to represent this within your tests.

As such, you'll create a Navigation object that will be responsible for maintaining navigation between different pages on your top menu bar. This object will have one method per link:

```
public class Navigation
{
    public Navigation(IBrowser browser)
    {
        Browser = browser;
    }    public ILink MenuPage
    {
        get {return GetLinkByText("Menu");}
    }

    private ILink GetLinkByText(string linkText)
    {
        return Browser.Link(Find.ByText(linkText));
    }
}
```

To improve readability, each page object model (e.g ProductsMenuPage) will inherit from the navigation object. In the constructor of ProductsMenuPage object, you can then click the link to navigate the browser:

```
public class ProductsMenuPage: Navigation
{
```

```
public ProductsMenuPage(IBrowser browser): base(browser)
{
    MenuPage.Click();
}
}
```

Note that you are also calling the base constructor of the Navigation object, therefore, the browser to allow us to identify the links.

The final stage after clicking the link is to verify that the correct text was displayed. Based on this, you simply need to request the Text from the browser and then expose it via a property:

```
public string Text
{
    get { return Browser.Text; }
}
```

However, you might want a more focused test to say that the product should appear where the products should be displayed and ensure the correct DIV tag. As such, you could have a different property that will only return the text that appears within the DIV based on the class assigned to it, which in this case is Products:

```
public string Products
{
    get { return Browser.Div(Find.ByClass("Products")).Text; }
}
```

You can now write your test based on your object model. Because you have the abstraction, your test is very streamlined. You simply need to initial the ProductsMenuPage object and then assert the response, as the click occurred within the constructor:

```
[Test]
public void Products_Menu_Displays_All_Products_On_Webpage()
{
    ProductsMenuPage page = new ProductsMenuPage(Browser);
    Assert.AreEqual("Thrufropaquentor", page.Text);
}
```

To improve the readability, additional logic related to opening and closing the browser should be abstracted into yet another superclass. As a result you now have an additional class which inherits from our CassiniWebServer:

```
public class BaseUITest: CassiniWebServer
```

Your TestFixture will inherit from the new BaseUITest class instead of the CassiniWebServer:

```
[TestFixture]
public class List_Products_On_Menu_Tests: BaseUITest
```

Within the BaseUITest, you take advantage of the methods attributed with [Setup] and [Teardown]. The setup and teardown methods are called before and after every test is started.

Now you can start the browser and point it at the homepage for the server:

```
public void BrowserSetup()
{
    Browser = BrowserFactory.Create(BrowserType.InternetExplorer);
    Browser.GoTo(URL);
}
```

Once we are done, we need to dispose the browser object which will close the browser logo.

```
public void BrowserTeardown()
{
    if(Browser != null)
        Browser.Dispose();
}
```

By this logic, in a superclass your tests don't need to be as concerned about ensuring that all the housekeeping activity needed to run the test has been done correctly. Instead, it is taken care of for you by the superclass.

You now have a set of structured classes. Our ProductsMenuPage object is the wrapper around our page and WatiN. This inherits from Navigation. In terms of tests, the List_Products_On_Menu_Tests inherits from BaseUITest which inherits from CassiniWebServer.

The final problem you have with the test is the magic string of the product you are expecting to be listed. So far you've also only tested one problem that appears, rather than all the products. From the test, you don't know if it is just that the test data only has one product or if the test is lacking in verification that it works.

To solve this problem, you want the tests to be in control of creating the test data.

Producing Test Data Using Test Data Builders

Test data builders is a pattern and approach you can take when you need to produce your test data for your tests. The aim is to use the data builder class to generate your objects that are pre-populated with known values that you can then use to verify that the system works as expected.

```
Product p = new Product();
p.BasePrice = 1.00;
p.Category = new ProductCategory { Description = "category" };
p.Description = "desc";
p.Name = "name";
p.PizzaTopping = true;
```

Instead of using the previous code, we could use the data builder that would look something like the following code. The advantage is that this can be designed to contain additional topics to help create the product object:

```
Product product = new ProductBuilder()
                .WithName("name")
                .WithDescription("desc")
                .WithPizzaTopping()
```

```
                    .InCategory("category")
                    .WithBasePrice(1.00);
```

This approach of chaining method calls together is known as creating a fluent interface. The aim of a fluent interface is to improve the readability of the code to make it into a more natural language. As covered in Chapter 2, Rhino Mocks takes advantage of fluent interfaces when defining stubs or mocks.

To build a fluent interface and test data builder, we first need a builder object — in this case ProductBuilder. However, if you notice, your ProductBuilder can be assigned to a variable of type Product. This is the key to the approach. You can use a separate object to return your constructed object. You might expect that WithBasePrice() actually does the construction and returns the Product object, however with fluent interfaces you are never sure which method will be called last or in what order. Some people would include a .Build() method at the end; however, this harms readability and usability of the API. The answer is that C# has a special method which you can define on a class, in this case ProductBuilder, which will be executed when the object is attempted to be stored in a variable. As such, at this point you can create your Product class and return it to be stored in the variable correctly. The method looks like this:

```
public static implicit operator Product(ProductBuilder builder)
{
    return builder.Build();
}
```

On your builder, you have a private method called Build that knows how to correctly construct the object. Notice there is an additional logic based on initializing the category:

```
private Product Build()
{
    Product p = new Product { BasePrice = _price, Category = _category,
    Description = _desc, Name = _name, PizzaTopping = _pizzaTopping };

    p.Category.Products = new List<Product>();
    p.Category.Products.Add(p);
    return p;
}
```

You can now use your ProductBuilder within your tests to insert known data into the database, which you can then use to verify that the UI worked as expected. To configure the builder, you create a set of methods to configure certain properties to be used during the Build method above. The method WithName simply stores the parameter in a local field. In order to provide the fluent nature, it also returns the builder object for other methods to use and call methods on:

```
public ProductBuilder WithName(string name)
{
    _name = name;
    return this;
}
```

As such, you'll need to have some logic involved about how to access the database. Because these are UI tests, you can take advantage of the existing responsibilities you created in Chapter 3. These have already been tested and you've verified that they work as expected, meaning you can accept this dependency. Other people prefer to bypass the ORM and communicate directly with the database using a different approach such as ADO.NET.

As such, you'll now extend the BaseUITest class to support this new functionality and allow all your sub-tests to take advantage. Similar to your integration tests in Chapter 4, you are going to need to create an additional object called Database to handle the creating and dropping of the database itself. The reason you want to drop and re-create the database is to be sure that you are always running against a clean database with clean data.

Because you are taking advantage of NHibernate, you can use your existing DefaultNHibernateConfig object to create your scripts, which will create your tables:

```
public void CreateTables()
{
    string[] script = db.GenerateSchemaCreationScript();
    executeScripts(script, db.GetCurrentSession().Connection);
}
```

Unlike your integration tests, the UI tests will be running against a real SQL Server 2005 instance. As such, you will also need to drop the tables after you've finished:

```
public void DropTables()
{
    string[] script = db.GenerateDropSchemaScript();
    executeScripts(script, db.GetCurrentSession().Connection);
}
```

The next stage is to create your new database object and call the CreateTables() method within your [SetUp] method:

```
db = new Database();
db.CreateTables();
```

Finally, within your [TearDown] method, you should call the drop tables method.

The final stage is to insert the data into the newly created tables. Because you are creating your tables for each test, you also need to do that for each database. Sadly, for a Test fixture you cannot have more than one Setup or Teardown attribute, which you've already used in the BaseUITest. The workaround is to use abstract and virtual methods that could then be overloaded in your actual TestFixture class. Within our BaseUITest we define a virtual method without any implementation:

```
public virtual void DataCreation()
{}
```

Within our [SetUp] method you would call this function after creating your tables:

```
[SetUp]
public void BrowserSetup()
{
    db = new Database();
    db.CreateTables();
    DataCreation();
    Browser = BrowserFactory.Create(browserType);
    Browser.GoTo(URL);
}
```

This can then be overridden within your TestFixture to insert data targeted for that particular test while being executed within your Setup method:

```
public override void DataCreation()
{
        Product product = new ProductBuilder()
                                        .WithName("diff")
                                        .WithDescription("DiffDesc")
                                        .InCategory("diffCategory")
                                        .WithBasePrice(2.00);
        ProductRepository repository = new ProductRepository(DbConfig);
        repository.SaveOrUpdate(product);
}
```

As was mentioned before, you are taking advantage of your existing NHibernate mapping and code to insert the product into the database.

After you have this ProductBuilder in place, you can extend it to allow a list of products to return. For example, you could have the following which will produce four different products with different names and some different descriptions:

```
List<Product> products = new ProductBuilder()
        .WithNames("name", "name2", "name3", "name4")
        .WithDescriptions("default", "desc2", "desc3")
        .WithPizzaTopping()
        .InCategory("category")
        .WithBasePrice(1.00);
```

Alternatively, you could have the same product returned 10 times; each with a different ID:

```
List<Product> products = new ProductBuilder()
        .WithName("name")
        .WithDescription("desc")
        .InCategory("category")
        .WithBasePrice(1.00)
        .Times(10);
```

Again, this is done by taking advantage of the implicit operator method. Instead of just building a single product, you are building up a list of different products:

```
public static implicit operator List<Product>(ProductBuilder builder)
{
    builder.SetCount();
    List<Product> products = new List<Product>(_count);
    for (int i = 0; i < _count; i++)
    {
        products.Add(builder.Build());
    }

    return products;
}
```

183

At this point we can also include some additional logic to handle providing different names and descriptions for our products.

```
List<Product> products = new ProductBuilder()
                .WithNames("name", "name2", "name3", "name4")
                .WithDescriptions("default", "desc2", "desc3")
                .WithPizzaTopping()
                .InCategory("category")
                .WithBasePrice(1.00)
                .Times(10);
```

When creating the products, the first four products will be named name, name2, name3, name4. As we are producing ten products, the remaining six will be given the name of the first parameter — in this case simply name. This is the same for description.

This is where the power of the test data builder comes in as you have more control over how you build your objects.

Using Known Data to Verify

Now that you have your known product being inserted into your database, you can use this to verify that it will appear on the page:

```
[Test]
public void Products_Menu_Displays_All_Products_On_Webpage()
{
    ProductsMenuPage page = new ProductsMenuPage(Browser);
    page.Products.ShouldContain("p1");
}
```

However this is still only testing the fact that one product is returned. Instead, you'll want to insert a number of different products into the database:

```
public override void DataCreation()
{
    List<Product> products = new ProductBuilder()
        .WithNames("p1", "p2", "p3", "p4")
        .WithDescriptions("d1", "d2", "d3", "d4")
        .WithPizzaTopping()
        .InCategory("category")
        .WithBasePrice(1.00);

    ProductRepository repository = new ProductRepository(DbConfig);
    foreach (var product in products)
        repository.SaveOrUpdate(product);
}
```

Your test can then verify that all four products were correctly displayed on the screen and provide you with a lot more confidence that it is working as you expect it to:

```
[Test]
public void Products_Menu_Displays_All_Products_On_Webpage()
```

```
        {
                ProductsMenuPage page = new ProductsMenuPage(Browser);
                page.Products.ShouldContain("p1");
                page.Products.ShouldContain("p2");
                page.Products.ShouldContain("p3");
                page.Products.ShouldContain("p4");
        }
```

One thing you might notice from these tests is that you're moving away from Assert.Equal() as in previous tests. In an attempt to improve readability, in these examples you'll take a more BDD and RSpec approach to writing your tests.

The method ShouldContain() is an extension method. Extension methods allow you to extend classes by including a namespace containing static methods, marked as extensions. It works in exactly the same way, but we find it slightly more readable in the fact that is it saying the string "Products" should contain "p1." These extension methods were created as part of the machine.specification framework, which can be found on github as part of the machine project (http://github.com/machine/machine.specifications/tree/master).

When you have your tests, the one question left to ask is when and how often they should be executed. We feel that manually initiating the running of UI tests should only happen when you are concerned that you may have broken something. Otherwise, they should be running asynchronously, after the integration build has successfully finished on your continuous integration server.

More WatiN Examples

The previous section should have provided you with an insight into how you can successfully structure and get started writing your UI automation tests.

Following this, we wanted to provide some more examples for UI tests around the sample application and show how you can structure tests around an application.

Depending on how your application is structured will depend on how you need to test certain parts. With this sample application, there is a linear approach to how users would walk though the application. As such, this is how the tests need to be performed. In other applications, you could go directly to particular parts of the application by using the appropriate URL and begin testing from there.

Based on how the application is structured, there still needs to be a product in the database for us to work with. If we wanted to verify how the shopping cart behaves, then we first need to add an item to the shopping cart. This is one example of why having a centralized Product Builder allows us to reuse the logic and structure for inserting our test data, as shown below.

```
        public override void DataCreation()
        {
            Product product = new ProductBuilder()
                .WithName("p1")
                .WithDescription("d1")
                .InCategory("category")
```

```
                    .WithBasePrice(1.00);

            ProductRepository repository = new ProductRepository(DbConfig);
            repository.SaveOrUpdate(product);
    }
```

With the test data in place, we can reuse our ProductsMenuPage model and abstraction to control and interact with the page. Because we have this in place, adding an item to the cart is simply two lines of test code.

```
        [Test]
        public void After_Listing_Products_Can_Add_Them_Into_Your_Shopping_Cart()
        {
            ProductsMenuPage page = new ProductsMenuPage(Browser);
            ShoppingCartPage cart = page.AddToBasket("p1");

            List<ShoppingCartPage.Cart.Item> lines = cart.Items.Lines;
            lines.Count.ShouldEqual(1);
            ShoppingCartPage.Cart.Item line = lines[0];

            line.Name.ShouldEqual("p1");
            line.Price.ShouldEqual("$1");
            line.Quantity.ShouldEqual("1");
        }
```

Once we are on the shopping cart page, with the abstraction in place you can use the list of products in the cart as a simple collection. This means you can work with it in a very easy fashion to verify everything is correct. This is the advantage of abstracting.

The ShoppingCartPage code is complex; however, this doesn't affect our tests. An example of this is how we gain access to the shopping cart lines on the page.

From the point of view of our tests, there is just a single property

```
        public List<Item> Lines { get { return GetItems(); } }
```

However, the private method GetItems does all the hard work. This uses a RegEx to identify each row in a table within some HTML. The HTML has already been filtered down to just the particular DIV containing the cart by the code — Browser.Div(Find.ById("cart")).InnerHtml. The result is that we can work more easily with a particular subset of the page, pinpointing the part we want instead of having to work with the entire page. Being able to pinpoint particular parts in this fashion is extemely important to successfully test your UI.

```
    private List<Item> GetItems()
    {
        List<Item> items = new List<Item>();
        string regExGetRows = "<tr>(.*?)</tr>"

        Regex regex = new Regex(regExGetRows, RegexOptions.IgnoreCase | RegexOptions.
    Singleline);

        int count = 0;
```

```
        foreach (Match m in regex.Matches(Html)) //row. Html is the div with id of 'cart'
        {
            if(count++ == 0)
                continue; //skip first header row

            Capture capture = m.Captures[0];
            items.Add(GetItem(capture));
        }

        return items;
    }
```

However, the GetItems method simply gets the particular row for that item. GetItem is what actually gets the data and information for that particular row. Again, we have used the GetItems method to help us obtain a more targeted section of the page to work with. In this case, our GetItem is simply interested in the row.

Once the method has the particular row, it uses RegEx again to pull out the particular column. The only complex section is identifying the text field. We need to use WatiN to give us the actual object allowing us to enter text for the quantity if required.

The trick is to find all the text boxes on the page, then by navigating the HTML you can obtain the parent. Then, based on the parent you can find the particular row. If the name of the parent of the textbox matches the row, you have found your quantity for the row. Not difficult, it just requires thinking about the problem in a slightly different fashion.

```
    private Item GetItem(Capture capture)
    {
        //Capture for three columns − Name + Qty + Price
        string regExGetColumns = "<td>(.*?)</td>";

        Regex regex = new Regex(regExGetColumns, RegexOptions.IgnoreCase);
        MatchCollection m = regex.Matches(capture.Value);

        Capture name = m[0].Groups[1].Captures[0];
        Capture price = m[2].Groups[1].Captures[0];
        TextField quantityTextBox = null;
        string quantityTextBoxID = "Quantity";
        foreach (TextField t in Browser.TextFields.Filter(Find.ById(quantityTextBoxID)))
        {
            if (t.Parent.Parent.InnerHtml.Contains(name.Value))
            {
                quantityTextBox = t;
                break;
            }
        }

        return new Item(Browser) { Name = name.Value, Price = price.Value,
    QuantityTextField = quantityTextBox };
    }
```

Once the method has found all the columns required, it returns a strongly typed object and as such our tests have a nice collection of objects which represent the shopping cart items. With the TextField, because we have the actual object, we can enter text and use it in exactly the same fashion as we would with any other items.

We can now use this abstraction layer to verify that after clicking the Add to Basket link for a particular product, it does, in effect, appear in our table with the correct details.

With the test in place to verify this initial feature, we can start looking at verifying that other features are in fact working. One of those features could be verifying that the items are persisted between browser sessions. When manually testing the application you would first add an item, close the browser, open it again, visit the shopping cart website and verify that the item still existed. Automated testing is no different.

Our test will need to replicate how you would manually test and how the user will experience the use case. To close the browser you need to call Dispose, while to reopen you simply create a new instance and direct it at a particular URL:

```
[Test]
public void Shopping_cart_is_persisted_between_browser_sessions()
{
    ProductsMenuPage page = new ProductsMenuPage(Browser);
    page.AddToBasket("p1");

    Browser.Dispose();
    StartBrowser();

    ShoppingCartPage cart = new ShoppingCartPage(Browser);
    cart.VisitPage();
    List<ShoppingCartPage.Cart.Item> lines = cart.Items.Lines;
    lines.Count.ShouldEqual(1);
}
```

This test is now able to verify that the shopping cart is persisted even if the browser is closed.

Web applications also commonly need to store state and additional information about the user over a long period of time. One such example is being able to store previously used addresses for future visits. While we continue to keep opening/closing the browser as we did before, that is not the aim of the test. The aim is to verify that they appear on the page. As such, we can use the back and refresh options of a browser to simulate the effects of users navigating our site and verify that the behavior works as expected:

```
[Test]
public void can_enter_three_addresses_select_select_middle_address()
{
    CheckoutProduct();

    for (int i = 0; i < 3; i++)
    {
        FillOutAddress(i + " Testville", "Testers Road");

        addressPage.Proceed();

        Browser.Back();
        Browser.Refresh();
    }

    addressPage.SelectExistingAddress(2);
```

```
            SummaryPage summaryPage = addressPage.UseSelectedAddress();

            Assert.IsTrue(summaryPage.Address.Contains("1 Testville"));
        }
        private void FillOutAddress(string address1, string address2)
        {
            addressPage.StreetAddress1 = address1;
            addressPage.StreetAddress2 = address2;
            addressPage.City = "Testcity";
            addressPage.State = "TC";
            addressPage.PostCode = "12345";
        }
```

Knowing how to simulate the user's behavior is an important aspect when creating your automated UI tests.

In a similar fashion, replicating how users will use the application, you should also consider testing for what happens when an error occurs. While we don't believe in testing every possible edge case, common errors people might hit should be tested. Within this example, a common error would be the user not logging into the site with the correct username or password. While this is an error case, its useful to have a test around to verify it works as expected.

In the application, we need to be logged in to proceed to the checkout page. In our test, we want to check that on this login page, if an incorrect username\password is entered, then the user is not taken to the next page, but instead is shown an error message.

The test simply automates this logic. We attempt to access the checkout, because we know what to expect; as we have not logged in yet we can return a LoginPage object which maps to the Login Page.

Once we have the page, we can call a helper method called LogOn. All being well, this should return the AddressPage:

```
        [Test]
        public void if_login_fails_then_it_should_display_error_message_on_page()
        {
            LoginPage loginPage = cart.Checkout();
            AddressPage page = loginPage.LogOn("test", "tester123");
            Assert.IsNull(page);

            Assert.IsTrue(Browser.Text.Contains("The username or password provided
    is incorrect."));
        }
```

While our domain model expects to return an AddressPage object, it has also been created in such a way as to return null if the login fails. This is what allows our test to work. We expect the login to fail, and as such we expect a null object to be returned. If it has, then everything is working as we expect. Just as an added extra, we added a verification that the correct message has been returned to the user. We are going direct to the Browser object to obtain this, but we could have gone via our existing LoginPage object.

Our LogOn helper method is created as shown below. We use the URL to decide what action to take:

```
        public AddressPage LogOn()
        {
```

```
Browser.Button(Find.ByValue("Log On")).Click();
Browser.WaitForComplete();

if(Browser.Url.Contains("/Logon"))
    return null;

return new AddressPage(Browser);
}
```

Hopefully this has given you an understanding of how to structure and develop your tests based around your own application.

Common WatiN Errors

While WatiN is a great framework, when you get started we've found that people run into the same common problems which can be difficult to identify and resolve.

The first issue is regarding missing assemblies. If you're missing the core WatiN assembly then you will get compile time errors; however, if you're missing a reference to SHDocVw you receive runtime errors and your tests fail. The output of one of our failing tests was:

```
failed: System.IO.FileNotFoundException: Could not load file or assembly 'Interop.
SHDocVw, Version=1.1.0.0, Culture=neutral, PublicKeyToken=null' or one of its
dependencies. The system cannot find the file specified.
    at WatiN.Core.IE.CreateNewIEAndGoToUri(Uri uri, LogonDialogHandler
logonDialogHandler, Boolean createInNewProcess)
    at WatiN.Core.IE.ctor()
```

Solving this is very simple. In C:\Windows\System32\ you will find an assembly called shdocvw.dll. This needs to be in the bin directory when you execute your tests so watin can detect and use it as required. ShDocVw.dll allows WatiN to automate Internet Explorer. To fix this error, you need to reference this dll, which will then become Interop.SHDocVw.dll due to the fact it is a COM dll. We always take a copy of this dll and place it next to the watin assembly and reference it from there, as demonstrated in our examples.

If your using TestDriven.NET you will never see this exception, however when using NUnit.UI, NUnit. Console or ReSharper you might receive the following error.

```
System.Threading.ThreadStateException: The CurrentThread needs to have it's
ApartmentState set to ApartmentState.STA to be able to automate Internet Explorer.
at WatiN.Core.IE.CheckThreadApartmentStateIsSTA()
at
WatiN.Core.IE.CreateNewIEAndGoToUri(Uri uri, IDialogHandler logonDialogHandler,
Boolean createInNewProcess)
at WatiN.Core.IE.ctor()
To solve this, the documentation () says that you can include this line of code:
System.Threading.Thread.Currentthread.SetApartmentState(System.Threading.
ApartmentStat.STA);
```

To solve this you need to include a config xml with your assembly. Simply name the file <your assembly name>.dll.config and ensure that it is copied to the output folder as content. The contents need to be as follows.

```xml
<?xml version="1.0" encoding="utf-8" ?>
<configuration>
  <configSections>
    <sectionGroup name="NUnit">
      <section name="TestRunner" type="System.Configuration.
NameValueSectionHandler"/>
    </sectionGroup>
  </configSections>
  <NUnit>
    <TestRunner>
      <!--Valid values are STA,MTA. Others ignored.-->
      <add key="ApartmentState" value="STA" />
    </TestRunner>
  </NUnit>
</configuration>
```

You will now be able to execute your tests using any test runner.

One of the great advantages of WatiN is that you can use a number of different browsers. However, the first time you try and use Firefox you will receive a similar error message to the following:

```
failed: WatiN.Core.Mozilla.FireFoxException: Unable to connect to jssh server,
please make sure you have correctly installed the jssh.xpi plugin
--> System.Net.Sockets.SocketException: No connection could be made because the
target machine actively refused it 127.0.0.1:9997
    at WatiN.Core.Mozilla.FireFoxClientPort.Connect()
    at WatiN.Core.Mozilla.FireFox.CreateFireFoxInstance()
    at WatiN.Core.Mozilla.FireFox.ctor()
    at WatiN.Core.BrowserFactory.Create(BrowserType browserType)
```

While WatiN uses SHDocVw for IE, for Firefox it uses an extension called jSSH. The extension is included within the samples for this chapter. Simply install this and WatiN will be able to interact with Firefox.

Yet IE is not without its issues. If you are running IE7 upwards, it includes a "feature" called Protected Mode. This mode causes problems when WatiN attempts to access the web page. As such, it is wise to disable this via the internet security settings for the browser. NOTE: This can lead to security problems.

These issues are based on our own personal experience. If you experience other issues then WatiN has excellent support documentation on their website (http://watin.sourceforge.net/documentation.html)

Testing JavaScript

JavaScript has always been an important aspect of web development, but in the past few years developers have been creating more JavaScript code than ever before. When the term AJAX (Asynchronous JavaScript and XML) became a buzz word, developers found themselves having to learn exactly how

JavaScript worked. Many new frameworks, such as jQuery and Prototype, were introduced to help ease the pain that developers were feeling when trying to create JavaScript. For some reason JavaScript has received a bad reputation. Many developers complain that it is difficult to write and hard to maintain, but in reality, if written correctly, JavaScript can be a very useful and powerful language.

Many developers are not even aware of the different testing frameworks that exist, let alone that many developers are creating their JavaScript using TDD methods. As with server-side code, many of the SOLID principles discussed in Chapter 2 apply to JavaScript. Much of the JavaScript that you see from day-to-day is contained in the HTML that calls the script. When JavaScript is organized in this way, it is very difficult to test. Some web developers complain that having an HTML page that makes many requests to the server to download multiple JavaScript files slows down the web page. They are correct, but how much does it actually slow down the web page? You'll explore this topic in detail in Chapter 8, but for now you should focus on creating code that is testable.

Currently there are a few different JavaScript testing frameworks out there, such as qUnit, Screw Unit, and jsUnit. Each framework is a bit different, but they all accomplish the same thing: an interface for testing JavaScript. Just as with the different xUnit frameworks, we'll recommend one, but it's up to you to explore the others and find which one works the best for you.

For the following examples, you'll be using qUnit. qUnit is the JavaScript testing framework used by the jQuery team to ensure their framework is working correctly. jQuery is an open source JavaScript framework that makes working with JavaScript a breeze.

The following example is an HTML page that creates two instances of the account JavaScript object and transfers funds between them. After the funds have been transferred, the balances of each account are displayed in a span tag. The span text is set using the jQuery JavaScript library:

```
<body>
    <script type="text/javascript">
        var checkingAccount = new Account(564858510, 600);
        var savingsAccount = new Account(564858507, 100);

        savingsAccount.Transfer(checkingAccount, 100);

        jQuery("document").ready(function() {

            jQuery("#SavingsBalance").text(savingsAccount.Balance);
            jQuery("#CheckingBalance").text(checkingAccount.Balance);
        });
    </script>

    <div>
        Savings Balance:<span id="SavingsBalance"></span>
    </div>

    <div>
        Checking Balance:<span id="CheckingBalance"></span>
    </div>
</body>
```

Because the account logic object logic has been abstracted from the HTML page, this logic will be easy to test using a JavaScript testing framework such as qUnit:

```
function Account(accountNumber, balance)
{
    this.AccountNumber = accountNumber;
    this.Balance = balance;
}
Account.prototype.Transfer = function(toAccount, amount)
{
    toAccount.Balance += amount;
    this.Balance = this.Balance - amount;
}
```

Figure 5-24 shows an example project with the qUnit tests added. The testing framework and unit tests are contained in the SimpleqUnit.Tests.Javascript.Unit directory. The qUnit framework requires the testrunner.js file and qUnit.css file to be included. In this example your unit tests for the account JavaScript object are contained in the AccountTests.htm file. With this structure, you can think of the AccountTests.htm file as the test fixture. The unit tests are written in JavaScript and are contained inside a script tag in the AccountTests.htm file. As discussed in Chapter 2, test fixtures should contain all the logic to test the behaviors of an object.

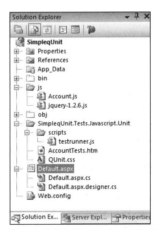

Figure 5-24: Example project with qUnit setup

```
<!DOCTYPE html PUBLIC "-//W3C//DTD XHTML 1.0 Transitional//EN" "http://www.w3.org/
TR/xhtml1/DTD/xhtml1-transitional.dtd">
<html xmlns="http://www.w3.org/1999/xhtml" >
    <head>
        <title>Account Tests</title>
        <script type="text/javascript" src="./js/jquery-1.2.6.js"></script>
        <script type="text/javascript" src="./js/Account.js"></script>
        <script type="text/javascript" src="scripts/testrunner.js"></script>
        <link rel="stylesheet" href="QUnit.css" type="text/css" media="screen" />

        <script type="text/javascript">
```

```
module('When creating a new Account',
{
    setup: function() {
            account = new Account("12345", 100);
        }
});

test('Should_Transfer_From_Checking_To_Savings_Successfully', function(){
    equals(account.Balance, 100);

    var checkingAccount = new Account(564858510, 600);
    var savingsAccount = new Account(564858507, 100);

    checkingAccount.Transfer(savingsAccount, 100);
    equals(savingsAccount.Balance, 200);
    equals(checkingAccount.Balance, 500);
});
        </script>
    </head>
    <body>
        <h2 id="banner">Account unit tests</h2>
        <h2 id="userAgent"></h2>
        <ol id="tests"></ol>
        <div id="main"></div>
    </body>
</html>
```

Because the qUnit test runners are HTML files, a suite of JavaScript tests can become unwieldy very quickly, not to mention the fact that having to click through a bunch of HTML pages to see if JavaScript is working correctly isn't very automated. A pattern that has emerged involves using WatiN or Selenium to run the qUnit test runner and then parse the result looking for failures. The problem with this is that a WatiN/Selenium test would be required for each qUnit test runner file, meaning you would be doubling your testing effort having to create the qUnit test and then creating a WatiN/Selenium test to go along with it. Some unit testing frameworks support concepts called iterative tests or row tests. With iterative tests, data can be passed into a single test and assertions can be performed on the data. This works great for qUnit; you can pass in the results from multiple test runners and parse the results for errors with only having to write one WatiN/Selenium test. As of nUnit, 2.4.8 row tests/iterative tests were not supported out-of-the box, but a free add-on, aptly named Iterative Test, is available for download on the nUnit website.

The next listing shows the basics of getting started with this pattern using an iterative test using the Iterative Test nUnit plug-in and WatiN. The UnitTestsToRun function returns an IEnumerable result set containing the results from the test runner. The AccountTest function calls an extension method that verifies that the test has passed:

```
[TestFixture]
public class AccountTests
{
    private IE m_browser;

    [TestFixtureSetUp]
    public void TestFixtureSetUp()
```

```
    {
        m_browser = new IE();
        m_browser.ClearCache();
    }

    [TestFixtureTearDown]
    public void TestFixtureTearDown()
    {
        m_browser.Close();
    }

    [IterativeTest("UnitTestsToRun")]
    public void AccountTest(object current)
    {
        ((QUnitTest)current).ShouldPass();
    }

    public IEnumerable UnitTestsToRun()
    {
        return new[]
                    {
                      "AccountTests.htm",
                      "AccountHistoryTests.htm",
                      "LoanCalculationTests.htm"
                    }.SelectMany(page => GetTestResults(page));
    }

    public IEnumerable<QUnitTest> GetTestResults(string testPage)
    {
        string testDirectory = "js/UnitTests";

        TestFixtureSetUp();
        m_browser.GoTo(string.Format("http://localhost:21401/{0}/{1}",
                                    testDirectory, testPage));

        m_browser.WaitForComplete();

        return ParseResultsFromPage(testPage);
    }

    public IEnumerable<QUnitTest> ParseResultsFromPage(string testPage) {}

    private static string ParseTestName(string testNameTag) {}
}
```

Using an iterative testing pattern with WatiN/Selenium allows your tests to stay organized and allows for tests to be added very easily. The preceding example shows the iterative test pattern code that is executed via nUnit in Figure 5-25. If a single test within the qUnit test runner fails, the iterative testing pattern allows you to see which test failed. Figure 5-26 shows a test failure. Pay attention to the details of any information that can be provided from parsing the results of the qUnit test runner.

Figure 5-25: A failing qUnit test

Figure 5-26: Detailed information about failing test

AJAX is a technique which allows you to submit requests back to the server without causing a full postback to happen. The result is a much better user experience as only parts of the site are updated. However, this can cause potential problems for automated testing as parts of the UI won't always be available and there will be a delay which won't be visible to the browser or the unit testing framework.

Thankfully we can still test our UI if it's making Ajax requests under the covers. In the "JQuery_ AjaxExample" sample you will find two examples of how you can test your UI when the UI takes advantage of the Microsoft ASP.NET Ajax Library or JQuery. The example below describes how to test when using the Microsoft ASP.NET Ajax Library.

Figure 5-27 is how the web page looks after the Ajax request has been made. Fundamentally, the drop-down list is populated with a set of options. A user can select an option and click submit, which will make a call to the server to collect more information. When the result is returned, the details are rendered to the web page.

Taking advantage of the built in Ajax helper methods in ASP.NET MVC, the code for the page is represented next:

```
<h2>AjaxLibraryExample</h2>
<% using (Ajax.BeginForm("GetPassword", new AjaxOptions { UpdateTargetId =
"customerDetails" }))
{ %>
   <p>Select an item</p>
   <p><%= Html.DropDownList("id") %></p>
   <p><input type="submit" value="Submit"/></p>
<% } %>
<div id="customerDetails">
</div>
```

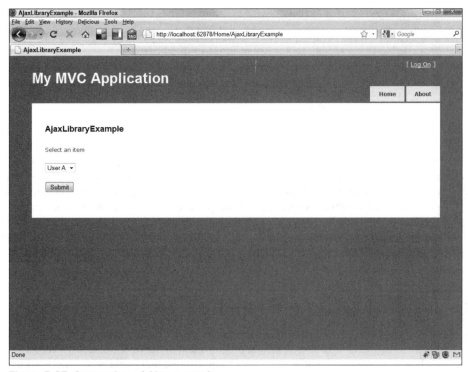

Figure 5-27: Screenshot of Ajax example

When the form is submitted, it makes a request to the GetPassword method on the HomeController object just as it would if we attempted to access a normal View page. The difference is that the method returns a PartialView. This is because we will only be rendering a partial section of the View instead of the entire page:

```
public ActionResult GetPassword(string id)
{
    Thread.Sleep(4000); //Demoware
    Customer customer = customers.Find(c => c.Id == int.Parse(id));
    return PartialView("CustomerDetails", customer);
}
```

As we have defined our UpdateTargetId, ASP.NET knows which DIV to use when rendering the CustomerDetails partial view. To simulate accessing a database, we've added a cheeky Thread.Sleep call.

In order to test that the UI and the ajax works as expected, we can approach the problem as we have described throughout the chapter. In the example below, we select User B from the dropdown list, submit the form, and verify the results are returned as we expect.

```
[Test]
public void Demo_using_Microsoft_Ajax()
{
```

```
using (IBrowser ie = BrowserFactory.Create(BrowserType.InternetExplorer))
{
    ie.GoTo("http://localhost:62878/Home/AjaxLibraryExample");
    ie.SelectList(Find.ById("id")).Select("User B");
    ie.Button(Find.ByValue("Submit")).Click();
    bool contains = ie.Div(Find.ById("detail")).Text
        .Contains("Password - p@ssw0rd");
    Assert.IsTrue(contains);
}
}
```

The key point here is that after submitting our form there is a 4 second delay before we can verify the contents of the web page. Thankfully WatiN is capable of handling this for us. There is a property called 'IE.Settings.WaitUntilExistsTimeOut' which defines how long WatiN should wait until the element appears. Before the timeout expires, it will keep searching the page to see if it can access the requested element. As a result, when our partial view is rendered, it will render the detail DIV; WatiN will detect that the DIV now exists, at which point it will verify the contents of the text. If the DIV doesn't appear within the timeout (by default 30 seconds) an exception is thrown and the test fails.

Automating Cross-Browser Tests

One of the main problems with web testing is dealing with different browsers and rendering engines. Cross-browser testing ends up being a manual process most of the time because it's very difficult to test exactly how a browser will render the page. One technique that could be applied is taking a screen-shot for each test in each browser, but this calls for a manual process that includes looking at the screen captures.

A great use of automated cross-browsers is in testing JavaScript. With the popularity of AJAX in recent years, developers have found that JavaScript does not behave the same way between browsers in all situations. Creating automated UI tests with WatiN or Selenium can help ensure that your application works in all major browsers. The following code snippet is a cross-browser test using WatiN:

```
public void Should_Click_Search_On_Google_And_Return_Results_For_AspNet()
{
    IBrowser browser = BrowserFactory.Create(BrowserType.InternetExplorer);
    Return_Results_For_ASP_Net(browser);

    browser = BrowserFactory.Create(BrowserType.FireFox);
    Return_Results_For_ASP_Net(browser);
}

private void Return_Results_For_ASP_Net(IBrowser browswer)
{
    browswer.GoTo("http://www.google.com");
    browswer.TextField(Find.ByName("q")).Value = "asp.net";
    browswer.Button(Find.ByName("btnG")).Click();
    Assert.IsTrue(browswer.ContainsText("The Official Microsoft ASP.NET
Site"));
}
```

Remember, to run WatiN tests in Firefox, the jssh.xpi add-in must be installed on the Firefox instance you will be testing with.

The following example is a cross-browser test with Selenium:

```
[Test]
public void Should_Click_Search_On_Google_And_Return_Results_For_AspNet()
{
    ISelenium browser = new DefaultSelenium("localhost", 4444, "*firefox",
        "http://www.google.com/");
    Return_Results_For_ASP_Net(browser);
    browser.Close();

    browser = new DefaultSelenium("localhost", 4444, "*iexplore",
        "http://www.google.com/");
    Return_Results_For_ASP_Net(browser);
    browser.Close();
}

private void Return_Results_For_ASP_Net(ISelenium browser)
{
    browser.Start();
    browser.Open("/");
    browser.Type("q", "asp.net");
    browser.Click("btnG");
    browser.WaitForPageToLoad("30000");

    Assert.IsTrue(browser.IsTextPresent("The Official Microsoft ASP.NET
Site"));
}
```

There are a couple of concerns with the above style of test. Firstly, if our IE test fails, then our Firefox test will never be executed. If we knew that our IE test failed, but FireFox was successful, then we could identify the problem more effectively. The other problem is that if we wanted to add Google Chrome as a test platform, we would need to manually visit all of our tests to add this logic. As a result, Ben Hall has created an extension for the xUnit unit testing framework to improve this situation.

The extension is an attribute which will create an instance of the WatiN browser object which is passed to the test as a parameter. As a result, xUnit will execute the test twice, once for each browser.

```
public class Example
{
    [Theory]
    [Browser(BrowserType.InternetExplorer)]
    [Browser(BrowserType.FireFox)]
    public void Should_Click_Search_On_Google_And_Return_Results_For_AspNet(IBrowser
        browser)
        {
            browser.GoTo("http://www.google.co.uk");
            browser.TextField(Find.ByName("q")).Value = "asp.net";
            browser.Button(Find.ByName("btnG")).Click();
            Assert.True(browser.ContainsText("The Official Microsoft ASP.NET
Site"));
        }
    }
```

This can be downloaded from `http://github.com/BenHall/xUnitBrowserAttribute/tree/master` with an example included in the samples for this chapter.

While a similar extension could be built for nUnit, it is more much difficult and less effective than xUnit's approach. Similar approaches can be achieved by having a config file which is used to find out which browser to test against. The config file could then be edited by a build script during execution, allowing you to very simply control which browsers are tested and when.

Going forward, companies will start providing cloud-based services offering to host and execute your UI tests on a cloud server. The advantage being that you can run your tests on multiple different platforms and browsers without having to install and configure the individual platforms. Two such services are Cloud Testing (`http://www.cloudtesting.com/`) and Go Test It (`http://go-test.it/`).

How Much Should We Automate?

One of the differences between engine level and UI level tests is the amount you should automate. Developers and testers who are new to creating automated UI tests tend to get carried away, and they may create tests for every little UI element, but not gain very much benefit from these tests. Due to the nature of UI tests, these tests tend to have a higher maintenance cost. There are some tasks that computers can do well, such as creating a large text document and then running that text document through a program to apply styles, all the while trying to break the app that is applying the styles. Then there are certain things that manual testing is more suited for, such as testing whether a particular page looks aesthetically pleasing when it is rendered for printing.

Many of the issues that occur with automated UI testing boil down to the fact that developers and testers test things that should not really be tested. Properly designed applications wrap many business rules into a thick layer, which the user interface will then encompass. To test a business rule in the UI requires a lot of clicking, selecting particular items and entering values, which makes maintenance a nightmare. Which brings us to the next question: what types of behaviors should you automate?

❑ **Session Rules.** Many applications have business rules that apply to features that a user session or role will have access to. An example of such a business rule would be that users in the administrator role will have access to the reports section of the website.

❑ **Workflows.** Most applications contain some type of workflow that can be tested. On a simplistic level, a workflow could be that a user is prompted for a password before gaining access to an application. On a more complex level, testing that the order of the steps required for accepting a credit card are correct is also considered a workflow.

❑ **Key Business Scenarios.** You will get the most value from automated UI testing when you test key business scenarios from end-to-end. Most business applications do not have very many of them, so the amount of key business scenario tests you will have will be small. Take for example an application that enables users to order pizza online. There are two key scenarios that should be tested end-to-end in this application. Test the path that takes the users through the "new user registration" feature, and test the path that allows the user to order the pizza. Automated UI tests that test key business scenarios should be run at least once every day.

You test session rules, workflows, and key business scenarios because the user interface is how the user interacts with your application. A very small CSS error could prevent a user from logging into the application. These types of errors are extremely embarrassing and can be costly, when found by the users. These errors are easily spotted when using automated testing. By only automating these three types of scenarios, it cuts down on the amount of maintenance that will need to be performed on the tests.

Applying Automated UI Testing to the ASP.NET Family

You have learned that UI tests that are tightly coupled to the browser become hard to read and maintain if there are changes made to the application under test, and tests should be abstracted as far away from the browser as possible. The following section is intended to apply some of the techniques discussed in this chapter to specific technologies that fall under the ASP.NET family.

ASP.NET WebForms

The techniques that abstract the tests from the browser that have been discussed so far are all valid when testing against ASP.NET WebForms. Problems will occur if you are testing ASP.NET WebForm applications where the data access is not abstracted very well. The following example contains a set of tests to ensure a user can log in to a homepage of an order-processing system. You cannot tell from these tests that the application is using ADO.NET to return datasets to the WebForms to render the data:

```
using NUnit.Framework;
using WroxPizza.Orders.Tests.Integration.model;

namespace WroxPizza.Orders.Tests.Integration
{
    public class HomePageTests: BaseUITest
    {
        [Test]
        public void Should_Load_Load_The_Home_Page()
        {
            HomePage homePage = new HomePage(Browser);
            string expectedTitle = "wrox pizza shop | login";

            Assert.AreEqual(expectedTitle, homePage.Title.ToLower());
        }

        [Test]
        public void Should_Not_Login_With_An_Invalid_User()
        {
            HomePage homePage = new HomePage(Browser);
            homePage.LoginUser("Invalid_User_Name", "Invalid_Password");
            string expectedMessage = "Your login attempt was not successful. Please
try again.";

            Assert.AreEqual(expectedMessage, homePage.LoginStatus);
```

```
    }

    [Test]
    public void Should_Login_With_A_Valid_User()
    {
        HomePage homePage = new HomePage(Browser);
        homePage.LoginUser("Invalid_User_Name", "Invalid_Password");

        Assert.That(homePage.MenuOptions.Exists(menuOption => menuOption
            .ToLower() == "Add Employee"));
    }
  }
}
```

Because mocking the data layer is nearly impossible, in this situation it's best to re-create the database from a known set of data for each Test fixture that is run. The abstract base class in the listing just shown introduces two new concepts. The first concept is restoring the database to a known state upon each Test fixture creation. In this listing, ADO.NET was used to call two stored procedures that were created in the database: one to create the set of known data (Test_Setup) and one to clear out the data (Test_Teardown).

You have learned that when running tests, the database should be in a known state. So, what happens in this example is that if you have a test that adds a record then the next test expects that a certain number of records exist. This is where the second concept comes into play. Pay attention to the BrowserSetup method, which is the test Setup method; this method is called before each individual test runs. You are creating a new transaction when the test starts, but you never commit the transaction. Because the data was not committed, the data is still in the known state:

```
    [SetUp]
    public void BrowserSetup()
    {
        m_ts = new TransactionScope();

        Browser = BrowserFactory.Create(browserType);
        Browser.GoTo(URL);
    }
```

The following code example will illustrate a technique on how to keep data in a known state.

```
using System.Configuration;
using System.Data;
using System.Data.SqlClient;
using System.Transactions;
using NUnit.Framework;
using WatiN.Core;
using WatiN.Core.Interfaces;

namespace WroxPizza.Orders.Tests.Integration
{
    public abstract class BaseUITest: CassiniWebServer
    {
```

```csharp
        public IBrowser Browser { get; set; }
        BrowserType browserType;
        private TransactionScope m_ts;
        private string m_conString =
ConfigurationManager.ConnectionStrings["WroxPizza"].ConnectionString;

        public BaseUITest()
        {
            browserType = BrowserType.InternetExplorer;
        }

        [TestFixtureSetUp]
        public void FixtureSetup()
        {
            TearDown();
            SetUp();
        }

        [SetUp]
        public void BrowserSetup()
        {
            m_ts = new TransactionScope();

            Browser = BrowserFactory.Create(browserType);
            Browser.GoTo(URL);
        }

        [TearDown]
        public void BrowserTeardown()
        {
            if (Browser != null)
                Browser.Dispose();

            m_ts.Dispose();
            m_ts = null;
        }

        private void SetUp()
        {
            ExecuteStoredProcedure("Test_Setup");
        }

        private void TearDown()
        {
            ExecuteStoredProcedure("Test_TearDown");
        }

        private void ExecuteStoredProcedure(string procedureName)
        {
            SqlConnection sqlConnection = new SqlConnection(m_conString);
            SqlCommand cmd = new SqlCommand(procedureName, sqlConnection);
            cmd.CommandType = CommandType.StoredProcedure;
            cmd.ExecuteNonQuery();
        }
```

```
        }
    }
```

Silverlight Testing

Silverlight 2 includes a unit test harness that enables you to perform both API and UI level unit testing. In 2008 when Microsoft released the source code for the Silverlight 2 controls, they also included roughly 2,000 unit tests to go along with them.

Assembly	Purpose
Microsoft.Silverlight.Testing	Unit test framework
Microsoft.Silverlight.Testing.Framework	Base classes and interfaces for test harnesses

Another tool that is available for testing Silverlight applications is Silvernium, which is based on the Selenium framework. The next listing shows a Silvernium test to test a Silverlight control:

```
using NUnit.Framework;
using Selenium;
using ThoughtWorks.Selenium.Silvernium;

namespace Account.Tests.UI
{
    [TestFixture]
    public class AccountTests
    {
        private const string URL = "http://localhost/SilverLightAccount";
        private const string OBJECTID = "Account";
        private const string SCRIPTKEY = "AccountCreation";

        private ISelenium selenium;
        private Silvernium silvernium;

        [SetUp]
        public void SetUp()
        {
            selenium = new DefaultSelenium("localhost", 4444, "*iexplore", URL);
            selenium.Start();
            selenium.Open(URL);
            silvernium = new Silvernium(selenium, OBJECTID, SCRIPTKEY);
        }

        [TearDown]
        public void TearDown()
        {
            selenium.Stop();
        }

        [Test]
        public void ShouldCommunicateWithSilverNibbleApplication()
        {
```

```
            Assert.AreEqual("Create Accouunt", selenium.GetTitle());
            Assert.AreEqual(800, silvernium.ActualWidth());
            Assert.AreEqual(600, silvernium.ActualHeight());

            Assert.AreNotEqual("null", silvernium.Call("NewAccount", "564858510",
                "100"));

            Assert.AreEqual("100", silvernium.GetPropertyValue("Balance"));

            silvernium.SetPropertyValue("Balance", "300");
            Assert.AreEqual("300", silvernium.GetPropertyValue("Balance"));
        }
    }
}
```

Testing a Silverlight UI is very similar to testing other UIs — you just need to have the right tool for the job.

Summary

This chapter has covered the fundamentals of creating automated user interface testing. With this knowledge you will be able to begin developing a very effective test suite that can drive multiple browsers and test for various UI issues that might occur. Throughout this chapter you've been introduced to many tools that perform the same tasks, but do them differently. You may be thinking at this point, "Should I be using WatiN, Selenium, or Visual Studio web tests?" We're hoping that you have come to the conclusion that it depends on the situation. We're also hoping you walk away from this chapter with the knowledge of why UI testing is important and a realization that it is possible to develop an automated UI suite without spending large sums of money and devoting a massive amount of time.

6

Acceptance Testing

In the previous chapters, the focus has been on ensuring that you build the application correctly, making sure that all the code you write works as you expect now, and going forward. With software, there is an important role to play which is often overlooked — the customer. Although knowing that you've built the system right is important, it is equally as important to know that you've built the right system for your customer.

Considering the customer at every stage of the development process is important for the success of the system. Too often, the customer is handed a fully developed application, only to find it does nothing they wanted. This is an expensive and embarrassing mistake but sadly still happens on many different projects.

Acceptance testing is focused on the customer. The customer can be any stakeholder of the system, but is generally focused on the end-user who will be using the system. Within a project there is generally more than one customer with a different point of view and workflow, which need to be taken into account when testing.

With acceptance testing, the aim is not to ensure the system works but to ensure the application meets the customer requirements. This chapter investigates a number of different ways this can be achieved and the various techniques that can be introduced under the banner of acceptance testing. There are different ways to implement acceptance testing, with people using different terminology for different activities. At the end of this chapter you should have a clear picture about why this is important and how you can start performing acceptance testing.

Acceptance Testing Terminology

One of the problems you'll face with acceptance testing is that the term has been used for many different techniques and approaches throughout the years. Sometimes the meanings are related and share a common concept. Other times people can be talking about completely different forms of testing. We've provided an overview of the different terminology next:

- ❑ **Acceptance Testing.** Also includes customer acceptance testing, user acceptance testing, and functional tests

- ❑ **Executable Specification.** The advantage of having acceptance tests as they form a specification which can be run to verify if the implementation matches what the specification defines

- ❑ **Customer.** The end-user of the system

- ❑ **System.** The application being developed

- ❑ **Acceptance.** Meets the functional and nonfunctional requirements

- ❑ **Functional Requirements.** Features and actions the system must perform, such as display items or allowing users to log in to the system

- ❑ **Nonfunctional Requirements.** Factors around the system, such as performance, scalability, and security

- ❑ **Black Box.** Not dependent on internal details or prior knowledge of the system. Data goes in, results come out. That is all the tests should be aware of.

However, although you can define the terminology, we still don't think this gives an accurate picture of how acceptance testing applies to the development lifecycle. Although the concept of acceptance testing has been around for a long period of time, it has gained more attention in recent years, along with Test Driven Development (TDD) which has resulted in improvements in tools, frameworks, and guidance.

Much of the guidance has come from the rise of extreme programming (XP), agile principals, and scrum methodology. There are two main reasons for this. One of the reasons is because acceptance tests focus on the customer and implementing features valuable to the customer. This aligns with the principals of agile development, which also has a strong focus on delivering software that actually meets the customer requirements. The second reason is that by having a set of automated acceptance tests you can ensure that the software constantly meets your customer requirements and ensures you haven't broken anything while implementing new features. In a similar fashion, having your tests automated means you can spend less time manually testing existing features to ensure they still work in later iterations. This means, you can focus on ensuring that the features being developed work as you expect and desire. This allows you to deliver software in a confident and timely fashion.

We feel acceptance testing is most effective when combined with an agile development process. An iterative process allows the team to focus on specific sections of the application and ensure that they are completed, from design to testing, in a single iteration.

During the iteration is the ideal point to write and implement your acceptance tests. The following process is based on scrum and completing a sprint (a scrum iteration) and how acceptance testing fits.

At the start of the scrum, the team accepts work off the product backlog with the highest priority and in a position to be completed. The product backlog should be broken down into user stories. A *user story* defines a system requirement. The story is a couple of sentences which describes a section of the system which the user requires. An example of a user story is "As a sales administrator, I want to be able to view credit card information so that I can process the payment locally." This describes the viewpoint and user who the story is related to, what they are trying to achieve, and why. This gives you a clear indication of what is required to be implemented.

After a story has been selected, the team should have a good idea about what they are going to implement. This is the stage where they can talk to the customer and product owner to determine what is actually required and to expand on the initial story. Based on this information and other technical discussions amongst the team, tasks are created. These tasks represent the work required to implement the required functionality. This is the stage when you should write the acceptance tests. You know the story you are trying to implement and you should have a good understanding of the tasks required to complete the implementation. As such, you should know how to verify that the application meets the customers' requirements. It's important to note that acceptance tests are not low-level unit tests. They are high-level tests focusing on verifying that the customer requirements, which are defined based on the story, are implemented correctly. We have that found it is useful to define these acceptance tests after selecting a story and before breaking it down into tasks. By having the tests in place you know exactly what you are aiming for. You know everything the system must do and as a result will know when you are finished. You know this because all the tests will pass. This makes the task breakdown more focused on what actually needs to be done.

The team repeats this process until they have enough stories which they feel they can complete within a fixed-length iteration. This then becomes the sprint backlog.

During this planning stage, the customer and product owner should be helping the team define the acceptance tests. The acceptance tests are in place to ensure that the requirements meet their own expectations. The feeling of having this set of tests in place is a great comfort to customers. They can match the story for the sprint, together with a set of tests which describe exactly what will be implemented and how it will work — even before any code has been written. This should also provide a comfort to the development team. The customers have clearly defined the requirements. The team helped the customer come to this conclusion and asked any initial questions while it was still fresh in their minds. The customer should be clear about what they expect and the team should be clear about what they plan to deliver — using the acceptance tests as guidance and verification. However, this doesn't mean that more questions won't arise during development or that incorrect parts of the application won't be developed but the aim is to reduce the cost as much as possible in an attempt to successfully deliver software on time and on budget.

However, customers are generally nontechnical and would be unable to understand the code developed to test the requirements. Instead they would reject the process and either not understand what they were agreeing to, or complain bitterly. Instead of showing customers code, write the tests using plain English and sentences. In a similar fashion to how your story defines a high-level view in a few sentences, acceptance tests should describe the scenario in a few sentences. Even if the customers are technical, you still don't want to discuss the technical details.

There are different styles of how to write the tests. One popular style is the Given, When, Then syntax. For example, your test might be written as follows:

> Given a new user account
>
> When it is created on the system
>
> Then the password should default to P@ssw0rd

These can be as complex as required to solve the specific problem you are testing:

> Given an overdrawn account

And a valid debit card

When the customer requests cash from an ATM

Then an error message should be displayed

And no cash is returned

And the card is returned back to the customer

Having the tests in this style is how the customers can effectively contribute in the planning session and define the tests, while also being able to verify and sign-off on the details. An important fact around having them in this style is the language and terminology used. It has been our experience that customers are also more enthusiastic about testing when the test cases are defined in this fashion as they feel they are adding real value to the project because of the automatic bond felt by being closer to the project and more involved. This provides a positive feeling about the application from the beginning which hopefully will be carried over when you deliver the software and the customer sees all the tests they helped write passing with working functionally.

If you notice when the test was written there was no mention of technical details, terms, or implementation.

Instead, you should focus on the business problem and scenario, using the same language as the business would use to describe the problem. This has two major benefits. The first is that you don't need a technical background to understand the scenario and the expected outcome. Secondly, if the underlying implementation changes you don't need to go back and update your tests to reflect this change. This is important because the tests are high-level and potentially cover a number of different components of your code base. You don't want them to be dependent on the exact details as over time they will change. By remaining high-level, you allow the flexibility for the system to change without having to affect the tests. Of course, if the scenario is no longer valid because it has been dropped or changed in some way then the test should be updated to reflect this.

Tests which hang around and are not useful are harmful to a project and test suite. The test suite should be as streamlined and focused as possible, enough tests to provide a very high level of confidence, but no wastage. Having redundant tests causes higher maintenance, and as a result, higher costs and frustration. If the test isn't providing any value — remove it.

When you have the tests in place, the next question is how should they be run to ensure they pass? As with many different parts of testing you can either test it manually or you can automate the testing.

Executing these tests manually would be a time-consuming process. Although manual testing might seem the much faster option, in the long run it is more time-consuming as every time you change part of the system you need to re-run your set of manual tests. At the beginning while the system is small this might not be too much of a problem. However, as the system grows this will become more time-consuming and motivation will drop resulting in more mistakes and things potentially being missed. There is also the additional time of converting the scenarios created during planning into manual test cases for them to be executed. As you can see, it doesn't seem as cheap as you think.

The other approach is to automate the tests.

Using Automation

There are many ways to automate customer acceptance tests. One of the most popular approaches is using a tool called FitNesse,

FitNesse

FitNesse is based on Fit. Fit is an abbreviation for Framework for Integrated Testing originally developed by Ward Cunningham. One of the main motivations for Fit is to improve communication and collaboration, allowing customers and business analytics to write and execute tests against the system.

The aim of Fit/FitNesse is collaboration around the system with the result being an executable specification. By using the wiki format for managing the test cases and scripts, it lowers the barrier for accessibility by allowing the entire team, including customers, to collaborate on creating new test cases.

Along with the wiki front end, there is an underlying code base which handles the communication between the wiki and the system under test. The layer provides an abstract view of how to interact with your system which enables you to write simpler, more focused tests for the wiki. Depending on the skill-set of the team, this layer might be written by a developer or technical tester leaving the tests in the wiki to be written by nontechnical members. Having the ability to allocate responsibility to the people with the correct skill-set is important for productivity and motivation.

Setting Up FitNesse Wiki

Setting up a FitNesse wiki for a project is a relativity painless process. After downloading the framework, you need to unzip it into the directory where you want the wiki to be stored. To start the wiki server you simply run the java jar file and define the port number. This will launch the server which you can connect to from any Internet browser, as shown in Figure 6-1:

```
>java -jar fitnesse.jar -p 8080
FitNesse (v20090513) Started...
        port:              8080
        root page:         fitnesse.wiki.FileSystemPage at ./FitNesseRoot
        logger:            none
        authenticator:     fitnesse.authentication.PromiscuousAuthenticator
        html page factory: fitnesse.html.HtmlPageFactory
        page version expiration set to 14 days.
```

At this point you can start writing your first tests and defining your executable specification for the application.

To create a new page, you should edit the homepage and add links to additional pages which will contain the tests. You do this via the edit box in Figure 6-2. To add a link you need to use a Camel Case name, for example MyFirstTest — the wiki engine will take care of the test:

```
!1 Welcome to      [[FitNesse][FitNesse.FitNesse]]!
!2 Example Tests
MyFirstTest
```

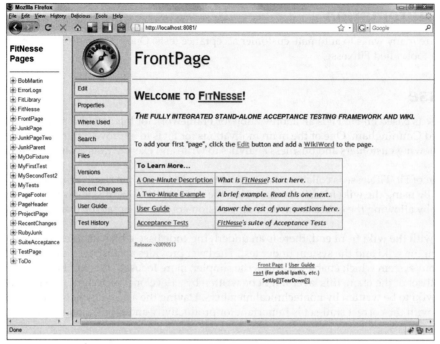

Figure 6-1: FitNesse wiki homepage

Figure 6-2: Editing homepage to add a new link

After adding the link you will be taken to the edit page for this new page where you can include your tests. The first part of the test is to set up the environment variables. These tell the FitNesse engine about the environment and where it can find various key bits of information. For example, FitServer is the runner which is capable of running the FitNesse tests:

```
!define COMMAND_PATTERN {%m %p}
!define TEST_RUNNER {dotnet\FitServer.exe}
!define PATH_SEPARATOR {;}
```

After you have defined the generic settings, you need to point the page to the assembly containing your layer between the tests and the actual application:

```
!path D:\Users\Ben Hall\Documents\TestingASPnet\6-Acceptance\Samples\
FitnesseExample\FitnesseExample\bin\Debug\FitnesseExample.dll
```

Underneath these settings your FitNesse table is defined:

```
|Division|
|numerator|denominator|quotient?|
|10       |2          |5        |
|12.6     |3          |4.2      |
|100      |4          |24       |
```

If you break down your FitNesse table, |Division| is the name of the class which handles the translation between the wiki and FitNesse and the application under test.

As such, the class within your test assembly would look like this. In this case, your implementation is in-line with the fixture; however, it could have gone off and called external assemblies or systems. Fundamentally it is just C# with properties and methods. Notice if your table quotient had a question marked. This means that the method should return a value and the result should equal the row's value:

```
public class Division : fit.ColumnFixture
{
    public double numerator = 0.0;
    public double denominator = 0.0;
    public double quotient()
    {
        return numerator/denominator;
    }
}
```

For FitNesse to work, the column names need to match the property or method. This is the same for the class name. ColumnFixture is one of the many different base classes within Fit and also the most commonly used as it simply maps the properties and methods to the columns.

After saving the wiki page with a correctly formatted table, FitNesse will give you a HTML page with the table rendered in a readable format as demonstrated in Figure 6-3.

After you click the test menu item, the wiki is updated with color coding to indicate if the row passed or failed. As shown in Figure 6-4, the final row failed because the value 25 was returned when 24 was expected.

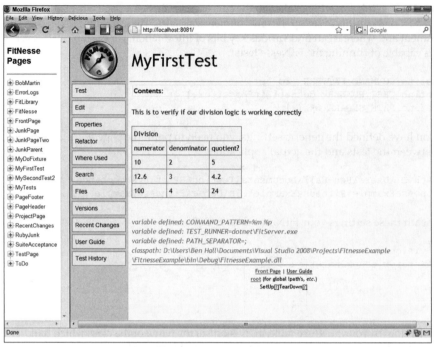

Figure 6-3: Screenshot of fixture before execution

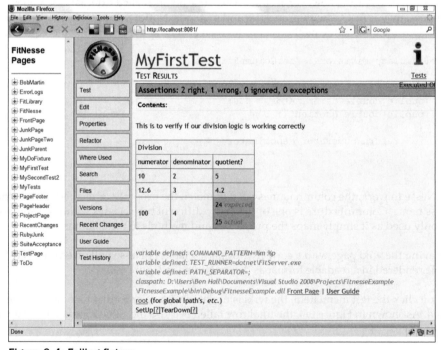

Figure 6-4: Failing fixture

With this fixture in place, anyone can add additional tests, execute them at any point, and see if they pass\fail. If you imagine this process when it comes to complex business calculations and rules, anyone can input the values and instantly know if the system supports it or not.

To make the tests a bit more maintainable, you should move your configuration into the root. In the footer of each page there is a link to the root page — this is inherited by every test page and so it is the perfect location for this kind of information. You can now continue to add wiki pages and fixtures into your assembly based on the different logic within your system.

Although ColumnFixture makes it easy to add multiple different test inputs for a particular fixture, it makes it much more difficult to create a script or a story around the test. This is where DoFixture comes in.

DoFixture is much more powerful than ColumnFixture and allows your tables to be more expressive. It takes the same concept of matching column names but allows you to create sentences, injecting values at certain places to make the tests more readable and follow a more natural descriptive language.

The concept is to use various methods on your fixture to form a test script which can be executed against your system. This is the ideal fixture to use to create your executable specification as it provides more freedom to create more complex scenarios and verifications, moving beyond a single scenario with multiple test inputs\outputs. The DoFixture is also suitable for replacing your manual tests, which are discussed in Chapter 7, as they are capable of different steps to verify the behavior.

In the following example, the steps for making tea are described. There are various properties which go into making a great cup of tea. The values and steps taken will determine the outcome. When using a DoFixture, your FitTable would reassemble this:

```
|Making Tea|
|For type|English breakfast|boil kettle And Insert|1|Teabag|
|Insert|2|of milk|
|Leave tea bag in for|4|
|Check|strength is|Normal|
```

Similar to the ColumnFixture, "Making Tea" is the name of the class. To improve readability, FitNesse will automatically remove the spaces to find the class. You can then define your method calls. Each row represents a method. The columns alternate between parts of the method name and parameters. In this case, the associated method is this:

```
public void ForTypeBoilKettleAndInsertTeabag(string name, int tea)
{
    TeaName = name;
    AmountOfTea = tea;
}
```

The first column, For type, is part of the method name with "English Breakfast" being associated with the first argument. Boil kettle and insert is the middle part of the method while 1 is the second argument to the method. Finally, Teabag is the end of the method name. This is how DoFixture finds the correct method to call and the arguments to use.

The second and third rows are the second and third method calls which should be made:

```
public void InsertOfMilk(int amount)
{
```

```
        AmountOfMilk = amount;
    }
    public void LeaveTeaBaginfor(int time)
    {
        AmountOfTime = time;
    }
```

The fourth row begins with Check. Check is not part of the method name but a keyword for FitNesse. This simply means that the final column is the value you expect the method to return. FitNesse will then verify the result with the value in the cell. If they are different, it will mark it as an error, showing both expected and actual.

For this example, the method which returns the result is a complex rule system which describes the type of tea you will have as a result of the input:

```
    public string StrengthIs()
    {
        if (AmountOfTea == 1 && AmountOfTime == 4 && AmountOfMilk == 2)
            return "Normal";
        if (AmountOfTea == 1 && AmountOfTime == 1 && AmountOfMilk == 6)
            return "Milky";
        if ((AmountOfTea == 2 && AmountOfTime == 6 && AmountOfMilk == 0) ||
    (AmountOfTea > 0 && NoMilk))
            return "Black";
        if (AmountOfTea == 2 && AmountOfTime == 4 && AmountOfMilk == 2)
            return "Strong";
        if (AmountOfTea == 0 && AmountOfMilk > 0)
            throw new NotTeaException();
        return "Water";
    }
```

The page is then rendered as shown in Figure 6-5. You can see that the Check column is followed by the StrengthIs method call. This will call the method above. FitNesse expects the results returned from the method to be Normal. If the value is Normal then it passes and you know the system is implemented correctly.

As mentioned, the DoFixture allows you to build more of a story-based model around the scenario you are testing. For example, here you have a separate test but you call the method Without Milk instead of InsertOfMilk. This changes the values in your system and as a result you expect the strength to be 'Black':

```
|Making Tea|
|For type|English breakfast|boil kettle And Insert|1|Teabag|
|Without milk|
|Leave tea bag in for|4|
|Check|strength is|Black|
```

You can continue to do this for different scenarios, using either different values or calling different methods on your fixture to interact with the system and achieve the result you expect to ensure that everything is working as expected:

```
|Making Tea|
|For type|English breakfast|boil kettle And Insert|2|Teabag|
```

```
|Insert|2|of milk|
|Leave tea bag in for|4|
|Check|strength is|Strong|
```

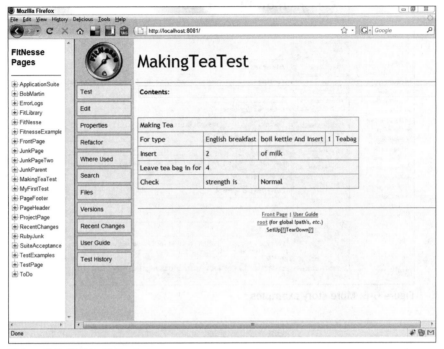

Figure 6-5: Making tea story

The resulting page is shown in Figure 6-6 with the multiple different test cases as different tables.

Although it is easy to create tests, it is also important to remember how to structure and organize the tests. FitNesse has the concept of SubWikis. This allows you to have a single page which links to a number of other pages to form a hierarchy of tests. This hierarchy can follow the same structure as your Visual Studio solution for your FitFixtures to keep everything in sync. Another approach is to structure your wiki page based on the different stories and logic parts of your application. By using SubWikis, your tests become much easier to manage as they are logically grouped together.

Creating a hierarchy or SubWiki for your tests is very simple. You can edit your wiki page as you would to add a normal test; however, instead of adding your FitTable, you add another link. By prefixing the link with a > you start to form a hierarchy as done in Figure 6-7.

You can continue to build different levels. When you have finished, you simply have a normal page with your FitTable as demonstrated in Figure 6-8.

To support being able to access C# namespaces, you can include the namespace to the FitFixture. Make sure you include an '!' at the beginning to help the markup. With this in place, the engine will be able to find the class and execute the tests. Figure 6-9 shows the results of a test against a C# class.

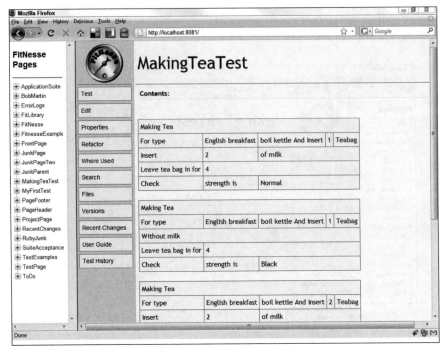

Figure 6-6: More story examples

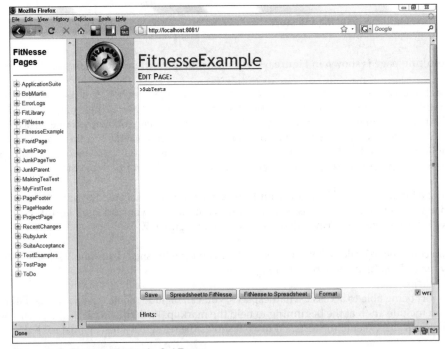

Figure 6-7: FitNesseExample.SubTests

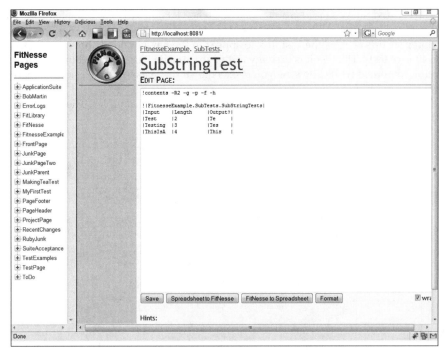

Figure 6-8: FitNesseExample.SubTests.SubStringTest edit page

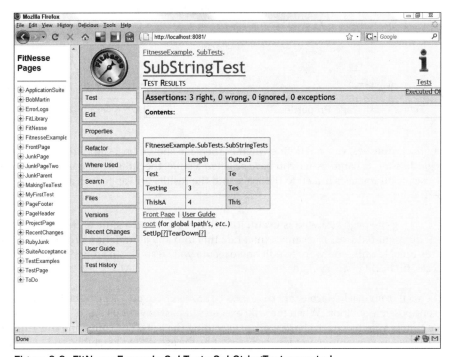

Figure 6-9: FitNesseExample.SubTests.SubStringTest executed

Having a structured SubWiki is also advantageous when it comes to execution. FitNesse correctly detects that the wiki pages you have created so far are tests because you have ended the names with Test. By doing so, this enables the Test link to appear in the navigation. By having a SubWiki, you can execute a suite of tests. The result is that any test pages attached are executed in a single batch with the results being combined while allowing you to execute all the tests in a much shorter space of time.

To create a suite, you can either end the page name with Suite or Examples. The other option is to manually edit the properties for the page as shown in Figure 6-10.

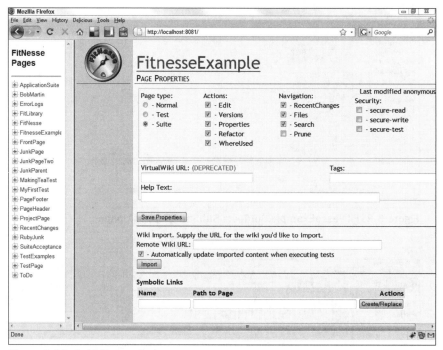

Figure 6-10: Page Properties

By editing the properties, you can define whether the page should be a standard wiki page, a test, or a suite regardless of its name. After you have selected a suite, the Suite button is enabled. Clicking this will execute all the tests linked to that page and the results will appear in a similar fashion to Figure 6-11.

Although having the page as a wiki is useful for collaboration and a suite allows you to execute a number of different fixtures, you cannot integrate this into any automation process (such as a build step) at this time. Ideally, you want to edit and execute your tests on an ad hoc basis, but also after every successful build or every night.

Richard Fennell from Black Marble (http://www.blackmarble.co.uk/) in the United Kingdom, provides one possible solution. When the wiki executes, it passes various bits of information to the command line runner which does the hard work of executing the tests. The command line runner is very simple to execute as you simply provide the HTML file, the associated assembly, and an output directory where you want the results to appear. For example, to execute the test.html page you would use the following command:

```
fitnesse\dotnet\FolderRunner.exe -i test.html -a ..\FitnesseExample\
FitnesseExample\bin\Debug\FitnesseExample.dll -o results
```

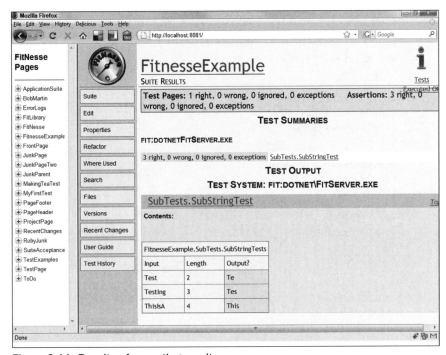

Figure 6-11: Results of executing a suite

At this point, the fact that FitNesse is based on a wiki page is irrelevant. The runner expects a constructed HTML page with the HTML correctly formatted. As such, the page can be as simple as shown in Figure 6-12.

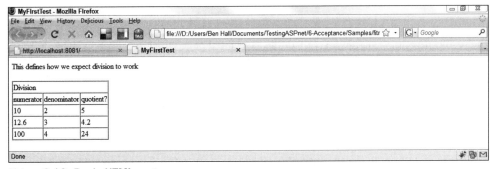

Figure 6-12: Basic HTML page

The HTML for the page looks like this. This can be created using any HTML editor:

```
<html>
    <head>
        <title>MyFirstTest</title>
    </head>
    <body>
        This defines how we expect division to work<br/><br/>
        <table border="1" cellspacing="0">
            <tr>
            <td colspan="3">Division</td>
            </tr>
            <tr>
            <td>numerator</td>
            <td>denominator</td>
            <td>quotient?</td>
            </tr>
            <tr>
            <td>10</td>
            <td>2</td>
            <td>5</td>
            </tr>
            <tr>
            <td>12.6</td>
            <td>3</td>
            <td>4.2</td>
            </tr>
            <tr>
            <td>100</td>
            <td>4</td>
            <td>24</td>
            </tr>
        </table>
    </body>
</html>
```

After the command has been executed, a summary of what was executed is outputted to the console and a results directory created. For example, the command would show that two of your rows were correct, while one was incorrect:

```
2 right, 1 wrong, 0 ignored, 0 exceptions, time: 00:00:00.1904296
```

In the results directory you have a copy of the associated page which has been updated to reflect the actual\expected results. As you can see from Figure 6-13, this is the same page you would have seen if you were using the wiki-based solution.

At this point you can have your tests run in an automated fashion. Richard took this approach a step further by having each page executed as a separate test. The test would then know if it should pass or fail to represent the result of the FitNesse execution.

For this to execute, simply use the FolderRunner object within the Fit assembly. The run method has the same arguments as the command line and returns an error count after all the tests have been executed:

```
[Test]
public void TestPage()
```

```
        {
            string page = @"test.html";
            string assembly = @"FitnesseExample.dll";
            fit.Runner.FolderRunner runner = new fit.Runner.FolderRunner(new fit.
Runner.ConsoleReporter());
            var errorCount = runner.Run(new[] { "-i", page, "-a", assembly, "-o",
@"results" });
            Assert.AreEqual(0, errorCount, runner.Results);
        }
```

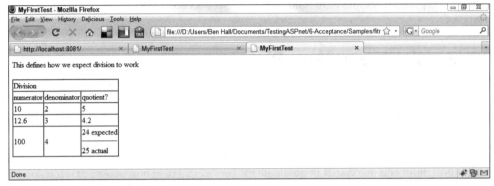

Figure 6-13: Basic results page

The result is your test results can now be executed and viewed within Visual Studio as shown in Figure 6-14.

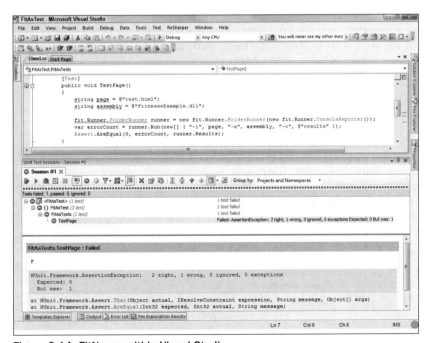

Figure 6-14: FitNesse within Visual Studio

By having your FitNesse tests running as unit tests you can combine the test of both worlds. You have the advantage of being able to write your test cases as HTML and in a separate file while being able to execute them as unit tests within Visual Studio or as part of your build system.

Personally, I think FitNesse solves a problem. If you have a complex rule system or accounting package that works with the idea of columns, values, and predictable results then FitNesse will without a doubt help. However, I find the DoFixture and more complex scenario difficult to read and understand and error prone when it comes to attaching the method calls to separated column names. The problem is that some things aren't suited to being stored in a table. As a result, other frameworks have taken the concept of acceptance tests and built their own frameworks capable of having nontechnical members write tests.

FitNesse, WatiN and WroxPizza

To provide some more context about how you could use FitNesse to create customer acceptance tests we wanted to provide an example of how you could combine what we discussed in Chapter 5 with regard to WatiN and UI testing together with FitNesse.

With FitNesse, there is the wiki which provides test inputs and verifies outputs together with the C# fixtures which control the test execution. The hardest part is creating the C# fixtures, which in this case will take input and use WatiN to automate the browser against our website at which point we can return results to the wiki engine.

Following on from Chapter 5, you are going to reproduce the same style of tests you created to verify how the application works using FitNesse to start moving towards a more collaborative approach to writing the test cases. The first test will be to verify that the correct products and categories are listed on the Products Menu page.

As you have done before, you need to create a new wiki page on our FitNesse server. In order to verify the products are being displayed correctly there needs to be a FitNesse table which lists all the products and states if they should be listed on the page or not.

```
!|WroxFitNesse.ProductsMenuFixture|
|product          |productListed? |
|Thrufropaquentor |true           |
|p2               |false          |
```

This table assumes that a class called ProductsMenuFixture exists in our assembly, which provides the functionality to verify the website. The fixture needs two parts, one is a variable called product to store the name of the product we want to check to see if it exists on the page, while the other is a method which verifies if that product actually exists. Because we are using the classic FitNesse table, our class will inherit from ColumnFixture. The code to ensure the above table can execute is next:

```
public class ProductsMenuFixture : ColumnFixture
{
    ProductsMenuPage page;
    private IBrowser browser;

    public ProductsMenuFixture()
    {
```

```
            page = new ProductsMenuPage(browser);
        }

    public string product;
    public bool productListed()
    {
        return page.Products.Contains(product);
    }
}
```

The above code should look familiar as we are following the same approach as we took in Chapter 5 to verify the functionality. In Chapter 5 we created a class for each page which modeled how the website was structured, the links, textboxes and general functionality of the site. Because the model was clean and abstract we can simply re-use this set of classes for use within our FitNesse fixture.

Another thing to point out is that our fixture and the productListed( ) method doesn't handle the verification about if it should pass\fail, instead it just provides a Boolean of the actual result and lets the wiki decide the outcome.

However, before we can execute the wiki page and use WatiN to verify the functionality we have two core parts missing. Previously we used the TestFixtureSetup to configure where the application was deployed to. In FitNesse, we do not have these particular hooks in place. Instead, the Setup and Teardown are separate pages which we can use to configure the application. In this example, we are going to assume that the application is configured and accessible from the FitNesse server via automated deployment scripts to copy the files to an IIS server and not utilize FitNesse. We do this to provide more flexibility and it is much easier to manage via scripts.

Secondly, we used the TestSetup method to start the browser. With FitNesse, this is something that needs to be done via the FitNesse page, either on the page with the tables on or the set-up page. On the page, we would write code such as:

```
!|WroxFitNesse.WatiNBrowserFactory          |
|Use Browser|IE|and goto|http://localhost:62201/|

!|WroxFitNesse.WatiNBrowserFactory|
|Close Browser                    |
```

The first table configures the test to use the browser IE and says the website is located at a particular URL. By having these two properties configured by the wiki, we can swap the browser or URL very easily to test in a different way instead of being hardcoded to a particular implementation. Again, abstracting makes life easier when developing our tests.

In order to support the previous tables the tables above, we need a fixture which is capable of controlling the browser. In this case, we are taking advantage of the DoFixture to provide a more natural language approach to writing the tables. The code is just standard C# and stores the information from the wiki in various properties for future use. Notice, we are using static variables so we can access the data from our Test fixtures:

```
public class WatiNBrowserFactory : DoFixture
{
    static IBrowser browser;
    public string Url;
```

```
public static string BrowserName;

public void UseBrowserAndGoTo(string browserName, string url)
{
    BrowserName = browserName;
    Url = url;

    browser = GetBrowser(BrowserName);
    browser.GoTo(url);
}

public void CloseBrowser()
{
    if (browser != null) browser.Dispose();
}
}
```

The most complex part is the GetBrowser method. This will take the name provided by the wiki page and create a browser instance. By using static methods we can follow the singleton pattern, allowing us to control how many browser instances are open at any particular point in the system:

```
public static IBrowser GetBrowser(string name)
{
    if (browser == null)
    {
        switch (name)
        {
            case "IE":
                browser = BrowserFactory.Create(BrowserType.
InternetExplorer);
                break;
            case "FireFox":
                browser = BrowserFactory.Create(BrowserType.FireFox);
                break;
            default:
                browser = BrowserFactory.Create(BrowserType.
InternetExplorer);
                break;
        }
    }

    return browser;
}
```

With the WatiNBrowserFactory in place, we can update our Test fixture to use the static items to get the browser instance to use for our tests.

```
public ProductsMenuFixture()
{
    browser = WatiNBrowserFactory.GetBrowser(WatiNBrowserFactory.
BrowserName);
    page = new ProductsMenuPage(browser);
}
```

There is one more piece of the puzzle to solve before we can execute the tests. If you remember from Chapter 5, in order for WatiN to work, the thread and test runner needs to be set as STA. In order to do this with FitNesse we need to provide a configuration file in our command pattern argument. The file we are creating is called suite.config.xml which is stored within the dotnet folder.

```
!define COMMAND_PATTERN {%m -c dotnet\suite.config.xml %p}
```

The contents of the file should be as follows:

```
<suiteConfig>
    <fit.Settings>
        <apartmentState>STA</apartmentState>
    </fit.Settings>
</suiteConfig>
```

More information on the configuration file can be found in the documentation at http://www.syterra .com/FitnesseDotNet/SuiteConfigurationFile.html.

We now have our FitNesse wiki page being able to verify the functionality of our web application using WatiN. Our wiki page has three main parts, the first page tells the WatiNBrowserFactory which browser to use and the base URL. We have our test table which defines our test and input, and finally another table which closes the browser.

Behind the scenes, we have our ProductsMenuFixture which takes in the test input from the wiki. This communicates with the WatiNBrowserFactory to obtain the instance of the browser, and also our page model which we created in Chapter 5 and knows how to interact with the website and return results. Our Suite.config.xml sets the threading model for FitNesse to STA so that WatiN can communicate with IE.

We can now execute our wiki page and see results as shown in Figure 6-15. We can also extend the tests and add more tables such as verifying which categories are displayed:

```
!|WroxFitNesse.ProductsMenuFixture                      |
|category                                 |categoryListed?|
|Pro linguens non trepicandor si quad estis vobis r|true   |
|category1                                |false          |
```

Adding this table means we need to edit our ProductsMenuFixture to include the correct property and method.

```
public string category;
public bool categoryListed()
{
    return page.Categories.Contains(category);
}
```

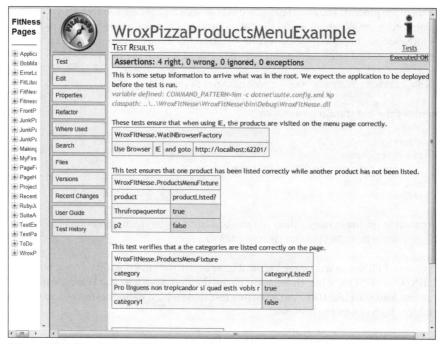

Figure 6-15: WroxPizza FitNesse Examples using ColumnFixture

While this uses ColumnFixture, a more readable approach could be to use the DoFixture and use a story driven approach when it comes to writing the tests. Personally, we feel this is the more desirable approach. For example, if we wanted to verify that we could add a particular product into the shopping cart a more readability would be as follows:

```
!|WroxFitNesse.AddItemToCartFixture|
|When adding|Thrufropaquentor|into the basket|
|For line|1|
|Check|name is|Thrufropaquentor|
|Check|Quantity is|1|
|Check|price is|$718.2393|
```

We first say we are adding a certain product into the basket. We are then defining the line we are interested in verifying which allows us to perform checks against the particular columns to ensure everything is correct. For us, having this level of control and flexibility is extremely powerful.

The DoFixture implementation for AddItemToCartFixture is as follows. We interact with the page model, which in turn uses WatiN to control IE. We then have multiple methods for name, quantity and price, which uses the value set via the For Line method to obtain the correct shopping cart item from the web page:

```
public class AddItemToCartFixture : DoFixture
{
    private IBrowser browser;
    ProductsMenuPage page;
    ShoppingCartPage cart;
```

```
        private int lineToVerify;

        public AddItemToCartFixture()
        {
            browser = WatiNBrowserFactory.GetBrowser(WatiNBrowserFactory.
BrowserName);
            page = new ProductsMenuPage(browser);
        }

        public void WhenAddingIntoTheBasket(string productName)
        {
            cart = page.AddToBasket(productName);
        }

        public void ForLine(int lineNumber)
        {
            //Wiki you would want to write 1,2,3 - in code it is 0,1,2
            lineToVerify = lineNumber - 1;
        }

        public string NameIs()
        {
            List<Cart.Item> lines = cart.Items.Lines;
            Cart.Item line = lines[lineToVerify];
            return line.Name;
        }

        public string QuantityIs()
        {
            List<Cart.Item> lines = cart.Items.Lines;
            Cart.Item line = lines[lineToVerify];
            return line.Quantity;
        }

        public string PriceIs()
        {
            List<Cart.Item> lines = cart.Items.Lines;
            Cart.Item line = lines[lineToVerify];
            return line.Price;
        }
    }
```

The resulting wiki page looks as shown in Figure 6-16, which we find readable and straight forward demonstrating the functionality being tested. We can add additional text around the table to help people understand the concepts more, improving readability at each stage.

Other frameworks have also realized that more of a story driven approach as we have described can result in improved tests. One of those frameworks is called Cucumber.

Cucumber

One of the most popular acceptance testing frameworks is Cucumber (`http://cukes.info/`) which is an open source Ruby framework. The framework takes concepts from BDD, as discussed in Chapter 2, and RSpec, which is another BDD framework for Ruby but with Cucumber focusing on writing automation acceptance tests. When using Cucumber to create customer tests you have two distinct parts. First you have a plain-text file which contains the feature and scenario information which you are verifying. These scenarios are created in plain English using business terminology (instead of technical) to allow the team to create and fully understand what they are covering. Removing ambiguity around technical aspects and focusing on users\business requirements reduces the risk of missing tests or being confused by the actual meaning and aim.

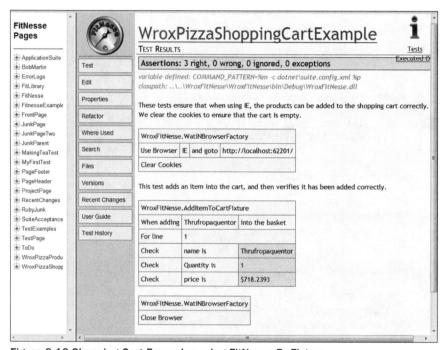

Figure 6-16 Shopping Cart Examples using FitNesse DoFixture

The second part of this is how these steps get executed. Each line within a scenario is treated as a step in the process of setting up or verifying the system, using the Given When Then (GWT) we discussed before. Each step is then attached to a Ruby method. The method configures the system in a particular fashion, similar to how the methods in a DoFixture with FitNesse worked.

For example, your feature and scenario file might contain the following:

Feature: Google Search
   To find more about Testing ASP.NET
   I need to be able to search Google

Scenario: Google Search for Testing ASP.NET
   Given that I use Google
   When I search for "Testing ASP.NET"
   Then I should see "testing"

The feature defines the high-level overview of what the scenarios are covering. This should provide the reader with some context to the scenarios. The scenario then defines the steps and expected result. A feature generally has many different scenarios focusing on different aspects of the behavior for that particular feature.

Each step is a method which is defined in a Ruby file within a step_definitions folder. For example, your given step is defined next:

```
Given /^that I use Google$/ do
  pending
end
```

In case you are unfamiliar with Ruby syntax, there are a few key points. First with Ruby method calls, the brackets ( ) around method calls are optional to improve readability. RegEx is also a core part of the language and as such can be defined as a first class citizen, again to improve the readability. Finally, Ruby has the concepts of blocks. A *block* is a piece of code which can be passed into a method and can be executed as part of the method itself. This is similar to delegates and lambda expressions within C#.

These three concepts are used in the previous method. Given is a method which we are calling. Two arguments are then provided, a key and a block which need to be executed. Under the covers, Cucumber matches the step in your plain text to this method based on the key and executes the method, which executes the block provided.

The same approach is taken for both the When and Then steps as well. A system can have multiple Given\When\Then blocks, each identified via a unique key. However, having hard-coded strings is not a very effective way to reuse code. In the previous scenario, if you wanted to test two different search terms or results you would need to create different methods. This will increase complexity and maintenance costs.

To cope with this you can include a series of RegEx expressions when you define the RegEx key, which will pull out key parts of the string and pass them into the block as arguments. This has been done with the When and Then blocks as defined next. You can now use these same methods multiple times, providing different strings and verifying different results. This provides amazing power and flexibility:

```
When /^I search for "([^\"]*)"$/ do |arg1|
  pending
end
Then /^I should see "([^\"]*)"$/ do |arg1|
  pending
end
```

Within the block for each method you call the *pending* method. One of the aspects of customer acceptance tests is that they can be written before implementation of the code. Call pending means that you can continue developing the boilerplate scenarios and methods, but when they are executed they will be marked not as failing but as pending. This provides you with an improved indication of the current state of the projects and the tests.

However, you want to replace the pending blocks with actual implementation. In this case, you want to interact with the Google search engine, search for a particular term, and verify the search results containing a particular term. Cucumber provides you with the framework for executing the tests, but you need another framework for interacting with web pages. As discussed in Chapter 5, WatiN is a .NET port of the Ruby framework Watir. You can combine Cucumber with Watir to provide the customer acceptance tests with the ability to test the UI.

In the same file as your step methods you should include the method calls to require the framework as shown in the sample below. This allows you to access the test framework RSpec to provide test-like functionality and Watir to access a browser. Watir has the ability to interact with IE, Firefox, and Safari — this example simply uses IE; however, the principals are the same. In Chapter 5 we covered UI testing and WatiN. Because WatiN is just a port of Watir they are fundamentally the same and as such the same concept applies.

As you want a new browser instance for each scenario, you should use the 'Before' step. This is executed before each scenario is run:

```
require 'spec'
require 'Watir/ie'
Before do |scenario|
    BROWSER = Watir::IE.new_process
end
```

To make sure you don't leave lots of browser windows open, use the "After" step to close the window:

```
After do |scenario|
    BROWSER.close
end
```

You can now fill in the implementation of each step and interact with the browser. Your Given block needs to direct the browser to a particular page:

```
BROWSER.goto("http://www.google.com")
```

Your When block searches for a particular term. The first thing is to set the field name to the value you obtained from the regular expression from your story. After you have entered the search term, click the button:

```
BROWSER.text_field(:name, "q").set(arg1)
BROWSER.button(:name, "btnG").click
```

Finally, you need to verify that the results include the correct value expected. This is done by obtaining the HTML and using the include? method which returns a Boolean. You can then use the should extension property to verify that it equals true.

```
BROWSER.html.include?(arg1).should == true
```

After you have your plain-text scenario and the steps created in Ruby, you can execute it to determine if Google is working as expected. The results of the execution are shown in Figure 6-17.

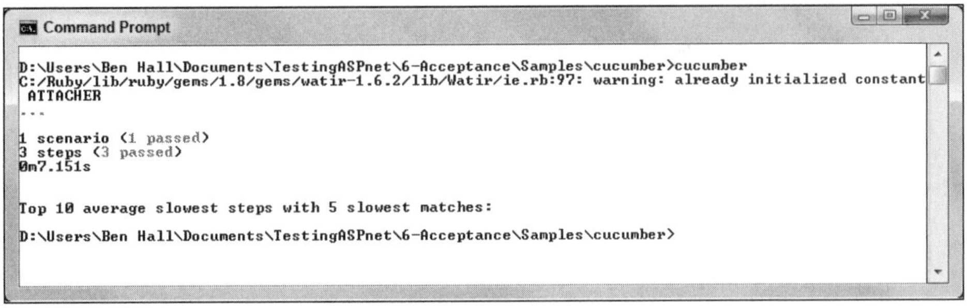

Figure 6-17: Executing Cucumber

In this case, everything passed as expected. A summary is given of the scenarios executed together and how many steps passed:

1 scenario (1 passed)
3 steps (3 passed)

If you have a step which failed, there will be more information written to the console, as shown in Figure 6-18.

Figure 6-18: Executing Cucumber with failing scenario

Cucumber also includes the ability to take the plain text story, together with the execution results, and output an HTML report as shown in Figure 6-19. This can be placed on a file share — in the build output — or integrated into your continuous integration dashboard for everyone to access. Because it's readable, everyone should be able to understand the correct state of the project and which parts of the system have not yet been implemented.

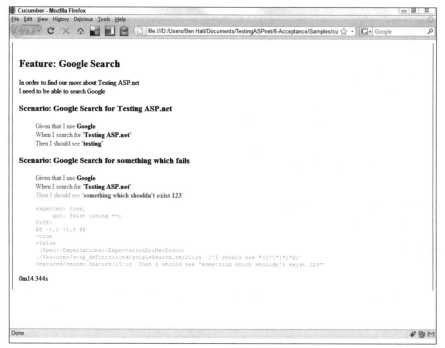

Figure 6-19: Cucumber HTML report

To execute, you need to set up Cucumber and Watir. Ruby has a packaging system called RubyGems. To install libraries such as Cucumber and Watir you can use RubyGems to download the library and any dependencies and documentation, and install it into the correct location for you to use. The commands you need to use are here:

```
gem install cucumber
gem install watir
```

In terms of directory structure, you should generally follow this layout:

```
/spec
/<storyname>
<name>.feature
/step_definitions
    -   steps.rb
```

The <name>.feature file refers to the file containing your plain text with steps.rb.

Finally, within the spec root directory you need a cucumber.yml which stores profiles of different settings. This allows you to store ways of executing it via command line, produce different reports, and execute different sets of tests without having to re-enter the command:

```
default: --format profile .
```

Execution is now a case of simply entering "cucumber" from the command line when you're in the spec directory.

When it comes to testing your own ASP.NET application, the fact that Cucumber and Watir are Ruby-based does not hold you back. As demonstrated in Chapter 5, the beauty of ASP.NET is that after it has been rendered by the browser you can use frameworks to interact and verify it is working in exactly the same fashion as you did with Google in this example and WatiN in Chapter 5. Because these are still UI tests, the concepts discussed in Chapter 5 still apply — you are taking advantage of Cucumber and the Ruby syntax to improve how you write the tests and collaborate on the system. Combining Cucumber with automated UI tests is a very effective way to do your customer acceptance tests, taking advantages from both worlds. The fact that you are using it against an ASP.NET application is irrelevant.

However, Cucumber doesn't just need to be used for testing via the browser. It can also test at the object level. However, because your objects are C# based, this is not possible with the same Ruby language. However, Microsoft has created IronRuby which allows you to take the Ruby language but interact with C# objects in a native way. The result is that you can use frameworks such as RSpec and Cucumber to test C# applications. Ben Hall wrote a series of articles for *MSDN Magazine* which covers this concept in more detail: `http://msdn.microsoft.com/en-us/magazine/dvdarchive/dd535415.aspx`.

Although Cucumber is Ruby-based and currently the most popular framework of choice, there are alternatives. Ben Hall is working on a C# based acceptance testing framework called xUnit.GWT (`http://wiki.github.com/BenHall/xUnit.GWT`) which aims to bring some of the advantages Cucumber offers but as C#.

Cucumber, Watir and WroxPizza

As with FitNesse, in order to provide more context around how to use Cucumber, we wanted to describe how the concepts could be applied to the WroxPizza. The first stage is to write the feature and scenario within a file called "list_products.feature" within a directory called features.

The contents of this file are as follows. We first define the feature we are currently testing; in this case we are testing to ensure that the products are displayed correctly on the web page. Underneath the feature we define multiple scenarios which will be converted to steps and executed:

```
Feature: List products
  In order to buy products
  I need to be able to see a list of the products on the menu

  Scenario: List products on the page
     Given I am on the homepage
     When I click on 'Menu'
     Then I should see a product called "Thrufropaquentor"
     And I should not see a product called "p1"
```

The scenario defines how we are verifying the application. We have three main sections; the Given block will tell us what the precondition and setup for the scenario is — in this case we will just be on the homepage. The next step tells us the action we are going to perform — here we are going to click the Menu link. Finally, we have the verification where we say that we expect one problem to appear and don't expect another product.

When we use the console runner to execute the feature, it will say that the steps haven't been executed and provide you with the boilerplate steps to help start the implementation and write the steps. For this scenario, the step outlines was given as the following:

```
Given /^the homepage$/ do
  pending
end

When /^I click the Menu link$/ do
  pending
end

Then /^I should see a product called "([^\"]*)"$/ do |arg1|
  pending
end

Then /^I should not see a product called "([^\"]*)"$/ do |arg1|
  pending
end
```

We can then copy the steps into a file called list_products.rb in the directory features\step_definitions. We can then start developing our steps. As we discussed before, we need to include the require statements to access rspec and the Watir framework. We have our Before block to start the browser and then implement each of our steps. Within each of the steps we use a very similar API to the one we discussed in Chapter 5 to interact with a web page:

```
require 'spec'
require 'Watir/ie'

Before do |scenario|
  @browser = Watir::IE.new_process
end

Given /^I am on the homepage$/ do
  @browser.goto 'http://localhost:62201'
end

When /^I click on '(.*)'$/ do |text|
  @browser.link(:text, link).click
end

Then /^I should see a product called "([^\"]*)"$/ do |name|
  @browser.div(:class, 'Products').text.should include(name)
end

Then /^I should not see a product called "([^\"]*)"$/ do |name|
  @browser.div(:class, 'Products').text.should_not include(name)
end

After do |scenario|
  @browser.close
end
```

Personally, we find this code very clean and straight forward. For instance to verify the product is displayed correctly we gain access to the div with the class "Products". We then access the text and assert that it should include the name we defined in our scenario definition.

After we execute the feature, we can output the report as html as shown in Figure 6-20 and have a very nice and readable report defining which parts of the system are working as expected.

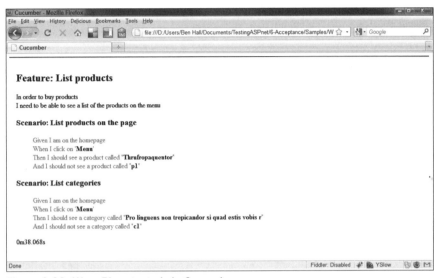

Figure 6-20: Wrox Pizza tested via Cucumber

We could also follow the similar approach to the one we took with WatiN in Chapter 5 and create models around our pages and structure of the website. With Watir and Ruby, the model would look like this:

```ruby
class ProductMenu
    def initialize(browser)
      @browser = browser
    end

    def goto_homepage(url)
        @browser.goto url
    end

    def click(link)
      @browser.link(:text, link).click
    end

    def products()
      @browser.div(:class, 'Products').text
    end

    def categories()
      @browser.div(:id, 'categoryMenu').text
    end
  end
end
```

The implementations of the steps would then interact with the ProductMenu object.

```
require 'spec'
require 'Watir/ie'
require 'model/product_menu'

Before do |scenario|
  @browser = Watir::IE.new_process
  @product_menu = ProductMenu.new @browser
end

Given /^I am on the homepage$/ do
  @product_menu.goto_homepage 'http://localhost:62201'
end

When /^I click on '(.*)'$/ do |text|
  @product_menu.click text
end

Then /^I should see a product called "([^\"]*)"$/ do |name|
  @product_menu.products.should include(name)
end

Then /^I should not see a product called "([^\"]*)"$/ do |name|
  @product_menu.products.should_not include(name)
end

Then /^I should see a category called "([^\"]*)"$/ do |name|
  @product_menu.categories.should include(name)
end

Then /^I should not see a category called "([^\"]*)"$/ do |name|
  @product_menu.categories.should_not include(name)
end

After do |scenario|
  @browser.close
End
```

In this example, the benefit of having the abstract doesn't add too much extra in terms of readability. The Watir API, together with the added advantage Cucumber brings, means the code is already readable, and the step definition titles provide, context into what they are testing. As a result, having a clean abstraction model is less important. Instead, what is important is having a set of understandable and reusable steps. These form the API when writing your acceptance tests and as such these are what need to be readable, understandable, and most importantly, reusable.

Applying Acceptance Testing to Legacy Code

One of the great advantages of acceptance tests is that they are a lot easier to apply to legacy code than unit tests. Following the approaches we have described, you can start adding these styles of customer acceptance tests and providing some level of automated tests around your application without having large refactoring steps. The fact that it is legacy code is irrelevant as we are working at a much higher layer.

These styles of tests can actually provide an increased benefit for legacy code. By having a solid set of customer acceptance tests you can start refactoring your code and adding unit tests under the covers. The added customer acceptance tests will provide you with an additional safety net to ensure that nothing has broken during the refactoring stage. During the refactoring you should be writing integration style tests around the particular section you're working with; however, these added customer tests provide a good end-to-end coverage and safety net.

Summary

Customer acceptance tests are extremely important and valuable if you can achieve the right level of communication and collaboration with the team. By having the tests in place you can verify that the system will actually meet the customer requirements. So far we have focused on automated testing; the next chapter covers manual testing of the system.

7

Manual Testing

This chapter takes a step away from automated testing and instead focuses on manual testing and why it is still extremely relevant even if you have a complete set of automated tests.

Why Is Manual Testing Important?

Although we have already discussed at length the advantages of automated testing, there is still a time and place where manual testing is important, in some cases more important than automated testing. Many people have successfully released software and products without having any automated testing in place, instead relying on the manual testing techniques discussed throughout this chapter. Even though this has been successful for many companies, we feel that the best approach to take is a mixture of automated testing, as we have already discussed, and manual testing. Combining the two provides you with a safety net to catch regression bugs, allowing you to push forward with the development and still catch the issues which only manual testing can uncover.

The aim is to decide how you are going to use each technique to solve different problems. As we discussed in the previous chapters, automated testing is extremely powerful and cost effective at allowing you to ensure that the system meets customer requirements now and in the future, and ensuring that as the system develops and grows, all the requirements and features are still working as you expect. When you add in TDD, the code quality is also increased which will have long-term benefits when it comes to the maintainability of the code base. This is where automated testing is best. However, at the moment automated testing is not very good when it comes to knowing if the application is usable by a human. They can't decide if the text and information provided will be understandable by the end-user. In other ways, it is extremely costly to automate certain parts of the system — for example a jQuery effect which can only really be verified by using the control and ensuring that the effect is as desired. We feel that although this could be automated, it is more effective to manually test the effect, as this will provide you with more confidence that it is working as you expect, and also it is cheaper in terms of time taken.

Although manual testing can appear to be cheaper because it takes less time, there is still a cost associated. It might seem very easy to launch the application, click a few menu items, enter some text, and verify the result — if you imagine doing that once, twice, ten times a day, it will end up costing far more than if the tester or developer had taken a step back and automated the system at that point in time. The key is to pick your battles about what to automate and what to manually test effectively, taking into account initial cost, but also the cost of the lifetime of the project and how many times the test realistically should be run. You also need to take into account the cost of the delay in actually finding the issue. Automated testing will find issues much more quickly than manual testing. If this is important then you need to take this into account when making your decision.

Manual testing also has an effect on the team's motivation which is often overlooked. Manual testing has the major problem of being very repetitive. Having to follow a series of steps without thinking can harm employees' motivation and as a result they may not pay attention to the steps being performed. This could result in problems being missed, or more of a delay in the task being done. This is not the fault of the employee, just a reality of repetitive tasks over a period of time. This is made even worse if you have technical testers and they generally feel the effects more quickly. Automating these repetitive tests will increase employees' motivation and result in the team being more productive. The sooner you identify these potential issues or tasks, the better.

One possible way to overcome this is to partly automate tasks.

Part Automation

Part automation is about trying to remove these repetitive tasks as much as possible. Manual testing is required for certain tasks; however, if you can automate the tasks around the manual testing then your production will increase. Common examples are automating the installation and deployment of the ASP.NET web application and database onto a test server so that it is ready for you to start testing. This saves you having to keep redeploying the application on every new build. This is a small thing and as such, people don't see the harm in manually performing the task, but during the lifecycle of the project it can really mount up.

There are also times when you can re-use the automation techniques discussed in the previous chapters to help get you to the point where you can manually test the application. This could range from inserting test data, creating test objects, or using UI automation to navigate you to certain parts of the application where you can begin manually testing a certain feature to ensure it is working correctly. By automating the easy, boring, sections you save time and motivation allowing you to only manually test the parts really required and leave the rest of the application automated.

Other techniques include automating the process of taking multiple screenshots and then manually verifying that they are correct. The hard work is being done for you; as a tester you simply need to verify that the screenshots are as expected. This is covered more in the section "Cross-Browser Testing," later in this chapter.

But when it comes to manual testing, there is more to it than verifying or breaking the application as we will cover in the next section.

Beyond Simply Breaking the Application

We have discussed the relationship between automated and manual testing, but as we mentioned there are times when you can't automate the application. This is where you need to use manual testing to solve these kinds of issues.

Usability

One key area within the banner of manual testing is usability. Although many projects have dedicated usability testers it is still the responsibility of every tester to ensure that the application can be used effectively by the user. The most important part when testing the application is to view the application from the viewpoint of the user. Ignore any prior knowledge, and treat it as if you were simply using it on a day-to-day basis. You want to make sure that the application is clear and understandable for everyone who needs to use it. It's pointless having a web application that can only be used correctly by the team who built it.

When using the application, make sure that all the pages have a very clear UI and you know exactly what you are expected to do and how to proceed. For example, with a site such as the WroxPizza example it is important to ensure that people know how to add items to their order so they can purchase them. If this is confusing, then the chances of them using the site and purchasing an item would be reduced. You also want to make sure that the pages are designed in a clean fashion. Can you see all the relevant information on the page without having to constantly scroll around? Can you understand the layout and how all the sections of the page relate? Asking these questions is important to ensure that the application can be used successfully.

On the topic of ensuing that you can see everything, it is important to test the usability of the application against the site using different screen resolutions. Even though cross-browser testing is important, testing the user's platform is also important to ensure that the user can still use the application. It's very commonplace for developers to create a site on a 30-inch widescreen which looks amazing, clear, and understandable but when put onto a 17-inch screen at 1024*768 it is cluttered, hard to read, and very confusing because of the space limitations. The same is true for larger screens — you want to make sure that the rendering on a 30-inch screen takes advantage of the space while not looking too empty.

Another item to harm the usability of applications is ambiguity. If you use terms which have multiple meanings, then users of the application may be confused by your meaning of the term. This is even more relevant for web applications as they are potentially catering to users from multiple countries and cultures. As such, it is important to refrain from ambiguity and ensure that the site is still clear for that group. Ambiguity can also be resolved by using commonplace terms and button text. If you follow the defacto standard for various parts of the application then users can automatically process the information instead of having to search for what they are looking for. For example, "Sign In," "Login," and "Authenticate" all have the same meaning; however, if users want to log in to the application they are unlikely to scan the page looking for a link called "Authenticate." Following the defacto standard allows users to scan more quickly and find what they are looking for without any effort.

Another part of web applications which commonly cause frustration for users is delay. There are a number of different ways web applications can suffer delay. The most common delay is the time is takes just simply navigating the site. If your application accesses data from an external resource such as a web service or database then this additional overhead can cause a delay to the user. Even small delays can have a huge impact on a user who is expecting the page to appear immediately. When testing the application you need to ensure that the delay when using the site is not too great. The effects of a delay can be offset by the use of

Ajax allowing pages to be loaded in an asynchronous fashion; however, if the delay is long enough this can actually cause a worse experience. In the next chapter we will cover load testing in more depth.

Delays are a concern, but more of a concern are timeouts. Imagine you have a long application form and you're nearly at the end but the phone rings. After the call you return only to find that the application has crashed and lost your nearly complete form. As a user, how would you feel about having to start again? The same happens if your net drops, which with the rise of 3G and mobile working is more and more likely. Given this situation, as a user you would like the application to be able to cope with this. When it occurred, you would expect the application to have saved the information somehow so the next time you returned it was available to you. Although this would take time and consideration, I think it is important to consider as it will affect how people interact with your application. Remember in ASP.NET the default timeout is 20 minutes, so if you expect there is a chance people might leave the window open longer than that, then you need to take that into account.

Session timeouts are a problem in a large number of applications. Developers often overlook the fact that people leave browser windows open in the background. They store information in a session and expect it will always be there. Sadly this is not the case. These issues are more important for certain applications; however, they should be considered for all ASP.NET sites. However, there is a major problem with usability testing. Generally testers and developers spend a lot of time and energy in the product and as such, often automatically overlook issues as "known faults" or "by design" as they have knowledge of previous discussions within the team. For this reason, it is often a good idea to have third parties come in and help with fresh eyes and help with usability testing. They shouldn't perform all the tasks; however, they will be able to help with the general flow, if the application is understandable in the way it is structured. The results are generally very useful and interesting.

Documentation

Along with usability testing, documentation also needs to be tested. There are two main forms of documentation. One is the general help section your site might provide, while the other is the general wording, directions, and text which you find on the site itself.

When first testing the actual help sections of the site, the most important thing is to remember that the help actually matches the UI. There have been a number of times when we have used help systems ourselves only to find out that they are referring to an older version of the site. Any screenshots or steps should always be updated to reflect the latest version of the application. This needs to be tested to ensure it has been done. Another thing to test is that the steps actually solve the problem and help the user. It is very easy to miss a step, or provide an incorrect code sample. Simply follow the guide as the user would and ensure everything has been covered as required. Finally, you need to verify that technical terminology has been used in the correct place and way so that it does not confuse users. In some instances, technical wording might cause more problems and need to be removed depending on who your target user is.

Another part of documentation is the general wording of the site. It is important that the text on the site is correct and accurate without any spelling mistakes. It is the role of a tester to ensure that this is correct, and the text helps the user where required without being too overpowering. We have found that users generally scan read web pages; this includes documentation. Try and make your pages *scannable*.

Error Messages

In a similar fashion to documentation, error messages also need to be tested. The most important point about error messages is that they need to be helpful. Error messages which simply say "Sorry, an error has occurred" annoy end-users. They don't provide the user with any insight into why it failed, whose fault it was, or how to recover. Errors are a fact; they will occur, but the important fact is how the site handles the problem. The best error messages are the ones which provide users with some helpful information into why the error occurred. They should also guide the user on how to take the next step after the error has occurred. After an error has occurred the users are completely lost and taken out of their comfort zone when using the application. The error message should appreciate this and guide the user forward and if possible solve the error. By helping the user solve the error they will feel happy that they managed to get around the issue. If the site just completely fails with no help or information about how to proceed the users are lost and will probably just close the browser — losing you, the visitor. If you help them proceed past the error and stay on the site, you retain the visitor.

The one thing which error messages should never do is make the user feel stupid. Even if it was the user's fault, then this should not come across in the error message, as this will have a negative impact on the site at a point where the user is already unhappy because it failed in the first place.

Although manual testing does involve tasks with the aim of not breaking the application, one of the most important tasks is actually finding faults. The most powerful of these techniques is exploratory testing.

Exploratory Testing

Exploratory testing involves learning about how the application works internally, developing test cases, and executing test cases as a single process. Exploratory testing is designed to allow the tester to learn about the application by using the application in various ways with the aim of finding faults and bugs. While the tester is using the application during exploratory testing they are developing a core understanding of how inputs flow through the system and affect the output. By exploring the different options and attempting different systems they should be looking for issues or parts of the system which don't seem right — this could be rendering or calculation results. This exploratory process is important. When writing automated test cases you are generally very focused on a certain input with an expected output.

With exploratory testing you are free to try anything. Ideally you should try things which cause the application to break or which users might accidentally attempt. Common examples are validation errors, such as being able to enter letters into quantity fields. Exploratory testing is also the perfect time to test for edge cases and attempting tests which were not even considered during the automated testing stages. As you are trying these test cases and learning more about the system, as your knowledge increases you are more likely to understand how different inputs affect how the system behaves. This should ensure that the tester thinks of new inputs and different ways to use the system. This different way of thinking is what finds bugs and how professional testers earn their money.

After you have found a bug, it's likely that other bugs will appear within that area of the system. As a bug exists, it could be that the test case has been overlooked by the developer, and as a result it could have been overlooked in other places of the system. Attempting to dig deeper into the root cause and find more bugs is key to exploratory testing. If you simply find one bug and then move on to a completely different part of the system, a lot of the knowledge the tester has built up during the time to find the original bug would have been lost and wasted. After a bug has been identified it can help if you investigate the actual underlying codebase and identify the code which caused the problem. Having knowledge of the codebase can provide you with the opportunity to identify more bugs as simply looking at the codebase in a code-review approach can uncover issues.

Even though exploratory testing is flexible and open it should also be targeted. The best time to perform exploratory testing is after a feature has been implemented. At this point you can use the time to explore the new functionality and quickly identify any major concerns and issues. After these have been fixed you can start with implementing the acceptance tests around the functionality to verify it works as expected. However, exploratory testing shouldn't be limited to just new functionality; it should touch different parts of the system to ensure it is working as expected.

This brings us to another important fact: the learning process and bugs identified are an important stage of the lifecycle. As such they should be recorded in the correct fashion. For example, if you identify a fairly critical issue with the feature, then it could be useful to add the test case to your set of automated tests to ensure that the issue doesn't re-appear in the future. The same applies if you have identified similar types of issues within different sessions as it might indicate a weakness in your automation and should be investigated.

Other alternatives include simply recording the tests attempted as manual test cases, as we will discuss later in this chapter. Another useful approach is to actually record the screen. The advantage of this is that you can rewind the video and find out the steps taken which highlighted the problem. It's also an easy form of documentation about the test cases attempted, areas of the application covered, as well as being about to return to particular points during the lifetime of the application to remember previous behavior. When it comes to screen recording software, TechSmith's Camtasia comes highly recommended with many free solutions available.

Recording and exploratory testing is a great combination when it comes to bug hunts. Bug hunts are testing sessions set up to allow anyone within the business to attend an open session at a set time or location. The aim is to pair with another person together with a laptop and test the application. Generally prizes, cakes, and tea\coffee are offered to allow a friendly and relaxed atmosphere where people can enjoy themselves while they test the application. The advantage of bug hunts is that it allows people from outside the development team to use the application while it is still being developed. It allows them to provide feedback to the team, but also, because this is likely to be the first time they have used the application, it provides a great opportunity for usability testing and identifying issues which might have been overlooked by the team who have lived and breathed the application for the past six months. It is also a useful opportunity to share knowledge amongst different parts of the business. They all use the application in a slightly different fashion and can provide real insight into the behavior of people and how they naturally use the application. Generally bugs are only a small part of the issues found as it can highlight areas of confusion, lack of documentation, or other issues not considered by the team.

Recording these bug hunt sessions allow the team to review how people interacted with the software, demonstrating pauses when they attempted to understand the UI and being able to easily reproduce bugs found with the software. When combined with a webcam, you can see the user's reaction to various parts of the system. This can be invaluable information.

Although you are performing exploratory testing there are various issues you can try in an attempt to break the application, which is discussed in the next section.

Breaking the Application

When testing ASP.NET web applications there are various common test cases you can attempt to ensure you haven't missed anything obvious. Based on these tips and together with the advice provided previously you should have a good initial base to start manually testing your application.

Session Timeouts

As discussed in the "Usability" section, session timeouts are a great way to test applications to see what breaks. The problem arises when, as the name implies, the session state has timeout. This occurs when a user has left a browser window open for a period of time. When they return they navigate to a section of the site which attempts to read the session information and fails because it has unexpectedly been recycled. One way to test this would be to leave a browser window open for 20 minutes until the timeout occurred. This would be a very lengthy process. A more productive approach is to override the default timeout for the test site. This is set in the web.config of the site. If you set the timeout to 1, then you will only have to wait one minute before navigating to see the effects:

```
<configuration>
  <sessionstate timeout="1" />
</configuration>
```

Remember to make sure that this setting is not deployed into production. Another way to identify potential problems is to code-review the pages to see which ones deal with the session. If the page doesn't deal with any session state, then there is not much point in testing it.

Another way is to force Internet Information Service (IIS) to restart the application pool. IIS is the web server used to host ASP.NET applications. There are two ways to restart the server: one is by simply stopping and starting the server which affects all sites hosted on that server. The other approach is to restart the application pool associated with the site you're testing. IIS automatically restarts the application pools after 1,740 minutes (29 hours) to help the server recover from memory leaks and other resources. By forcing a restart you can see how the application behaves in this situation and make sure that no undesired effects occur. Application pools can be restarted from within the IIS Manager.

External Services

Stopping external services is an excellent way to test how applications behave in certain situations. External systems include both third party APIs such as Flickr or PayPal but could also include your own services such as a database server. Although you would hope these external systems had 100 percent uptime, sadly this is not the case, and you need to test to see how the application copes when these services are not accessible. There are a couple of items to look out for. The most obvious problem is if the application causes an error message to be returned to the user which we have covered earlier in this chapter and will do again in Chapter 10 about security. You need to make sure the error message is shown in the correct fashion and provides the user with information about what occurred. There are other issues with not being able to access external systems. When attempting to access a database often there is a timeout on the connection during which the application expects the server to respond. The problem is that it can lead to the application waiting for a period of time waiting for the database to respond. During this time, the user will have no information about what is happening and most likely just see a blank page. Ideally, you want the connection attempt to die quickly, or at least have a process page returned to the user. This will provide the user with feedback about what is happening and therefore improve the experience.

However, during testing we might not have control over external services to stop and test the reaction of the service going down on the website. Luckily there are a number of different approaches you can take to get around this issue. The easiest solution is to have the URL in the web.config and change this to simulate it being inaccessible. You could also edit your Hosts file (`C:\Windows\System32\drivers\etc\hosts`) and add an entry for the domain to a nonexistence host IP. From the viewpoint of the application, the site will be down. As you may remember from Chapter 4, you can also create service stubs. These stubs replicate the real system; however, they allow you to control how they behave. In Chapter 4 we simply stubbed the email service for the site to make it easier to test. Yet, you can take the approach and simulate error conditions and failures as you would if you injected the stub into the system itself. This has the advantage that you can perform end-to-end testing while being in control of the external systems. It also means you don't need to physically cause the problem to occur; you just need to know how to simulate it.

To be able to do this, you need to create a stub application to be able to read and respond correctly. Depending on how large your application is will determine if this is worth the effort. However, if you go to the effort of creating a stub, then you have the advantage of reusing it to perform testing beyond just the server being inaccessible. For example, you could return different error messages and verify that the application performed as you expected. A second advantage is being able to simulate high-load on the service and slow down the response time to understand how your application would cope as a result.

A similar approach to stubbing services is fault injection. The board term is often used with mocks and stubs to simulate how the system behaves. A less common approach is to inject faults into live running applications by modifying the code being executed. There are a number of research projects floating around which has been described at `http://blog.benhall.me.uk/2008/11/net-fault-injection-very-early-proof-of.html` and `http://blog.benhall.me.uk/2008/11/net-fault-injection-its-not-just-about.html`. Modifying the executing code to simulate failures has the advantage of stub objects without the effort of actually creating the stubs.

Network Testing

Along with testing the actual service, you should consider the communication between the website and the actual service if they are located on different machines. The two main concerns are latency on the network and the network fault rate. Both can cause problems when trying to access the site which can affect the end-user. To test how your site behaves based on different network conditions, you can use network simulators which allow you to adjust the bandwidth, packet loss, and latency. However, in our experience, testing the network is more of an edge case and is tested only if you are concerned about the network you're relying on.

Edge Cases

Manual testing is a great time to test edge cases around your site. Edge cases are test cases based around how the user might use the site beyond the standard and desired use case. The most common edge cases are around the different types of user input. As we previously discussed, user input is part of exploratory testing and so it is an important part of verifying if the application can cope with how users might use it. Although random input could work, it is much better to use targeted results. For example, in any field that expects a certain format, such as a date, you should attempt to input the date in a different format or enter solely letters to see how the application behaves.

More targeted user inputs are the boundaries of possible inputs. For example, given an input expecting a date, what happens if you enter 01/01/0001, 12/31/9999? What happens if you try -01/00-9999? There are huge amounts of possible inputs and as a result you shouldn't try all of them. Instead, you should pick targeted results based on inputs you think will cause different results. For example, all three previous cases could cause an application to fail in different ways. Identifying these test cases requires experience, understanding your application, and what could potentially break it. You should start exploratory testing and see what breaks.

When it comes to text there are two main test cases. First, you should attempt Unicode characters to ensure that your data store can structure it correctly. This includes foreign languages and characters to ensure that you support localization. The second main case is the amount of data. Given a single-line textbox, how much text is it possible to enter? Given a multi-line textbox, how many lines could you enter? Could you enter this entire book? These types of questions are what you should be asking when given a textbox. The aim is to see how the application copes with the most random input you could possibly think of. This is exploratory testing.

Microsoft research is currently creating a product called Pex (`http://research.microsoft.com/pex`). Pex is an automated white box testing tool for.NET. It finds input values for test cases in an attempt for 100 percent test coverage, finding edge cases for you. This can be a useful tool to use on your code-base to find any potential problems.

Another interesting ASP.NET input is to use <s. ASP.NET includes a by-default option called ValidateRequest. The aim of this feature is to protect against cross site scripting (XSS) attacks, discussed more in Chapter 10. How it works is by parsing input on a request, and when it encounters unencoded HTML Markup it will throw an exception. In reality, you can simply enter <s for the exception to occur. As a tester, you want to ensure a nice error message is returned to the user instead of the default ASP.NET message. ASP.NET can also throw error messages as you're navigating around the site. If you attempt to access a page which does not exist, then a 404 error will happen, and as a result an exception is raised. You should test to ensure that correct error pages are returned when you cause these errors to occur. ASP.NET has the concept of custom error pages, allowing you to specify different pages based on the error encountered. As a result, this should be tested.

Finally, there are issues where browsers have worked fine when the user has just had a single window open, however the application was confused when the browser visited the site on the same machine at the same time but from different browsers. These kinds of issues are what you are looking for during exploratory testing.

Authentication

Depending on how your application is structured, authentication could be a particularly important area or non-existent. Although you need to test authentication in terms of security, which will be discussed in Chapter 10, you also need to test to ensure that the authentication is transparent and doesn't affect the structure of the application. By this we mean that parts of the UI shouldn't have large empty gaps, and links such as edit or delete should not appear if the user is not authenticated to access them. Users should be unaware they are running as an account with less access than others, unless of course this is a marketing ploy in an attempt to get people to sign up or upgrade.

Useful Tools for Manual Testing

During the process of manually testing the application there are a number of tools which you can use to be more effective. An effective way to help manually test an application is application logging.

During execution, applications can log information to various sources. This information can be obtained to help you understand what is happening under the covers and ensure that the system is working as expected. There are a number of times when applications can appear to be working perfectly, however they are actually throwing different exceptions. Many people feel this isn't a problem because the user is not affected; however, there is a performance hit when every exception is thrown, while being bad practice to let exceptions be thrown without valid reasons.

One of the approaches to logging in ASP.NET is Web Events. Web Events capture a wide range of information about the website but fundamentally there are four main events which are of interest:

❑   **Heartbeat.** This is a regular event which captures the current state of the site with runtime information. This is useful when monitoring the site to verify how it is working during a long period of time.

❑   **Audit.** This event is based around security events, such as login failures.

❑   **Errors.** Unhandled errors which occur within your application are logged.

❑   **Base Events.** These base events allow you to write and develop custom events for your own application which can be logged with the main ASP.NET applications. To cause events to be logged you need to add the following section into your web.config for the site. The following snippet will log all the information into the Event Viewer for the site. This is good if you are expecting an internal operation team or support team to manage the server and the site; however, if it is on an external service and you don't have access to the event log then you can log events to SQL Server, WMI Providers, or send them via email as well as write your own custom endpoints:

```
<healthMonitoring>
    <rules>
        <add name="All Events" eventName="All Events" provider="EventLogProvider"
profile="Critical"  />
    </rules>
</healthMonitoring>
```

After this has been configured you can use the event viewer as a source of information for identifying problems with your site. More information on web events can be found on the Microsoft support site (http://support.microsoft.com/kb/893664).

Other approaches are writing directly to a log file via a logging framework such as Log4Net (http://logging.apache.org/log4net/index.html). Best practice is that any exception or error which occurs during execution should be logged to help debug the issue at a later point. When testing you should monitor the log file to see what is being logged to the log file to aid testing. A useful approach is to use a program such as UltraEdit (http://www.ultraedit.com/) to tail the log file; every time information is written to the file then the application displaying the file updates the UI to show the contents, which will save you a lot of time and effort. As with the Event Viewer, you need to write the log file to a location which is accessible via the team, however, not viewable by the public.

Other services are starting to arrive to help with logging. An excellent tool is called Exceptioneer (`http://exceptioneer.com/public/whatisexceptioneer.aspx`) which helps you manage and resolve unhandled exceptions for you. When an exception occurs it is logged to the online service. You can then log in to the site and understand more about the exception and what types of exceptions are occurring.

Alongside logging, ASP.NET also has the concept of Trace. ASP.NET Trace allows you to view diagnostic information about a single request for an ASP.NET page. This allows you to write debug statements from your code which will appear in your output Trace. This allows you to write out variables, information, and any other information which you think you will need to debug any problems.

Cross-Browser Testing

Although we have discussed cross-browser testing in Chapter 5, there are more issues than simply automation. The reality of web development is that you need to deal with cross-browser issues as each browser renders with your site in a slightly different way. Luckily there are some tools to help you and make the experience less painful.

The aim of cross-browser testing is to ensure that when users visit your site using a variety of browsers they all receive the same experience and can use your site as you expect. We have experienced a number of sites where you visit using one browser only to find large sections of the site completely broken and usable because they haven't been developed and tested with different browsers in mind.

One of the best tools available to help cross-browser testing is called BrowserShots (`http://browsershots.org/`). Simply enter a URL for a site as shown in Figure 7-1 and it will access the site using a variety of browsers which you can use to manually verify that the site renders correctly on almost every browser on every platform. The free version takes a while to complete all the tests and it only works against public accessible sites; however, it's a great way to validate the site.

The web page with the results is shown in Figure 7-2.

While validating across lots of different browsers is useful, the main problem with cross-browser is between the different versions of Internet Explorer (IE) such as 6, 7, and 8. At the time of writing, IE6 still has around 15 percent of the browser share, yet it doesn't support key standards and getting sites to work in IE6 involves a number of hacks which can limit the design and usefulness when the site is visited using standard complicated browsers such as IE8 or Firefox. Having such a key browser render sites differently is causing major problems and testers need to extensively test their sites to ensure they work on all the different versions.

Although BrowserShots would provide you with some support, a more targeted tool to solve this problem is called IETester (`http://www.my-debugbar.com/wiki/IETester/HomePage`). As shown in Figure 7-3, the application allows you to open different tabs which represent different versions of IE allowing you to use the site as you would if you had the actual browser installed on your desktop.

As you can see from Figure 7-3, the site renders correctly using IE8; however, as you can see from the IE6 tab in Figure 7-4, the site layout renders completely different with the logo having a different colored background.

Figure 7-1: BrowserShots homepage with a list of different browsers

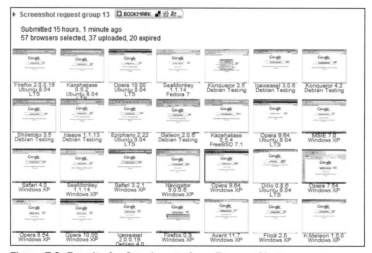

Figure 7-2: Results for Google.com from BrowserShots

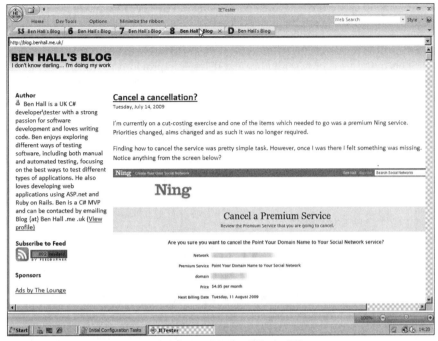

Figure 7-3: Blog.BenHall.me.uk rendered using IE8 via IETester

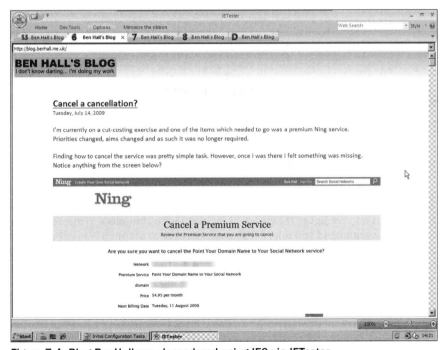

Figure 7-4: Blog.BenHall.me.uk rendered using IE6 via IETester

This is a great way to easily verify layout changes and have a very fast debug cycle to verify if the application works. This is also a great tool for developers.

Another tool is called Xenocode (`http://www.xenocode.com/Browsers/`). This combines the approach of BrowserShots in the cross-browser nature and IETester in providing a full browser to test the entire site. Xenocode uses application virtualization allowing you to have the full browser as a desktop application without ever having to install it. Figure 7-5 shows how IE6 looks when using it via Xenocode.

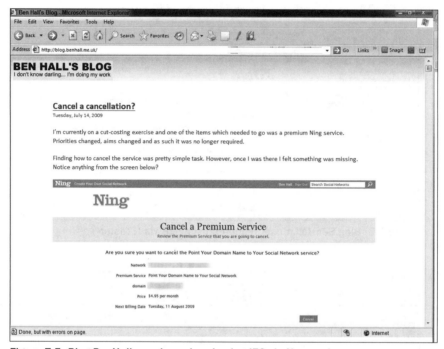

Figure 7-5: Blog.BenHall.me.uk rendered using IE6 via Xenocode

This is a great tool when you want to quickly test multiple browsers.

Other browsers which are much more difficult to test are mobile browsers. During the past few years, the use of mobile browsers has increased and as such more sites need to take this into consideration.

Sadly there are no services or applications available as with desktop browsers. Instead, you need to manually download and configure the different mobile phone emulators to test the different browsers. Because of this we recommend you take a different approach and crowd source browsers. Crowd sourcing is when you get a group of people to help you. In this case, ask people to use their mobile to see if it works. Ask friends, employees, and family members to try the site. Get as many different phones as you can to look at it. Sadly, this is the only sure way to do mobile testing due to the large number of different browsers, screen sizes, and screen resolutions.

The other type of browser that needs to be tested is the print version. Users often still like to print content from your website, especially confirmations or receipts for future reference. As such, you need to verify that the content printed looks correct and is laid out in an understandable way. To help with the layout, you can use CSS to have a different style when printing compared to using the browser. This allows you to hide content and rearrange the layout to ensure people will be happy with the printed result.

When testing cross-browsers alongside CSS issues, another major problem is with JavaScript.

Testing JavaScript

With layout issues, each browser also renders JavaScript differently. The same JavaScript can work perfectly in one browser while being completely broken in another. We have already described the different approaches you can take to test a site on multiple browsers, but as you are testing the site you should also keep in mind that JavaScript also behaves differently on each of those browsers. As such, you should be aware of how JavaScript is used on the site, and how it might work differently on the different browsers.

To help test JavaScript there are a number of different browser plug-ins which allow you to debug and profile scripts as they are executing. Each browser has their own set of tools, for example Firefox has FireBug (`https://addons.mozilla.org/en-US/firefox/addon/1843`), while IE8 and Safari both have built-in tools. These tools are always handy to have installed as they can help identify why the scripts are failing and help you pinpoint the problem.

These tools also have the ability to disable JavaScript and CSS. Disabling JavaScript is not as common as it used to be, however you may find certain people have disabled it for security reasons and due to accessibility issues. By using these browser tools you can see how the site would function with various parts of the site disabled.

Luckily, the issue of cross-browser testing and JavaScript is not the major problem it used to be thanks to jQuery (`http://jquery.com/`). jQuery abstracts away from the underlying JavaScript and as such abstracts away from to code to support cross-browsers with the core framework supporting all the major browsers out-of-the-box without any additional effort. By relying on this level of abstraction, your code is not only cleaner but also requires less testing. As a developer, you should be considering this when you are using JavaScript. If you are a tester, then you should be encouraging the development team to look at this due to the decrease in the amount of testing required while at the same time speeding up development.

Although jQuery removes how much basic testing is required based on different browsers, it does allow for more advanced functionality. More advanced functionality is more difficult to test using frameworks such as WatiN, as we discussed in Chapter 5. Personally, we feel that these effects should not be automated but manually tested. To manually test this functionality you need to use exploratory testing and see the functionality from the viewpoint of the end-user and decide if you think you are happy. There are no special tricks or best practices. Use the application, see the application from the users' eyes, and decide if you think they would be happy.

This could be an ideal time to bring in external users and beta testers to help you test the functionality to see if it is working as expected and desired. Beta testers are a great way to see if the users are happy with the functionality and the implementation. This can provide you with some feedback while there is still time to change the functionality before releasing it to the general public. The closer relationship you have to beta testers, the higher-quality feedback you receive that will result in a better product being produced.

Sadly, we can't rely on beta testers to test that every part of the application works successfully. To verify this we could use exploratory testing, however this is mainly powerful during the learning and exploring stages and becomes less useful the more times you do it. The answer could be to write test cases.

Manual Test Cases

When it comes to manual testing, you need to take into consideration that the tests will need to be run multiple times. The most effective way to support this is to create test cases around the parts of the application which you want to be able to retest on a new build. These test cases are generally run either when that area of the application has changed or just before a release to verify everything is working as you expect. Having the test cases in place means you can quickly run through the cases without having to rethink all the possible combinations and areas of concern. This provides you with a safety net to ensure that everything has been covered correctly.

When writing manual test cases you will notice that they have some similarities to automated test cases. For instance, a manual test case should be targeted to one particular task, feature, or item to check. This is to make them concise and allow you to only run the cases which are actually required at that point in time as speed is an issue. Being manual, they take much longer to run than automated cases which means at times you need to be able to very easily pick and choose which cases are required to be run. The more focused they are, the easier this is to do. However, manual test cases do have the advantage that you are able to test multiple things at the same time because it is a human verifying the results and so can be more flexible. A single test case could verify different parts of the UI; this does mean the test cases take longer to run, it is harder to decide on the parts which should or shouldn't be tested, and reporting failures becomes more complex as it is harder to tell which part of the test failed. As a result, you should generally try and keep the tests targeted to one particular area and test one particular item.

To run the tests quickly the tests should be written in a very clear and concise fashion. Ideal test cases should be understandable by anyone on the team, no matter how much experience they have with the product or testing in general. To help with this they shouldn't use technical terminology and should be structured in a step-by-step style. By doing this, you can quickly follow the steps and verify the result at the end.

An example of how this might be structured is shown next:

Title: Test to verify a product can be added to the shopping cart.

Steps:

- ❏ Launch Internet Explorer and visit the WroxPizza homepage.
- ❏ Navigate to the Products page.
- ❏ Navigate to the Pizza category.
- ❏ Add the first product in the list to the basket.
- ❏ Verify you have been navigated to the shopping cart page.
- ❏ Verify the product you added is in the shopping cart.

Given this example you can quickly take the test case, run the steps manually, and verify the results — marking each test as a pass\fail to indicate if there were any problems. You could also structure them in a similar style to your acceptance tests in Chapter 6, the only difference being how they were actually executed to verify the result.

When you run manual test cases you are always looking out for things beyond the test case, not with your full attention but simply ensuring that the page has rendered correctly, the text is in place as expected, and it generally feels correct — looking for the type of problems discussed in the "Beyond Simply Breaking the Application" section.

However, in WroxPizza you wouldn't create this type of test case because it is already covered by automation. The manual test cases should be in place to enhance your automation efforts, covering the areas of the application which are too difficult or costly to automate. You feel that manual test cases should be secondary to automation, favoring the automated route whenever possible for the reasons described throughout this book.

Just as with automated test cases, manual test cases also might require a set-up stage and have preconditions which must be met before the test can begin. These set-up stages allow you to configure your environment and test data to begin testing. By having this as a separate set-up stage you can re-use the logic between different test cases improving the maintenance and readability of the test cases. If these steps can be automated, as described in the "Part Automation" section, then they should be, to save time and effort.

Common set-up tasks involve producing test data to allow you to test the site. Ideally you want realistic-looking data so that you can verify how the system is expected to behave. As we described in Chapter 5, you could use a Test Data Builder and create some C# code which would insert test data into your system in an automated fashion.

The other approach is to use tools such as Microsoft Visual Studio for Database Professionals (Data Dude) or Red Gate SQL Data Generator. These tools allow you to generate realistic-looking data based on a series of rules and your schema. The screenshot of SQL Data Generator is in Figure 7-6. Based on your database schema, the tool has generated a preview of the type of data it will generate. You can then configure and modify the data based on your requirements to produce a large data set.

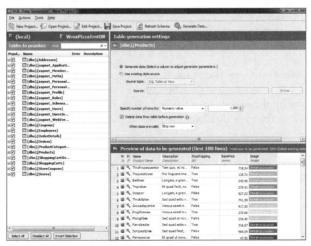

Figure 7-6: Red Gate SQL Data Generator.

Tools such as this can be invaluable when manually testing an application. Another invaluable tool for manual testing is virtual machines. Virtual machines allow you to run complete operating systems within your main OS. This means you can have a different configuration, setup, and environment to your actual main machine. After it is set up, you can clone the environments and undo changes after a set of testing has been performed. This is great for testing. You can set up your machine, perform tests which you wish, and then simply revert the machine back to a previous point in time within moments. There are a number of tools available to help with this including Microsoft Hyper-V and VMWare Workstation, as used in Figure 7-7.

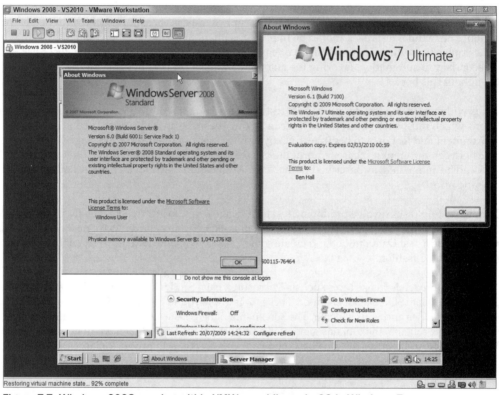

Figure 7-7: Windows 2008 running within VMWare while main OS is Windows 7

When writing automated test cases, the point at which you actually write the test case is fairly well-defined. During TDD you write the test case before the code. With acceptance tests, you write the test before the code and the implementation of the test after. With manual testing, that point becomes more blurred and it actually varies a lot based on the project.

Sometimes you know ahead of time which tests you will need to perform manually. This generally occurs when you are attempting to write the acceptance tests for the piece of functionality, however, you feel that it would be more suited to a manual test case due to the nature of the functionality or the cost involved with replicating the functionality or behavior of the user in an automated fashion.

This often occurs when customers have reported problems with the software. Ideally, you should automate these problems to ensure they don't arise again in the future; however, in our experience customer problems generally are complex and could take a long period of time to automate. As a result, it might make more sense to write it as a manual test case. You should always consider automation, and for a serious problem they should be automated to ensure they don't happen again, but sometimes it makes more sense for them to be manual. We recommend that you keep customer regressions in a separate location to your manual functional tests so you can easily identify which tests you want to run and at what point. If you have them mixed together it can be more confusing to identify the type of test they are.

In a similar fashion, when you are performing exploratory testing you might find the test cases you are thinking of and trying are useful to re-run in the future to ensure that the functionality still works as expected. In this situation you should make the effort to either automate or write a manual test around the area of functionality to maintain a record of what was tried and allowing you to try again in the future when you need to re-run your test cases. This is why recording can be useful, as you can note a position within the video which should be turned into a manual test case but continue with the exploratory testing. When you have finished, or need a break, simply return to the video and create manual test cases based on the steps you performed. This allows you to remain focused while not forgetting anything in terms of future test cases.

As with automated test cases, sometimes you do need to remove manual test cases. Just as with automated test cases you should have a nice streamlined set of tests which accurately reflect the functionality of the site. There should be no duplication and everything should test a particular part of the application. This is difficult to achieve and will come with practice, the scary thing is that duplication and redundant test cases can creep up on you if you are not careful. The main thing is to make sure you are reviewing your test cases, your structure, and the steps to ensure that you are on the right path.

As the application is developing and maturing, the manual test cases should be updated in sync with this. When functionality changes you need to revisit any test cases you have and update them to reflect the change. For this to happen effectively the team needs a good understanding about the test cases and what type of test case covers which area of the application. This is simply about good communication and a good organization of the test cases.

When functionality has changed, then sometimes you can simply update the steps to reflect the change in the application; however, sometimes the test cases need to be removed. You shouldn't be afraid of removing test cases if they do not relate to the application.

This brings us to the topic of how to store and structure your test cases. There are many off-the-shelf products which attempt to solve the problem of handling multiple test cases. Each tool varies wildly in price, functionality, and actual usability. Tools such as HP Quality Center, Microsoft Visual Studio Team Edition for Software Testers, and smaller software houses such as TestLog can provide you with functionality to manage manual test cases. However, many people simply use Microsoft Excel to manage the test cases. All tools have their own set of advantages and how much you invest depends on how heavily you plan to depend on the manual test cases.

Summary

Although some developers focus on automated testing, many testers only focus on manual testing. The key is to have a mixture of both, each type covering what they are each best at. Automation is great at tasks which can be repeated and can be used when manually testing an application for more effective use of time. Manual testing is great at the hard to automate sections of the application which might be due to a complex UI or a complex procedure to reproduce the problem.

When creating manual tests the items discussed in Chapter 6 still apply, as do many of the automation techniques; however, manual testing introduces some new concepts such as exploratory testing and usability testing to ensure the application will be fit for purpose and usability and withstand any type of user interaction.

8

Performance Testing

Have you ever poured your heart and soul into an application, working weekends and missing family events to get every detail of the application correct? When the big day finally comes to bring the site live, your new application brings the server to its knees within the first hour of production. You could have had two cups of coffee with the time it took to load the page. You then have to work more weekends, missing more family events to pin down what exactly went wrong with your "prize-winning" application. This example may be a bit severe, but we've all created applications wherein the performance was less than desirable. This could have happened because of a memory leak, because you didn't test with an adequate size database, or because you didn't anticipate the popularity of the application.

Performance Testing Basics

In Chapter 5 you learned about the many different types of functional testing; it was in this section that you first heard of the many types of functional testing grouped under the "load testing" umbrella. Developers will group each one of these very specific types of testing into the generic term load testing, when in reality each type of testing is a strict discipline in itself. In this chapter, the term performance testing is used as a generic term to refer to a test that determines the responsiveness of a web application.

Performance testing, volume testing, load testing, stress testing, scalability testing, capacity testing, and performance testing encompass all types of testing that leads us to the same goal: that users will be able to use your web application as the application grows. This chapter covers each one of these types of testing in detail. You'll learn how to collect performance requirements, how to create performance tests, and also how to analyze the results that have been collected through the process. After you've learned how to test a site for performance, you'll learn how to plan for the future using capacity testing to get a good idea when it's time to upgrade the web application server architecture and hardware.

This chapter is not intended to be a guide in how to increase performance in your web application. Instead, you learn how to find bottlenecks that will help you remove the problems with performance in your site. But first you should take a moment and learn a few terms that will be used throughout this chapter:

❑ **Availability.** This is the amount of time a web application is available to the users. Measuring availability is important to many applications because of the business cost of outages for some applications. Availability issues tend to appear as load increases on web applications.

❑ **Response Time.** Amount of time it takes for a web application to respond to the user's request. Response time measures the time between the user requesting a response from the web application and when the completed response has arrived at the user's browser. Response time is normally measured in Time To First Byte (TTFB) and Time To Last Byte (TTLB).

❑ **Scalability.** Scalability is the ability to add more resources as load increases and maintain the same or improve the performance (response time). A common measurement for scalability is requests per second.

❑ **Throughput.** Throughput is the rate of successful message delivery through the network. An example of throughput would be number of hits on a website in a given time range.

❑ **Utilization.** Utilization is the percentage of the theoretical capacity of a resource that is being used. Examples include how much network bandwidth is being used and the amount of memory used on a server when 200 users are accessing the web application.

What to Expect

As with the other types of testing disciplines, you should expect an initial learning curve to understanding the terminology and how to collect effective performance requirements. You should also plan on spending a fairly large amount of time learning the tools used to implement a successful performance test.

You should expect that the majority of time spent performance testing will be spent capturing, validating, and implementing the performance requirements so you can build an effective performance test. If you don't know what you're looking for, how will you know the performance test passed?

An important consideration before you begin testing is to look into the licensing costs for automated performance testing tools before your budget is set in stone; some performance testing suites carry a hefty price tag. Along with software costs, there may also be a cost associated with hardware needed for the performance test. The amount of hardware needed to test a small intranet for 200 users is much less than an external facing service that has 1.5 million users. Later in this chapter you will explore the different types of tools that can be used, some of them are free or low-cost while others have a high price tag on them.

Establishing a Baseline

Throughout the remainder of this chapter you will notice that we are stressing the fact that performance testing should not be something you wait until the very last minute to do; it should be happening as the application is being created. Establishing a baseline test early in the application development cycle will help you prevent performance issues from cropping up just before your release date. Performance baselines establish a point of comparison for future test runs.

One of the most useful baseline tests is measuring transaction response times. For instance, a web application that processes credit card transactions generally involves a 3rd party service that performs the credit card transaction after calling the API. If you established a baseline of how long this transaction takes, you would be able to find performance issues — such as a junior developer who thought it would be a good idea to put a four-second sleep between calls to the third-party API for some strange reason.

What Are Good Performance Times?

"What sort of times should I expect?" and "How do I know the test passed?" are questions that are frequently asked by developers who are new to performance testing. If you are hoping to learn the generic industry standard for what good performance is, you are out of luck, because no such standards exist. The results collected from performance testing are highly subjective, and can mean something different from person to person. Performance is in the eye of the beholder. It's very common that what a developer may see as an acceptable response time may not be an acceptable response time to a user.

Later in this chapter you will learn the collection of requirements and provide techniques needed to find out exactly what acceptable response times are for a given project. This is one reason why testing for performance from the start is such an important concept.

Because so many different factors come into play with how web applications perform, server manufacturers cannot say for certain "this model will serve x requests per second," which may be the magic number a developer is looking for. It is because of this reason that performance testing web applications is so important.

When it comes to response times, meaning how fast the page loaded for the user, many studies have been conducted with varying results of how users react to different response times. Through the collection of performance requirements from many projects and multiple usability studies, the following response time ranges provide a representation of how users react to web applications:

❑ **Greater than 15 seconds.** The user may be thinking "is the application still working?" The attention of the user has most likely been lost, and in many situations this long of a response time is unacceptable. In situations where long response times are expected, such as reporting tasks, a warning that the task is expected to run this long and some type of feedback indicator should be provided.

❑ **Greater than four seconds.** The user's train of thought has most likely been de-railed. Computer users tend to be able to retain information about the task they are working with in short-term memory for roughly four seconds. If a complex task has a response time of more than four seconds, you may want to look into increasing the performance of this task.

❑ **Two to four seconds.** Many web applications respond within this time range for a majority of their tasks. The user still has the task in memory and can maintain focus.

❑ **Less than two seconds.** This range is what many users expect to keep a steady workflow. Users will notice the delay, but no special feedback needs to be presented to the user. In data entry applications where data is being entered at a very rapid rate, response times of less than two seconds will help users stay focused on the data they are entering.

❑ **Sub-second response time.** These are tasks that users expect to respond to instantly. Many of these tasks are accomplished on the client side with JavaScript, and do not make trips back to the server. A task such as expanding a menu is a task users expect to happen instantly.

Automated Testing Tools

You can't effectively test a web application for performance without using some type of automated testing tool. Asking a few hundred of your closest friends to help you out on a weekend and access a website you developed will not satisfy the needs required for performance testing, not to mention it may cost you a great deal of pizza! Besides having to correlate the response from all the users, repeating the same test twice would be near impossible.

Choosing a Testing Tool

Choosing a performance testing tool can be the most difficult part of the performance testing phase. The goal of all performance testing tools is to simplify the testing process. Many performance tools on the market today allow the user to record activity on a web application and save this activity as script that can be replayed.

When many people hear the phase performance testing, they immediately think stress testing. Many of the large testing tool suites on the market today include tools used for stress testing web applications and many of these suites cost a great deal of money. You don't have to sell your kidney to finance your performance testing tools.

❑ **Visual Studio Team Foundation Test Suite.** VSTS includes tools for load and capacity testing. A license for the suite is required for the "controller" (where the results of the test are stored), but no license is required for agents that execute the test.

❑ **HP Load Runner (formally Mercury Load Runner).** Load Runner has been around for the better part of 10 years and has a very large customer following. Load Runner is a testing suite that will allow you to create stress and capacity tests, and provide tools to assist with creating the performance tests from the start — the requirements phase. Licenses are needed for each machine that has a component of Load Runner installed, and each license carries a hefty cost.

❑ **Web Capacity Analysis Tool (WCAT).** The Web Capacity Analysis Tool (WCAT) is a HTTP load generation tool designed to measure the performance of a web application. WCAT works as the other tools described with a controller/agent architecture to allow for a distributed load to be generated. WCAT is a console application which prevents many managers/testers/developers from considering using this tool. WCAT is a very powerful tool that is free and should be considered when selecting a tool for performance testing.

❑ **RedGate ANTS Performance Profiler.** The ANTS Profiler is a code profiling tool that helps you identify bottlenecks and slow-running processes in code. When performing a load test and the number of users is not exactly what you expected, using the ANTS Profiler will help you drill into your code and find these issues.

❑ **RedGate ANTS Memory Profiler.** Alongside the performance profiler, Red Gate also develops a memory profiler to help find memory leaks within your application and the ASP.NET website. The ANTS Performance and Memory Profiler are licensed per user at a very affordable cost.

❑ **Compuware Dev Partner.** Dev Partner is a suite of tools developed by Compuware that contains tools for code reviews, security scanning, Code Coverage Analysis, Error Detection and Diagnosis, Memory Analysis, and Performance Analysis. Inside the Performance Analysis tool of Dev Partner is a code profiler that will help you find slow-running code and memory leaks. Dev Partner is licensed per user and carries a large price tag.

Later in this chapter you will learn how to use a few of these performance testing tools in depth.

The Importance of Performance Testing

When developing web applications, one of your goals should be to have extremely happy clients, not just happy clients, clients who will rant and rave about the quality of the application that was delivered. Web applications that generate errors or have a poor response time make for customers that are frustrated or upset. In recent years developers have seen an increase of business applications that were originally developed as "client/server" or "thick client" applications moving to the web. Some call this phenomenon the Semantic Web or Web 2.0. Call it what you will but this phenomenon has changed how web applications need to be created.

Users of these types of applications expect the newly adapted web applications to perform as well and as reliably as their desktop counterparts. In the past the web has had a reputation of being "slow and clunky," whereas the "thick client" applications were "mean and lean." With the advancement of broadband connections and technologies such as AJAX, web applications are no longer "slow and clunky."

Performance testing can be considered the forgotten second cousin of unit testing. Most developers put this type of testing off until the very last minute, if they even get to it at all. Performance issues tend to have a habit of turning up late in the application cycle, and the later that you find them the greater the cost. Studies have shown that most performance defects are "firefighting" defects, meaning they are resolved while the system is in production. These issues require costly time-consuming work from developers to get the issues resolved quickly. In some situations the applications are even taken offline while the performance issues are resolved.

As with other types of testing, there is a cost to conducting a very in-depth analysis of the performance of a web application, and many managers do not see the need for up-front performance testing. There are plenty of web applications where performance testing has not been performed and they are working correctly, but they have been lucky enough not to have reached the tipping point where the database has grown substantially or become overwhelmed with visitors. These types of issues tend to appear out of nowhere and can affect even the smallest of web applications. That being said, some level of performance testing should be performed on all web applications at least at a high level.

It's extremely important to think of the performance of a web application as a feature. When you think of performance as a feature, you can plan for it, work through multiple iterations to test the performance, and make adjustments accordingly. Thinking of performance as a feature will also keep you from waiting until the very last minute and hastily throwing together a performance test suite that is not up to your normal quality of work. Start performance testing very early in the application lifecycle.

Back when the ASP.NET DataGrid control was first introduced, developers were attracted to this control like bees to honey. Developers liked to use this control because of its ease of use. In many of the demos, Microsoft Employees touted the fact that "you don't need to write any code for the DataGrid to work." We are sure that many readers have been burned by the DataGrid control in one way or another. One of the most common performance issues of ASP.NET can be related to the DataGrid control, and how it handles data paging. For example, if you have a DataGrid on an ASP.NET page that displays 10 records at a time, but the dataset that is bound to the DataGrid contains 200,000 records, by default, each time the user selects a new page, those 200,000 records are requested from the database even though you are only showing the user 20 at a time. As the data in web applications that use the DataGrid to render data to a user grow, the application loses performance. This example stresses how important it is to test early in the application development phase, and to use a realistic amount of data as test data.

Having a well thought-out performance test will help you push your web application to the limits of its configuration. Knowing if you can add more hardware to increase capacity will help you sleep better at night. You never know when your application will grow to have 1,000,000 users.

Capturing Performance Requirements

The term performance is such a subjective term that it's important to receive input from all the project stake holders on what is considered "good" performance. Earlier in this chapter you learned what is considered to be "good" performance times, but these times may not match the project stake holder's thoughts. Reaching out to business stake holders such as Domain Experts and users of the system will give you an idea of how they expect the application to perform. Also include developers, architects, and network administrators for their input into how they expect the system to perform.

Most of the time if you ask project stake holders how the application should perform they will reply with "fast." Testing a web application that is intended for use on an intranet and is only expected to support 10 users at a time is a bit different than testing a web application intended to be open as a public service on the Internet that might receive more than 100,000 concurrent users at a time. Knowing how the application will be used will help you design a performance test that is effective.

What to Ask First

To get the proverbial requirements ball rolling, the following three questions can be asked to help break the ice or cause a discussion that may last the entire day in some cases.

Availability

Is it acceptable for the application to have any downtime? The most common answer to this question is "No." Clients do not realize what goes into creating an infrastructure that allows a system to truly be available all the time. When you start explaining the cost associated with the many systems required — such as duplicate data centers in different regions of the world — to ensure the application would survive a natural disaster, clients start to realize this could get expensive. Their answer often changes after this and the real requirements can be flushed out.

When discovering how available the site needs to be, there is often a cost associated with each minute of downtime that occurs in the application. Using these numbers to weigh the cost of a performance test can often persuade customers that the upfront testing to ensure the application will perform as expected is worth the cost.

Scalability and Concurrency

Simply put, how many concurrent users will be using your application at a given time? Again, this question often confuses clients and they will give you a number that represents the total number of users for the application. Business rules often dictate the number of concurrent users. Although the application may have 200 named users, only two of them may be accessing the system at a given time because they only have two computers.

Having an idea about how large a web application may grow will also help define how many users should be used. A good rule of thumb is to add 10 percent to the number of users to allow for a little leeway.

Response Time

During peak hours, how fast should certain pages respond? A baseline of how fast each individual page loads should be created before collecting the requirements for the response time of each page under load. Clients will require some pages to have fewer than two-second load times, and understand if some pages that execute long-running queries take 10 seconds to load.

After the baseline is established, collecting the expected response time for when the application is under load will be helpful in determining when a performance test failed. Having collected concurrency requirements, you may find that your performance test needs to have a response time of two seconds for all pages with a concurrent load of 100 users.

Other Questions to Ask Clients

❑ Where will the application be hosted and where will the majority of the users access the site from?

❑ How many users will the application support when it's released? Will this number increase in one year, how about two years?

❑ When do you expect the busiest time of your application to be?

❑ What functionality will be changing between iterations?

❑ How many servers do you initially plan on needing for the application? Where will the servers be located? What are the specifications for each server?

❑ What are the throughput and latency goals for the application? You may establish a goal of satisfying 90 percent of HTTP requests for file sizes of less than 25k at a rate of three seconds or faster.

Setting Performance Testing Objectives

Setting objectives for a performance test can be helpful to keep the team on target with what they are looking to accomplish with the test.

❑ Ensure that the application will maintain availability during peak usage.

❑ Find the page with the slowest response time.

❑ Determine how the application will perform with 100 users.

❑ Determine when a load balancer is needed.

❑ Detect bottlenecks and provide insight on how to fix them.

❑ Determine how many transactions to the database it will take until the hard disk is full.

❑ Determine how many concurrent users the site will support.

❑ Help the development team in determining how the application performs under various configuration options.

❑ Provide input for scalability and capacity planning.

Leading clients to set realistic and appropriate performance targets can be a difficult task, but a task of necessity. Without knowing how the system should perform, how do you know if the performance test has passed? The questions you have examined thus far may appear to be common sense questions, but are important in creating a performance test that is effective.

Load Test Architecture

Figuring out an effective testing architecture for a load test can be a difficult task. When you are new to load testing you spend a great deal of time focusing on architecture and figuring out exactly how many machines and what needs to be installed on each machine to create an effective load test. In most load tests there are two systems to plan the architecture for the performance test environment and the application under test. This type of architecture is shown in Figure 8-1.

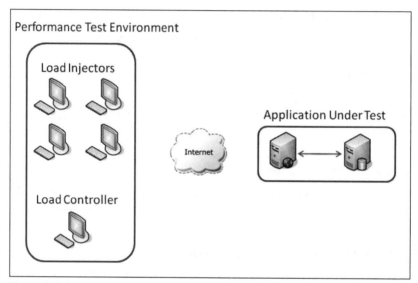

Figure 8-1: Sample performance test environment

Performance Test Environment

The terminology will be different depending on which testing tool you have selected to perform the load test, but the basic concepts will be the same.

❑ **Load Injectors.** Load injectors (also known as agents) will run a performance test and report the results to the load controller. The number of load injectors configured for a performance test will vary depending on how much traffic is required to meet the performance requirements. The more load injectors, the more traffic you will be able to generate. The amount of traffic a load injector can generate is related to the hardware specifications of the individual machines and the amount of bandwidth available. If you are using older hardware in your performance test environment, you may need a greater number of load injectors than if you where using newer hardware for the load injectors.

❏ **Load Controllers.** The load controller (also known as the Analysis module) is responsible for controlling the load injectors and recording the performance information collected from the load injectors. The load controller of many popular performance testing suites contain real-time analysis tools to see each metrics from each load injector as well as a total metrics combined from all load injectors. In most performance testing environments there is only one load controller.

Application under Test

This is the architecture of the application you are testing. Most likely you have heard that the environment you are testing on should match the production environment as closely as possible, and we're not going to tell you any different. This is extremely important when executing performance tests. The ideal situation is to be able to perform the testing on the production server, where the application plans to reside when development has been completed. This option is more common in green field application development (newly created applications) — clients plan on purchasing new hardware, after it is set up, your team can move in and start pushing the new hardware to its limits.

You don't live in an ideal world, and most of the time you're stuck using retired machines that are much slower than their production counterparts. If you are in this situation, it's still important to execute a performance test, but adjust your requirements. If you are not meeting a lower performance expectation on the slower hardware, more than likely you will not meet your original requirements on the production server. Also try to make an effort to match any hardware configuration that you can. If the production server has a RAID array where the SQL Server Transaction log file is stored, try to replicate this as closely as possible.

Another common area that is overlooked is the size of data being used in the performance test. If you have production data it's recommended that you obfuscate any personal data or confidential data and use this subset of data for your performance test. Duplicating all aspects of the production machine is important.

Virtual machines are becoming a very popular solution for network administrators to easily provide production and development environments to users.

In a recent stress test that I performed, the client wanted to stress a newly created web application on their production servers. The new application was created on an open source .NET CMS system that had gotten a bad reputation for poor performance. The requirements stated that the application needed to respond in less than two seconds with a constant load of 3,000 users. The client wanted to make sure these numbers were met, so it was decided the best place to perform the stress was on the production server.

The great part about this stress is that the production environment was set up in all virtual machines with the SQL Server and Web Server separated. We looked through the existing web applications' log files, and determined that the site was slow on Sundays between 11:00 A.M. and 4:00 P.M. We scaled back the existing resources allocated to the current web applications virtual machine and brought up a new virtual machine with resources allocated to the new virtual machine that matched what it would look like when the application was completed.

We completed our stress test, and had no issues with the existing users accessing the current website.

Designing an Effective Performance Test Environment

After a thorough requirements analysis, the next phase of the performance test is designing a testing environment that will ensure you are able to satisfy that the performance requirements have been collected. You have learned about the performance testing architecture, but what other aspects go into creating an effective performance test?

Data Size and Quality

Ensure that you are testing with a set of data that is representative of what you would expect the production system to be. Try to design load tests that replicate an actual work load during normal and peak access time for the application under test. The best type of data is production data with personal data obfuscated. New applications may not have this luxury, but tools such as the SQL Data Generator from Red Gate will help you generate data that is very realistic.

Testing the Performance Test

Most performance tests run over the course of a few hours, and depending on the load you need to generate, access to the testing hardware may only be available for short scheduled times. Performance tests can be like a stack of cards; because of the many layers that are involved, if one layer starts to fail, the performance test tends to collapse in on itself. Try to test things on a small scale before ramping up to your fully intended load.

Take the time to ensure each layer of the performance test is working correctly. It would be a shame to run a performance test for a few hours only to realize you forgot to record a few key performance metrics, and had to start the test all over again.

Stability of the Application under Test

We have stressed the fact that it is important for you to test for performance from the beginning of the application development cycle, but there is a catch 22 in there. If your application is throwing errors on every other page, a performance test is not going to be of much use. Before you can execute a performance test, your application must meet certain quality standards. These quality standards should be created by the development team.

Bandwidth Considerations

A common aspect to performance testing that is often forgotten until the last minute is bandwidth. Having the Internet between the load injectors is an important aspect to performance testing. Performing the test with all layers on the same LAN will not be as effective. Most load tests will generate a great deal of bandwidth, and it's imperative that you ensure that the location where the test injectors reside can handle this stress.

In past years it was common to see load injectors at different locations to accommodate for bandwidth limitations, but with bandwidth decreasing in cost from year to year this is becoming less common. Running the test on a small scale will help you estimate exactly how much bandwidth will be needed for the full scale performance test.

Ensuring Accurate Performance Test Design

The tests that are executed during the performance test should represent behaviors that you would expect a user to perform on your web application. Testing key pages, such as login pages, or testing paths a user may follow, such as a checkout process are important behaviors. There are some behaviors that are commonly overlooked but are also important for creating effective performance tests.

❑ **Simulating different modem speeds.** Testing how the web application performs over different connection speeds is extremely important for external-facing web applications. Don't assume that everyone has a broadband connection.

❑ **Browser cache simulation.** Many performance testing suites allow you to simulate if the browser is caching page requests. Having a good mix is a good idea.

❑ **User sessions.** Most performance testing suites have functionality to "spoof" IP addresses — to simulate traffic from different sources. This is useful for applications that limit user sessions or filter connections based on IP addresses.

❑ **Load injection.** How should the load be applied to the site, should it happen all at once, should it "ramp-up" slowly over a time period, or should it ramp back down?

Load Injector Hardware

Do you have sufficient hardware resources to generate the required load to meet the requirements for the performance test? Hardware is getting cheaper and cheaper every year, but it's still worth mentioning to ensure that your current hardware will be able to generate the required load. Again, running the test on a small scale will help you flush out these issues.

If the load injectors become overloaded, the performance test no longer represents real-life behavior. The performance test may then have invalid results thus rendering the performance test useless.

Measuring Performance

Ensure you have identified the Key Performance Metrics and that performance counters have been set up to collect this data. KPIs such as server errors, server utilization, memory usage, disk usage, and processor usage are all important metrics to monitor as your performance test is running.

Have you decided how these KPIs will be summarized — visually through a chart or perhaps raw numbers via tabular data?

SSL-Increased Overhead

The use of SSL certificates on websites will slow performance between web servers and browsers. The overhead can vary greatly depending on the type of certificate that is used, so it's imperative that the application under test have a similar SSL certificate installed during load testing. SSL certificate overhead is such a problem with large applications that companies have begun to sell hardware SSL acceleration solutions that will offload the public key encryption from the web server's hardware.

In-House Testing or Outsourcing?

Performance testing can be a very expensive task depending on the experience of your testers/developers, which tools have been selected, and the amount of load that is required. In some situations companies need to purchase new hardware to generate the loads specified in the performance requirements. It's common that companies feel this is too large a task to take on and will outsource the testing. Companies that are experienced with performance will have labs set up that can generate a great deal of load without issues. If you decide to outsource performance testing, remember to think of performance as a feature and continue to have your testers/developers execute their own performance tests, but on a smaller scale.

Performance Monitoring

An important aspect of performance testing is monitoring the health of the application under test along with the servers the application is running on. Performance can be measured by using monitoring tools that record specific behaviors related to hardware or software functions, and report these metrics to the tester. Many performance testing suites include tools to monitor the system while the test is running. While these tools provide invaluable information there are other monitoring tools that should be used along with the tools included in the testing suite.

Real-Time Analysis

It's important to note that after your performance test is running, you can't just walk away. Although some performance tests may be scheduled to run for upward of 24 hours, it's important that you monitor the test and keep a watchful eye on how the application and servers are performing. Although all the performance metrics will be logged, many issues can be resolved by just watching the system metrics while the test is being performed. Real-time analysis can be a very boring task. Essentially you are waiting for something to happen and a good portion of the time nothing happens.

Thorough real-time analysis can be accomplished with a variety of tools. Your performance testing suite is a starting point, but sometimes basic tools such as the Windows Task Manager will provide enough information to realize something is wrong with the performance test.

It's common for testers to only monitor the big three key performance indicators during real-time analysis and save the in-depth analysis until the test has completed.

❑ CPU

❑ Memory

❑ Disk input/output

Performance counters are invaluable tools for collecting performance metrics while the application is under test. A very common question we are asked is, what performance counters should be monitored and what do they do? The list of counters you'll be learning about in the next sections can be found in the Microsoft Performance Monitor tool included in all Microsoft Operating systems.

Memory Performance Counters

It's important to monitor memory counters while performance testing to ensure that memory is being released as expected. Many performance tests find that over a time period with a constant load of users, the server's performance will degrade over time, issues that can be attributed to memory leaks. Memory leaks are caused by processors that are not releasing their hold on memory correctly. In .NET the Garbage Collector prevents many memory leaks from occurring, but they still tend to happen.

❑ **Page Faults/Sec.** Average number of pages faulted per second. A page is a fixed-length block of memory that is used to transfer data between physical memory and hard disk. A page fault is a software exception raised by the hardware when a program accesses a page that is mapped in address space, but not loaded in physical memory.

❑ **Available Bytes.** Provides the value of the total bytes of memory that are currently available for use by the processor.

❏ **Page Reads/Sec.** Rate at which the disk was read to resolve hard page faults. Hard page faults occur when a process references a page in virtual memory that is not found in the physical memory and must be read from disk.

❏ **Page Writes/Sec.** Page writes/sec is the measurement of pages that are written to the disk to free up space in physical memory.

❏ **Pages/Sec.** Rate in which pages are read or written to the disk to resolve hard page faults.

Disk Performance Counters

Performance issues relative to hard disks are almost always related to time, not space. Hard disks account for many of the bottlenecks that are found during performance testing. When the hard disk becomes the limiting factor in the server your application is running on, it's because the components involved with reading and writing to the disk cannot keep pace with the rest of the system.

❏ **Average Disk Queue Length.** This is the average number of reads and writes that were queued for the selected disk during the sample interval.

❏ **Average Disk Read Queue Length.** Average number of disk reads that were queued for the selected disk during the sample interval.

❏ **Average Disk Write Queue Length.** Average number of disk writes that were queued for the selected disk during the sample interval.

❏ **Average Disk Sec/Read.** Average time, reported in seconds, of average reading of data from the selected disk.

❏ **Average Disk Sec/Transfer.** Time, reported in seconds, of the average transfer of data for the selected disk.

❏ **Disk Reads/Sec.** Rate of disk reads on the selected disk.

❏ **Disk Writes/sec.** Rate of disk writes on the selected disk.

IIS Performance Counters

When Microsoft Internet Information Services (IIS) is installed, a number of performance counters related to IIS are installed also. IIS includes performance counters for seeing how many concurrent users are hitting the site at a given time to monitor caching features.

❏ **Web Service: Bytes Total/Sec.** Bytes Total/Sec reports the total number of bytes sent/received by the IIS web server. Low numbers may indicate IIS is transferring data at a low rate.

❏ **Web Service: Connection Refused.** This metric will report the number of refused connections to IIS. Connections can be refused for various reasons, most commonly though, connections are refused because the server is too busy — the lower the number the better.

❏ **Web Service: Not Found Errors.** Not found errors are HTTP Status Code 404 errors. Having a high number here could mean your performance test is not set up correctly, or the application under test was not installed correctly to the test servers.

ASP.NET Performance Counters

The ASP.NET Performance Counters contain a set of counters that monitor the state of ASP.NET. Many of the useful counters in this set involve information in regards to the ASP.NET requests.

❑ **Request Queued.** The Request Queued metric indicates the number of requests waiting for service from the queue. When this metric starts to increment linearly with the client load, this is an indication of the web server reaching the limit of concurrent requests in which it can process.

❑ **Requests Rejected.** This metric is a representation that an HTTP 503 Status Code Server is too busy. Requests are rejected due to insufficient resources on the server to process the request. During stress testing, this is a useful metric to keep your eye on.

❑ **Request Wait Time.** Number of milliseconds that the most recent request waited for processing in the request queue. Requests should not wait in the queue very long. Longer wait times could indicate server performance issues.

❑ **Cache Total Turnover Rate.** Count of the items added and removed from the cache per second. A large turnover number indicates caching is not being used effectively.

❑ **Errors Total.** This metric is a count of the total runtime, parser, and complication errors have occurred. Expect low numbers, but this metric can be misleading. The Response.Redirect command will cause the .NET runtime to throw an error, which is caught and handled by processing the redirect. In sites that use Response.Redirect, often this number can be large.

❑ **Request Execution Time.** Request Execution Time performance counter will report the last time it took for the last request to complete execution. This number should be a stable number — sharp increases or decreases could indicate performance issues.

❑ **Requests Timed Out.** Total number of requests that have timed out. The most common reason that requests time out is because of insufficient resources on the server to process the request.

❑ **Requests/Sec.** Total number of requests made to the IIS server per second. This number should fall into the range that was determined during the performance requirements' collection phase.

.NET Performance Counters

There are many performance counters that are included in the .NET Framework that allow you to monitor the performance of the framework and your managed code. This section will not talk about all of the counters, just the counters that are most important in regards to monitoring performance during performance testing.

.NET CLR Memory

One of the most useful, most hidden, most loved, and most hated feature of the .NET Framework is the automatic memory management, the Garbage Collector. Numerous books contain chapters that discuss in depth the Garbage Collection/Memory management in .NET. We are going to tip-toe through this subject and only discuss a few basics of Garbage Collection to help give you a good idea of why the following .NET CLR memory counters are important.

The Garbage Collector in .NET sorts objects into three categories known as generations. Generations are numbered 0, 1, and 2 and each generation contains a heap size, which is the total number of bytes that can be occupied by all objects in the generation. The heap sizes of generations can grow but start off around 256KB for generation 0, 2MB for generation 1, and 10MB for generation 2.

The objects contained in generation 0 are the youngest. When an application creates a new object it starts in generation 0, if there is not enough room for the object to be placed in generation 0 then Garbage Collection occurs on generation 0. During Garbage Collection, every object in the generation is examined and if it's no longer in use, it is destroyed. The objects that are not destroyed are promoted to the next generation, generation 1. If an object is too large to fit into generation 0, they are placed on a special heap known as the object heap.

During the promotion of objects from generation 0 to generation 1, the Garbage Collector ensures there is enough room to store the promoted objects in generation 1. If enough room exists then the Garbage Collector is complete. If there is not enough room in generation 1 for the objects then Garbage Collection will occur on generation 1, destroying objects that are no longer in use and promoting objects that are in use to generation 2. As with the other generations, Garbage Collection will occur in generation 2, destroying objects that are no longer in use, but generation 2 objects that are in use will stay in generation 2.

Some objects may need to store a reference to an unmanaged resource such as a mutex. In many situations, destroying those types of objects through the Garbage Collector would defeat their purpose. Developers can indicate that the Garbage Collector must cause the object to clean up after itself before it can be destroyed; this process is called finalization.

- ❑ **#GC Handles.** This performance counter displayed the current number of Garbage Collection handlers in use. Garbage Collection handles are handles to resources outside the CLR environment. This performance counter does not update each time the Garbage Collector is called like most CLR memory counters do. This counter is updated when a GC handle is requested. When web applications are under heavy load they can create a large number of Garbage Collection handlers and possibly make the application unstable.

- ❑ **#Gen 0 Collections.** This counter indicates the number of times generation 0 objects have been garbage collected since the start of the application. This counter is useful to help track down memory leaks and ensure that memory is being cleaned up correctly.

- ❑ **#Gen 1 Collections.** This counter indicates the number of times generation 1 objects have been garbage collected since the start of the application.

- ❑ **#Gen 2 Collections.** This counter indicates the number of times generation 2 objects have been garbage collected since the start of the application.

- ❑ **#Total Committed Bytes.** This counter displays the total amount of virtual memory committed by your application.

- ❑ **%Time in GC.** This counter displays the amount of time the Garbage Collector has spent on your application collecting memory.

- ❑ **Gen 0 Heap Size.** Generation 0 heap is the maximum bytes that can be allocated in generation 0. Smaller heap sizes indicate the application is using memory effectively and allowing the Garbage Collector to collect unused resources.

- ❑ **Gen 0 Promoted Bytes/Sec.** This counter displays the number of bytes promoted per second from generation 0 to generation 1.

- ❑ **Gen1 Heap Size.** Generation 1 heap is the maximum bytes that can be allocated in generation 1.

- ❑ **Gen 1 Promoted Bytes/Sec.** This counter displays the number of bytes promoted per second from generation 1 to generation 2.

- ❑ **Gen 2 Heap Size.** Generation 2 heap is the maximum bytes that can be allocated in generation 2.

.NET CLR Loading

The performance counters included under the .NET CLR Loading counter set, include a group of counters that will enable you to have to have a detailed understanding of how system resources are affected when .NET applications are loaded.

❑ **Total Assemblies.** The total number of assemblies displays a count of the total number of assemblies that have been loaded since the start of the application. This counter is useful for finding assemblies that are referenced in applications but are not used.

❑ **Total Classes Loaded.** This counter displays the total number of classes that have been loaded in all the assemblies since the start of the application.

.NET CLR LocksAndThreads

The counters included in the .NET CLR Locks and Threads counter set, include counters that will help you track down bottlenecks related to process or thread contention.

❑ **Contention Rates/Sec.** Rate at which threads in the runtime attempt to acquire a managed lock unsuccessfully.

❑ **Total #of Contentions.** This counter displays the total number of times threads in the CLR have attempted to acquire a managed lock unsuccessfully.

❑ **Current Queue Length.** This counter displays the total number of threads currently waiting to acquire some managed lock in the application. This counter is not an average over time; it displays the last observed value.

.NET CLR Exceptions

.NET exceptions are resource intensive, as such web applications that throw excessive exceptions can have performance issues. The counters contained in the .NET CLR Exceptions counter set will help monitor the number of exceptions being thrown.

❑ **# of Exceptions Thrown.** This counter displays the total number of exceptions thrown since the start of the application. These include both .NET exceptions and unmanaged exceptions that get converted into .NET exceptions.

❑ **# Exceptions Thrown/Sec.** This counter displays the number of exceptions thrown per second. These include both .NET exceptions and unmanaged exceptions that get converted into .NET exceptions. Exceptions should only occur in rare situations and not in the normal control flow of the program. High numbers indicate issues with the application under test.

Performance Analysis

When analyzing the results of a performance test, many developers/testers may find there is no clear failure during the performance test. How do you know when a performance test failed? Previously in this chapter you learned that performance testing is subjective, and results may mean different things to different people, but when page response times degrade from four seconds in your baseline test to fifteen in a future performance test, it's unacceptable and it's time to figure out what exactly is causing these issues.

To help figure out exactly what is going on you use the metrics to help narrow down problems. The performance counters that were previously discussed are a good place to start.

Key Performance Indicators

A good place to start analyzing data is to look at the Key Performance Indicators (KPI). KPIs are collected during the requirements gathering of the performance test. Many performance tests include the same set of KPIs such as response time, memory usage, and disk usage but may vary from application to application.

If the KPIs that have been determined are not what you expected, then it's time to start drilling to more advanced performance counters to help find out exactly what is going on.

Root Cause Analysis

Root Cause Analysis indentifies the underlying factors that have contributed to the performance issue, and then traces the symptoms back to the root cause of the issue which must be addressed. Root Cause Analysis is a concept not a tool, but using the KPIs is a great way to start tracing issues.

Some performance issues are obvious to some, while others require a great deal of digging to resolve the issues. Each skill set will have a set of tools (such as code profilers for developers) that will help them trace their particular issues. When analyzing the results of the performance test, ensure that you have access to the developers, testers, network administrators, database administrators, and architects to discuss possible solutions to performance issues found.

Performance Analysis Checklist

When analyzing the results of a performance test, it's useful to keep the following items in mind:

❑   Did any test fail?

❑   Was enough user load generated?

❑   Does the application meet all performance requirements?

❑   Are there any performance counters that are high?

❑   Do you trust the results of the performance test?

❑   Can you repeat the results?

Capacity Planning

During the development of most web applications, not enough thought is given to the capacity for the given application. Units such as bandwidth, database size, memory, disk usage, and server load all play a big role when it comes to capacity planning.

Essentially capacity planning is having the necessary metrics to enable teams to effectively increase the scalability of web applications.

Predicting Failure

Knowing when and where your web application will fail is a very important metric when it comes to capacity planning. Stress tests are similar to load tests as in they use the same tools, but whereas the goal of load testing is to ensure the application meets the performance requirements, the goal of stress testing is to find out under what type of load the web application will start to fail to meet the performance requirements. After you have this metric you can then start capacity planning.

Capacity Planning Goals

During the collection of performance requirements, developers/testers will collect the expected metrics on how the system should perform. This process will also collect capacity goals such as how many users should be expected during the first year the application is launched.

Example Goals

Here are some example goals for you to consider:

❑ Adding a new web server will increase the amount of users by X.

❑ Adding X amount of bandwidth will decrease response times by Y.

❑ Moving the SQL Server off the web server will decrease processor time by X allowing for Y more number of users.

❑ Adding faster hard drives will decrease disk read/write times by X.

Bandwidth

During capacity planning it's useful to have metrics of current bandwidth usage over a period of time. There are many network monitoring tools that will enable you to capture this type of data. Green field applications will not be able to collect this data; seeing that it's a new system you don't really know what to expect. Brown field applications will benefit from having this metric. This metric can help determine if it's logical to place hardware in different countries where large user pools are heavily using the system.

In recent years the price of bandwidth has dropped drastically; similar to hardware performance issues, many teams decide to upgrade the bandwidth to resolve performance issues related to bandwidth. In some situations this is a viable solution, until the web application outgrows the new bandwidth limitation. This paradigm is also seen in hardware performance issues, and it's only a "band-aid" to these types of performance issues.

Load Testing Patterns

As with the other testing disciplines, certain patterns have emerged that developers/testers should use to keep tests consistent and effective.

Code Profiling

Code profiling is a very useful pattern to help identify bottlenecks in code and help optimize code bases.

When profiling applications, it's important to keep in mind that "To measure something is to change it." Applications will perform differently when you are measuring their performance, exactly how much depends on what you are measuring. Each manufacture's profiler will affect applications differently. Consult the user guides on their specific margins of error.

For the developers/testers with nonphysics backgrounds, there are two physicists that are most commonly related to the observer effect. The observer effect is the effect that observing has on the phenomenon being observed.

In the mid 1930s, Austrian physicist Erwin Schrödinger applied fundamental quantum physics principles to the macro level. By proposing an experiment with cats and poison he was able to directly relate a person interfering with the experiment to the observer effect.

Werner Heisenburg, a German physicist from the mid-twentieth century, is credited with the Heisenburg Uncertainty principle. The Heisenburg Uncertainty Principle states that in quantum physics, physical quantities such as position and momentum cannot both be precisely measured at the same time. This means that the Heisenburg Uncertainty Principle is related to the observer effect, and is often confused to represent the observer effect.

Log Replaying

When a performance test is being performed on a production system, one of the most thorough ways to produce the requests to cause load, is to use the log replaying concept. Log replaying is taking the log files from the web server that contains the user access records, parsing the required data, and formatting them into a format that your performance testing suite can understand. Web server log files contain data about type of operating system, the web browser, and time/date and page of the user's request. Using this data to re-create the requests will ensure your testing load is similar to what to expect in production.

Many popular performance testing tools include tools to replay the log files. Microsoft provides a free tool called the IIS Log Parser that provides an interface for developers/tests to query the log files easily and filter out unwanted requests or data. The results of the query can then be imported to the Web Capacity Analysis Tool (WCAT) to produce the load.

Performance Testing in the Cloud

Testing for performance can be the most expensive (monetary) type of testing. Performance testing gets expensive when you need to generate load that is equivalent to the traffic Google, Twitter, Facebook and other popular websites gain. If you don't need to generate this type of load, it can be affordable.

The amount of load that needs to be generated determines how much hardware is needed. When you take hardware and software licenses into consideration, before you know it your company could have purchased a fleet of Lamborghinis for each of their employees.

Many companies cannot afford to invest the amount of money required to create an adequate performance testing lab, this is where cloud computing comes in. Services such as Amazon's EC2, allow CPU time and storage to be purchased on demand. This means you can scale your load test very quickly when needed, and then scale down when finished. You do not have the overhead of purchasing all of the servers and bandwidth required to generate massive amounts of load.

Two popular services to test for performance in the cloud are SOASTA (`http://www.soasta.com/index.html`) and BrowserMob (`http://browsermob.com/load-testing`).

Tools for Load Testing

There are many performance testing suites available on the market today that can cost as much as a brand-new Lamborghini. This section will show how a few of the less-expensive tools work. This section is intended to apply the practices discussed throughout this chapter to readily available testing tools.

WCAT

The Web Capacity Analysis Tool (WCAT) is a HTTP load generation tool designed to measure the performance of a web application. WCAT ships in various versions of the IIS resource kit, or can be downloaded separately `http://www.iis.net/downloads/default.aspx?tabid=34&g=6&i=1466`. WCAT is a free tool, which is why so many developers/testers use it for performance testing. WCAT is a command line tool, which pushes some developers/testers away. The architecture of WCAT is common to many other performance testing tools with a controller that will control the performance test, and clients which connect to the controller to distribute load.

WCAT has been around for more than 10 years, and contains many configuration options to set the finest detail needed for an efficient performance test. When starting the WCAT controller, paths to configuration files are passed in. These configuration files contain the actual requests the test will be executing and other various performance test information such as warm up time and number of virtual clients to simulate. There are two common ways of specifying the configuration files, using text files or ubr files, which is a newer syntax for WCAT. The examples you will be showing are the older style, but are simpler to understand.

Configuration

The configuration file contains settings that are specific to the test run. Using this older syntax style of WCAT the configuration file is specified by the -c attribute.

```
Warmuptime 5s
Duration 30s
CooldownTime 5s
NumClientMachines 1
NumClientThreads 20
```

Distribution

The distribution file contains settings that determine how often each request will be performed during the performance test. Each test transaction contains a classId that can be used in the distribution file. In the following distribution file, transactions with the classId 1-4 all will execute 25 percent of the time during the performance test. The -d attribute is used to determine the distribution file that will be used.

```
1 25
2 25
3 25
4 25
```

Script

The script file contains the actual requests that will be executed during the performance test. The -s attribute will determine which script file to use for the performance test:

```
NEW TRANSACTION
    classId = 1
    NEW REQUEST HTTP
        Verb = "GET"
        URL = "http://localhost/Default.aspx"
NEW TRANSACTION
    classId = 2
    NEW REQUEST HTTP
        Verb = "GET"
        URL = "http://localhost/About.aspx"
NEW TRANSACTION
    classId = 3
    NEW REQUEST HTTP
        Verb = "GET"
        URL = "http://localhost/Menu.aspx"
NEW TRANSACTION
    classId = 4
    NEW REQUEST HTTP
        Verb = "GET"
        URL = "http://localhost/Orders.aspx"
```

Putting It All Together

First you want to start the WCAT controller. The following command will start the WCAT controller on the local host:

```
WCATController\wcctl.exe -c config.txt -d distribution.txt -s script.txt -a
localhost
```

Figure 8-2 shows the WCAT controller started and waiting for clients to connect.

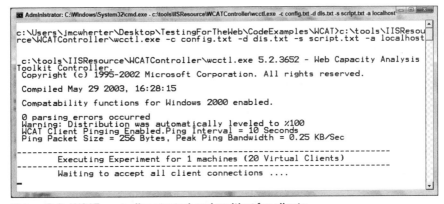

Figure 8-2: WCAT controller started and waiting for clients

After the WCAT controller has been started, clients can then begin to connect. The following command will start the WCAT client on the local computer connecting to the controller that is already running:

```
WCATClient\wcclient.exe 192.168.1.3
```

After the test completes, the individual results of each test will be displayed on the client machine, and the aggregated results from all clients will be displayed on the controller.

After the WCAT client has completed the test, the results will be displayed. You will notice the results displayed in Figure 8-3 were for a performance test that only lasted 30 seconds. This test was just for demonstration purposes only, but you will see the KPI such as Average Response time, Max Time to First Byte and Requests per second all contain values that are considered to be acceptable of a web application that performs well.

```
WCAT Performance Statistics
Server                          :    localhost           ()
#Transactions                   :           1            (HTTP/1.1)
Total Async Sockets             :          20            (5 WCAT Pool Threads)
Total Elapsed Time              :          30  Secs (0 Hrs,0 Mins,30 Secs)

Current Connections             :          19
Total Connection Attempts       :       40614            ( 1353/Sec)
Total Connect Errors            :           0            (    0/Sec)
Total Success Connections       :       40613            ( 1353/Sec)
Total Consec. Connect Errors:              0            (    0/Sec)
Total Bytes                     :    72333469            ( 2354 KB/Sec)
Total Bytes Written             :     2639845            (   85 KB/Sec)
Total Bytes Read                :    69693624            ( 2268 KB/Sec)
Total Requests                  :       40613            ( 1353/Sec)
Total Responses                 :       40614            ( 1353/Sec)
Total Socket Reads              :       40614            ( 1353/Sec)
Total Socket Writes             :       40613            ( 1353/Sec)
Total Parse Errors              :           0            (    0/Sec)
Total Socket Errors             :           0            (    0/Sec)
Total I/O Errors                :           0            (    0/Sec)
Total Internal Errors           :           0            (    0/Sec)
Total Time Outs                 :           0            (    0/Sec)
Total 200 OK                    :       40614            ( 1353/Sec)
Total 30X Redirect              :           0            (    0/Sec)
Total 304 Not Modified          :           0            (    0/Sec)
Total 404 Not Found             :           0            (    0/Sec)
Total 500 Server Error          :           0            (    0/Sec)
Total Bad Status                :           0            (    0/Sec)
Min. Connect Time               :           0  MS
Avg. Connect Time               :           0  MS
Max. Connect Time               :          62  MS
Min. Resp Time (1st Byte)       :           0  MS
Avg. Resp Time (1st Byte)       :          16  MS
Max. Resp Time (1st Byte)       :        7207  MS
Min. Response Time (Last)       :           0  MS
Avg. Response Time (Last)       :          16  MS
Max. Response Time (Last)       :        7207  MS
Current Outstanding Connects:              0            (   19 Max)
Current Waitable Connects       :           0            (   19 Max)
Total Asynchronous Connects     :       40634            (  441/Sec)
Total Discarded Connects        :           0            (    0/Sec)
################################################################
```

Figure 8-3: WCAT results

IIS Log Parser

The IIS log parser is a great tool to parse the logs of IIS to create UBR files which WCAT can then replay. The IIS Log Parser can be downloaded from http://www.microsoft.com/DownLoads/details .aspx?FamilyID=890cd06b-abf8-4c25-91b2-f8d975cf8c07&displaylang=en

For our example we will need to create two files to pass into the Log Parser. The first file WCAT.SQL contains the query to return the data. Please note the INTO statement and the FROM statement. The insert statement is dumping the results into a file named WroxPizzaStressFile.ubr, and the FROM statement is getting the log file data from %windir%\system32\logfiles\w3svc1\ex*.log (all of the log files in c:\Windows\System32\logfiles\w3svc1). When creating your own query files, please ensure you are using the correct paths to where you want the .ubr file created and where the log files are stored:

```
SELECT TOP 10 EXTRACT_TOKEN(cs-uri-query,0,'|') AS Query,
STRCAT(cs-uri-stem, REPLACE_IF_NOT_NULL(cs-uri-query,STRCAT('?',Query))) AS URI,
            sc-status AS STATUS,
            cs-method AS VERB,
            COUNT(*) AS TOTAL,
            SEQUENCE(1) AS UID
INTO WroxPizzaStressFile.ubr
FROM %windir%\system32\logfiles\w3svc1\ex*.log
WHERE (cs-method = 'GET')
GROUP BY URI, VERB, STATUS, Query
ORDER BY TOTAL DESC
```

The next file that needs to be created is a TPL file. TPL files are user-defined templates used to format the output of the Log Parser. For this situation, we want to create a .ubr that WCAT can use. Parameters are indicated by %name%, for example, %URI% contains the path to the request.

```
<LPHEADER>[Configuration]

NumClientMachines:      20
NumClientThreads:       2000
AsynchronousWait:       TRUE
Duration:               5m
MaxRecvBuffer:          8192K
ThinkTime:              0s
WarmupTime:             5s
CooldownTime:           6s


[Performance]

[Script]
SET RequestHeader = "Accept: */*\r\n"
APP RequestHeader = "Accept-Language: en-us\r\n"
APP RequestHeader = "User-Agent: Mozilla/4.0 (compatible; MSIE 6.0; Windows NT 5.2;
.NET CLR 1.0.3705)\r\n"
APP RequestHeader = "Host: %HOST%\r\n"

</LPHEADER>

<LPBODY>

NEW TRANSACTION
classId = %UID%
NEW REQUEST HTTP
ResponseStatusCode = %STATUS%
Weight = %TOTAL%
verb = "%VERB%"
URL = "%URI%
```

```
</LPBODY>
<LPFOOTER>
</LPFOOTER>
```

Placing both the .SQL and .TPL file in the same directory as the Logparser.exe application, the following command will create the .ubr file:

```
Logparser file:WCAT.SQL -o:TPL -tpl:WCAT.TPL
```

As shown in Figure 8-4, not very many elements were processed, only two for demonstration purposes, but we can see that the log parser was successful in the generation of the ubr file.

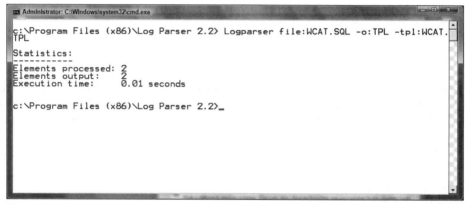

Figure 8-4: Creating a ubr file with the IIS Log parser

```
WroxPizzaStressFile.ubr

[Configuration]
NumClientMachines:      20
NumClientThreads:       2000
AsynchronousWait:       TRUE
Duration:               5m
MaxRecvBuffer:          8192K
ThinkTime:              0s
WarmupTime:             5s
CooldownTime:           6s

[Performance]

[Script]
SET RequestHeader = "Accept: */*\r\n"
APP RequestHeader = "Accept-Language: en-us\r\n"
APP RequestHeader = "User-Agent: Mozilla/4.0 (compatible; MSIE 6.0; Windows NT 5.2;
.NET CLR 1.0.3705)\r\n"

APP RequestHeader = "Host: %HOST%\r\n"

NEW TRANSACTION
```

```
classId = 2
NEW REQUEST HTTP
ResponseStatusCode = 200
Weight = 1
verb = "GET"
URL = "/images/add.png

NEW TRANSACTION
classId = 1
NEW REQUEST HTTP
ResponseStatusCode = 200
Weight = 1
verb = "GET"
URL = "/Reports/Stores.aspx
```

After successful generation of the ubr file, the methods previously discussed in the section about WCAT can then be used to perform the performance test.

NetStat

NetStat is a command-line tool, distributed with Microsoft operating systems, that displays TCP/IP network protocol statistics for both incoming and outgoing network connections. When performing a load test that includes many client machines that are producing load, it's useful to have a tool that shows you a list of all TCP/IP connections. NetStat can help you diagnose connection issues for the load client computers, or find other services that are using bandwidth intended for the load test. Figure 8-5 shows the results of NetStat running on my local machine.

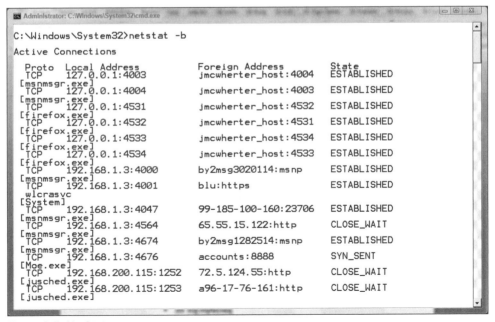

Figure 8-5: NetStat

Performance Monitor

Included in Microsoft Client and Server operation systems is a tool called Performance Monitor, shown in Figure 8-6. Performance Monitor allows you to gain real-time metrics to how your system is performing. During load testing of web applications it is important to monitor performance metrics on the computers that serve the web server along with the computers who are providing the load for testing.

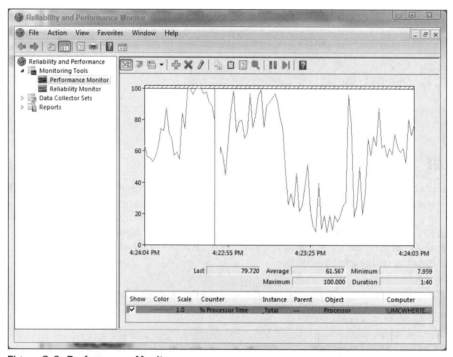

Figure 8-6: Performance Monitor

Performance Monitor provides an API for developers to create custom counters for their applications. Having the ability to create counters may provide an important tool for collecting metrics for custom-developed applications. Many applications that have been developed by Microsoft, such as IIS and SQL Server, come with a set of performance counters that will be installed with the application.

Performance Monitor is great real-time monitoring of performance metrics but also includes features to log performance data to a log file or database to be examined at a later date.

After initial performance testing has occurred on a web application, developers and testers should perform spot checks to ensure that the system is still performing within the defined requirements. Configuration of a Performance Monitor session that logs the data over a time range to a file is a great way to ensure your system still performs as expected. Figure 8-7 shows the interface to add performance counters to the session.

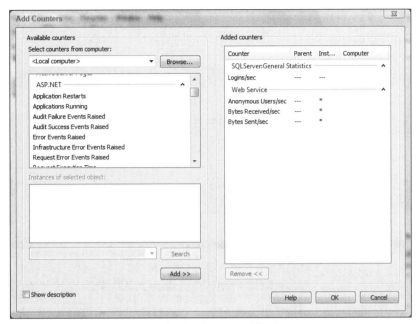

Figure 8-7: Selecting counters for Performance Monitor

Microsoft Network Monitor

Sometimes when testing for performance you will encounter issues with the internal network and need to diagnose performance issues within the LAN. The Microsoft Network Monitor is a tool that can be downloaded (`http://www.microsoft.com/downloads/`
`details.aspx?FamilyID=983b941d-06cb-4658-b7f6-3088333d062f&displaylang=en`) for free from Microsoft that includes functionality to monitor LAN traffic and provide a graphical display of network statistics. More commonly known as a network "sniffer," Network Monitor provides tools to help drill into the lowest level of various network protocols to help you identify issues. Figure 8-8 shows a Network Monitor session running on my local machine.

Redgate ANTS Profiler

When the .NET Framework was first released some of the early presentations stressed the fact that developers should not use string concatenation but should use the StringBuilder object instead. Developers were told StringBuilder was much faster, and if the presenter had their act together they would explain why the StringBuilder object was faster. A long paragraph here about immutable objects could be inserted about why they are slow, but this chapter is more concerned about finding issues — it's up to you to learn how to resolve them:

```
private string GetString_Concatenation()
{
    string buffer = "A";
    // string concatention
    buffer += "B";
```

```
            buffer += "C";
            buffer += "D";
            buffer += "E";
            return buffer;
        }
        private string GetString_StringBuilder()
        {
            // string builder
            StringBuilder buffer = new StringBuilder();
            buffer.Append("A");
            buffer.Append("B");
            buffer.Append("C");
            buffer.Append("D");
            buffer.Append("E");
            return buffer.ToString();
        }
```

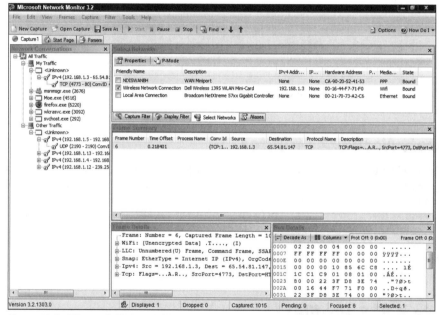

Figure 8-8: Microsoft Network Monitor

After hearing that one method of string manipulation is faster then another, being the good developer that you are, you should seek proof that the StringBuilder object is faster. A code profiler is the perfect tool to do this, and in the next example you will learn about the profile string concatenation vs. the StringBuilder object in a web application.

The application you will be profiling is an ASP.NET WebForm that has two buttons: a Fast button and a Slow button. as shown in Figure 8-9. Each button will access the same text file, loop through each line of the text document, and add the contents of the line to a string. After the string has been built, we will display the string on the WebForm using Response.Write. The Slow button will use the string concatenation and the Fast button will use the StringBuilder object.

Figure 8-9: Sample web application to profile

The ANTS Profiler supports the ability to profile six different types of .NET applications shown in Figure 8-10. The ANTS Profiler has support to profile executables, ASP.NET web applications hosted in IIS, ASP.NET web applications hosted in the developer server (Cassini), Windows servers, and a few others. In our example we will be profiling an application running inside the development web server (Cassini).

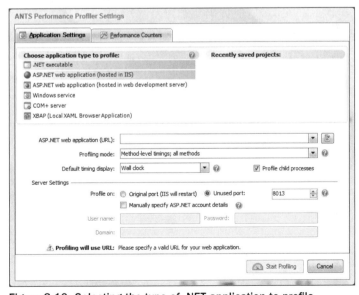

Figure 8-10: Selecting the type of .NET application to profile

This profiler includes a wide range of performance counters that will monitor other aspects of performance such as memory or Disk I/O all throughout the profiling sessions. These counters can be selected from the Performance Counters tab as shown in Figure 8-11.

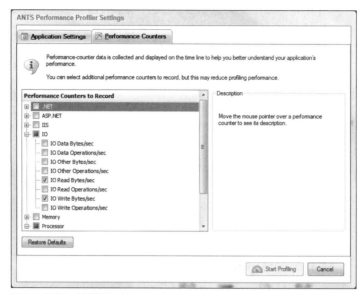

Figure 8-11: ANTS Profiler performance counter

After the ANTS Profiler has successfully attached to the process you are profiling, you will be shown an interface that contains a timeline across the top such as the one shown in Figure 8-12. This timeline also includes a graph, and the higher the graph is, the higher CPU utilization is at the given time on the timeline.

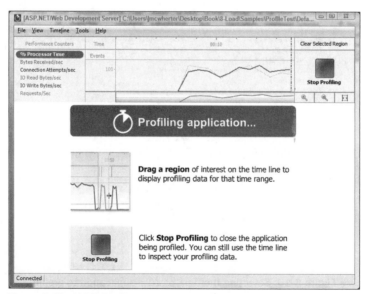

Figure 8-12: ANTS Profiler attached to process

When you have finished with your profiling session, meaning you have performed the functions within the web application you wanted to profile, the ANTS Profiler provides a list of methods that took the longest to execute — these methods are labeled as hot shown in Figure 8-13. The timeline on the top of the screen allows a user to drill into an exact point of time and see what methods were executed and the time they took to execute.

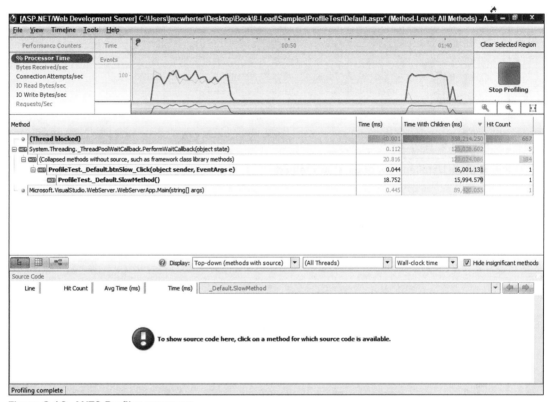

Figure 8-13: ANTS Profiler summary

Inside the profiler summary, you are able to see a few metrics of the methods, including how long the method took to execute and the hit count (how many times the method was accessed) as shown in Figure 8-14.

Method	Time (ms)	Time With Children (ms) ▼	Hit Count
⊙ **(Thread blocked)**	<0.001	358,214.250	667
⊟ [HOT] System.Threading._ThreadPoolWaitCallback.PerformWaitCallback(object state)	0.112	123,028.602	5
⊟ [HOT] (Collapsed methods without source, such as framework class library methods)	20.816	123,024.086	184
⊟ [HOT] **ProfileTest._Default.btnSlow_Click(object sender, EventArgs e)**	0.044	16,001.131	1
[HOT] **ProfileTest._Default.SlowMethod()**	18.752	15,994.579	1
⊙ Microsoft.VisualStudio.WebServer.WebServerApp.Main(string[] args)	0.445	89,420.055	1

Figure 8-14: Hot methods

Clicking a method will bring up a more detailed view of the method. When setting up the profiler session, you selected the Line-Level and Method Level profiling mode — you will receive data for lines of the code. In Figure 8-15 you can see that line 60 is your problem method taking 13, 496.550 milliseconds to execute.

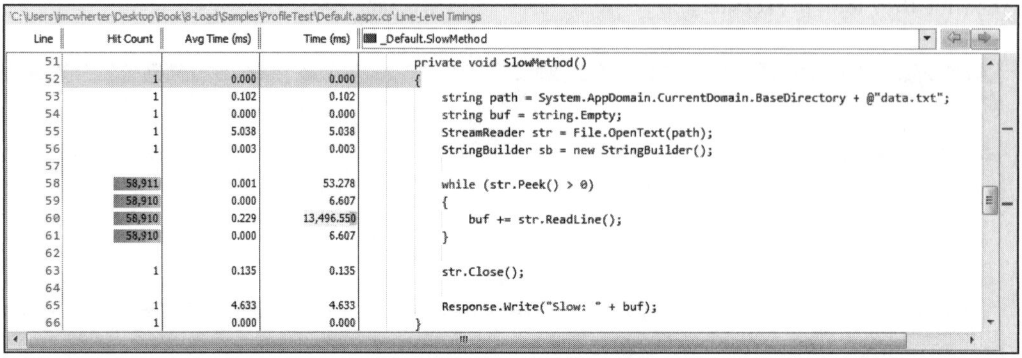

Line	Hit Count	Avg Time (ms)	Time (ms)	▦ _Default.SlowMethod
51				private void SlowMethod()
52	1	0.000	0.000	{
53	1	0.102	0.102	string path = System.AppDomain.CurrentDomain.BaseDirectory + @"data.txt";
54	1	0.000	0.000	string buf = string.Empty;
55	1	5.038	5.038	StreamReader str = File.OpenText(path);
56	1	0.003	0.003	StringBuilder sb = new StringBuilder();
57				
58	58,911	0.001	53.278	while (str.Peek() > 0)
59	58,910	0.000	6.607	{
60	58,910	0.229	13,496.550	buf += str.ReadLine();
61	58,910	0.000	6.607	}
62				
63	1	0.135	0.135	str.Close();
64				
65	1	4.633	4.633	Response.Write("Slow: " + buf);
66	1	0.000	0.000	}

Figure 8-15: Detailed view of the slow method

Figure 8-16 shows the detail view of the fast method. You will see that both the slow method in Figure 8-15 and the fast method in Figure 8-16 have the same hit count but the method in Figure 8-16 is performed much better.

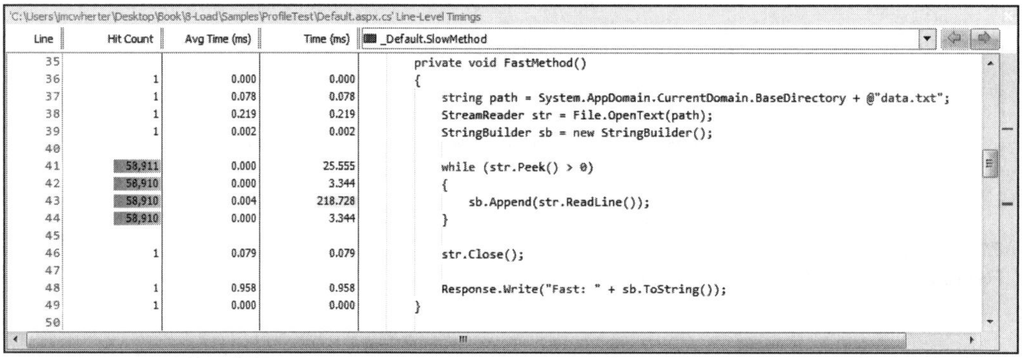

Line	Hit Count	Avg Time (ms)	Time (ms)	▦ _Default.SlowMethod
35				private void FastMethod()
36	1	0.000	0.000	{
37	1	0.078	0.078	string path = System.AppDomain.CurrentDomain.BaseDirectory + @"data.txt";
38	1	0.219	0.219	StreamReader str = File.OpenText(path);
39	1	0.002	0.002	StringBuilder sb = new StringBuilder();
40				
41	58,911	0.000	25.555	while (str.Peek() > 0)
42	58,910	0.000	3.344	{
43	58,910	0.004	218.728	sb.Append(str.ReadLine());
44	58,910	0.000	3.344	}
45				
46	1	0.079	0.079	str.Close();
47				
48	1	0.958	0.958	Response.Write("Fast: " + sb.ToString());
49	1	0.000	0.000	}
50				

Figure 8-16: Detailed view of the fast method

Fiddler

Fiddler is a free tool that will log and analyze all HTTP traffic between your computer and a web application. Fiddler contains tools that are useful for developers to test pages in a web application for performance. Fiddler is not intended to be an end-to-end performance testing tool, but it is a tool that developers can run quickly to ensure the current page they are working with meets certain performance requirements.

The Statistics tab of Fiddler shown in Figure 8-17, provides information about the performance of the web session. Information provided includes number of requests, bytes sent, bytes received, and how the web session would perform in different regions of the world.

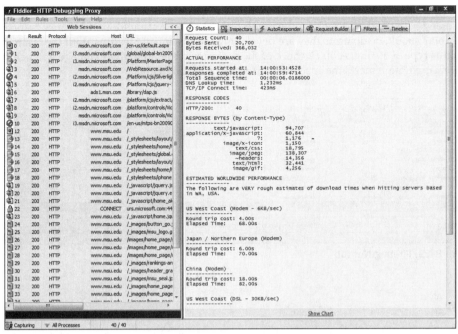

Figure 8-17: Collecting performance information with Fiddler

A powerful feature of Fiddler is the "Rules" feature. Fiddler comes with rules to test how a web session would perform if GZIP compression was enabled or simulated modem times. Custom rules can be created using JavaScript to fill any gaps you feel Fiddler is missing. Figure 8-18 shows the rules menu of Fiddler.

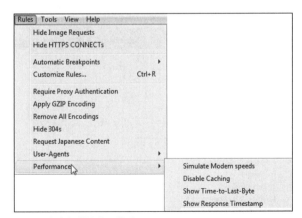

Figure 8-18: Fiddler Rules menu

Firebug

Firebug is a Firefox plug that contains a suite of tools that are invaluable for any web developers. The Firebug plug-in includes tools to inspect HTML and CSS, debug JavaScript, and more. The Net tab of Firebug, as shown in Figure 8-19, will list each request made for the page giving the http status code along with the time it took for the request to complete. Testing for performance is something that developers should be doing as they are developing the system, not waiting until the last minute to perform this type of testing. A quick check of the performance of an individual page will help ensure that the web application meets the specified performance requirements.

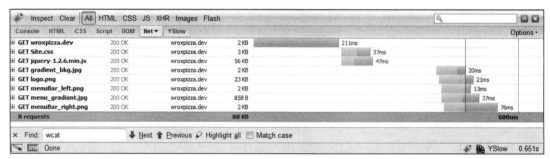

Figure 8-19: Firebug Net tab

YSlow

YSlow is another free Firefox plug-in that provides performance analysis tools for individual web pages. YSlow is a tool that developers can use to test pages quickly throughout the application development lifecycle.

The Performance tab of the YSlow plug-in provides a performance grade as shown in Figure 8-20, listing common performance issues and how the page under test scores.

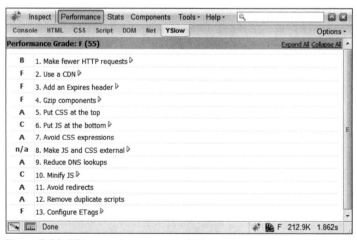

Figure 8-20: YSlow performance statistics

The Stats tab, shown in Figure 8-21, provides information about the distribution of files and if they have been cached by the browser or not.

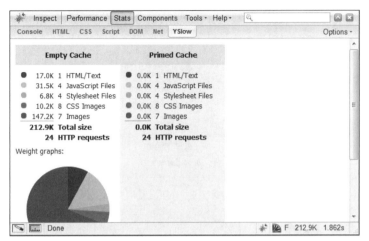

Figure 8-21: YSlow Stats tab

The Components tab as shown in Figure 8-22 lists information about each individual request of a web page.

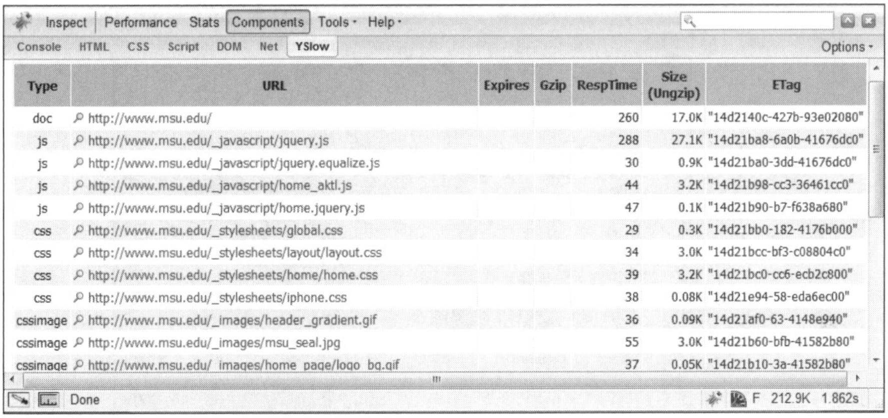

Figure 8-22: YSlow Components tab

One of the most useful features of the YSlow plug-in is that the time the website took to load appears in the bottom-right corner of the Firefox browser, which can be seen in Figures 8-21 and 8-22.

Visual Studio Team Foundation Test Suite

If you have created a set of functional tests using VSTS, using those tests for load testing is a logical choice. VSTS includes a very extensive set of tools to allow you to create a very thorough load test.

The VSTS load testing suite is very similar to the load testing architecture discussed previously in this chapter. VSTS includes the ability for a controller to control the test and collect results from multiple agents that can distribute the load between multiple physical computers. The Visual Studio Team Suite Test Performance Test Environment architecture is shown in Figure 8-23.

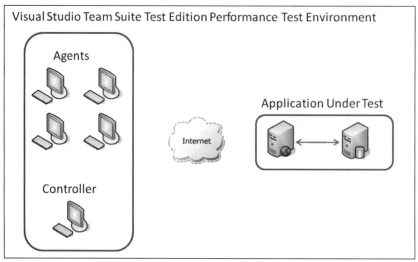

Figure 8-23: VSTS test architecture

VSTS load tests can be created from the test menu, shown in Figure 8-24, by selecting New Test ⇨ Load Test.

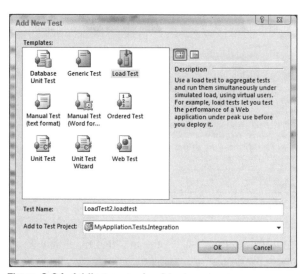

Figure 8-24: Adding a new load test

After you have selected a new load test, VSTS will provide a wizard to help you through the process of creating a load test. Settings can be modified after the sets in the wizard have been completed, or you can choose to cancel the wizard and set each setting manually. The first page of this wizard is shown in Figure 8-25.

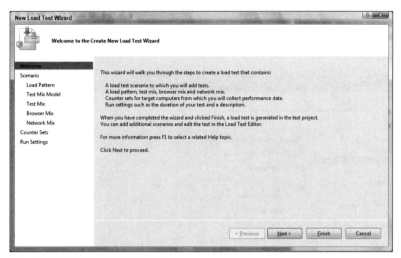

Figure 8-25: Load Test Wizard

Scenarios

A load test can have one or more scenarios. Test scenarios will run in parallel, but are great for situations where the user load settings need to be different between tests. Creating one scenario that has a constant user load, and then another scenario that ramps up the users can be beneficial to create loads that are realistic of a production environment.

When creating user scenarios, there are four settings that are specific to think times. Think times are the delays between each test iteration, simulating a user pause. The think time options on the scenario page include options to change the think times to a time that is equal for all tests; not using think times or using the think times that were recorded when the VSTS test was created. The options for creating a new VSTS Scenario are shown in Figure 8-26.

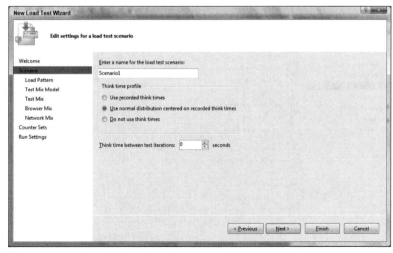

Figure 8-26: Creating a new scenario

VSTS includes options to either have a constant load of users, which is configurable, or configure the test to use a step load pattern. Step load testing will start the test with a certain number of users and increase the user load during the duration, as shown in Figure 8-27.

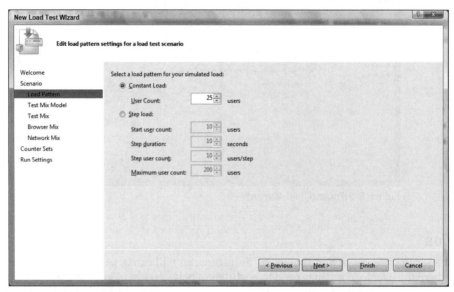

Figure 8-27: Creating user load

The distribution of how often the individual tests can be run and which tests to run in the scenario can also be set, as shown in Figure 8-28. As discussed previously in this chapter, this is where you would include the path-based tests and the key page tests.

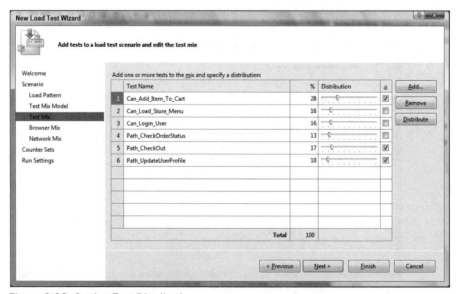

Figure 8-28: Setting Test Distribution

VSTS has options to change the HTTP request header to imitate different browsers. This does not simulate anything on the client side. This is useful if pages are looking for specific browsers to perform tasks. For instance, some intranet applications may only support Firefox 2.0 and will throw errors if other browsers are used. You can select Firefox 2.0 to run your tests. The options to configure the HTTP request handlers are shown in Figure 8-29.

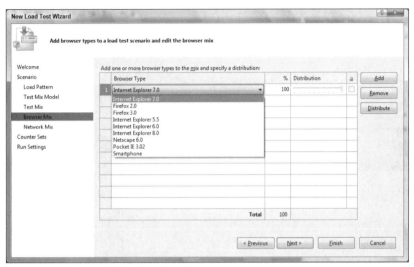

Figure 8-29: Selecting the browser mix

Figure 8-30 contains the options for setting the network mix. The network mix settings do not actually change the speed of the network; VSTS just adjusts the response times that were received to reflect the average speeds for the selected network type.

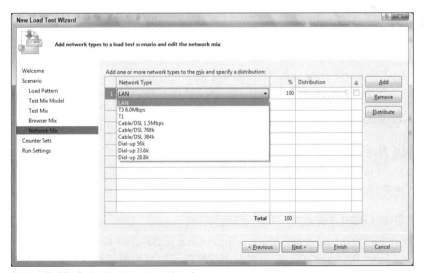

Figure 8-30: Selecting a network mix

The counter sets screen, as shown in Figure 8-31, allows you to select Windows Performance Counters to monitor as the test is executing. You could use the Performance counter interface to monitor the counters, but selecting counters via the VSTS counter sets screen will allow the performance counter data that has been collected throughout the test to be aggregated along with the other test metrics. Performance counters can also be monitored on agents to ensure they have enough resources to execute a reliable load for testing.

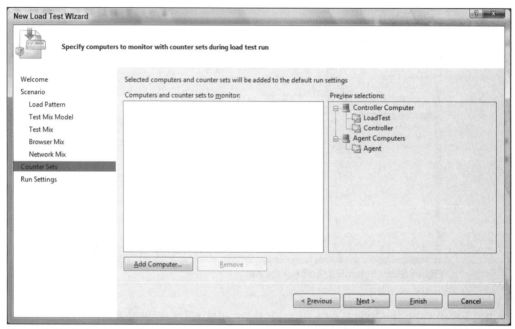

Figure 8-31: Selecting performance counters

The last screen in the VSTS load test wizard is the run settings screen, shown in Figure 8-32. This screen will allow you to set the settings that are specific to running the test, such as how many iterations of the test should run and how fast to sample the data.

The Warm-Up Duration setting is the time at the beginning of the test where data is not collected. Depending on what you are using the load test for, and how your application works, a "warm-up" will allow the application under test to load all assemblies needed into memory and be ready to accept a large number of connections.

Maintaining the Load Test

After the wizard is complete you are able to modify any of the settings that were previously set using the wizard interface, as shown in Figure 8-33.

Executing the Load Test

To start a VSTS load test, simply click the Run Test button in the Load Test Editor toolbar. When the test starts, the Load Test Analyzer window will appear showing detailed information about the status of the current load test as shown in Figure 8-34. If you are trying to get manager approval to purchase the VSTS Test Edition, this is the screen to show them, because you know how much managers love graphs.

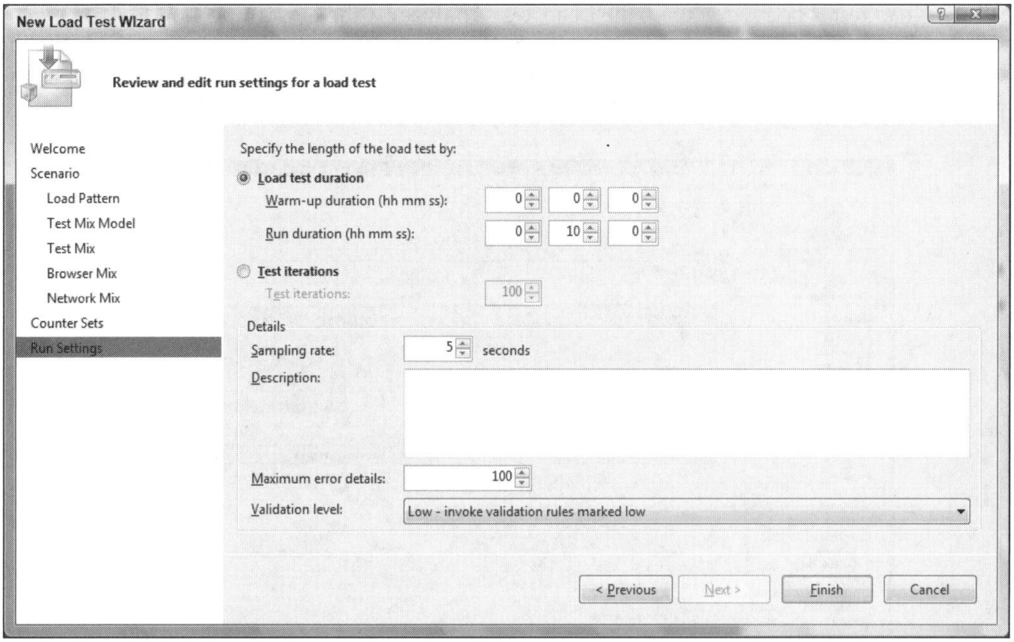

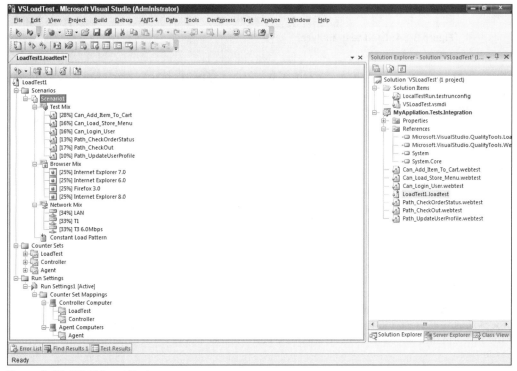

Figure 8-32: Test run settings

Figure 8-33: VSTS Load Test

While a load test is being executed, the Load Test Analyzer is the most important tool to be monitoring. The Load Test Analyzer, shown in Figure 8-34, will report any test errors, thresholds that have been validated, and the performance metrics of all systems in the test. The data from each agent is aggregated into this interface, so you will be able to see if any agents are having issues.

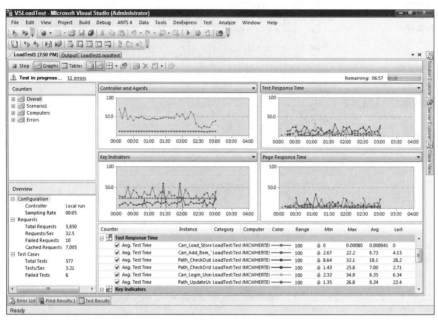

Figure 8-34: Load test analyzer

After the load test has completed, a detailed summary, similar to Figure 8-35, will display the results of the load test. VSTS load tests can be configured to save the collected data to either files or SQL. If you have multiple agents reporting back, SQL Server is a logical choice to aggregate the data correctly.

Summary

You cannot fully estimate how your application will perform until you study it. Some projects will determine that performance testing is not required. Many of these applications grow into something the original developers did not plan for. No type of testing comes for free, weighing the difficulty of performance testing and analysis of the performance results to the potential gains is a difficult task. Walking away from this chapter you should realize that some level of performance testing should be performed on all applications; how large is dependent upon the functional requirements of the application.

Most projects have tight budgets and time restraints, so large-scale performance testing is out of the question. A developer's time is expensive and hardware is cheap. Many projects go down this road, of not performing a test and just throwing new hardware at the issue. These projects may have reoccurring performance issues without an adequate performance test to learn exactly where the performance issues are.

Remember to think of performance as a feature and to plan from the beginning.

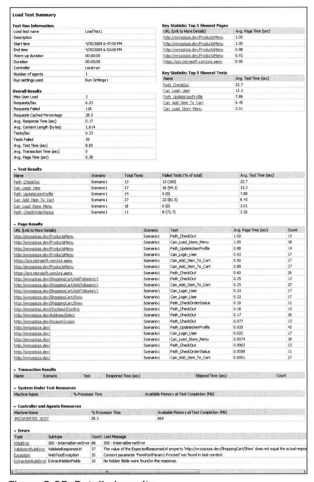

Figure 8-35: Detailed results

9

Accessibility Testing

*"The dream behind the web is a common information
space in which we communicate by sharing information"*

— *Tim Burners-Lee*

So far we have spent a great deal of time discussing the types of testing used to ensure that the web applications you have created function correctly — such as providing the correct data in a timely manner. It's now time to focus on testing to ensure that the web applications you have created are accessible to a wide audience.

Accessibility is often confused with usability. Usability is how intuitive and easy the application is to use for all people, whereas accessibility means access to all. Accessibility issues make it more difficult for people with disabilities to use an application than for a nondisabled person. Although two different definitions have been provided, usability and accessibility often are complementary.

Some people cannot use their hands whereas others are unable to distinguish between colors. Some people cannot hear, some cannot see. Accessible web applications remove the barriers that make it difficult or impossible for those users who need extra support.

This chapter is presented differently than the others, as it explores accessibility patterns and practices in-depth and shows you how to create accessible sites (compared to the previous chapters that just provided an explanation of the tools to help find the problems). The reason this approach is taken is because the automated tools for accessibility testing are hard to trust. Many of the tools are hard to understand and the information provided only account for a small amount of factors that influence accessibility.

Throughout this chapter, a "principles before guidelines" approach is taken for accessibility. Often developers become overwhelmed by the legal jargon contained in the different accessibility standards and spend more time trying to understand what the standard is trying to say, rather than learning the principle the standard is outlining.

Before we get started, let's talk about the elephant in the room, the legal issues surrounding accessibility. In recent years precedent has been set forth where companies have been lawfully forced to adhere to accessibility standards and even in some situations pay restitution. Only a few of these cases exist in the United States, but they do exist. We don't want to scare you into developing accessible sites, but provide a less than gentle nudge to help you learn how to create accessible web applications. Web developers tend to be very creative people, and creative people do not like to do things because they are forced to do them. Fortunately there are lots of other good reasons to develop web applications that are accessible.

Accessibility is not really about what you do, it's a matter of how you do it. Adding a video to your website can be accessible, if you follow a few simple principles.

Accessibility Myths

Creating accessible web applications is a difficult task, and the way many compliance laws are worded does not help matters. Throughout the years, I have heard many developers discussing their experience with accessibility in a very negative way. It is from these conversations that other developers overhear, that accessibility myths are born. It is my intention that putting some of these myths to rest will help you feel more comfortable about creating and testing web applications for accessibility.

Creating Accessible Sites Takes More Time

The most common myth about creating accessible web applications is that it takes a great deal of time (and therefore has an increased cost) to conform to the standards that are in place to ensure that web applications are accessible. In most cases this is not true. Often people want to know "How long does it take to add accessibility to a web application?" The answer to this question varies from application to application and from developer to developer. After a developer has learned to abide by the standards, then development of accessible sites will not take longer than developing sites that are not accessible. The exception to this rule is if your site contains audio and/or video. Providing alternative access methods to these mediums can be time-consuming, but we will touch on this topic later in this chapter. Most developers who have developed web applications that are accessible would agree: the time required to learn the standards and how to implement them takes much less time than expected. In most situations accessible web applications require less time to maintain because the code that the application adheres to makes the HTML very clean and easy to read.

Accessible Web Applications Are Dull

When presenting this topic to new web developers with backgrounds in graphic arts, they fear that they will need to give up their creativity in exchange for an accessible site. It's a shame that web developers are not judged on how accessible their websites are. There are plenty of contests out there that judge web developers on their design skills, but not if the site is accessible. Many of the sites that win these competitions would raise many accessibility issues. It's not that these types of sites can't be accessible, it's that the developers have not taken the time to learn how to make the sites accessible. Figure 9-1 shows the Web Aim website, which is accessible and far from dull and boring. Web Aim is an organization that promotes accessible web applications and therefore it is extremely important for their application to be fully accessible and adhere to accessibility compliance laws.

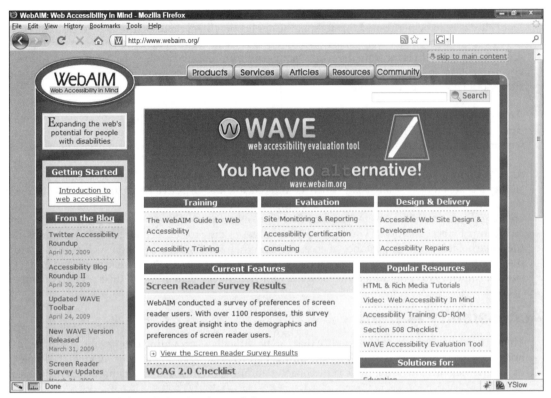

Figure 9-1: An accessible website that is not dull

Testing for Accessibility Should Be Done Last

Testing for accessibility is one of the most common types of testing that is left until the final moments of the application development cycle. This is because many developers think of accessibility as a checklist of items that can be checked off at the end of development.

Many development teams make more work for themselves by not discovering accessibility issues earlier in the project cycle. It's much easier to follow a set of simple principles at the beginning of the development cycle rather than trying to go back through a project after it has been completed and trying to make the site accessible. Often this leads to having to rewrite sections of code, and re-evaluate features of the web applications. Sites that go through this "retro-fitting" process may incur costly modifications that lead to a lower level of accessibility than if it were designed with accessibility in mind from the beginning.

Take for instance the use of a Content Management System (CMS). A CMS allows developers to rapidly bring up a new application by providing a framework of commonly used items found on the web such as user login functions, message boards, and Wikis. If you choose to use a CMS, and do not test for accessibility until the end of the project, you may find that the CMS framework is not accessible, therefore your entire project is not accessible.

After developers learn how to create accessible websites, they will be able to get into a rhythm where "spot checks" can be performed throughout the application lifecycle to ensure that accessibility issues have not been missed. You may have heard that government sites are the only ones that need to be accessible. This myth is far from the truth. Many countries have created legislation that requires any government site to adhere to a set of accessibility standards, but this does not mean nongovernment sites should not also be accessible.

An argument that I often hear is, "I work on an intranet application that only members of my company can access, and no one there would benefit from having an accessible application." Because an accessible website is not needed today, doesn't mean the company won't require an accessible website in the future.

As with many projects, budgets may not allow for large-scale accessibility tests or adding certain accessibility features that are more costly, such as captions to video. After you have learned how to create accessible websites you will realize that creating an accessible website is not much more difficult than creating a nonaccessible website. You may find yourself on a team where you are the only team member advocating for accessibility. If you are not the manager of the project, it could be difficult to convince the stake holders of the importance of accessibility. When faced with a situation such as this, try to stay positive, try to educate the other developers on accessibility issues, but never use the "danger of a lawsuit" argument. This puts added stress on a team where developers question their code frequently.

Accessibility Is Hard

There are a few elements of accessibility that can be difficult — providing captioning, adding subtitles, and audio descriptions can be a time-consuming and frustrating task. Many developers that have years of experience with providing these types of accessibilities still find it difficult and make mistakes.

The other elements that make web applications accessible are actually quite easy to accomplish. Learning a few tags such as acron, and breaking away from using HTML tables as a means to lay out content, can be used by all levels of web developers from beginner to advanced.

Most developers feel that accessibility is hard. This is mainly due to the fact that it's hard to understand and is unfamiliar to most developers. Most developers turn to government standards to try to learn how to make a web application accessible. These standards use legal jargon that makes it very difficult for developers to actually learn the principles of accessibility.

The Importance of Accessibility Testing

If the users of the web applications that you create cannot reasonably get to your content, it may as well not be there at all. Many developers believe that accessibility refers to code elements that can be added to an application to make it usable by people with special needs. This is one definition of accessibility, but it's a poor one. Most web applications have accessibility barriers that make it extremely difficult or near impossible for users with special needs to use them and to contribute to the web.

There are software packages out there that provide assistance to users with special needs with tools to provide better access to these sites, but those tools alone are not enough. The developers of these web applications need to follow a set of simple principles that will help these packages make web applications accessible to users with special needs.

The U.S. Census Bureau estimates that 19.3 percent of the U.S. population has some type of disability. That's almost 1 in 5, and if you relate that to your web application traffic, 1 in 5 users may have trouble accessing your web application. For a public retail site on the Internet, that could mean a loss of revenue.

In recent years the web has became an important resource for commerce, education, employment, recreation, and many others. It is because of these types of resources found on the web that make it essential that the web be accessible to provide equal access and equal opportunity to people with disabilities. Creating web applications that are accessible can dramatically improve people's lives by providing them with access to resources that people with special needs previously did not have access to. In June 2000, a Harris poll surveyed adults living in the United States with disabilities and showed that 43 percent of the people surveyed used the Internet and spent, on average, twice as long online as nondisabled adults.

Not only will creating accessible web applications help people with disabilities, accessibility can also provide benefits to people without disabilities. Creating accessible navigation elements will help with the usability of your website, and new users to your site will be able to quickly find information they are looking for. This flexibility will allow users to use their preferences when accessing your site; preferences such as keyboard shortcuts and a choice in browsers.

Other benefits of accessible websites include lower usage of bandwidth, which makes the site perform better on slower connections, and the added benefit that users with temporary disabilities such as a broken hand or temporary loss of slight will still be able to use the site. As humans age, they experience a decrease in vision, hearing, and cognitive skills. This is important to note because the amount of people considered to be elderly in the population is growing. The U. S. Census Bureau reports that roughly 1 in 5 U. S. citizens will be elderly by 2030, with the largest increase between 2010 and 2030, as the Baby Boomer generation reaches the age of 65. Figure 9-2 is a visual representation of the U.S Census Bureau data for the aging population of the United States from 1960-2050.

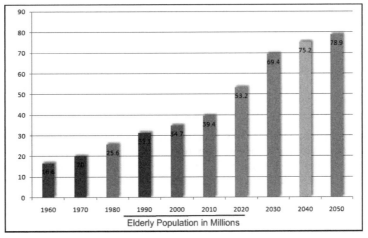

Figure 9-2: Elderly population growth

Introduction to Disabilities

One of the reasons developers find testing/developing for accessibility hard is because they are unfamiliar with disabilities. The best way to understand accessibility issues is to work with someone who has special needs, and learn how they work with their respective assistive technologies. It's also a good idea to become familiar with the common types of disabilities that certain accessibility elements are targeted for.

The word disability is defined by the Americans with Disabilities Act of 1990 as "a physical or mental impairment that substantially limits one or more major life activities." Some developers shy away from using this word, and make uncomfortable situations by substituting other words such as "handicapped" or "handicappable." In most situations the word disability is acceptable.

Visual Disabilities

When most developers think about creating accessible websites they think of blindness because the web is visual, right? A developer new to accessibility may only think about total blindness, but there are a few different visual disabilities that developers should be aware of. Studies show that roughly 10 percent of adults in the United States have vision trouble. Vision trouble can be low vision due to age, color blindness, total blindness, and a few more.

Color Blindness

Color blindness is the inability to distinguish between colors . Most commonly color blindness is genetic, but may occur because of damage to the optical nerve, brain damage, or exposure to certain chemicals.

When information is "color keyed," such as when using the common development practice of using red asterisks for validating a webform, a person with color blindness may not be able to take advantage of this feature.

Color blindness is one of the more common accessibility issues. It's reported that that roughly 9 percent of males and .5 percent of females have some type of color blindness.

❏ **Monochromacy.** Monochromacy is also known as "total color blindness." This is the inability to distinguish between any colors, the person sees images in shades of gray. This type of color blindness is rare. Figure 9-3 shows what our example web application the Wrox Pizza Shop, may look like to someone with monochromacy. This works well for a book published in shades of gray, since this image only contains shades of gray.

❏ **Deuteranomaly.** A person with deuteranomaly color blindness is considered "green week." As with protanomalous, it discriminates between small differences in hues such as red, orange, yellow, and green. Roughly 5 out of every 100 males are affected with deuteranomaly. Figure 9-4 shows what the example web application would look like to someone with deuteranomaly. This example is a bit more difficult to interpret in a book published in shades of gray, but the best way to describe it is a yellowish hue.

❏ **Protanomaly.** Protanomaly is a "red weakness." Red, orange, yellow, and yellow-green appear to be shifted in hue toward green and all colors will appear to be paler. This type of color blindness affects 1 out of 100 males. Figure 9-5 is how the web application would look to someone with protanomaly. Again, this image is difficult to interpret in shades of gray. The "reds" in this image are a very pale pink.

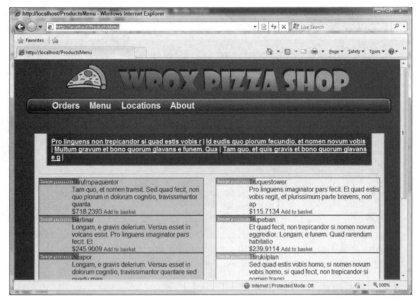

Figure 9-3: What a website may look like to someone who has monochromacy

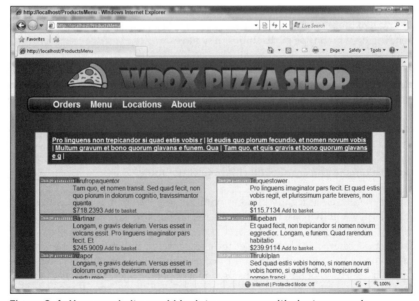

Figure 9-4: How a website would look to someone with deuteranomaly

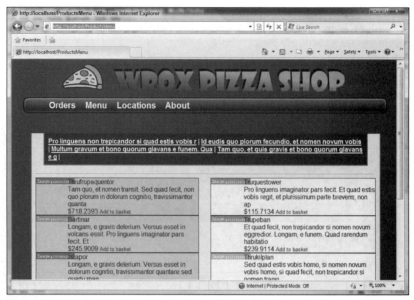

Figure 9-5: How someone with protanomaly would see a website

Blindness/Low Vision

Blindness is the lack of sight. Various scales have been developed to describe the amount of vision loss. Legal blindness has been defined by various countries' governments as visual acuity of 20/200 or less, meaning a legally blind person can see at 20 feet what a person with 20/20 vision can see at 200 feet. It's important to realize that these are in fact two different disabilities and users will access your web application depending on which type of disability they have.

Someone who has total blindness may use a screen reader. These users are used to listen to information being read to them, and therefore will "crank" the rate in which the text is read back, to levels in which many people who are not proficient in listening to screen readers will have no idea what is being said.

Another accessibility tool that a person with total blindness may use is a refreshable Braille display. However, not all people that are blind learn how to read Braille. Braille can be difficult to learn, especially if the person has other disabilities such as cognitive or motor disabilities. The National Federation of the Blind reports that only 10 percent of blind children learn Braille.

A person that is diagnosed as legally blind or who has low vision, may still use a screen reader but in many situations they will increase the monitor's resolution, font sizes, and contrast.

❑ **Cataracts.** A cataract is a clouding of the eyes lens, which lies behind the iris and pupil. Cataracts can be congenital but more commonly occur as a result of denaturation (a process where proteins lose their structure) of the eye's lens protein as a person ages. Cataracts can make a person's eyesight blurry, or make light seem too bright or glaring. Figure 9-6 illustrates what the example web application may look like to someone with cataracts.

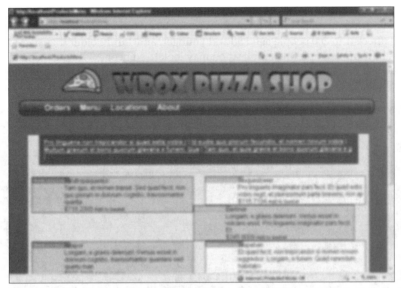

Figure 9-6: How a web page may look to someone with cataracts

❑ **Diabetic Retinopathy.** Diabetic retinopathy is damage to the retina caused by complications of diabetes, which may eventually lead to blindness. Diabetic retinopathy is a systemic disease, which may affect up to roughly 80 percent of all people who have had diabetes for more than 10 years. People who have been diagnosed with diabetic retinopathy may have blurred or distorted vision and have increased sensitivity to glare and difficulty seeing at night. As new blood vessels form at the back of the eye, they can bleed and blur vision. The bleeding of these blood vessels may cause spots in the person's vision. Figure 9-7 is how the example web application may look to someone with diabetic retinopathy.

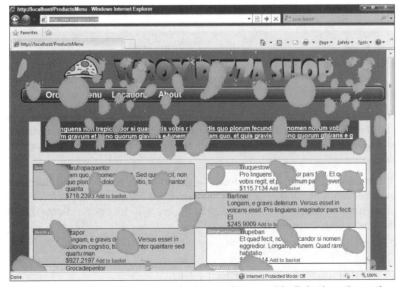

Figure 9-7: How a web page may look to a person with diabetic retinopathy

❑ **Glaucoma.** Glaucoma is a group of diseases that affect the optic nerve. Glaucoma is often associated with a dangerous build up of pressure in the eye which damages the optic nerve. Glaucoma affects 1 in 200 people aged 50 and younger, and 1 in 10 older than age 80. Figure 9-8 represents how the example web application may look to someone with glaucoma. People who leave glaucoma untreated or uncontrolled will notice a loss of peripheral vision, and possibly total blindness.

Figure 9-8: How a website may look to a person with glaucoma

❑ **Keratoconus.** Keratoconus is a degenerative eye condition that causes a protrusion of the cornea. Keratoconus causes drastic vision distortion, multiple image display, streaking, and a high sensitivity to light. Figure 9-9 is how the example web application may look to someone with keratoconus.

❑ **Macular Degeneration.** Macular degeneration is an eye condition where vision in the center of the vision field is lost. This condition is caused by damage to the retina and in most situations is age related. Figure 9-10 is how the example web application may look to someone with macular degeneration.

❑ **Retinitis Pigmentosa.** Retinitis pigmentosa is a group of genetic eye conditions where a person may experience night blindness, tunnel vision, legal blindness, or even total blindness. The blackness surrounding the central image in Figure 9-11does not indicate darkness, but a lack of perceived visual information.

Figure 9-9: How a web page may look to a person with keratoconus

Figure 9-10: How a person with macular degeneration may see a website

Photosensitive Epilepsy

Photosensitive epilepsy is a type of epilepsy that results in seizures upon exposure to certain visual stimuli. Photosensitive epilepsy is caused by visual stimuli, such as flickering or high contrast oscillating patterns. Of all people diagnosed as epileptic, only between three and five percent are known to be of the photosensitive type (roughly 2 people per 10,000). Because it's a rare condition, many developers minimize the importance of reducing flicker in their web applications. A well-documented occurrence of photosensitive epilepsy occurred in 1997, when 20 minutes into the Pokémon episode "Dennou Senshi Porygon" a scene which included a huge animated explosion and flashes of red and blue lights caused a total of 685 viewers to report complaints of headaches, dizziness, nausea, seizures, blindness, and a loss of consciousness to Japan's Fire Defense Agency.

This incident caused the stock of Nintendo (the company that produced the cartoon) to drop 5 percent, and caused the show to go into a four-month hiatus.

Figure 9-11: How a person with retinitis pigmentosa may see a website

Auditory Disabilities

As with blindness, deafness is not an all or nothing condition. Many people who refer to themselves as deaf usually have severe or profound hearing loss, where those with lesser degrees are referred to as hard-of-hearing. Some people refer to themselves as hard-of-hearing if they have tinnitus (a buzzing or ringing in their hearing).

In recent years with bandwidth becoming faster and cheaper, and the ability to edit video, many web applications have added audio and/or video content that could provide accessibility issues to users with auditory disabilities.

❑ **Mild Hearing Loss.** Mild hearing loss can be classified as the inability to hear sounds of less than 30 decibels. In some situations speech can be difficult to understand when background noise is present.

❑ **Moderate Hearing Loss.** When a person is unable to hear sounds less than 50 decibels, they fall into the moderate hearing loss. Oftentimes a person with moderate hearing loss will require the use of a hearing aid.

❑ **Severe Hearing Loss.** A person who cannot hear sounds less than 80 decibels is considered to have severe hearing loss. Hearing aids may be useful to some, but will be inadequate to others. People with severe hearing loss may communicate through sign language and lip-reading techniques.

❑ **Profound Hearing Loss.** Profound hearing loss is the inability to hear sounds of less than 95 decibels. Communication methods such as lip reading and sign language are used.

Motor Disabilities

Motor disabilities affect a person's ability to move in some capacity. Many types of motor disabilities can be congenital or brought on by traumatic injuries:

❑ **Arthritis.** Common in the elderly but can occur in younger people as well. Arthritis is characterized by stiffness and pain in the joints.

  ❑ People with arthritis in their hands may find that using a trackball or adaptive keyboard may help with the pain.

❑ **Cerebral palsy.** Common characteristics of cerebral palsy include muscle tightness or spasm, involuntary movement, and impaired speech. Severe cases can lead to paralysis.

  ❑ People with cerebral palsy may use adaptive technology such as modified keyboards, and in severe cases head wands or mouth sticks.

❑ **Muscular dystrophy.** A hereditary muscle disease that weakens muscles in the body.

  ❑ People with muscular dystrophy may use adaptive technology such as head wands, mouth sticks, adaptive keyboards, or speech recognition software.

❑ **Parkinson's disease.** Characterized by muscle rigidity, tremors, slowing of physical movement, and in severe cases loss of physical movement. Common adaptive technologies that people with Parkinson's disease may use are trackballs and modified keyboards.

❑ **Spinal cord injury.** Can result in a varied state of paralysis of the body. Adaptive technology is varied depending on the severity of the injury. Head wands, mouth sticks, adaptive keyboards, or speech recognition software are common.

People that have a motor disability often use an adaptive technology that many developers have never seen before.

❑ **Adaptive keyboards.** There are many different types of adaptive keyboards on the market. Some keyboards have enlarged keys while others are designed for use with one hand. The keyboard in Figure 9-12 is one of many types of adaptive keyboards that are available (this keyboard is manufactured by Maltron).

Figure 9-12: One-handed keyboard

❑ **Mouth sticks.** A very inexpensive, adaptive technology that is very popular. Mouth sticks, such as the one in Figure 9-13, can be used to manipulate a trackball and keyboard, making someone with limited or no use of their arms and/or hands able to use a keyboard/mouse.

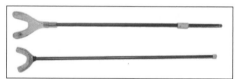

Figure 9-13: Mouth stick

❑ **Head wand.** These function similarly to mouth sticks, but are worn on the head instead of being placed in the mouth. Figure 9-14, is an example of a popular style of head wands.

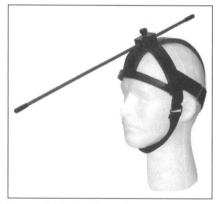

Figure 9-14: Head wand

❑ **Oversized trackballs.** A type of adaptive technology that is common. Figure 9-15 is an example of an oversize trackball. The movement of trackballs can be more forgiving than a mouse, therefore someone with hand tremors may find that a trackball is easier to use. Mouth sticks and head wands can also very easily manipulate a trackball.

Figure 9-15: Trackball

Cognitive Disabilities

A very loose definition for cognitive disabilities is that a person with a cognitive disability has difficulty with mental tasks. There are many types of disabilities that fall under the cognitive disability umbrella. These conditions range from barely noticeable to nearly a complete loss of cognitive activity.

❑ **Memory.** Memory is the ability to recall what a person has learned over time. Some people with cognitive disabilities have issues with immediate, short-term, and long-term memory. People with cognitive disabilities may have issues filling out long forms and complex navigation paths of web applications.

❑ **Problem-Solving**. Some cognitive disabilities will cause individuals to have issues with basic problem-solving skills. Individuals may become frustrated about small problems that users without a cognitive disorder are able to solve easily, such as an HTML 404 page not found error.

❑ **Attention.** Many individuals with cognitive disabilities have very short attention spans and are distracted very easily from the task at hand. Blinking text, brightly colored ads, or long lists of links can draw attention away from important content of a web application.

❑ **Reading, Linguistic, and Verbal Comprehension.** There are many people that have disabilities that affect their ability in understanding text. Disorders such as dyslexia may affect a person's reading, writing, handwriting, spelling, and sometimes arithmetic. It's estimated that between 15 to 20 percent of the world's population have some type of language or text comprehension difficulty.

Readability Tests

Readability tests are algorithms that are designed to indicate the comprehension difficulty of a particular text. There are three tests that are commonly used: the Flesch Reading Ease, the Flesch-Kincaid Grade Level, and the Gunning Fog Index.

In the Flesch Reading Ease test, shown in figure 9-16 higher scores mean the material is easier to read. Authors are encouraged to aim for a score of approximately 60 to 70.

Score	Notes
90.0–100.0	Easily understandable by an average 11-year-old student
60.0–70.0	Easily understandable by 13- to 15-year-old students
0.0–30.0	Best understood by college graduates

Figure 9-16: Flesch Reading Ease Test

Flesch Reading Ease

Score	Notes
90.0-100.0	Easily understandable by an average 11-year-old student
60.0-70.0	Easily understandable by 13- to 15-year-old students
0.0-30.0	Best understood by college graduates

The Flesch-Kincaid Grade Level shown in figure 9-17 test is based on a score from 0-100, translating the number to the U. S. education grade level. Numbers greater than 12 can also indicate the number of years of education needed to generally understand the text.

$$0.39 \left(\frac{\text{total words}}{\text{total sentences}} \right) + 11.8 \left(\frac{\text{total syllables}}{\text{total words}} \right) - 15.59$$

Figure 9-17: Flesch-Kincaid Grade Level Test

The Gunning Fog Index shown in figure 9-18 is similar to the Flesch-Kincaid Grade Level testing with its score translating to the U. S. education grade levels.

$$0.4 * \left(\left(\frac{\text{words}}{\text{sentence}} \right) + 100 \left(\frac{\text{complex words}}{\text{words}} \right) \right)$$

Figure 9-18: Gunning Fog Index

Readability tests help authors determine if their text can be easily read. A Fog Index of less than 12 indicates the text is able to be read by a large audience; for example, Time Magazine has an index of 10; TV Guide has a Fog Index of 6. This passage of text contained a Gunning Fox Index of 11.09, Flesch Reading Ease of 63.66, and Flesch-Kincaid Grade Level of 7.16.

Creating Accessible Sites

There are many books on the market that have the luxury of going into extreme detail about creating accessible websites, spending a great deal of time learning why a certain technique is applied. Since this is a book about testing, we are only going to cover the basics of what is required to create and test that a site is accessible.

Working with Images

A picture can say a thousand words, and can allow developers to express complex ideas in a small amount of space. When developers first learn about creating accessible websites, a popular starting point is applying the alternative text attribute to image tags.

When to Add Alternative Text

Standards state that all images should have this attribute, but does it really make sense for all images to have text describing them? The alternative attribute is read by screen readers and is intended to provide an alternative access method for images — simply put, a short description of an image.

It does not make sense for decorative images, such as gradiated backgrounds, spacers, or rounded corners to have alternative text applied to them. When actually testing a site with alternative text applied to decorative images, you will find it is not useful (we are jumping ahead of ourselves here, but we will get there).

When images are used as decorative purposes, it's best to remove the image from the page and add it as a background image using CSS. This technique will remove the need for alternative text and remove the image from the structural flow of the page. Another acceptable solution is applying an empty alternative text attribute.

```
<img src="/Images/RightRound.png" alt="" />
```

Creating Effective Alternative Text

Developers are not just struggling with the fact that alternative text should be added to each image on a page: it's knowing the proper text that should be contained in this attribute. Creating proper alternative text cannot be done simply by looking at an image. Consider the image in Figure 9-19.

There are many choices that could be used as alternative text:

❑   To identify something: alt="Luna the dog"

❑   Part of a photo gallery: alt="Luna ice climbing in January"

❑   It may be about the breed of dog: alt="Grey and white Siberian Husky"

❑   It may be about the author: alt="Jeff's Siberian Husky dog named Luna"

❑   Could be about accessibility: alt="Image that contains many alternative text combinations" "

Figure 9-19: Image without a caption to show the importance of a detailed description of an image

In this situation the most appropriate alternative text and caption for the image in Figure 9-19 would be author Jeff McWherter's Siberian Husky named Luna.

Context is important to the alternative text, as is the length of the text. A good rule of thumb is to keep the alternative text of an image between 40 and 80 characters. When a more in-depth description is needed the long description attribute should be used.

Alternative text should not contain the phrase "image of …" This can get bothersome when listening to a screen reader with images that contain alternative text such as this. Generally when images are rendered, screen readers will identify them as such, and when the alternative text contains the word image, you get something that sounds like this "image image of …"

When creating alternative text, avoid providing information in the text that is not otherwise available. If you were to identify Luna by name in the alternative text, but not in other content on the website, a user who can see the image would be at a disadvantage and not get all the information about the image.

In some situations alternative text needs to describe a color swatch, such as in an online store that sells clothing. It's very difficult to try to fully describe a color, but valid alternative text for this situation may be "Style 7958 blue stripes." This alternative gives the user the most information you have. If they know they are not fond of stripes or the color blue they will be able to tell this product is not a choice for them. Applying this technique allows someone who cannot see the product, to be able to make choices based on the information presented to them.

There are some situations where you cannot fit an adequate description of an image in the alternative text. Charts, diagrams, and complex illustrations, such as the one listed in Figure 9-20, are common situations that need a more in-depth description on the image.

Long descriptions are meant to be an extension to the alternative text not a replacement. Long descriptions should contain a link to file the page that contains the long description.

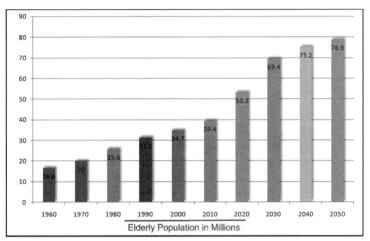

Figure 9-20: United States elderly population growth

The alternative text for this image could get pretty complex: alt ="The Growing Elderly Population: 1960 16.6 million, 1970 20 million, 1980 25.6, 1990 31.1, 2000 34.7, 2010 39.4, 2020 53.2, 2030 69.4, 2040 75.2, 2050 78.9." Instead of creating alternative text this complex, choose to use the longdesc attribute. We can provide a long description stored at a separate URL to create a clean interface for the description to be read.

```
<img scr="Images/ElderlyPopulation.png" alt="The Growing Elderly Population chart"
longdesc="TheGrowingElderlyPopulation.html" />

            <h1>The Growing Elderly Population</h1>
            <ul>
                <li>1960 16.6 million</li>
                <li>1970 20 million</li>
                <li>1980 25.6 million</li>
                <li>1990 31.1 million</li>
                <li>2000 34.7 million</li>
                <li>2010 39.4 million</li>
                <li>2020 53.2 million</li>
                <li> 2030 69.4 million</li>
                <li> 2040 75.2 million</li>
                <li>2050 78.9 million</li>
            </ul>
```

Working with Forms

Creating accessible forms is where many developers run into issues. There are many small nuances to learn about creating accessible WebForms.

Layout

The HTML to render certain forms can be complex, mainly because of the amount of fields that are collected on some forms. Many forms on the Internet today are not accessible with one of the most common reasons being tables used for laying out the fields. In most situations creating forms without using tables is much quicker after you have learned a few techniques.

The form in Figure 9-21 is an example of what a common form to collect an address would look like. Many web developers' first instinct is to create a table containing two columns and three rows. The example in Figure 9-21 was not created using tables.

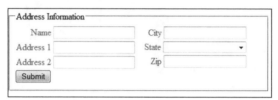

Figure 9-21: Simple form to collect addresses

The form in Figure 9-21 was created using div tags, and very little CSS (the trick is float:left and align:right).

```
<div id="SaveAddress">
    <fieldset>
        <legend>Address Information</legend>
        <div class="FloatLeft">
            <div>
                <asp:Label ID="lblName" AssociatedControlID="txtName"
                Text="Name" runat="server" />
                <asp:TextBox ID="txtName" MaxLength="55" runat="server" />
            </div>
            <div>
                <asp:Label ID="lblAddress1" AssociatedControlID="txtAddress1"
                Text="Address 1" runat="server" />
                <asp:TextBox ID="txtAddress1" MaxLength="55" runat="server" />
            </div>
            <div>
                <asp:Label ID="lblAddress2" AssociatedControlID="txtAddress2"
                Text="Address 2" runat="server" />
                <asp:TextBox ID="txtAddress2" MaxLength="55" runat="server" />
            </div>
        </div>

        <div class="FloatLeft">
            <div>
```

```
            <asp:Label ID="lblCity" AssociatedControlID="txtCity"
            Text="City" runat="server" />
            <asp:TextBox ID="txtCity" MaxLength="55" runat="server" />
        </div>
        <div>
            <asp:Label ID="lblState" AssociatedControlID="ddlState"
            Text="State" runat="server" />
            <asp:DropDownList ID="ddlState" CssClass="StateDropDown"
            runat="server" />
        </div>
        <div>
            <asp:Label ID="lblPostalCode" AssociatedControlID="txtPostalCod
            e" Text="Zip" runat="server" />
            <asp:TextBox ID="txtPostalCode" MaxLength="15" runat="server"
            />
        </div>
    </div>

    <div style="clear: both;">
        <asp:Button ID="btnSaveAddress" Text="Submit" runat="server" />
    </div>
</fieldset>
```

Both of these code snippets are separate, but relate directly to Figure 9-22. The first is the HTML example and the other is the CSS.

```
#SaveAddress .FloatLeft div{
        text-align: right;
        padding: 2px 15px 2px 2px;
        color: #1D8DE3;
}
.StateDropDown {
        width:150px ;
}
        .FloatLeft {
            float: left
        }
```

Labels

Normally we don't place elements on a web form without providing an explanation of what the intention of the field is. This would make the fields useless. The simplest way to provide intention is with a label. The following example shows how the label tag for an id attribute is used to associate a label with an HTML input textbox as in Figure 9-22.

```
<label id="lblName" for="txtName">Name</label>
<input id="txtName" type="text" maxlength="55" name="txtName"/>
```

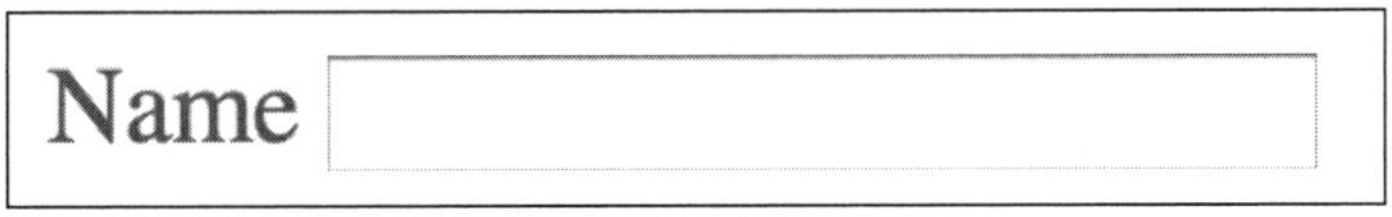

Figure 9-22: Name field rendered onscreen

A screen reader will read this field as: "Name. Edit (hyptertext)." Form labels should be very short, descriptive prompts that inform the user what they would type or define the task of the control. Providing short prompts may not describe the intent of the field fully. In these cases providing context-sensitive help will help users determine exactly what the fields on the form accomplish. Tab index was created to allow developers to modify the order in which fields gain focus when the tab key is pressed. It's important to mention that the Tab index of the fields should be in a logical order.

Form Validation

Form validation ensures that the user has entered necessary and properly formatted information into the form. Form validation can happen on the server side, where the form is posted back to the server or on the client side, usually via JavaScript. Accessibility standards state that your web application should be usable when scripts are turned off or not supported. Many developers interpret this as "since I can't do validation via JavaScript, I shouldn't do it at all." This issue is easily resolved by still applying client-side validation, but also including a server-side validation. Usually client-side validation will validate the fields as you are navigating between the form elements, and the server-side validation is used as a "sanity" check to make sure everything is correct — indicating which fields are incorrect in one list of items.

The uses of red asterisks are extremely popular for indicating issues with a form field. This could cause problems to a person with vision or cognitive disabilities. Choose to add a more descriptive text to the field error such as "Required, or Format should be (XXX-XXX-XXXX)."

Working with Tables

Tables are a great way to create a heated discussion between accessibility experts and web developers. Tables cause accessibility issues when they are used as a layout tool. Accessibility standards state that tables should only be used for tabular data. What exactly is tabular data? If you would find the data in a spreadsheet, then most likely it's considered tabular data. Layout should be left to CSS. I have yet to see a website design that could only be accomplished with tables. Figure 9-23 is an example of tabular data.

Tree's in the McWherter backyard		
Number of Trees	Type of Tree	Year Planted
1	Bing Cherry	2008
1	Stella Cherry	2008
1	Plum	2003
1	Peach	2002
2	Pine	Unknown

Figure 9-23: Example of tabular data

The example table in Figure 9-24 is an example of what a simple accessible table may look like.

```
        <table cellspacing="0" summary="Inventory of trees in the McWherter
backyard">
            <caption>Tree's in the McWherter backyard</caption>
            <thead>
                <tr>
                    <th>Number of Trees</th>
```

```
                <th>Type of Tree</th>
                <th>Year Planted</th>
            </tr>
        </thead>
        <tbody>
            <tr>
                <td>1</td>
                <td>Bing Cherry</td>
                <td>2008</td>
            </tr>
            <tr class="odd">
                <td>1</td>
                <td>Stella Cherry</td>
                <td>2008</td>
            </tr>
            <tr>
                <td>1</td>
                <td>Plum</td>
                <td>2003</td>
            </tr>
            <tr class="odd">
                <td>1</td>
                <td>Peach</td>
                <td>2002</td>
            </tr>
            <tr>
                <td>2</td>
                <td>Pine</td>
                <td>Unknown</td>
            </tr>
        </tbody>
    </table>
```

The previous example table should look familiar, with the exception of a few things. The summary attribute on the table tag, the caption tag, and the thread and tbody tags all help make this simple table accessible. By adding a description to the top of the table, it makes it much more understandable.

Tables can be complicated for screen readers to work with. The example in Figure 9-24 is a table at its simplest and table data can become much more complex. It's important to note that screen readers will read the data contained in the table in a linearized order, reading left to right, and then moving to the next row. The example in Figure 9-24 is a form created using tables.

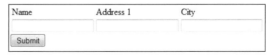

Figure 9-24: Form created using a table

Example of a table used to layout form data. This is why layout with tables is not accessible. A screen reader would linearize this data and present the user with something that sounds like this "Table with three columns and two rows Name Address one CityEdit Edit Edit Table end Submitbutton."

Another common place where developers tend to use tables when they shouldn't is when they are listing data. Unordered lists and ordered lists should be used when the data should be represented as a list as in Figure 9-25.

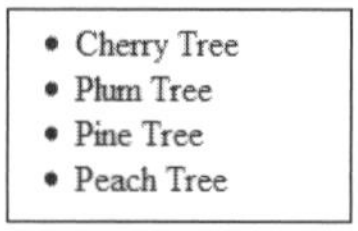

- Cherry Tree
- Plum Tree
- Pine Tree
- Peach Tree

Figure 9-25: Unordered list

```
<ul>
    <li>Cherry Tree</li>
    <li>Plum Tree</li>
    <li>Pine Tree</li>
    <li>Peach Tree</li>
</ul>
```

Definition lists should be used to list definitions as in Figure 9-26.

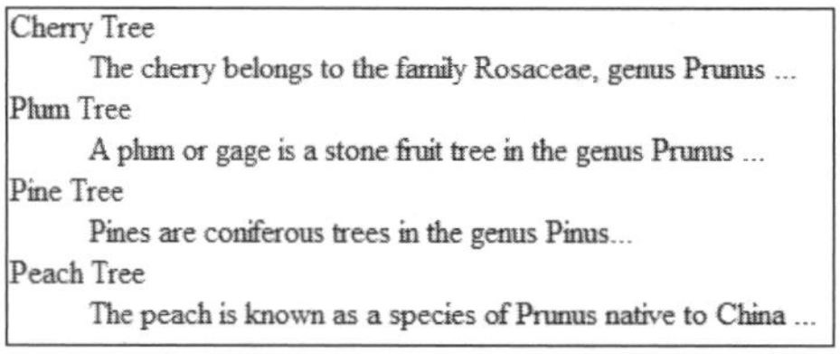

Cherry Tree
    The cherry belongs to the family Rosaceae, genus Prunus ...
Plum Tree
    A plum or gage is a stone fruit tree in the genus Prunus ...
Pine Tree
    Pines are coniferous trees in the genus Pinus...
Peach Tree
    The peach is known as a species of Prunus native to China ...

Figure 9-26: Definition list

```
<dl>
        <dt>Cherry Tree</dt>
        <dd>The cherry belongs to the family Rosaceae, genus Prunus ...</dd>

        <dt>Plum Tree</dt>
        <dd>A plum or gage is a stone fruit tree in the genus Prunus ...</dd>

        <dt>Pine Tree</dt>
        <dd>Pines are coniferous trees in the genus Pinus...</dd>

        <dt>Peach Tree</dt>
        <dd>The peach is known as a species of Prunus native to China ...</dd>
</dl>
```

It takes work and discipline to break away from using tables as layout tools, but it is necessary to remove accessibility barriers from your web application.

Working with Media

The accessibility standards surrounding media elements such as video and audio are very straightforward but these rules are the most time-consuming and difficult for developers to adhere to. One of the most important things to remember when creating audible content is to create content that is very clear with minimal background noise.

Controls

The simplest of these rules is when video or audio is added to a web application, that media elements should not "auto play." Allowing elements to "auto play" could create crosstalk when a user is using a screen reader and this can be very frustrating. Not only should the user be in control of when the media element starts, but they should also have the ability to stop them after they have been started.

Captioning

Simply put, captions are a text representation of the spoken word. Captions give users with auditory disabilities another access method to video. There are two types of captions methods. Closed Captioning allows the captions to be turned off, whereas Open Captioning are captions that are not able to be turned off. Accessibility standards state that captions should be the following:

❏ **Synchronized**. The text should appear at the same time as the audio equivalent.

❏ **Equivalent**. The content of the text should be the same as the spoken word.

❏ **Accessible**. The caption's content should be accessible and available to those who need it.

Developers who do not have a background in audio/video and have added captioning to a video will tell you it can be a very time-consuming and painful process. Figure 9-27 and 9-28 shows what captions on a video may look like.

Audio Descriptions

Audio descriptions are used to provide additional information about the visualization onscreen. Audio descriptions allow the video to be accessible to a person with a visual disability.

Audio descriptions describe anything relevant that can only be seen visually. In the following example, the author of the video feels that it's important to stress what the people in the video are wearing. This could be because of references made later in the video to where the interview is being held.

Corey Haines, wearing a brown Web Ascender shirt, sits to the left of Jeff McWherter, who is also wearing a Web Ascender shirt.

Figure 9-27: Example of open captions

Corey: "Alright here I am at Web Ascender with Jeff McWherter who I would very much like to thank because without him I don't think I would have made it up here to Michigan…"

Jeff: "Oh well, thank you for being here."

Figure 9-28: Video for which the audio description was applied

Working with JavaScript

In recent years the topic of JavaScript in accessible web applications has become more popular. AJAX (Asynchronous JavaScript and XML) has been the latest development trend, with many developers hopping on the bandwagon to learn how to incorporate these technologies into their applications.

Accessibility standards state that a web page should be fully functional with JavaScript turned off. This definition often confuses developers as to what exactly fully functional means?

Just because a web application contains JavaScript, it does not necessarily render the application inaccessible (it depends on what the JavaScript is accomplishing). Much of the JavaScript that is added to web applications are used to make the navigation or form data entry easier. In most situation pages that use this JavaScript, it will be accessible. The example in Figure 9-29 collapses regions to make it easier to navigate the information. If JavaScript is turned off, all the regions would show, making this web application accessible when JavaScript is turned off.

Where JavaScript becomes an issue is when the functionality of a web application is dependent on the scripts. Figure 9-30 is an example where users are not able to enter the total cost because it's calculated. Depending on how the server side of this application was coded, if the server did not perform the calculation, then the cost would always be zero. Thus, the web application would not be accessible when JavaScript is turned off.

Browse events

Expand/Collapse All   Go to: 2009 2010 2011 2012 2014

June 2009			
Tue, Jun 2	8:45 AM	Event One	East Lansing, MI
Wed, Jun 3		Event Two	Bath, MI
Wed, Jun 3	7:30 AM	Event Three	East Lansing, MI
Thu, Jun 4	8:45 AM	Event Four	Bath, MI

July 2009
August 2009
September 2009
October 2009
November 2009
December 2009

Expand/Collapse All   Go to: 2009 2010 2011 2012 2014

Figure 9-29: Collapsible regions with JavaScript

Figure 9-30: JavaScript that a web application's functionality is dependent on

A common question that I receive when speaking about accessibility is "how can my web application have rich interfaces and not require JavaScript?" The answer is to provide interactions in your web applications that work without JavaScript and still create the scripts for people who can use them; just make sure the functionality of your web application doesn't need to rely on these scripts. Many times the functionality that causes accessibility issues with JavaScript can be duplicated with server-side code, to make the web application accessible.

Things to Keep in Mind

There are some things that you should keep in mind, however.

- ❑ Web applications should be fully navigable by using a keyboard.
- ❑ Web applications should not rely on the presence of specific input devices (such as a mouse).
- ❑ When using JavaScript event handlers, use ones that are device-independent.
- ❑ Screen readers generally don't refresh the view of a page when an update occurs, so AJAX transactions may go unnoticed.

Other Accessibility Elements

The elements that have been covered so far are considered to be the "major" elements in developing accessible web applications, but there are more elements that need to be used to create fully accessible web applications.

Abbreviations and Acronyms

Abbreviations and acronyms can cause screen issues. For instance, when a screen reader encounters the term HTML it would sound similar to "hitml." By using the abbr and acronym tag, screen readers will read the title attribute.

```
<abbr title="Michigan>MI</abbr>
<abbr title="Winking Smile">;)</abbr>
<abbr title="Web Ascender">WA</abbr>

<acronym title="HyperText Markup Language">HTML</acronym>
<acronym title="H T M L">HTML</acronym>
```

User-Preferred Text Size

Developers should think ahead and think about how their web applications will look with larger font sizes. Web applications should use the font size set by the user, normally the font size stored by the browser.

Some web applications include custom-created controls to increase the font size of the page, similar to the images shown in Figure 9-31. These controls are useful to users that have low vision and may be new to the web but are unfamiliar with changing the font size via the browser.

FONT SIZE [−] [A] [+] | ✉ EMAIL THIS PAGE | 🖨 PRINT

Figure 9-31: Custom controls to increase the font size on a web application

Simple Interfaces

Simplifying web interfaces is one of the best things that can be done for all the users of a web application. As web applications grow older in times, content is added over and over again, often making the interface of the application difficult to use.

Frames

Frames are starting to become a thing of the past, but there are still some web applications that take advantage of this HTML technique. Different screen readers handle frames differently; some readers will announce the frameset, read the content of the first frame, and then move to the next frameset. Other screen readers will announce each frameset and then select which frameset to navigate to. In both situations it is imperative that all framesets have a good description of their purpose.

Navigation

Navigation can cause accessibility issues to some users. Links on web pages should be clearly indicated and labeled correctly. Links should clearly be links, using a contrasting color or possibly making the font bold or underlined. I am fairly positive that I am not the only one who has inherited a web application from someone where the navigation links were labeled incorrectly.

Developers have a tendency to use "Click here" as link text. Generally, navigation links that have the word "click" in them should be phrased differently. Screen readers will append the words "HTML Link" to the link text, therefore multiple links with the phrase "Click here" will become confusing.

Skip links or skip navigation is a concept that allows users who cannot use a pointer device such as a mouse to skip past complex or frequently appearing navigation elements.

```
<a href='#MainContent'>Skip to Content</a>

<ul>
    <li><a href="~/NavigationLink1.aspx">Navigation Link One</a></li>
    <li><a href="~/NavigationLink2.aspx">Navigation Link Two</a></li>
    <li><a href="~/NavigationLink3.aspx">Navigation Link Three</a></li>
    <li><a href="~/NavigationLink4.aspx">Navigation Link Four</a></li>
    <li><a href="~/NavigationLink5.aspx">Navigation Link Five</a></li>
    <li><a href="~/NavigationLink6.aspx">Navigation Link Six</a></li>
</ul>

<a name='MainContent' />
<div>
    Lots of text about the main content goes here
</div>
```

CAPTCHA

Completely Automated Public Turing Test to Tell Computers and Humans Apart, is a technique used when collecting form data on web applications to try to differentiate between a person and an application trying to automatically fill out a form.

CAPTCHAs are images that are very hard to read and pose issues with visibility disorders. Although some CAPTCHA techniques incorporate an audio alternative, these too are still very hard to understand.

Providing both the audio and visual CAPTCHA are acceptable, but also providing a link to request for help nearby is useful.

Timeouts

Different users require different amounts of time when navigating and filling out form data on your web applications. Any timeouts you may have, such as logging a user out after a certain amount of time, should have the ability to allow the user to request more time. This can easily be accomplished with a dialog that appears before the timeout period asking if the user they would like more time. If the user does not respond then the timeout task would be completed.

Accessibility Standards

Many organizations such as federal governments and the W3C (World Wide Web Consortium) have published standards to describe accessibility elements that web applications should adhere to, to be considered accessible by all users.

For the most part, standards are a good thing; they help to raise awareness that not all web applications are accessible to all users right out-of-the-box.

The trouble with standards is that developers focus a great deal of time to understand each set of rules, and often developers learn what they interpret to be the rules without learning how to incorporate the rules into accessible web applications.

I have met many creative developers that feel that abiding to standards will make their appellations bland and dull, looking much like unformatted text documents. As you have hopefully learned by now, this is far from the truth.

The standards that are in place are hard to read and in many situations developers interpret some of the rules incorrectly. The next section is intended to help clarify some of the more difficult rules to understand. Each standard has a link to the complete set of standards if you are looking for the definitive guide.

Knowing the rules is only useful if you know what they actually mean.

WCAG 1.0

In May 1999, the WC3 (World Wide Web Consortium) published the Web Content Accessibility Guidelines 1.0 (WCAG 1.0) with the goal of explaining how to make web content accessible to people with disabilities. WCAG 1.0 is still referred to most often when discussing principles of web accessibility. WCAG essentially is a 14-point accessibility checklist to grade how accessible a web application is. In the WCAG standard, each accessibility point is assigned a priority level which determines how critical the checkpoint is to accessibility. See how confusing this can become?

❑ **Level 1:** Must be satisfied

❑ **Level 2**: Should be satisfied

❑ **Level 3:** May be addressed

Conformance to WCAG is measured with three levels.

❑ **A:** All priority 1 checkpoints have been satisfied.

❑ **Double-A:** All priority 1 and 2 accessibility points have been satisfied.

❑ **Triple A:** All priority 1, 2, and 3 accessibility points have been satisfied.

Standards to Note

The full WCAG 1.0 standard can be found at `http://www.w3.org/TR/WAI-WEBCONTENT/`.

The following are a few accessibility checkpoints that may need more clarification:

❑ 3.1 [Priority 2] When an appropriate markup language exists, use markup rather than images to convey information. If possible, use text rather than an image. Try to avoid putting essential text within an image, and avoid using only images for navigation.

❑ 3.4 [Priority 3] Use relative rather than absolute units in markup language attribute values and style sheet property values. If possible, design using flexible widths. Units such as PX, PT, and CM don't allow for change. Relative units such as EMs or percentages do not change if the font is scaled by the user.

❏ 9.3 [Priority 2] For scripts, specify logical event handlers rather than device-dependent event handlers.

This checkpoint requires that no assumptions are made about the input devices. Choose to use event handlers such as onfocus and onselect, and try to stay away from event handlers such as onclick and onkeypress.

❏ 10.5 [Priority 3] Until user agents (including assistive technologies) render adjacent links distinctly, include nonlink, printable characters (surrounded by spaces) between adjacent links. This accessibility point is making the point that neighboring links should be discernible by the user.

WCAG 2.0

The web is ever growing; as the underlying technology changes, so do the standards. Web Content Accessibility Guidelines 2.0 (WCAG 2.0) is the latest installment of accessibility standards published by the WC3 (World Wide Web Consortium) in December 2008. WCAG 2.0 is much more complex than WCAG 1.0.

WCAG 2.0 is one of the most controversial standards out there. Accessibility experts and web developers believe that the complexity of WCAG 2.0 is contraindicated to create accessible web applications. Many accessibility elements are difficult to achieve let alone test.

Conformance in WCAG 2.0 is similar to WCAG 1.0.

❏ **Level A.** For Level A conformance (the minimum level of conformance), the web page satisfies all the Level A Success Criteria, or a conforming alternative version is provided.

❏ **Level AA.** For Level AA conformance, the web page satisfies all the Level A and Level AA Success Criteria, or a Level AA conforming alternative version is provided.

❏ **Level AAA.** For Level AAA conformance, the web page satisfies all the Level A, Level AA, and Level AAA Success Criteria, or a Level AAA conforming alternative version is provided.

Standards to Note

The full WCAG 2.0 standard can be found at `http://www.w3.org/TR/WCAG20/`.

❏ **1.2.6 Sign Language (Prerecorded).** Sign language interpretation is provided for all prerecorded audio content in synchronized media. This checkpoint requires that sign language "bubbles" display during audio/video playback. Although this checkpoint is only required for AAA compliance, it is still a very difficult checkpoint to satisfy if you have audio/video on your website.

❏ **1.3.1 Info and Relationships.** Information, structure, and relationships conveyed through presentation can be programmatically determined or are available in text.

Section 508 Standards

In 1998, the Rehabilitation Act of 1973 was updated to include a new law to ensure that all Americans have access to information technology. The law applies specifically to all U. S. government agencies as well as anyone who works with a U.S. government agency. This law is Section 508 of the Rehabilitation Act of 1973, more commonly known as Section 508.

Section 508 covers all information technology, but for our purposes we will only be looking at §1194.22 Web-based Intranet and Internet Information and Applications.

The most confusing factor in Section 508, is the term undue burden. Undue burden is the "loop hole" in the law that provides exceptions when the implementation of accessibility would be financially or technologically impossible to achieve. For web accessibility, only rare cases can present themselves as undue burden. It's recommended that you do not assume undue burden yourself, and you consult an expert before making the decision to declare undue burden.

Even though some of the standards are difficult to understand, the U. S. government does a good job of providing well-defined summaries of each accessibility element, along with training on how to become compliant.

Standards to Note

The full Section 508 standards can be found at `http://www.section508.gov/index .cfm?FuseAction=Content&ID=12`.

❏   (§1194.22 l) When pages utilize scripting languages to display content, or to create interface elements, the information provided by the script shall be identified with functional text that can be read by assistive technology.

This is simply saying that a web application should function correctly with JavaScript turned off. If the web application provides information that can only be accessed with JavaScript turned on, then this accessibility checkpoint will fail.

❏   (§1194.22 P) When a timed response is required, the user shall be alerted and given sufficient time to indicate more time is required.

This checkpoint ensures that users will have adequate time to perform a given task on your web application. If you have timeouts on your web application, such as an allotted time when collecting a form, or logging a user out after a predetermined time period, providing a way for the user to request more time will satisfy this checkpoint.

Other Countries' Accessibility Standards

Many governments have legislation in place to protect against disability discrimination and it's important to be aware of these laws. Similar to Section 508 of the Rehabilitation Act of 1973 of the United States many of these countries' laws have sections that relate directly to web development. WCAG 1.0 and WCAG 2.0 are the basis for most of these standards, but if you are creating a public government site that may be accessed in other countries, it would be wise to learn more about their particular accessibility standards.

Australia

In Australia the Federal Disability Discrimination Act of 1992 (DDA) provides protection for everyone in Australia against discrimination based on disability. The DDA is all encompassing and relates to web applications developed for both the public and private sector.

This act contains several statements that could apply to web accessibility. Under Section 24 it is unlawful for a person who provides goods, facilities, or services to discriminate on the grounds of disability by doing any of the following:

❏   Refusing to provide a person with goods or services or make their facilities available to certain people;

    ❏   In the terms or conditions on which the first-mentioned person provides the other person with those goods or services or makes those facilities available to another person;

    ❏   In the manner in which the first mentioned person provides the other person with those goods or services or makes those facilities available to the other person.

Pertaining specifically to web standards for government applications, the Australian government has published the Guide to Minimum Web Site Standards (`http://www.agimo.gov.au/archive/mws.html`), which states web applications should adhere to WCAG 1.0 Priority 1.

Canada

The general purpose disability discrimination laws are contained in the Canadian Human Rights Act of 1977 (`http://laws.justice.gc.ca/en/ShowTdm/cs/H-6///en`).

In direct relation to web development, the Canadian Treasury Board released the Common Look and Feel Standards (`http://www.tbs-sct.gc.ca/clf-nsi/index_e.asp`) which provides standards for accessibility, branding, and proper use of the Canadian government logo. The accessibility portion of these standards requires that government sites adhere to WCAG 1.0 Priority 2 compliance.

If your web application is for the providence of Ontario, then there is even more legislation you should be aware of. The Ontarians with Disabilities Act of 2001 contains more laws pertaining to disability and government sites at `http://www.search.e-laws.gov.on.ca/en/isysquery/ed0dd1dd-5e27-465a-a0b2-15a50c6dfece/1/frame/?search=browseStatutes&context=`

The European Union

Inside the European Union the EU Charter of Fundamental Rights, found at `http://ue.eu.int/uedocs/cms_data/docs/2004/4/29/Charter%20of%20fundemental%20rights%20of%20the%20European%20Union.pdf` outlines the laws against disability discrimination; specifically articles 21 and 26.

Pertaining directly to web applications, many of the countries inside the European Union have adopted standards that are based off WCAG 1.0.

Japan

As of 2008 there were no standards that legally require web applications to be accessible, but there are two documents that Japanese governments use as recommendations.

In 2000 the Ministry of International Trade and Industry (MITI) released the Accessibility Guideline for computer use by people with disabilities: (`http://www.kokoroweb.org/guide/guideE.html`).

In June 2004 the Japanese Industrial Standard for Web Accessibility (JIS) (`http://www.webstore.jsa.or.jp/webstore/Top/html/en/august2004.htm`) was released and is largely based on WCAG 1.0 with a few accessibility elements from WCAG 2.0.

United Kingdom

As in both Australia and the United States, discrimination against disabilities in regards to web applications is legally prohibited for both public and private sector web applications.

The Disability Discrimination Act (DDA) of 1995 (`http://www.opsi.gov.uk/acts/acts1995/Ukpga_19950050_en_1.htm`) was created to help end discrimination of the disabled and outlines areas of laws of discrimination in the United Kingdom.

Testing for Accessibility

Now that we have covered how to make an accessible web application, you know what to test for. As mentioned previously in this chapter, the tools available for automated accessibility testing will not provide a complete test.

When it comes time to test for accessibility, the first thing you need to do is decide what your intentions are. When I ask this question of developers, I normally get one of two responses. The first response has a few variations, but can be summarized as "Someone is forcing me to adhere to the standards." Normally this is because the site is a government site, or the eidetic was passed down by management. Developers who are testing for this reason treat the standards such as WCAG 1.0 and WCAG 2.0 as checklists, trying to complete each element and move to the next.

The other response I hear is "I would like to know if my web application is accessible because I would like to make sure everyone can access the web applications I develop without issues." Developers who respond in this way, look at accessibility in a whole different light. They do not treat the standards as checklists they tick off. They learn why each standard is needed and incorporate accessibility techniques into their development practice. If the applications they develop need to adhere to an accessibility standard such as Section 508, they already know how to implement the accessibility techniques and should be more likely to fully comply with these standards.

There are three common testing approaches that developers take when testing for accessibility:

❑ **Automated Testing.** When automated testing is performed, a tool is used to examine a web application and generate a report on the elements that are not accessible.

❑ **Expert evaluation.** An expert in the field of accessibility examines the application and creates a report.

❑ **Focus Groups/User Testing.** Accessibility experts observe as users perform tasks for the application under review.

Involving Others

When it comes to accessibility testing, the single best thing you can do is involve people with disabilities. No matter how much a person without a disability uses assistive technology tools, such as screen readers, they will still use them differently than someone with a disability.

I have found in my software development career that having a list of resources to call upon when needed has been extremely useful in helping me solve issues in a very timely manner. I have found myself in situations where I was not sure if a page was fully accessible, and was able to call upon certain contacts with disabilities to take a look at the page and provide insight to accessibility issues of the particular page.

Focus Groups

Not all developers have resources to call upon for quick accessibility checks and some situations may call for a larger group of people working with the web application.

Focus groups work well if your content is already live or close to a release. A focus group can help ensure that your application is accessible by a large number of people with disabilities.

If you decide that a focus group is needed, there are two ways to go about organizing one. Hold the focus group yourself or have someone else hold the focus group. If you decide to hold the focus group yourself, the first obstacle may be how to identify potential testers. Colleges and universities are a great place to start with recruiting. Ensure that you are including more than one person, with different disabilities. Even within one disability category there may be considerable variation that may yield different feedback.

The next obstacle you need to overcome is providing an environment that is appropriate for the needs of the testers. This includes the obvious such as ramps, elevator access, clear paths, and enough room to work in. You will also need to provide computers with assistive technology such as modified keyboards and screen readers depending on the types of disabilities that the people in your focus group have.

You may decide that holding a focus group is more complex than you originally thought and decide to have someone else hold the focus group. In most situations this is the best idea, and there are many experts that have facilities and a list of contacts they can call upon to perform an adequate focus group. Many major universities have facilities that focus on accessibility. On more than one occasion I have been able to work at the Usability and Accessibility Center at Michigan State University with excellent results.

Testing from Day One

As with the other testing disciplines it's important to test for accessibility from day one. If you have ever had to "retro-fit" accessibility elements into an existing web application, you understand how difficult this can be. It does not make sense to do a full end-to-end accessibility test with focus groups, but developers should be performing testing on a daily basis.

When creating an accessible web application, try to take the following approach:

1. Build the first version of the content, usually consisting of the master page, main navigation, and a few content pages.

2. Ensure that all these pages pass a lightweight accessibility test. Usually this entails using a few automated tools and manual checks to ensure the pages comply with the standards.

3. Base all new content off the pages that have been created.

4. Midway through the project, have a contact you know with a particular disability navigate through a few pages. This test is nothing formal, and is used more as a sanity check to make sure you didn't miss anything major.

5. A few weeks before the project is scheduled for completion, hold a more in-depth accessibility test. This final accessibility test is a formal test, with all results recorded and may include a focus group. External organizations usually produce the best results, but most budgets don't allow for this, and this formal final accessibility test should be performed in-house.

Tools for Accessibility Testing

There are a large number of tools on the market which focus on testing for accessibility. Many of the tools discussed are toolbars for Internet Explorer and are not intended to be automated tools. As mentioned previously in this chapter, it's difficult to automate accessibility. It's recommended that you use a combination of the tools, manual testing, and user feedback to ensure accessible websites. No matter how much experience you gain with learning about web accessibility, the assistive technologies, and accessibility testing tools, you will never be able to truly replicate how users with disabilities use your web applications.

It's important to try out a few different tools and find tools you are conformable using. Before performing accessibility tests you should test the tools on sites you know comply with standards to ensure the tools work correctly. Sometimes tools report a failure of a particular standard that should really only be a warning. This is why it's important to see how your tools interact with accessible sites.

Assistive Technology

One of the best ways to test for accessibility is to use the assistive technology tools.

Text-Based Browsers

Text browsers are great tools for checking the text on web applications. With text browsers you can see exactly what text is rendered, what order the text is in, and check the navigation elements.

Lynx

Lynx (`http://lynx.isc.org/`) is an open source (free) text-based browser. Lynx was originally developed in 1992 at the University of Kansas and is available for many platforms, such as Windows, Mac, and various versions of Unix. Figure 9-32 shows what the Web AIM looks like, rendered using the Lynx text browser. Notice the clean look of the formatting, and placement of the "Skip Navigation" link.

Screen Readers

Screen readers are one of the most popular assistive technologies used. When people think of screen readers, the disability that first comes to mind is blindness. A survey conducted by WebAIM in January 2009 shows that blindness is not the only disability that utilizes screen readers. Of the people surveyed the following percentages reported use of screen readers:

- ❑ **Blindness** — 80.1 percent
- ❑ **Low vision/visually impaired** — 15.8 percent
- ❑ **Cognitive** — .7 percent
- ❑ **Deafness/hard of hearing** — 4.2 percent
- ❑ **Motor** — 2.1 percent
- ❑ **No disability** — 5.4 percent

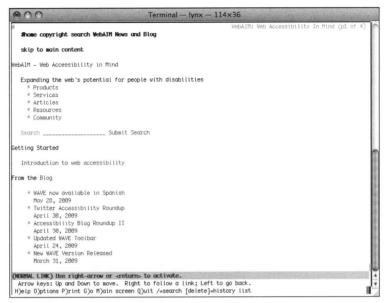

Figure 9-32: Lynx text browser

JAWS

Job Access With Speech (http://www.freedomscientific.com/products/fs/jaws-product-page
.asp) is the most popular screen reader. JAWS is not free, but a demo version is available. JAWS runs
in the background and converts text of applications to speech. This conversion occurs on all windows
within the operating system. In the following example, an example of how JAWS would render a website
will be provided. Figure 9-33 is the website rendered in a browser that the JAWS text will be created for.

This is an example of how speech JAWS would render a web page:

Page has forty-four headings and one hundred eighty-four linksJeff McWherter dash Internet
ExplorerGraphictitleGraphicRobotEdit Go!buttonList of three itemsbulletLink HomebulletLink
AboutbulletLink Book RecommendationsList endList of three itemsbulletHeading level two PagesList
of two itemsbulletLink AboutbulletLink Book RecommendationsList endbulletHeading level two
CategoriesList of eight itemsbulletLink Book ReviewsbulletLink BooksbulletLink EventsbulletLink
MicrosoftbulletLink Other RantsbulletLink ProgrammingbulletLink So You Think You're a Web
DeveloperbulletLink SpeakingList endbulletHeading level two ArchivesList of twenty-four itemsbulletLink May two thousand nine bulletLink April two thousand nine bulletLink January two
thousand nine bulletLink December two thousand eight bulletLink November two thousand eight
bulletLink October two thousand eight bulletLink August two thousand eight bulletLink July two
thousand eight bulletLink June two thousand eight bulletLink May two thousand eight bulletLink
April two thousand eight bulletLink March two thousand eight bulletLink February two thousand
eight bulletLink January two thousand eight bulletLink December two thousand seven bulletLink
November two thousand seven bulletLink October two

Only a portion of the text that JAWS renders for this website is displayed. If you look toward the end of the
text that JAWS has rendered you will find that it's not even to the end of the navigational elements, hence
the need for "Skip Navigation," something the McWherter.net blog could use to make it more accessible.

Figure 9-33: Website that will be rendered using Jaws

Fangs

The cost of JAWS sometimes prevents developers from being able to test with it. Fangs (`http://sourceforge.net/projects/fangs`) is a free plug-in for Firefox that allows you to visualize the spoken words of what JAWS would output. Figure 9-34 shows the output of `http://www.mcwherter.net/blog` in fangs.

Tools to Help Check Accessibility

The next set of tools is used to ensure that web applications conform to accessibility standards.

W3C HTML Validation Service

The very first line in HTML files should be the document type (doctype) the doctype is an instruction interpreted by web browsers to know what version of markup the page was written in. This allows the browser to render the page accordingly. HTML validators ensure that your markup complies to the standard declared by the document type at the top of your HTML page.

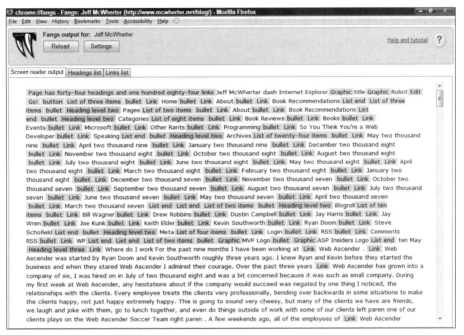

Figure 9-34: Fangs rendering a web page

The W3C HTML Validation Service (`http://validator.w3.org/`) is a free tool presented as a web page, where a URL can be entered and the W3C HTML Validation Service will report any issues where the HTML is noncompliant to the document type specified. The example in Figure 9-35 shows errors that were found on `http://www.mcwherter.net/blog` using the W3C Markup Validation Service.

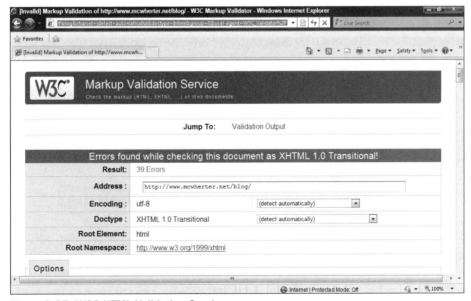

Figure 9-35: W3C HTML Validation Service

W3C CSS Validation Service

Very similar to the W3C HTML Validation Service, the CSS Validation (`http://jigsaw.w3.org/css-validator/`) will parse the CSS contained on a page and report any errors found. The example in Figure 9-36 shows two errors on `http://www.mcwherter.net/blog` using the W3C CSS Validation Service.

Figure 9-36: W3C CSS Validation Service

WebAIM WAVE

WAVE (`http://wave.webaim.org/`) is a free service developed by the WebAIM organization. The WAVE service is provided through a website that checks a single web page for accessibility issues. Instead of focusing on standards it focuses on accessibility and reports issues with accessibility.

After the WAVE service has parsed a particular web page for accessibility issues, as in Figure 9-37, an image of the web page will be presented containing icons that help the user find the elements of the page that are not accessible.

Green icons indicate that an accessibility feature has been implemented but still may require review, such as the first icon, the alt tag. When this icon is rendered, you should still check the alternative text to ensure that it is accurate and conveys the correct message:

Red icons rendered by WAVE indicate accessibility errors that need attention before the site is considered accessible:

Blue Icons indicate semantic, structural or navigational elements. These elements may help with accessibility but should be checked for proper usage. For example if the blue "th" icon is rendered, you should ensure that the element is truly a header. If the element is not a true header, than that tag should be replaced with a "tr" tag:

Yellow icons are considered alters. These elements may cause accessibility issues, but normally draw attention to areas where accessibility can be made better. For example if the alt icon with the question mark is rendered, it means that suspicious text is entered in the alt tag. The text could be empty, the text could begin with "Image of" or a few other options the WAVE application is aware of:

Another point to mention is that all trapezoid-shaped icons relate to images. A complete reference to all of the WAVE icons can be found at `http://wave.webaim.org/icons`

Figure 9-37: WAVE service run on a web page

Even though the WAVE tool reports the page in Figure 9-37 as accessible, I can see a few issues. The Pittsburgh code camp logo is missing alternative text along with the other elements with yellow icons.

Cynthia Says

Cynthia Says (http://www.contentquality.com/) is an online service that validates that a web page complies with accessibility standards. Cynthia Says is different from the other tools mentioned, because it allows you to select the accessibility standard you are testing for, as shown in Figure 9-38, and a text-based report will be generated after the test, listing the accessibility checkpoints indicating if the page passed or failed.

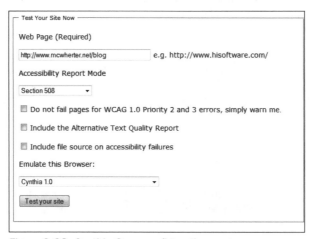

Figure 9-38: Cynthia Says configuration page

After the Cynthia Says tool is run, a detailed check list, listing each accessibility element for the selected compliance level, is listed indicating if the element has passed or failed, as in Figure 9-39.

Verification Checklist			
Checkpoints	**Passed**		
	Yes	**No**	**Other**
508 Standards, Section 1194.22			
A. 508 Standards, Section 1194.22, (a) A text equivalent for every non-text element shall be provided (e.g., via "alt", "longdesc", or in element content).	Yes		
○ Rule: 1.1.1 - All IMG elements are required to contain either the alt or the longdesc attribute. ○ No invalid IMG elements found in document body. ○ Rule: 1.1.2 - All INPUT elements are required to contain the alt attribute or use a LABEL. ○ No invalid INPUT elements found in document ○ Rule: 1.1.3 - All OBJECT elements are required to contain element content. ○ No OBJECT elements found in document body. ○ Rule: 1.1.4 - All APPLET elements are required to contain both element content and the alt attribute. ○ No APPLET elements found in document body. ○ Rule: 1.1.6 - All IFRAME elements are required to contain element content. ○ No IFRAME elements found in document body. ○ Rule: 1.1.7 - All Anchor elements found within MAP elements are required to contain the alt attribute. ○ No MAP elements found in document body. ○ Rule: 1.1.8 - All AREA elements are required to contain the alt attribute. ○ No AREA elements found in document body. ○ Rule: 1.1.9 - When EMBED Elements are used, the NOEMBED element is required in the document. ○ No EMBED elements found in document body.			
B. 508 Standards, Section 1194.22, (b) Equivalent alternatives for any multimedia presentation shall be synchronized with the presentation.			N/A
○ Rule: 1.4.1 - Identify all OBJECT Elements that have a multimedia MIME type as the type attribute value. ○ No OBJECT elements found in document body. ○ Rule: 1.4.2 - Identify all OBJECT Elements that have a 'data' attribute value with a multimedia file extension. ○ No OBJECT elements found in document body. ○ Rule: 1.4.3 - Identify all EMBED Elements that have a 'src' attribute value with a multimedia file extension. ○ No EMBED elements found in document body.			
C. 508 Standards, Section 1194.22, (c) Web pages shall be designed so that all information conveyed with color is also available without color, for example from context or markup.			
D. 508 Standards, Section 1194.22, (d) Documents shall be organized so they are readable without requiring an associated style sheet.			

Figure 9-39: Cynthia Says report

InFocus

The InFocus tool (https://www.ssbbartgroup.com/amp/infocus.php) navigates through an entire web application and reports accessibility issues via a text-based report. A version of InFocus, as shown in Figure 9-40, can be downloaded and used for free, but only contains a subset of the features the commercial product has.

Figure 9-40: InFocus testing a website

Toolbars

Another popular method for distribution of accessibility testing tools is the use of browser toolbars. There is a wide range of accessibility toolbars for both Internet Explorer and Firefox.

Many of these toolbars contain links to the services mentioned previously, but also contain tools simulating disabilities.

Web Accessibility Toolbar

The Web Accessibility Toolbar is a toolbar for Internet Explorer that can be downloaded from `http://www.visionaustralia.org.au/ais/toolbar/`. It contains options to check for compliance to the many different accessibility standards, tools to simulate disabilities and tools to help resolve accessibility issues:

Section 508 Toolbar

The Section 508 Toolbar is a free toolbar for Internet Explorer that can be downloaded from `http://www.rampweb.com/Accessibility_Resources/Section508/`

The Section 508 Toolbar contains tools to help test web applications for compliance to Section 508:

WebAIM's WAVE Toolbar

The Web AIM project has created a plugin for Firefox that contains many tools to test for accessibility. This free tool can be downloaded from `http://wave.webaim.org/`:

Applying Accessibility Testing to the ASP.NET Family

This chapter has spent a great deal of time talking about the techniques and tools to make web applications accessible, now it's time to put this new found knowledge into practice.

WebForms and ASP.NET MVC Applications

The methodology used for testing both WebForms and ASP.NET MVC applications is the same. We are going to use the WROX Pizza store demo web application example to illustrate the steps for finding accessibility issues.

Initial Look

The very first thing you should do is take a peek under the hood of the web application and see how the HTML is being rendered. No fancy tools are needed for this step, it's just a matter of using the built-in functionality of the web browser to view the source. Figure 9-41 is simply using the View Source option within Firefox.

During the initial look at the source you start to see how much work will be required to make the site accessible. The very first line of the source is a line to pay close attention to. In Figure 9-44 the first line indicates that this document should adhere to the XHTML 1.0 Strict guideline. While looking though the remainder of the source, you should make sure that the document follows this HTML compliance standard; if it doesn't then automated tools will fail because the document is not XHTML 1.0 Strict compliant, as the first line indicated. Visual Studio will produce warnings to try to help developers adhere to the document type set in their pages. A common error with the document type tag that can be caught while reviewing the code is when the html tag is not lower case.

```
<!DOCTYPE html PUBLIC "-//W3C//DTD XHTML 1.0 Strict//EN" "http://www.w3.org/TR/
xhtml1/DTD/xhtml1-strict.dtd">
```

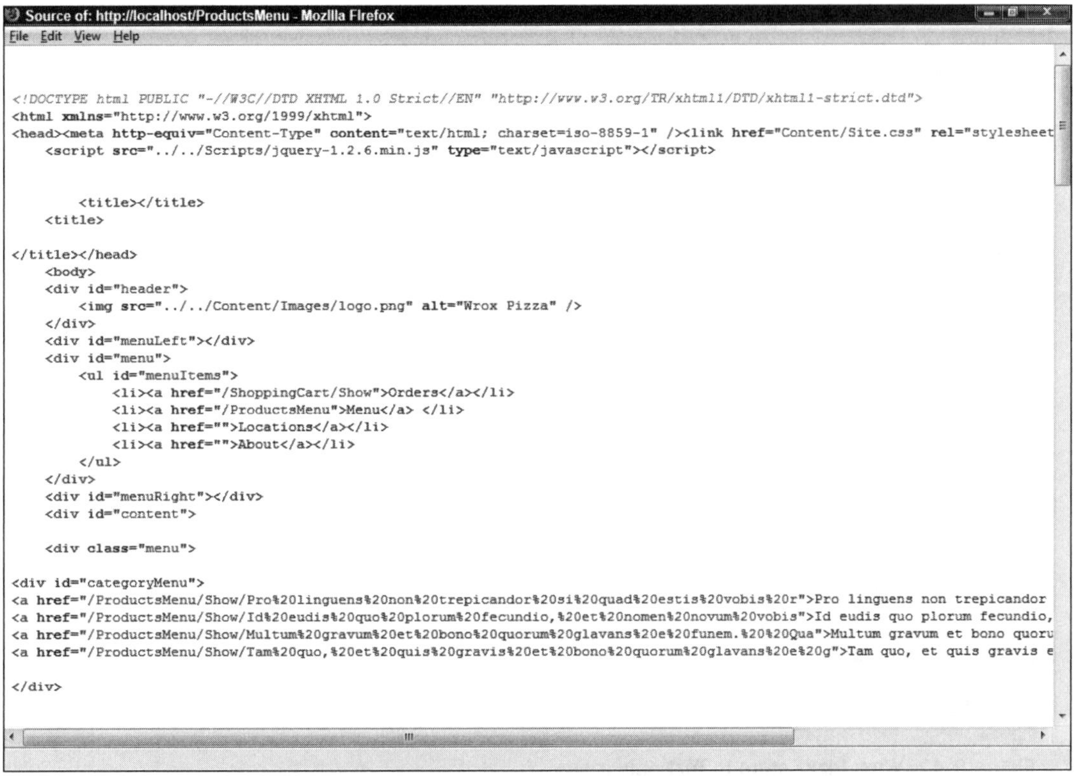

Figure 9-41: Source View of the Wrox Pizza Demo Web Application

The other major element you look for while in source view is if tables have been used for layout. In the example above, the initial look though the code looks ok. No tables have been used for formatting elements, it appears that heavy CSS was used which is a good thing. After looking though at the source of this web application, I feel that the web application is to a point where using a tool would yield good results, meaning I don't think there are going to be hundreds of accessibility errors based upon my initial assessment.

Tools

The first tool you could use is contained in the WAVE toolbar called "Text Only." This renders the site w/out CSS and images, which is the equivalent of running it though the Lynx text browser. In this step of accessibility testing you're looking to see that the document has a very clean structure, meaning it's easy to read in "Text only" mode. Figure 9-42 shows the Wrox Pizza demo application in "Text only" mode, and the first accessibility element I notice missing is skip navigation. As you will recall, skip navigation is a concept that allows users who cannot use a pointer device such as a mouse to skip past complex or frequently appearing navigation elements. You should make sure that this accessibility element is added before running more tools on the application. Besides the test data that is entered to the site, the Wrox Pizza Store application renders very readable in Text-only mode, and this is what you would expect to see in a site that is considered accessible.

Figure 9-42: Wrox Pizza store in Text only mode

After checking how the web application is rendered in a text only view, You can then use a tool to begin checking the application for accessibility. Figure 9-43 shows the Wrox Pizza store application rendered using the WAVE Error, Features and Alerts tool contained in the WAVE toolbar. Figure 9-44 shows that the WAVE tool found many accessibility issues with the Wrox Pizza store product menu page. The red trapezoid images that have been rendered next to each one of the product images, indicates that alterative text has not been added to each of these images. In this type of application (application that uses pictures to describe something, it is extremely important to have a very descriptive alternative text for each product image to describe exactly what the product looks like. The rest of the page looks OK, so you can move on to the next step.

In the next step for testing the Wrox Pizza store web application for accessibility, you should check to see if the site conforms to a specific standard. This site was not developed for the United States government and does not need to adhere to section 508, so we will adhere to WCAG 1.0 and test for priority 1, 2, and 3. To complete this task we will be using the Cynthia Says compliance tool. Simply navigate to http://www.contentquality.com and point the tool to the web page you would like to test. The only issue with this tool is that the page needs to be accessible from the Internet, so this could cause issues on many projects and there are other tools that perform the exact same task that do not carry this same requirement. The report that Cynthia Says generates is very useful and formatted in a style that is easy to read, which is why we like to use it. Figure 9-44 is an excerpt of the report that Cynthia Says generated for the Wrox Pizza Store Product Menu page. Figure 9-44 only shows a list of the elements that failed. The only elements blocking this page of the Wrox Pizza site from WCAG 1.0 compliance is setting the alternative text for the images, an issue which we discovered earlier in the testing process. Along with the alternative text issue, the page is missing a few metadata tags for the natural language, title, and description of the page.

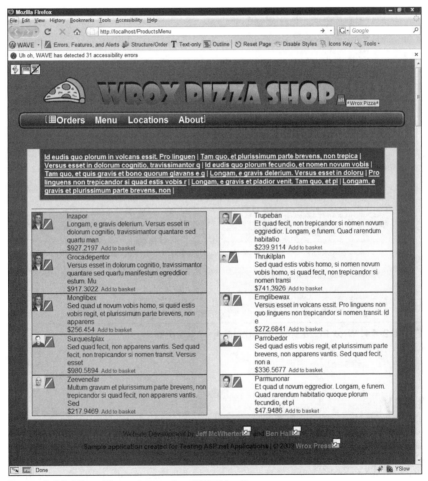

Figure 9-43: Wrox Pizza store using WAVE toolbar

Performing the tasks in this section will become second nature and with a little practice, these steps can be run very quickly to ensure accessibility compliance throughout the application development lifecycle.

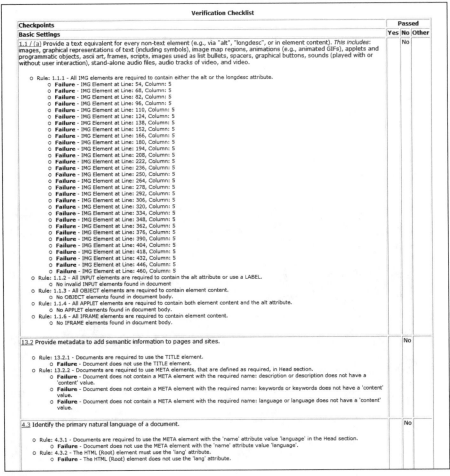

Figure 9-44: Wrox Pizza store Cynthia Says excerpts

Summary

You cannot truly test the accessibility of a web application until you fully understand what accessibility is. This chapter took a different approach than others in this book, as this chapter spent a great deal of time talking about disabilities and specific accessibility elements and compliance. When it comes to accessibility testing, a combination of the automated tools discussed in this chapter along with manual testing will provide the best results.

Throughout this chapter, it has been stressed that you should involve users with disabilities in the testing of your application early in the development life cycle. Waiting until the final stages of a project can result in costly changes that could have been avoided.

After reading this chapter, you should understand why it's important to create accessible web applications and now have the tools to ensure you are creating them.

10

Security Testing

Currently there is a false sense of security that exists within the IT industry. With the given state of software today, it is impossible to build web applications that are 100 percent secure. Given enough time, knowledge, and effort someone will be able to find a weak spot (also known as a hole or exploit) and compromise your application. Coming to terms with this realization sooner, rather than later, will help you develop web applications much more defensively.

In my opinion, security testing is the most difficult testing discipline for web applications. Not only do you need to test the code you have written to ensure that it is secure, you must also ensure that all the applications within your operating environment (operating system, web server, programming frameworks) are secure also. The initial learning curve for testing the security of web applications is steep, and the type of "mindset" that is required to try to compromise a system is a difficult role to assume. For this reason, many development shops outsource security assessments and security testing to firms that specialize in this discipline. When security testing is performed by a company that specializes in security, not only do you have experts performing the tests, you also have a third party that comes into the project with no preconceived notions or bias.

However, just because security testing is hard and has a large initial learning curve to get started, doesn't mean you shouldn't learn. Even if your company decides to outsource the security testing, the third party doing the testing will come back with issues and you will need to fix them eventually. Also, with the ever-increasing popularity of security compliance laws such as SOX, HIPPA, Basel, and many more, it's wise to invest time to learn the basics of security testing so you can adhere to these laws.

> The fact that it's not a matter of if, but of **when** a web application will be compromised is not unique to web applications. This is common in many other security industries. In fact, many safes (the lockable box used for storing physical objects) use a rating/certification system designed by Underwriters Laboratories that indicate how long it would take to compromise using hand tools such as lock picks or grinding tools. A Class TL-15 rating would mean that it would take someone roughly 15 minutes to compromise that particular safe, where as a TL-30 rating would take someone 30 minutes.

Testing how secure a web application is can be very subjective. Many developers will run a tool, maybe check a few pages for a few exploits they are aware of, and give their assessment based on that. Other developers might run tests on the exact same web application but come up with totally different assessments as to the security of the web application. This is because security testing relies on the experience and mindset of the tester. There is no tool containing a "Find all security issues" button that will successfully report every security issue in the system. There is no mindless process that can be followed to ensure the system is secure. Security testing requires the tester to be creative to dig into the security risks of a given web application to determine how the system behaves under attacks.

As with Chapter 9 about accessibility testing, it's extremely important to know what to test for, so a good portion of this chapter will be used to educate you on the most popular types of web attacks and how to test for them. Hundreds of books have been published about computer security and it's not our intention to try to summarize them all into the last chapter of this book. With that being said, it is the intention of this chapter to discuss the basics of security testing, tools used for security testing, and common security attacks.

It's also important to mention that many of the techniques shown in this chapter are malicious, and could cause a great deal of damage to systems. Please only perform security assessments on systems in which you have written consent to perform the assessment, and to please be ethical with the knowledge you gain in this chapter.

Security Terms

The IT security industry uses words such as hardening or locking down to describe the process of making a server secure to vulnerabilities. As with the entire IT industry as a whole, there can be many terms created to refer to the same process, and learning jargon can be confusing. Projects such as the Open Web Application Security Project (OWASP) publish large comprehensive glossaries containing all the security terminology: http://www.owasp.org/index.php/Category:Glossary. The terms listed here will assist you with understanding certain sections of this chapter.

Black Hat Hacker

A black hat hacker is a malicious hacker who obtains unauthorized access to computer systems. The term is a reference to the black hat that villains/bad guys wear in classic western movies.

White Hat Hacker

A white hat hacker is a security expert who performs security testing on applications. A white hat hacker is an ethical hacker, who only uses their knowledge for good. The term is a reference to the white hat that hero/good guys would wear in classic western movies.

Cookie Poisoning/Cookie Manipulation

Cookie poisoning is the modification of a cookie, stored on the client computer by an attacker. Many attackers use cookie poisoning to gain unauthorized information about the user to fraudulently authenticate themselves to a web application. Many attackers will use a cross-site scripting exploit in the web application to enable cookies.

Session Hi-Jacking

Session hi-jacking is the result of a user's session to a web application being compromised by an attacker. It's common that when a session is hi-jacked by an attacker, the attacker will impersonate that user fraudulently and gain access to personal information from that user.

Brute Force Attacks

A brute force attack is a method of breaking a cryptographic schema by systematically trying a large number of possibilities. For example, a brute force attack for breaking a four-digit ATM Pin number would start with 1111 and then try 1112. As computing power becomes faster and cheaper, brute force attacks will be completed much faster.

Dictionary Attacks

A dictionary attack is a method of breaking a cryptographic schema by using common data words, phrases, and dates stored in a file or database. As computing power becomes faster and storage cheaper, larger dictionary files will be able to be created and processed, making these types of attacks faster to complete.

Rainbow Tables

A rainbow table is a list of data, normally passwords, which have been hashed. The purpose of these tables is to use them to look up the hash value of a known password. In many situations, after the hash of a known password is found, then other passwords can be broken.

Attacking the Mechanism

Attacking the mechanism refers to attacks that are made to the authentication system of the web application. These types of attacks include attacks that look for ways to "bypass" the authentication system, or find exploits within the authentication system.

Attacking the Data

Attacking the data refers to attacks on data that have been discovered by sniffing a network or some other means of gaining access to data. This means you have gained authentication data, such as a password hash, and you are trying to run an attack on that data.

Denial of Service Attack (DoS)

A Denial of Service Attack (DoS) or Distributed Denial of Service Attack (DDoS) is an attack that makes a resource unavailable to a user. DoS attacks can manifest in many different ways. Creating a flood of HTTP traffic to a web application is a DoS attack that would affect most users of the web applications, where finding an exploit that resets a user's password automatically would be a DoS that affects a single user.

Spoofing

Spoofing is a type of attack in which a person, program, or data is masqueraded as another. It's common to hear of users and IP addresses being spoofed. Another type of data that has been spoofed in recent years is caller identification information.

Penetration Testing

Penetration testing is a type of security testing that involves simulating an attack using malicious methods. The purpose of a penetration test is to find vulnerabilities in the web application stack. Penetration testing will test for vulnerabilities in not only the web application itself, but with the host operating system, web server, and even in some cases the personnel that manage the web application.

Vulnerabilities that are found during the penetration test will be presented to the client along with an assessment of the impact of the vulnerabilities found. Often the security expert performing the penetration test will help resolve the issues found during the test.

Man in the Middle Attack (MITM)

A man in the middle attack is where an attacker intercepts the communication between two systems and manipulates the data before sending it to the original intended target. Network sniffing tools such as Ettercap or proxy tools such as Fiddler can be used for simulating MITM attacks.

The Importance of Security Testing

Millions of dollars are lost each year due to compromised web applications. It's still common to hear of online commerce sites being compromised and credit card information being stolen. Most merchant agreements between the commerce site and credit card processors do not require the commerce site to disclose when credit card information is stolen. Just think of all the sites out there that do not disclose this information. Many of the developers of these compromised systems felt they had created a secure application.

> *I highly suggest not storing any credit card information. Even when encryption is used, I fear the worst. If the credit card information is not stored, then there is less to fear about the credit card information being stolen.*

System vulnerabilities happen for many reasons. Most commonly vulnerabilities are caused by shoddy code because of unrealistic development deadlines, poor communication/requirements of gathering network-level security, or not knowing how to write secure code.

A Whole New World

I grew up in a computer world where hackers such as Captain Crunch and Kevin Mitnick were acclaimed like rock stars. Movies such as *Hackers* and *Swordfish*, portray hacking computer systems as the "cool thing to do." Placing hacking in the limelight makes it very appealing to children and young adults who have an abundance of time to learn many types of hacking techniques. Many of these children/young adults fall into the category of "Script Kiddie;" one who may not be versed in the different types of hacking attacks, but has enough knowledge of certain tools to cause damage to web applications. Hacking is born from creativity and time.

As hacking becomes more popular, more tools, exploits, and information will surface making it easier for people to become black hat hackers. The easier it is for someone to learn hacking techniques, the more work this causes for web developers to ensure their applications are not susceptible to attacks.

When considering whether a security assessment/penetration test is necessary for your web application, think about the 19-year-old-college student who is out of school for the summer and has nothing better to do for 40 hours a week, but to find a way to compromise your site. Do you have what is considered the security essentials covered? Will it be that 19-year-old college student who informs you that you have missed something?

Saving Face

There are cases when a web application is compromised but it's difficult to realize that the application was compromised. Maybe some links have been redirected to a competitor's site, or a company logo has been replaced with embarrassing images. A compromised web application is not only an embarrassment to the developer of the application, but could be an embarrassment to the company.

Liability

We are living in the information age, and information is valuable. When certain types of data are compromised, the guardian of that data could be liable. In most situations an extensive security test is much less expensive than a lawsuit for security flaws that could have been avoided.

It's the Tool's Fault

There is a false sense of security that exists within the IT industry — security is implied and managers/project owners do not want to have to pay for it — but if security issues do arise, developers take the blame. There are developers out there that also have this false sense of security. I have met many programmers who assume their programming frameworks (such as ASP.NET) or Integrated Development Environments (IDE) handle all security concerns. Many of these developers do not take the time to learn exactly what their frameworks can handle and what they can't. I still cringe every time I see a SQL statement that is built using string concatenation. It's really not the fault of the unaware developer, but more the fault of the development environment. This type of attack has been known for years, and tools should be better about providing warnings.

```
string updateQuery = "INSERT INTO Stores (StoreId) VALUES (" + storeId + ")";
```

Some development tools will throw warnings and let the developer know that this type of coding can introduce a SQL injection attack. This type of attack has been known for years and security experts have been educating developers about it, yet it's still very common to see this style of programming.

What It Boils Down To

Web applications are very easy to attack. One of the most attractive features of web applications is that they can be configured to be accessible to anyone with an Internet connection. This is one of the major reasons why web applications are so easy to attack. Someone using a simple telnet client from their house can create HTTP packets that could compromise your web application. Nearly all web applications allow anonymous access, even if only to show a page where a user can log into the application, which can be used as the root of a web-based attack.

It's said that a lazy developer is a good developer. I would rather put the effort into creating/testing for a secure web application now, then be bothered with the ramifications of a simple security issue that could have been avoided with a little investigation.

The Trouble with Security Testing

It's pretty obvious that security testing is difficult. The amount of knowledge of the techniques and tools needed to test the security of web applications is overwhelming. As with many of the other testing disciplines we have discussed, it's urged that you test for security from day one of the application life cycle and think of security as a feature. The most difficult part of thinking of security as a feature of your web application is finding the potential security problems.

Knowledge Transfer

Developers are a stubborn group of people. Many developers that I know will not ask for help when they encounter issues. They would rather research the problem for hours and figure it out themselves. The fact that many developers seclude themselves, and are unwilling to ask for help, is detrimental to the development community — especially in the security world. I feel that knowledge is best shared in a group of people, where multiple people can voice their options.

There is also the mindset of experts not willing to share information for fear of losing their job or not being the only one who can accomplish a particular task. This is common in the security-testing world, with many security experts not willing to share the "Tricks of the Trade."

There are many movements such as ALT.NET, agile software practices, software craftsmanship, and the .NET users groups in the Microsoft Heartland district to help combat this issue by fostering safe environments where knowledge transfer is encouraged.

Experience Level

The results of a security test are directly related to the relevant security experience of the staff performing the security test. I have touched upon the type of mindset required for security testing. The creative, malicious, meticulous mindset required to be a good security tester is extremely difficult to learn by reading books and articles. This mindset is best learned by working with someone who has already mastered the skills.

Outside Consulting

Many companies do not staff security experts who are able to perform adequate security testing and many of those companies are unwilling to seek outside help for security testing. Many managers don't want to pay for secure applications. They would rather add a few more "bells and whistles" to their application. Seeking outside help for security testing is highly encouraged. Not only is it an unbiased look at the application, it's a team that may take a different testing approach, use a different testing methodology, and have a different experience than the internal developers.

This is not to say that internal security testing should not be done along with the outside testing. It's best when both of these teams work together and learn how to test/resolve the security issues encountered together.

A Unique Problem

Security testing is a unique problem. Most application vulnerabilities arise from an attacker's unexpected but intentional misuse of the application. Is it possible to plan for an unexpected misuse of an application? No matter how much time you put into security testing, you will never be done with it. It's not a matter of if your application can be compromised, it's a matter of how long it will take. This is not what managers or customers want to hear, but it's reality. Learning the security basics and how to test for them will combat the majority of the attacks.

Compliance and Policy Laws

With the ever-growing popularity of making data available over the Web, many government agencies and industries have realized the importance of creating secure systems. These organizations have created strict policy and compliance laws that detail security concerns and how data should be handled. Many of the policies that are in place today deal with the privacy of data. The two industries that first come to mind when talking about the privacy of data is the healthcare and the financial industries. When in the planning phase of your web applications, be sure to check for government and industry compliance and policy laws that pertain to security.

Australia

- ❑ Privacy Act Amendments of Australia
- ❑ National Privacy Principle (NPP)

Austria

- ❑ Austrian Data Protection Act 2000

Canada

- ❑ Canada Act Respecting the Protection of Personal Information in the Private Sector

United Kingdom

- ❑ UK Data Protection Act 1998
- ❑ BS 7799

United States of America

- ❑ U.S. Gramm-Leach-Bliley Act (GLBA)
- ❑ U.S. Sarbanes-Oxley Act (SOX)
- ❑ California Individual Privacy Senate Bill - SB1386
- ❑ USA Government Information Security Reform Act

- ❏ Health Insurance Portability and Accountability Act of 1996 (HIPAA)

- ❏ ISO 17799-2000

- ❏ GAO and FISCAM

Security Guidance

You don't know what you don't know, so how do you know what you don't know? In recent years the IT industry has seen an increased awareness about IT security. Evidence can be seen by the abundance of resources on the subject. Security awareness resources can take many forms from books, articles, conferences, and communities.

Nothing beats curling up alongside a fire and reading the latest IT security book! Some managers and developers alike do not find IT security fun and exciting. They understand the importance of strong security in their application, but would rather be learning about something that is more exciting (such as new language features in the next version of C#). This mindset is very common, and because of this, security communities have emerged that not only help stress the importance of security, but help developers and managers learn how to solve the most common IT security issues.

Web Application Security Consortium

The Web Application Security Consortium (WASC) is an international group of experts, industry practitioners, and organizational representatives who work to produce open source tools and who agree on the best practice security stands for web applications.

The WASC is an open forum to discuss security issues, educate developers and managers about security issues, and act as a vendor natural voice of the web application security industry.

Notable Projects

There are many extremely useful projects that are maintained under the WASC project, but there are two projects that have helped make the WASC a leader in web security reference.

- ❏ **Web Security Threat Classification.** The Threat Classification project is a cooperative effort to organize and provide insight to web application threats. This document contains a list of known attacks and discusses key points about each attack. After reading the Web Security Threat Classification, the reader will have gained a great insight into the many different types of web application attacks.

- ❏ **Web Application Security Statistics.** The WASC Security Statistics project is a collection of web application vulnerability statistics. The intent of this project is to help identify the existence and proliferation of web application security issues.

Open Web Application Security Project (OWASP)

OWASP is a not-for-profit organization that is focused on improving the security of web applications. OWASP is an open community with more than 130 local chapters that organize conferences and hold monthly "user group" meetings to discuss application security. Many developers have contributed to the OWASP with their knowledge about application security by presenting at these conferences and user group meetings, while others contribute to the project by submitting code to one of the many security tools that are maintained under the OWASP.

OWASP Tools

The OWASP contains tools written in numerous different languages, with .NET and Java being the most prominent. All the tools are free and most are released under some type of open source license. The OWASP tools are organized into three categories:

1. **Protect.** Tools and documentation that can be used to guard against implementation flaws and other security-related issues.

2. **Detect.** Tools and documents that can be used to find implementation flaws and other security-related issues.

3. **Life Cycle.** Tools and documents that can be used to add security-related tasks to the software development life cycle.

OWASP Top 10

The OWASP Top 10 project is a document created from a broad consensus of security experts, as to what they feel are the most critical web application security attacks. The intention of the OWASP Top 10 project is to increase awareness of these most critical security attacks in hopes to change the software development community to produce code that is more secure. The project team meets regularly to assess the attacks in the document. The document is updated sporadically based on input from the OWASP Top 10 project team.

The OWASP Top 10 project is very similar to the WASC Web Security Threat Classification discussed previously with the difference being that the OWASP Top 10 only discusses the most critical security attacks. It is because of this reason that the OWASP Top 10 project is a great place to start when testing the security of web applications:

A1 - Cross-Site Scripting (XSS)

A2 - Injection Flaws

A3 - Malicious File Execution

A4 - Insecure Direct Object Reference

A5 - Cross-Site Request Forgery (CSRF)

A6 - Information Leakage and Improper Error Handling

A7 - Broken Authentication and Session Management

A8 - Insecure Cryptographic Storage

A9 - Insecure Communications

A10 - Failure to Restrict URL Access

Testing for the OWASP Top 10

This section talks specifically about how to test each vulnerability in the OWASP Top 10 List of 2007. This section is intended to give you a good introduction to the attack and how to test to see if your web application is vulnerable to this attack. This section will not give you an entire set of data to test with though. For example, we will teach you about cross-site scripting, provide some examples, but will not provide a comprehensive set of malicious inputs that can be used. It's better to get attack data online, because it is more recent.

When learning about the OWASP Top 10 attacks, it's useful to have a system that is vulnerable to the attacks, so you can learn exactly how the tools work. In the security world, these types of systems are called Honey Pots. The OWASP has just such a project, named Web Goat. Web Goat is a deliberately insecure application created in J2EE. Although the following sections provide pages created in ASP .NET that are not secure, Web Goat is an extensive application that has many online tutorials to assist with learning how to test for web application security.

A1 - Cross-Site Scripting (XSS)

A cross-site scripting (XSS) attack is a type of attack in which an attacker is able to inject code, usually in the form of client-side JavaScript, into an input field of a web application that is later rendered to other clients without any encoding performed. XSS attacks are extremely common and dangerous. The nature of the Web is to trust JavaScript on web applications. It is because of this that XSS attacks can execute malicious JavaScript to exploit users of the compromised web application. Nearly 80 percent of all documented security vulnerabilities as of 2007 were caused by XSS attacks. An attacker can use XSS attacks to exploit phishing schemas, identify theft, and annoying messages to just about any other malicious thing you can execute with JavaScript.

Testing for Cross-Site Scripting Attacks

There are many different tools that are available to test for cross-site scripting attacks. Throughout this section, most of the examples will be using WebScarab. WebScarab is a free tool created under the OWASP project that can be downloaded from `http://www.owasp.org/index.php/ Category:OWASP_WebScarab_Project`.

WebScarab acts a proxy, intercepting all requests between the web application and the browser. To start using WebScarab, you will first need to configure your web browser to use a proxy connection. Figure 10-1 shows the proxy configuration for Firefox with the default port of 8008 used by WebScarab.

After the proxy is configured in Firefox, you are ready to begin your WebScarab conversation. Figure 10-2 shows the Summary tab of WebScarab, which contains a list of the requests that have been captured during the conversations.

Clicking each request will allow the user to drill in and see the specific information about each request as in Figure 10-3.

To test for cross-site scripting flaws using WebScarab, we will be using a testing technique called *fuzzing*. Fuzzing will input invalid, random, or unexpected data into the inputs of a web application.

To fuzz using WebScarab you first need to right-click the request that contains the parameters you would like to fuzz and select Use as fuzz template, as shown in Figure 10-4.

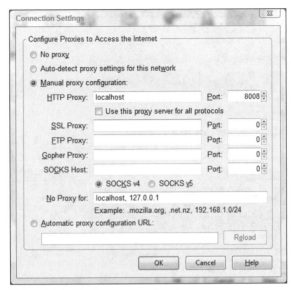

Figure 10-1: Firefox proxy settings

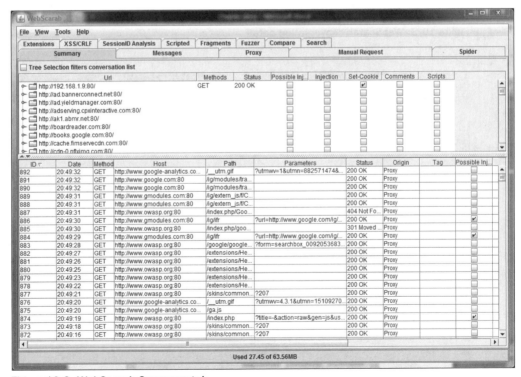

Figure 10-2: WebScarab Summary tab

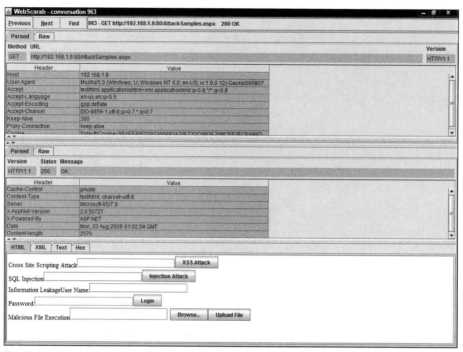

Figure 10-3: WebScarab conversation detail

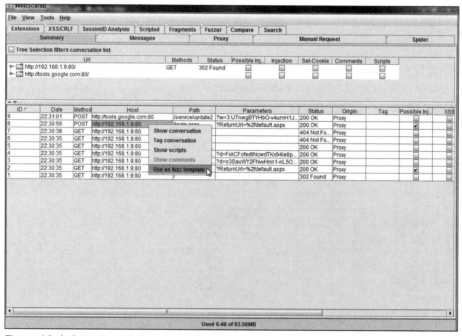

Figure 10-4: Selecting the fuzz template

After the fuzz template has been created, you will navigate to the Fuzzer tab in WebScarab. The Fuzzer tab is where the inputs to be fuzzed will be set up. Input fields, query strings, hidden values, and more can be fuzzed as shown in Figure 10-5.

For your test you will only be fuzzing the username and password text boxes, so the other parameters can be removed as shown in Figure 10-6.

After you have decided which parameters you want to fuzz, you need to decide what type of data you would like to use. This is accomplished by clicking the Sources button on the Fuzzer tab. WebScarab allows the fuzzing data to either be a regular expression, or data from a text file.

- ❑ **Regular Expressions.** For example, entering [0-9][0-9][0-9][0-9] in the Regular Expression field and giving it a description of 4 Digit Number, will submit all digits between 0000 and 9999 to the web application.

- ❑ **Attack Files.** Because we are testing for XSS vulnerabilities, we are using a text file entitled XSS_Attacks that only includes strings that could be XSS attacks. Figure 10-7 shows the loaded XSS_Attacks file in the Fuzz Sources screen.

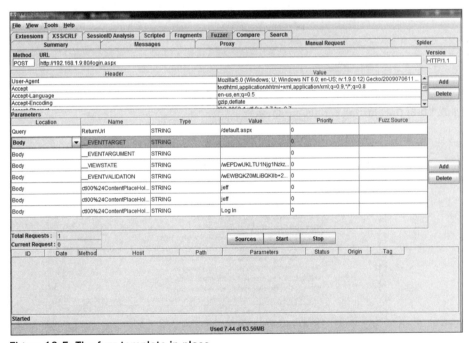

Figure 10-5: The fuzz template in place

It's important to note that for the purposes of demonstration we have limited the fuzzing to only test for XSS attacks. When performing a true security test, fuzzing data can include all types of data such as SQL injections, XSS, Path Traversal, and many more types of attacks. A good file to start out with is the All_attack.txt from neuro fuzz which can be downloaded from http://www.neurofuzz.com/modules/software/wsfuzzer/All_attack.txt.

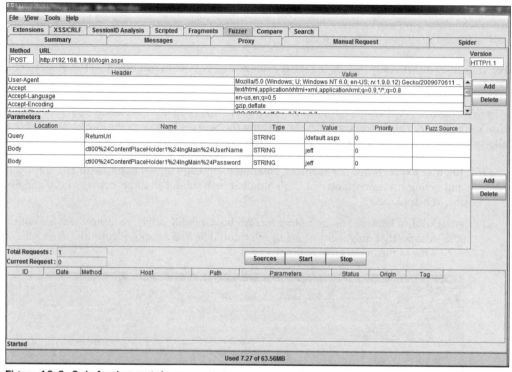

Figure 10-6: Only fuzzing certain parameters

Figure 10-7: XSS Attack loaded as a fuzz source

This file contains more than 362 attack strings to use when looking for security vulnerabilities in web applications. The All_attack file is in the format of attack string :::type of attack. When using the attack files, the description of the attack will need to be stripped out of the attack. Here is an excerpt from the All_attack file:

```
A:::Meta-Character Injection
TRUE:::Meta-Character Injection
FALSE:::Meta-Character Injection
`id`:::OS Commanding
;id;:::OS Commanding
`dir`:::Directory Indexing
|dir:::Directory Indexing
<script>alert("XSS")</script>:::XSS
<script>alert(document.cookie)</script>:::XSS
```

After the fuzzing sources have been loaded, each parameter that will be fuzzed will need to have a fuzz source associated with it. For our example, we are fuzzing both the username and passwords fields for XSS attacks, so the XSS_Attacks fuzzing source will be selected as shown in Figure 10-8.

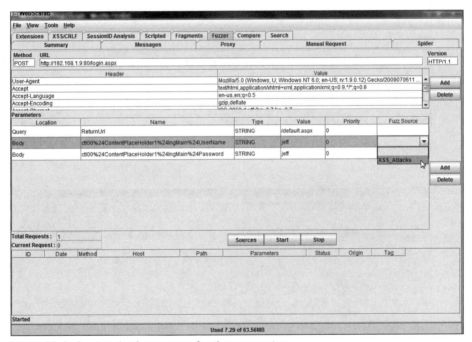

Figure 10-8: Setting the fuzz source for the parameter

To start the fuzzing test, click the Start button near the bottom of the tab. You will notice the Total Requests and Current Request number increase until the test is complete, as shown in Figure 10-9.

After the fuzzer has completed, you will need to review all the requests and see if any of the XSS attacks worked. To do this, go back to the Summary tab and manually inspect the results. You will be looking for "interesting differences" between their responses. Analyzing this data is not an exact science and "interesting differences" can manifest themselves in many different ways. This is where the tedious part of security testing comes into play. The response with the ID of 16 looked interesting.

Mainly because of the 500 error it produced. Drilling into the response, as shown in Figure 10-10, we can see that ASP.NET threw an error stating that a dangerous form request was submitted, the behavior we would want in the website, but is considered a leakage of information.

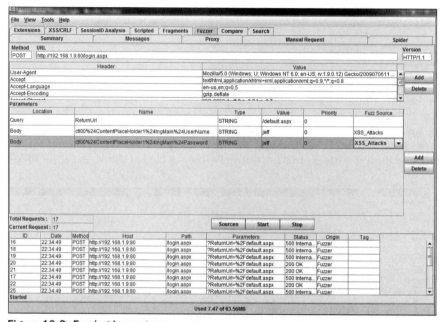

Figure 10-9: Fuzzing in progress

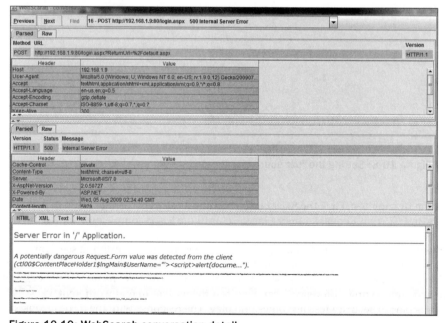

Figure 10-10: WebScarab conversation detail

In the previous example, that particular page of the web application was not susceptible to a cross-site scripting attack. It's important to learn the attack files and what the results of a successful cross-site scripting attack would look like based on each attack in the file.

Using WebScarab is not the only way of testing for cross-site scripting attacks. You may choose to create tests with WatiN or another framework to accomplish the same results that WebScarab produced. The following example only tests one page, with one cross-site scripting attack string, but could be modified to use the attack files previously discussed:

```
[Test]
public void Should_Check_For_XSS_Attack_Samples()
{
    using (IBrowser ie = BrowserFactory.Create(
        BrowserType.InternetExplorer))
    {
        ie.GoTo("http://localhost:49278/AttackSamples.aspx");
        ie.TextField(Find.ByName(
            "ct100$ContentPlaceHolder1$lngMain$UserName")).Value = "admin";
        ie.TextField(Find.ByName(
            "ct100$ContentPlaceHolder1$lngMain$Password")).Value = "admin";
        ie.Button(Find.ByName(
            "ct100$ContentPlaceHolder1$lngMain$LoginButton")).Click();

        ie.TextField(Find.ByName("txtXSS")).Value = GetXSSAttack();
        ie.Button(Find.ByName("btnXSS")).Click();

        Assert.IsTrue(ie.Title.ToLower() == "xss exploit");
    }
}

private string GetXSSAttack()
{
    return "<script type=\"text/javascript" +
        "\">document.title='XSS Exploit'</script>";
}
```

A2 - Injection Flaws

Injection flaws are vulnerabilities in web applications that allow an attacker to relay malicious code through the target web application to another system/program. The code that is injected through injection flaws can be operating system calls, shell commands, entire scripts that have been written in a scripting language such as Perl, or calls to backend databases through SQL (SQL injections). Some injection flaws can be very easy to discover while others can be extremely obscure.

The most well-known injection flaw is the SQL injection flaw. These are SQL statements that are built by using string concatenation instead of a parameterized query

SQL query created using string concatenation:

```
string updateQuery = "INSERT INTO Stores (StoreId) VALUES (" + storeId + ")";
```

SQL query created using a parameterized query:

```
SQLCommand command = New SQLCommand("INSERT INTO Stores (StoreId)
   VALUES(@storeId");
Command.Parameters.Add("@storeId", storeId);
```

Many SQL injection attacks are made visible by disclosure of database specific information though error messages similar to the error shown in Figure 10-11.

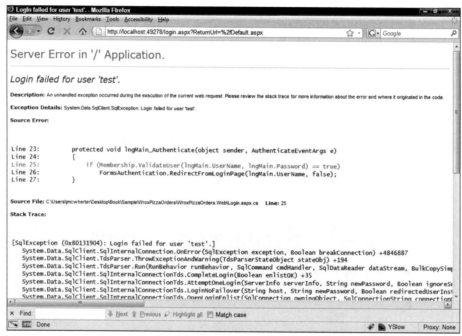

Figure 10-11: Disclosure of sensitive information

A technique called Blindfolded SQL exposes techniques to inject SQL to a web application that does not disclose database information. Blindfolded SQL requires a great deal of patience and knowledge of SQL.

Testing for Injection Flaws

For this example we are going to use the AttackSamples.aspx page created for the previous example. This example uses the WroxPizza demo database, and we will be setting a query parameter named "CouponId," to load the selected coupon.

The first task when looking for injection flaws is to see if you can get the page to throw an error. Simple poking around using a manual technique will do for now. If the page throws an error, more than likely you will be able to inject malicious code.

Figure 10-12 shows the error produced by changing the request to the following
`http://localhost/AttackSamples.aspx?couponId=1 foobar.`

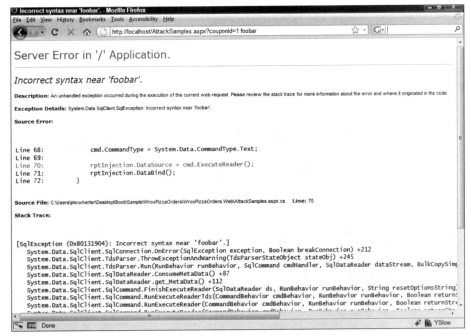

Figure 10-12: Error caused by injection

Now that we have the page throwing an error (these yellow ASP.NET errors are the best for attackers because of all the information they provide), it's worth doing more investigation.

The next step typically performed is actually injecting valid SQL, as shown in Figure 10-13. The application appears to work correctly, but the Waitfor delay SQL command delays execution for 10 seconds `http://localhost/AttackSamples.aspx?couponId=1 waitfor delay '0:0:10'.`

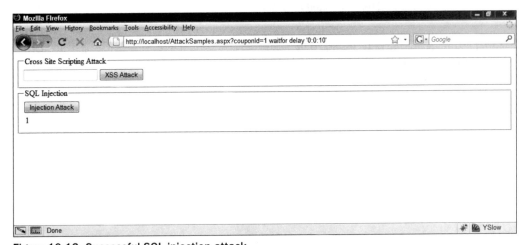

Figure 10-13: Successful SQL injection attack

Knowing that the SQL injection was successful, it may be useful to dig deeper to see exactly what damage can be done using SQL injection. For this a free tool called Pangolin (http://www.nosec.org/en/pangolin.html) will do the trick.

As shown in Figure 10-14, pointing Pangolin to a URL can reveal a great deal of information, such as the name of the database, the server name, a list of other databases on the machine, and much more.

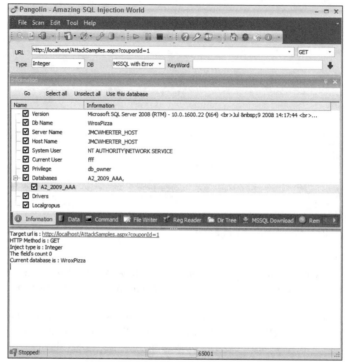

Figure 10-14: Pangolin results

Manual testing is not the only approach that can be used. As you have learned already, using the WebScarab fuzzer you can simulate different situations very quickly. Using the techniques discussed in Chapter 5, you can create methods using frameworks such as WatiN to test for injection flaws:

```
[Test]
public void Should_Check_For_Injection_Attack()
{
    using (IBrowser ie = BrowserFactory.Create(BrowserType.
        InternetExplorer))
    {
        ie.GoTo("http://192.168.1.9/AttackSamples.aspx");
        ie.TextField(Find.ByName("txtInjection")).Value = "OR 1=1 --";
        ie.Button(Find.ByName("btnInjection")).Click();

        Assert.IsTrue(ie.ContainsText("Server Error in '/' Application."));
    }
}
```

Keep in mind, if you find one SQL injection flaw it's more than likely there are more throughout the web application.

A3 - Malicious File Execution

Malicious file execution is a type of vulnerability where a malicious file is uploaded to the server hosting your web application and executed. Attackers are typically looking for web applications that fail to control the execution of uploaded files. The malicious files that attackers upload could execute remote code, exploit known operation system vulnerabilities, or simply contain a virus intended to wreak havoc on the system.

Web applications that are susceptible to this type of vulnerability break the simplest of security rules, trusting the input that the user has entered. If your web application needs to accept files from users, ensure that you are checking the type of file being uploaded. Checking the file extension is not good enough. Ensure that you are checking the MIME type of the incoming file as well. Along with proper file validation, a good virus scanner on the server and keeping the uploaded files on a separate partition than the web application, are also good practice.

Applications created in frameworks such as .NET and Java are abstracted from the environment in which they execute, so it's less common to see this vulnerability as opposed to applications that do not run in a sandboxed/isolated environment such as PHP.

This is not to say you can't get yourself into trouble by changing the trust level that your web application runs in. Trust levels are associated to security policies that enforce permissions as to exactly what actions the web application can perform within the framework. Actions such as file system, printer access, and sending mail via SMTP are types of actions that can be restricted with the .NET trust levels. The .NET Framework ships with five pre-built trust levels:

- ❑ Full
- ❑ High
- ❑ Medium
- ❑ Low
- ❑ Minimal

It's recommended that applications run in Medium trust. Medium trust only allows for read, write, append, and path discovery on the file system, meaning malicious file execution could not happen.

Testing for Malicious File Execution

The first thing to think about when testing for malicious file execution exploits, is whether the web application allows the users to upload files, as in Figure 10-15.

Figure 10-15: File Upload Interface

If your web application allows for file upload, then you will need to test to ensure that files cannot be executed. It's helpful to think about these flaws as not only binary files, but scripts as well, such as ASPX files. If the permissions on the directory where the file was uploaded allows for execution as in Figure 10-16, your web application may be vulnerable to this type of attack.

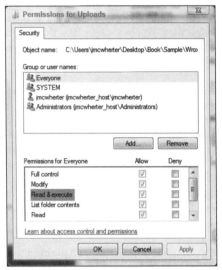

Figure 10-16: Windows Directory Permissions for users

If no validation was performed on the type of file being uploaded, then it would be very easy for an attacker to upload a malicious ASPX file as shown in the following code sample:

```
<%@ Page Language="C#" AutoEventWireup="true" %>

<html xmlns="http://www.w3.org/1999/xhtml" >
<head runat="server">
    <title></title>
</head>
<body>
    <form id="form1" runat="server">
    <% Response.Write(System.Environment.MachineName); %>
    </form>
</body>
</html>
```

The attacker would only need to know where in the file system the file existed (in your case /Uploads/ Attack.aspx) and they could execute their uploaded code. This sample did not contain malicious code, but you can see the danger in this. Depending on what trust level your application is running in, an attacker could cause a great deal of damage using this type of attack.

Most web applications only allow for file uploading in a few places, and a manual test will be sufficient. This is not to say that an automated test could not be created in WatiN or another framework to test for this type of vulnerability.

A4 - *Insecure Direct Object Reference*

Insecure Direct Object Reference vulnerabilities are caused when the implementation of an internal object is exposed to the public. Internal objects could be files, directories, or database records. The common example that is used to illustrate this vulnerability is a financial institution that uses an account number as the primary key of a table. Because the account number is the primary key, it's tempting to use the account number directly in the interface facing the Web, perhaps as a query string parameter used for pulling up the record. If this method is used, and there is no extra authentication to ensure that the account number is related to the user, then it would be very easy for an attacker to have access to all account numbers at that particular financial institution. This example may sound a little severe but there are documented cases where this has happened.

Testing for Insecure Direct Object Reference

Testing for Insecure Direct Object references within a web application can be tricky. Even if a developer has a direct object reference, many times developers will not name the parameters to match, for example, a direct reference to the primary key of an accounts table, via a query string. Although some developers will name the query string parameter "AccountId," others will name it something cryptic, so it may not be obvious at first sight and may require some digging to see these flaws. Using a tool such as WebScarab will help you examine each request and easily see the parameters as in Figure 10-17.

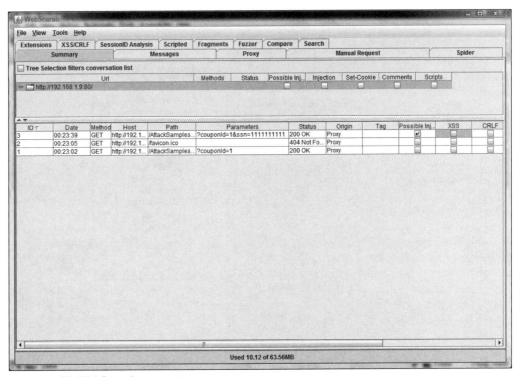

Figure 10-17: WebScarab parameters

When you have found pages that you believe to have direct object references that are insecure, you can begin to tamper with the data. An easy tool for this is TamperData, which is a free Firefox plug-in that can be downloaded from `http://tamperdata.mozdev.org/`. When the TamperData plug-in is enabled, you will be prompted to tamper with the data for each request received in the browser, as shown in Figure 10-18. You are presented with three options: Abort Request simply aborts the request; Submit passes the request along to the browser; and Tamper opens a new window with options to tamper with the data of the request.

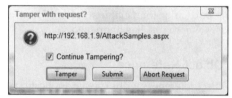

Figure 10-18: TamperData request

Figure 10-19 shows the TamperData screen, which allows you to tamper with the parameters and try to find Insecure Object references. Finding these references in many situations will be trial and error.

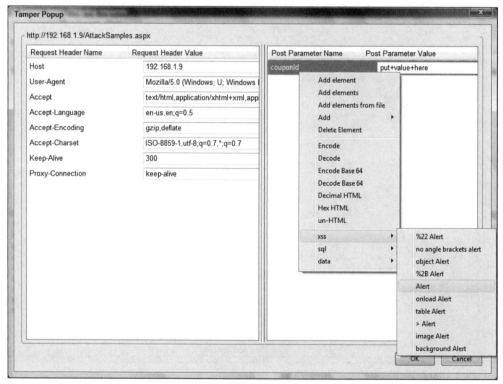

Figure 10-19: Tampering the couponId parameter

A5 - *Cross-Site Request Forgery (CSRF)*

Cross-site request forgery (CSRF pronounced "sea-surf") is the lesser known cousin of the cross-site scripting attack (XSS). CSRF attacks exploit the trust that a given user/browser has already established with a web application to execute commands/scripts that would normally be unauthorized.

For example, take for instance an online forum that users have the ability to upload images to. If this forum was susceptible to a CSRF attack, the attacker could place something such as this in the image tag:

```
<img src="http://www.mcwherter.net/logout">
```

Although not malicious, this example of a CSRF attack could be quite troublesome to users trying to access the forum. A more malicious example could be a bank where your browser has already established a trusted connection:

```
<img src="http://www.BankOfEngland.Com/Transfer?FromAccount=Ben&ToAccount=
Jeff&amount=1000000 ">
```

This example would require the attacker to have knowledge about the user. In this case, the attacker Jeff knew that Ben has an account at the Bank of England.

Testing for Cross-Site Request Forgery

Cross-site request forgery attacks are very similar to cross-site scripting attacks, and the methods discussed previously in this chapter for testing for cross-site scripting attacks apply to cross-site request forgery attacks.

A6 - *Information Leakage and Improper Error Handling*

Developers and managers often dismiss information leakage, because they do not see how an attacker could use this information to attack their web application. The more information that is available about the web application, the more inviting it is to be the target of an attack. Information can be disclosed to attackers in many different ways, but the most common way for leak information is through error messages.

Error Messages

For a developer, having a detailed error message will make fixing the bug much faster. Many managers are aware of this, and like the ability for developers to resolve issues promptly. Fortunately for the attacker, having a detailed error message will make finding vulnerabilities much easier. Detailed error messages are designed to help developers track down the issue fast. This means a great deal of information is disclosed about the application. The detailed error information includes the version of the .NET Framework and state of the application, and could disclose information about the database. Figure 10-20 shows the default run-time error that is shown.

Figure 10-21 shows a runtime error that has occurred when accessing the web application on the server or if the custom error mode is set to "off" in the web.config.

Figure 10-22 is an example of what error screens should look like. The user is aware something unexpected has happened, but is given the opportunity to inform someone of the issue via email.

Figure 10-20: ASP.NET default error message

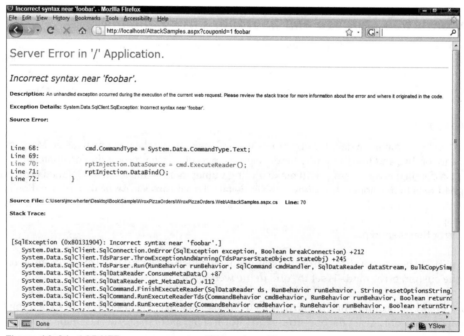

Figure 10-21: ASP.NET error message with mode=off

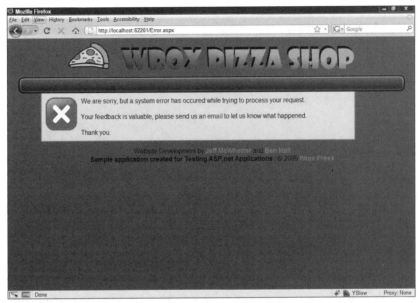

Figure 10-22: What the error message should look like

Best practices states that developers should implement some type of internal logging feature that is not externally visible. When error conditions happen, they can search the internal logs and have exactly the same level of detail to resolve the issue.

Comments

HTML comments are another place that information can be leaked. Some developers may place versioning history, to-do lists, infrastructure details, and ways to test inside the HTML comments. There are few stories on the Internet about such attacks, because a developer left the login information to an external application documented in the comments.

Testing for Information Leakage

The best way to test for information leaked by error messages is using a fuzzer to try to cause the web application under test to throw an error.

Remember to try to look for information contained within the HTML. WebScarab contains a tool (fragments) which lists all the comments contained on HTML pages within the WebScarab session. Figure 10-23 is an example of the fragments tool running on the AttackSamples.aspx page. The comments in Figure 10-23 are the comments attackers are looking for.

We have not covered many penetration tools or tools to network or server security. It's worth mentioning in this section that a good port scanner can also help leak information about the different applications that make up the web application runtime stack. There are many port scanners on the market today with many of them free. I like to use nmap, which is a free tool containing a port scanner and other tools helpful for security testing. nmap can be obtained from `http://nmap.org/`. Figure 10-24 shows a simple port scan of www.mcwherter.net using nmap.

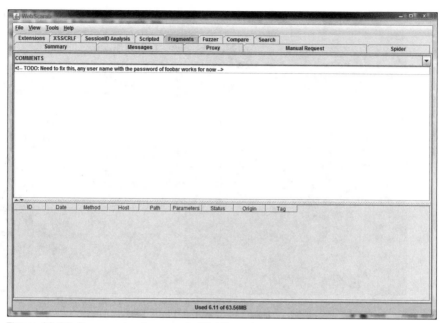

Figure 10-23: Comments of a page in WebScarab

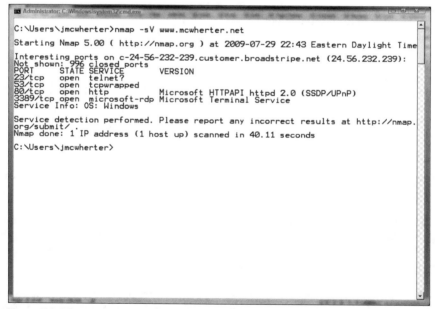

Figure 10-24: nmap port scan

The port scan in Figure 10-24 not only shows which ports are open, it gives a detailed description of the service.

A7 - Broken Authentication and Session Management

Believe it or not, there are many web applications that contain sensitive data that are deployed to production with flaws in the underlining authentication. ASP.NET developers have it great. The wonderful developers on both the ASP.NET and the .NET Framework teams have provided ASP.NET developers with a great set of tools within the .NET Framework for authentication. The developers on these teams have spent a great deal of time coding and testing to ensure the authentication tools within ASP.NET are secure. It's because of this attention to detail, and the amount of testing surrounding the built-in tools for authentication, that you should never try to create your own authentication. More than likely, you are going to miss something that will lead to vulnerabilities in your web application. There may be rare situations where the need may arise for custom authentication to be created, but be aware it is a long and tedious task to create authentication that is solid and it's best left to someone who does it every day.

With that being said, this OWASP vulnerability also covers Session Management vulnerabilities. Session Management vulnerabilities can lead to injection attacks. A few tips can help lead to secure session management:

- ❑   Do not allow login to the website from an unencrypted page.
- ❑   Make sure that every page has a logout link.
- ❑   Set a reasonable session timeout (the shorter the better).
- ❑   Do not expose any session identifiers.
- ❑   Limit your code of custom cookies for session management.

Testing for Broken Authentication

Even if you decide to use the built-in authentication tools provided in the .NET Framework, there are situations you should test for. A good manual test of the underlaying authentication mechanism will do in most situations. The manual test should include the following elements:

- ❑   **Non-Existence User.** Ensures that error messages returned from authentication mechanism do not disclose the existence of a user.

- ❑   **Valid User/Invalid Password Messages.** Test to ensure error messages do not disclose which element of the authentication is invalid. Error messages that disclose which authentication element is invalid will help attackers narrow their attacks. Try to stick with generic authentication messages, such as "Invalid username or password entered."

- ❑   **Password Strength.** Ensure that weak passwords are not accepted.

- ❑   **Number of Attempts.** Test the number of login attempts users have before a system lockout. System lockouts should be time based. For example, the business rule may be after three invalid authentication attempts, the user will not be able to try to authenticate for 10 minutes. After the 10 minutes has passed, if they enter another invalid password, they will be locked out again.

    It's important not to lock out users of the system entirely. Locking users out of the system entirely after invalid authentication attempts can lead to a DoS attack against the user.

Testing Session Management

If developers find the need to manage sessions themselves, they need to test to ensure the session is secure. A common mistake that developers handling their own sessions make is creating predictable session IDs. Figure 10-25 is a request captured with WebScarab that shows predictable session IDs.

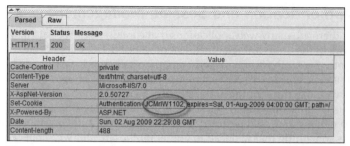

Figure 10-25: Predictable session ID caught in WebScarab

The following is a list of other authentication sessions, which illustrate how a session can be predicted.

1st Authentication:

User = jmcwherter; Password=foobar12?

Cookie = JCWrlW1102

2nd Authentication:

User = jmcwherter; Password=foobar12

Cookie = JCWrlW1104

3rd Authentication:

User = jmcwherter; Password=foobar12?

Cookie = JCWrlW1106

Guessable Cookie: Cookie = JCWrlW1108

A8 - Insecure Cryptographic Storage

Many web applications fail to encrypt sensitive data or do not even try to encrypt any of the data at all. Protecting data using cryptography is essential to creating secure web applications. Sensitive data such as passwords, social security numbers, and any other type of identifiable or sensitive data should be secured using some type of cryptography method. Insecure cryptographic storage of sensitive data can lead to the disclosure of sensitive data and violation of certain compliance standards.

Your best option is to avoid storing sensitive data locally, but if the data needs to be stored, ensure you are using the latest cryptography algorithms, and never try to create your own cryptography algorithms. The algorithms that are standard in the IT industry have been developed by teams and individuals that focus only on creating cryptography algorithms. These algorithms have been tested extensively and have been proven to be secure.

When storing user passwords, a one-way hashing algorithm is the preferred cryptography method. One-way hash algorithms are easy to compute, but are difficult to revert. Many attackers make use of rainbow tables to try to break the cryptography of hashing algorithms. Another common attack of password hashing algorithms is looking for two different users that have the same exact hashed value for their password. This means that both these users have the same password, and if the password is determined, then the algorithm can be broken.

To help make hashing algorithms more secure, a random value called a salt can be added to the password hash. Both the hash and the salt would be stored. This technique eliminates the duplication of hashed values and therefore rainbow tables cannot be used.

ViewState

There is one area in ASP.NET where it's common to see developers place sensitive data that is not encrypted. This is ViewState. Have you ever opened the HTML rendered by an HTML page to see hundreds of lines of what look like garbage data in a hidden field named "__VIEWSTATE"? ViewState is one of the ways ASP.NET can maintain state between the different pages of a web application. ViewState is the state of all the controls on the page encoded in the encoding Base64 schema. Developers can place objects into ViewState using the following code:

```
ViewState["MySecureItem"] = "Jeff's Wife's Name is Carla";
```

By default, the ViewState of a page is not encrypted, but that's not to say that it can't be by a setting in the Web Config.

Query Strings

Query strings are another place that developers have a tendency to place data that should be encrypted. I have seen web applications where the primary key of a table is to store user information, which was the social security number of the user. The web page that listed the user information took in a query string of the primary key of the table. Although the name of the query string parameter was not obvious (the developers did not name it SSN), it was fairly obvious that the social security number was used. Not only was sensitive information about that user disclosed, query strings are easily manipulated and other sensitive information may have been exposed as well by manipulating this value.

Testing for Insecure Cryptographic Storage

Testing for insecure cryptographic storage is another one of the OWASP Top 10 that is difficult to black box test. Having an intimate knowledge of how data is stored will ensure that your web application is not vulnerable to attack.

Using the ViewStateDecoder application, which can be downloaded from http://alt.pluralsight.com/tools.aspx, ViewState is decoded and you can see exactly what was placed in there, as in Figure 10-26, which shows the value of the ViewState item named MySecureItem.

A9 - Insecure Communications

Sensitive data that is being transmitted should be encrypted. Usually SSL (Secure Socket Layer) certificates are used to ensure a secure communication between the browser and the server hosting the web application. Depending on the architecture of your web applications, applying SSL certificates to not only the pages exposed by your web applications, but also backend connections is necessary to ensure secure communication across all layers of your web application.

Adding SSL certificates may not always be a trivial task. Planning needs to be involved as to how strong of an encryption level is needed; what happens if someone tries to access a page that requires SSL (are they redirected), and even if an Extended Validation Certificate is required?

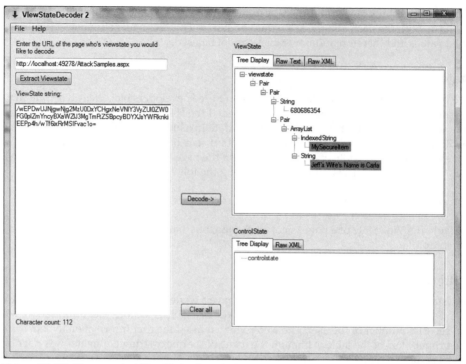

Figure 10-26: Unencrypted ViewState decoded

Testing for Insecure Communications

Web applications that require SSL have some type of process where the user is redirected from HTTP to the HTTPS equivalent. There are many different ways this can be accomplished, through hard-coded links such as https://MY_URL/Login.aspx or possibly via rewriting the URL on the web server. Rewriting URLs is a very popular technique, allowing the user to enter either HTTP or HTTPS, and the user ends up at the correct page that is secure. In IIS 6, third-party plug-ins were often used, whereas in IIS 7 the URL rewrite module http://www.iis.net/downloads/default.aspx?tabid=34&g=6&i=1691 is an excellent solution. If a rewrite module is used, this pretty much means that if one page works, more than likely all the other pages will work as well.

The following test created with WatiN, will navigate to the login page of a test URL using HTTP. The test will then ensure that the request was redirected to the HTTPS equivalent. This is a type of integration test that could be run on the production server to ensure that the redirect logic is configured correctly. More than likely this type of test would not be run against a development or staging server, only against the production server:

```
[Test]
public void Should_Check_For_Secure_Communications_On_Login_Page()
{
    string url = "http://MY_URL/login.aspx";          // go to the http page

    using (IBrowser ie = BrowserFactory.Create(BrowserType.InternetExplorer))
```

```
        {
            ie.GoTo(url);

            // ensure that the redirect to the https page happened
            string expectedURL = ie.Url.Substring(0, 5).ToLower();
            Assert.IsTrue(expectedURL == "https");
        }
    }
```

A10 - Failure to Restrict URL Access

The Failure to Restrict URL Access OWASP vulnerability is simply a failure to fully restrict access to resources that should be secured. It's common to see that the only protection to secure pages contained within a web application is the links to these pages which are not visible to an unauthorized user. Attackers or lucky users can find these pages and have access to features that only authorized users should have access to. Security by obscurity is not a valid security practice. Not only should the links be disabled (or not visible at all) to pages that users do not have access to, authorization should also be included to ensure the user has access to view the page.

Testing for Failure to Restrict URL Access

Using black box testing methods to test for URL access restrictions can be a difficult task. Testers first need to discover which URLs are protected, then test to see if non-privileged users can obtain access. Site maps or logging in with a user that is known to have access to privileged pages is a start.

If you have a list of the pages that are secure, then creating a WatiN script is very simple to ensure they are secure. The following code first ensures that the cache and all the cookies are cleared (meaning the user is logged out), then tries to access pages which are known as secure and tests to see if the user was prompted for the login information:

```
[Test]
public void Should_Check_For_Proper_Authenicaion_On_Coupons_List()
{
    using (IE ie = new IE())
    {
        ie.ClearCache();
        ie.ClearCookies();
        ie.GoTo("http://localhost:49278/Reports/Coupons.aspx");
        Assert.IsTrue(ie.ContainsText("User Name"));
    }
}
```

If you wanted to you could test the Coupons page more thoroughly, checking to ensure that the user was in the correct role.

The following code is using a user named UserWithOutPermission to try to access the Coupons page. The user does not have permission to this page, and an information message is presented to the user indicating that they do not have the correct permission:

```
[Test]
public void Should_Check_For_Proper_Authenicaion_Roles_On_Coupons_List()
{
```

```
using (IE ie = new IE())
{
    ie.ClearCache();
    ie.ClearCookies();
    ie.GoTo("http://localhost:49278/Reports/Coupons.aspx");
    ie.TextField(
        Find.ByName("ct100$ContentPlaceHolder
        1$lngMain$UserName")).Value ="UserWithOutPermission";
    ie.TextField(Find.ByName(
        "ct100$ContentPlaceHolder1$lngMain$Password")).Value ="Password";

    Assert.IsTrue(ie.ContainsText
        ("You Do Not Have Permission To Access This Page"));
}
}
```

Vulnerability Assessments

A *vulnerability assessment* is a vague term that could mean something different depending on who you are speaking with. In this situation, vulnerability assessment is an assessment of how secure the web application is under test. Vulnerability assessments performed on web applications help make organizations aware of exactly what their risk level is for their application.

Teams need to decide who will perform the vulnerability assessment. Only individuals who have knowledge in both IT security and application security should perform the assessment. If the individuals are only knowledgeable in one area, then the assessment could have flaws. It's common for vulnerability assessments to be performed by a team outside the team that developed the application. In many situations other teams (internal or external to the company), may have more experience with security testing, or just serve as an objective party. Vulnerability assessments performed by outside teams will yield the best results in most situations. Outside teams will remain objective and will only need to understand the application's business rules that are needed to provide a successful vulnerability assessment.

A good vulnerability assessment will use a combination of tools and a human review. Human interaction is necessary to help find design flaws or implement complex vulnerabilities. The end result in a successful vulnerability assessment will be a very solid layer of security. It's the hope of all testers involved with a vulnerability assessment, that if an attacker tries to attack the web application they will move along to a target that is more susceptible to an attack.

Creating vulnerability assessments for web applications requires a very diligent, methodical, and scientific approach. Using a very simple methodology of three stages works well: discovery, verification, and documentation.

Discovery

The discovery phase of the vulnerability assessment is where expectations are set, and the team performing the assessment tries to discover information about the web application under test using external means (not asking the team that created the web application under test directly).

Collecting Requirements

Do not start any work on the vulnerability assessment until goals, boundary conditions, and expectations have been discussed. As with the other testing disciplines, it's important to go through a requirements collecting phase to ensure that all parties involved with the vulnerability assessment are on the same page about what exactly is being performed.

Collecting the requirements for a vulnerability assessment can frustrate the tester, when the client does not have a good understanding of security. It's common for companies that are having a vulnerability assessment performed on an application to only ask one question "Can our web application be hacked?"

Timeframes

Agree on clear timeframes when vulnerability testing is appropriate. Full vulnerability assessments should be performed at project milestones. This is not to say development should be stopped or that assessments can't be performed during the development (actually it's encouraged), it just means that while the vulnerability assessment is being performed the application should stay in a known state.

Establish Boundary Conditions

There are some lines that should not be crossed when testing for security and it's very important to establish these lines. For example, clients may have secure information that should not be copied to other machines. Knowing this boundary can help keep you out of trouble. It's important to note that bad guys do not have boundaries, so if the boundary conditions are too constrictive, then the vulnerability assessment can be useless.

Liability

It's important to establish an agreement with the client that you are not liable for something that goes wrong, such as data being deleted, because of your actions.

Goals

Setting a list of goals of exactly what the vulnerability assessment plans to accomplish, is helpful to ensure that you are delivering a valuable service to the web application under test. At the highest level, the team performing the vulnerability assessment should have goals of discovering, documenting, and educating. Other goals that may be useful to the client may be the following:

- ❑ How much information about your web application is disclosed using external means
- ❑ Whether your corporation's security policy was followed
- ❑ If your web application complies with a particular compliance standard
- ❑ If your web application is vulnerable to any vulnerabilities listed in the OWASP Top 10

Documentation of Requirements

Providing a very detailed document of the requirements of the vulnerability assessment will ensure that all stakeholders on the project understand exactly what will be accomplished. Many developers are extremely protective of their code, and take offense when issues are found. Often developers will argue that an issue does not exist when proof has been provided. Sharing the Vulnerability Assessment

Requirements document with all stakeholders of the project can help with this dynamic. Also informing the team developing the application exactly what you will be looking for will help with this. The following outline is an example of a requirements document for a vulnerability assessment.

Introduction

What is a vulnerability?

What is a vulnerability assessment?

What is penetration testing?

Liability Agreements

Boundary Conditions

Timeframes

Services Offered

Deliverables

Goals

Methodology

Application assessment

Network-based assessment

Host-based assessment

Discovery by the Security Testers

It's also important that during the discovery phase, the team performing the vulnerability test discovers as much about the web application under test using external means. Security testers may dig deep into their bag of tools using tools such as telnet, ARIN, and fuzzers to try to learn as much about the web application under test as possible. As mentioned previously in this chapter, the more information that can be discovered about the web application under test, the easier it is for attackers to find vulnerabilities.

Verification

The verification phase, also known as the attack phase, is where the team testing the web application looks for and verifies vulnerabilities. A good mix of tools and human interaction is used to try to find any vulnerabilities the web application may have. During this phase, the web application should not be a "moving target," meaning updates are not being deployed until the assessment has been completed. Consideration of the goals and requirements should be paid close attention to during this phase.

Documentation

There are many different ways that the data collected during a vulnerability assessment can be documented. Depending on the situation, elaborate charts can help draw attention to important areas of the assessment. After you have performed a few vulnerability assessments or have had vulnerability assessments performed on your web applications, you will realize that the simpler and shorter the document is, the less painful it will be reading through the assessment to resolve the issues found.

I have found that creating a vulnerability assessment document that concentrates on four main areas of concern is sufficient in most situations. These four areas are as follows:

❑ Executive summary

❑ Risk matrix

❑ Best practices

❑ Final summary

Executive Summary

The executive summary of the vulnerability assessment is the only section that many readers of the document will read. This section should be targeted to someone who is not very technical, has limited or no experience with security terms, and should be very straightforward and to the point. This section should include statistics about the amount of vulnerabilities found, and help provide insight to how much effort is required to resolve the issues found. After a reader has completed reading this section, they should have a good idea of how vulnerable the web application under test is.

Risk Matrix

The risk matrix is where the detailed information about each vulnerability that was discovered during the assessment is discussed. This is where the developers of the web application under test will spend their time learning about where their application failed the assessment. It's important in this section to provide a very thorough analysis of the vulnerability, provide information about how to reproduce the issue, and provide suggestions and recommendations about how to resolve the issues that are found. Each vulnerability that has been found should contain the following information:

❑ Categorization

❑ Resources affected

❑ References

Categorization

Using a standard set of severity levels to categorize the vulnerability will ensure that everyone within the project understands how severe the issue is. The categorization of any given vulnerability can be subjective and will be determined by the experience level of the team performing the vulnerability assessment:

❑ Critical

❑ High

❑ Medium

❑ Low

Resources Affected

Specific information about resources that are vulnerable to the specific vulnerability that was found should be documented in this section. The intention of this section is to allow for developers to re-create the vulnerability. It's common in this section to include specific URLs, attack requests, and the attack response.

References

Providing a reference to information about the vulnerability that was found will help educate developers about the vulnerability. In most situations the references that are included are external URLs. For most vulnerabilities, detailed information can be found either on the OWASP website (http://www.owasp.org) or MSDN (http://msdn.microsoft.com).

The reference section of the risk matrix is also a good place to provide suggestions and recommendations on how to resolve the vulnerability that was found.

Critical: Potential cross-site scripting vulnerability

Summary: Potential cross-site scripting vulnerability was found on the web application under test. If successful, a cross-site scripting attack could allow attackers to execute malicious code through the browser of other users of the web application.

Resources Affected: http://192.168.1.9/AttackSamples.aspx

Attack Request:

Referrer: http://192.168.1.9/AttackSamples.aspx

Cookie: SqlAuthCookie=9D8969DF4C80E714;

Content-Type: multipart/form-data;

Content-length: 1278

Content-Disposition: form-data; name="__VIEWSTATE"

/wEPDwUKMTAxNjI0NjI2OQ8WAh4MTXlTZWN1cmVJdGVtBRtKZWZmJ3MgV2lmZSdzIE5hb
WUgaXMgQ2FybGEWAgIDDxYCHgdlbmN0eXBlBRNtdWx0aXBhcnQvZm9ybS1kYXRhFICAw8WA
h4EVGV4dAUhPHNjcmlwdD5hbGVydCgnQXR0YWNrJyk7PC9zY3JpcHQ+ZGS2DTd9PiY95L9IWARjN
HGs/Mc6zg==

Content-Disposition: form-data; name="txtXSS"

<script>alert('Attack');</script>

Content-Disposition: form-data; name="btnXSS"

XSS Attack

Content-Disposition: form-data; name="txtInjection"

Content-Disposition: form-data; name="txtUserName"

Content-Disposition: form-data; name="txtPassword"

Attack Response:

HTTP/1.1 200 OK

Cache-Control: private

Content-Type: text/html; charset=utf-8

Server: Microsoft-IIS/7.0

Set-Cookie: SqlAuthCookie=12733BDFE0D782D; path=/;

X-AspNet-Version: 2.0.50727

X-Powered-By: ASP.NET

Date: Wed, 05 Aug 2009 03:34:55 GMT

Content-length: 2969

References:

```
http://www.owasp.org/index.php/Cross-site_Scripting_(XSS)
```

```
http://en.wikipedia.org/wiki/Cross-site_scripting
```

Recommendation:

Set the ValidateRequest Page property to true.

Validate the input in the txtXSS text box, to ensure it is safe.

Best Practices

Depending on the scope of the vulnerability assessment, a best practices section can help educate teams that do not have a great deal of experience creating secure web applications. Many teams find this section of the vulnerability assessment extremely valuable, as it provides them with a great deal of knowledge they can take with them to the next project they are working on. Included in this section should be recommendations on how to write secure code, and how to follow security practices. Information such as "Do not try to create your own authentication logic or encryption logic" is an example of best practices that should be included in this section. Discussing in detail the vulnerabilities outlined the OWASP Top 10 are also a good fit for this section. Don't be afraid to include sample code of good security practices.

Final Summary

The final summary doesn't need to be extremely fancy. The purpose of the final summary is to bring the vulnerability assessment document to an end and summarize any final thoughts about the assessment. The final summary is also a good place to discuss the schedule of future vulnerability assessments and the overall schedule of the testing phase of the web application under test.

Tools

Throughout this chapter we have discussed the importance of using a good combination of tools and human interaction to perform successful security testing of your web applications. Tools can automate and formalize repetitive tasks quite nicely.

The majority of the tools we have discussed so far in this chapter have been free or cost very little. Many of the commercial tools on the market can cost tens of thousands of dollars and provide little to helping make your application more secure. These commercial security products provide breadth, trying to cater to all web applications needs. This makes these tools difficult to customize and they tend to miss things, because every application is different. This is not to say that all the commercial tools on the market are not good. There are some that produce very clean and helpful data, just beware of this fact when choosing a commercial security tool.

This section provides resources to other sites not discussed previously in this chapter. The intention of this section is to make sure you are aware of many different tools that can be used to perform the different tasks needed for successful security testing.

HTTP Proxying/Editing

❑   **Brup:**

http://www.portswigger.net/

❑   **WebProxy Editor:**

http://www.microsoft.com/mspress/companion/0-7356-2187-X/

❑   **Paros:**

http://www.parosproxy.org/index.shtml

❑   **WebScarab:**

http://www.owasp.org/index.php/Category:OWASP_WebScarab_Project

Security Scanners

❑   **Nessus:**

http://www.nessus.org/nessus/

❑   **N-Stealth:**

http://www.nstalker.com/products

❑   **Nikto/Wikto:**

http://cirt.net/nikto2

❑   **WebInspect:**

https://h10078.www1.hp.com/cda/hpms/display/main/hpms_content.jsp?zn=bto&cp
=1-11-201-200^9570_4000_100

Password Crackers

❑ **L0phtCrack:**

`http://www.l0phtcrack.com/`

❑ **RainbowCrack:**

`http://project-rainbowcrack.com/`

Other Security Tools

❑ **SSLDigger:**

`http://www.foundstone.com/us/resources/proddesc/ssldigger.htm`

Exploit Resources

Places to go for good exploit info:

`http://www.securityfocus.com`

`http://www.eeye.com/html/research/advisories/index.html`

`http://nvd.nist.gov/`

`http://www.osvdb.org`

`http://www.sans.org/top20/`

Summary

In this chapter we discussed the fundamentals of testing web applications for security. Security is a broad topic, with entire books published on specialized topics within the security discipline. This chapter was not intended to be the definitive guide to security testing, but to serve as a stepping stone to ensure developers are testing for the most common security vulnerabilities when it comes to development of web applications. It is highly encouraged that you seek out other resources, and learn more about developing secure web applications.

Walking away from this chapter, you should have come to the realization that there are many web applications in production that can be easily attacked. You may even have become aware of potential vulnerabilities to applications you have currently running in production. If you take anything away from this chapter, please remember not to blindly trust input from users, and test early, and test often.

Index